Agricultural Economics and Policy

World Scientific Lecture Notes in Economics and Policy

ISSN: 2630-4872

The World Scientific Lecture Notes in Economics and Policy series is aimed to produce lecture note texts for a wide range of economics disciplines, both theoretical and applied at the undergraduate and graduate levels. Contributors to the series are highly ranked and experienced professors of economics who see in publication of their lectures a mission to disseminate the teaching of economics in an affordable manner to students and other readers interested in enriching their knowledge of economic topics. The series was formerly titled World Scientific Lecture Notes in Economics.

Published:

Vol. 26: *Agricultural Economics and Policy*
by David Zilberman, Ruiqing Miao and Jian Rong

Vol. 25: *Handbook of Economy-wide Microeconomics: Theory, Applications, Tests and Extensions (In 4 Volumes)*
Volume 1: Existence and Uniqueness of Equilibrium
Volume 2: Stability and Optimality of Equilibrium
Volume 3: Comparative Statics and Applications
Volume 4: Tests and Extensions
by W. D. A. Bryant

For the complete list of volumes in this series, please visit
www.worldscientific.com/series/wslnep

World Scientific Lecture Notes in Economics and Policy – Vol. 26

Agricultural Economics and Policy

David Zilberman
University of California, Berkeley, USA

Ruiqing Miao
Auburn University, USA

Jian Rong
Auburn University, USA

World Scientific

NEW JERSEY • LONDON • SINGAPORE • BEIJING • SHANGHAI • TAIPEI • CHENNAI

Published by

World Scientific Publishing Co. Pte. Ltd.
5 Toh Tuck Link, Singapore 596224
USA office: 27 Warren Street, Suite 401-402, Hackensack, NJ 07601
UK office: 57 Shelton Street, Covent Garden, London WC2H 9HE

Library of Congress Cataloging-in-Publication Data
Names: Zilberman, David, 1947– author. | Miao, Ruiqing, author. |
Rong, Jian (Economist), author.
Title: Agricultural economics and policy / David Zilberman, University of California, Berkeley, USA, Ruiqing Miao, Auburn University, USA, Jian Rong, Auburn University, USA.
Description: New Jersey : World Scientific, [2025] | Series: World Scientific lecture notes in economics and policy, 2630-4872 ; vol. 26 | Includes bibliographical references and index.
Identifiers: LCCN 2024046677 | ISBN 9789811299162 (hardcover) |
ISBN 9789819801121 (paperback) | ISBN 9789811299179 (ebook) |
ISBN 9789811299186 (ebook other)
Subjects: LCSH: Agriculture--Economic aspects--United States.
Classification: LCC HD1761 .Z55 2025 | DDC 338.10973--dc23/eng/20241115
LC record available at https://lccn.loc.gov/2024046677

British Library Cataloguing-in-Publication Data
A catalogue record for this book is available from the British Library.

For any available supplementary material, please visit
https://www.worldscientific.com/worldscibooks/10.1142/14016#t=suppl

Desk Editors: Nambirajan Karuppiah/Geysilla Jean/Analyn Alcala

Typeset by Stallion Press
Email: enquiries@stallionpress.com

I dedicate this book to my teachers, and especially my students.
I learned more from them than they learned from me.

—David Zilberman

We dedicate this book to our parents.

—Ruiqing Miao and Jian Rong

About the Authors

David Zilberman holds the Robinson Chair in the Agricultural and Resource Economics Department at the University of California at Berkeley. He is the recipient of the 2019 Wolf Prize in Agriculture and was elected a member of the U.S. National Academy of Science in 2019. David served as the 2018–2019 President of the Agricultural & Applied Economics Association (AAEA). He's a fellow of multiple professional associations and has published in both professional and popular outlets. He has over 400 refereed articles in journals ranging from Science to *ARE Update* and has edited 25 books. In addition, he has served as a consultant to the U.S. Environmental Protection Agency, the World Bank, and the FAO. David's BA is from Tel Aviv University and his Ph.D. is from Berkeley. David is the co-founder of the Beahrs Environmental Leadership Program and the academic director of the Berkeley Master of Development Practice program. David's research analyzes water, innovation, supply chains, and the interactions between agriculture, energy, and the environment. He has researched the economics and political economy of agricultural biotechnology and the potential of the bioeconomy. In addition, he has been working on water policy programs and the economic impacts of the COVID-19 pandemic.

Ruiqing Miao is an associate professor in agricultural economics in the Department of Agricultural Economics and Rural Sociology at Auburn University. His research focuses on agricultural sustainability, innovation, and decision-making under risk and uncertainty. He studies the interaction between agricultural production and its environment, aiming to understand and quantify agriculture's impact on land use, water use, water quality, and biodiversity, as well as how agricultural production is affected by farmers' behaviors, public policies, agricultural innovation, technology adoption, and climate change. Ruiqing has served as a co-editor for *Choices* Magazine, and as an associate editor for *American Journal of Agricultural Economics, Agricultural Economics*, and *Natural Resource Modeling.* Ruiqing received his PhD in economics from Iowa State University in 2012.

Jian Rong is a senior lecturer in the Department of Agricultural Economics and Rural Sociology at Auburn University. In 2022, Dr. Rong was a visiting scholar in the Department of Agricultural and Resource Economics at the University of California, Berkeley, and a visiting lecturer in the Department of Agricultural and Resource Economics at the University of California, Davis. Dr. Rong has rich experience in teaching agricultural policy, agribusiness management and agribusiness marketing. She holds a PhD in Economics from Fudan University and an MBA from Iowa State University.

Contents

Prologue: The Uniqueness of Agricultural Economics

Agricultural economics has evolved as a distinguished discipline of economics. Economics, like any other discipline, has a core and many subdisciplines that tend to emphasize specific issues and develop their own agenda and methods to address specific challenges of the subdiscipline. Agricultural economics is among the largest economic subdisciplines. Agricultural economics has evolved over time as analytical tools and economic and political realities change. It applies, as well as develops, economic methodologies, and it incorporates notions and theories from other disciplines (e.g., life science, biophysical science, and psychology) to address the problems of agriculture and natural resources (Zilberman, 2019).

This book provides a review and some original results on various issues of agricultural economics and policy. The book contains lecture notes taught by David Zilberman in his PhD-level agricultural economics and policy course sequence at the University of California, Berkeley, augmented by lectures taught by Ruiqing Miao and Jian Rong at Auburn University. The book provides students and researchers in agricultural economics and related fields with a U.S. agriculture background, economic theories, applied models, and analysis of major agricultural policies in the United States and some other countries. The content of this book is broad, covering topics of agricultural history, production, demand, risk, technical innovation, adoption, welfare analysis, payment for ecosystem service, agricultural supply chain, the political economy of agricultural policies, and sustainable development in agriculture. Before we dive into these contents, let us first appreciate the uniqueness of agricultural economics. In this prologue, we will address the link between agricultural economics and economics, introduce some of the major fields of agricultural economics, commemorate the range of scholars who laid the foundation for advanced agricultural economics, and provide a perspective on its present and future.

The Diverse Field of Agricultural Economics

Adam Smith

Let us start with the beginning of the economic profession. Economics was spun off philosophy, and Adam Smith[1] was a professor of moral philosophy. Mathematics was introduced to explain the economy's behavior since "the laws of Nature are written in the language of mathematics" (Smith, 1776). Adam Smith introduced the notion of the invisible hand, showing that under perfect competition, markets will result in socially desirable outcomes. Later, economists used mathematical tools to refine the conditions under which Smith's results worked, and to understand the policy implications. The mathematical sophistication of economics was improved when von Neumann[2] and Morgenstern[3] introduced game theory, and Kuznets[4] and Frisch[5] introduced econometrics.

[1]https://www.econlib.org/library/Enc/bios/Smith.html.
[2]https://mathshistory.st-andrews.ac.uk/Biographies/Von_Neumann/.
[3]https://www.informs.org/Explore/History-of-O.R.-Excellence/Biographical-Profiles/Morgenstern-Oskar.
[4]https://www.nobelprize.org/prizes/economic-sciences/1971/kuznets/facts/.
[5]https://www.nobelprize.org/prizes/economic-sciences/1969/frisch/facts/.

John Maynard Keynes

John Maynard Keynes[6] was an economist and a trader. He developed an applied theory based on his experience in the real world. Based on observations, he developed new economic concepts, including risk premiums, non-equilibrating markets, and the role of government policy in stabilizing the economy. Keynes's macroeconomics became a major part of economic thought and policy analysis.

John Kenneth Galbraith

Agricultural economics was established in the early 20th century and was the result of a merger of the disciplines of farm economics and farm management. Farm management was more practical, emphasizing understanding farm behavior and helping farmers solve practical problems. Farm economics aimed to understand agricultural markets, prices, policy, and the "macro" of agriculture. The Keynesian thinking that contributed to government intervention during the Great Depression also led to agricultural policies introduced and shaped by farm economists. The new field of agricultural economics has combined theory and empirical work, and evolved with events and technology. One of the early leading agricultural economists was John Kenneth Galbraith.[7] He obtained

[6]https://www.econlib.org/library/Enc/bios/Keynes.html.
[7]https://www.econlib.org/library/Enc/bios/Galbraith.html.

his agricultural economics degree from the University of California, Berkeley, worked at the University of California, Davis on agricultural research issues, then moved to Harvard, played a major role in the government during the Second World War, and made major contributions to mainstream economics. He became a public intellectual, and his 1958 book, *The Affluent Society*, was influential. His career exemplified the major edge of agricultural economics, which is an applied discipline that works with farmers, businesses, and researchers, learns about the major problems on the ground, and develops ideas and techniques to modify them. In the process, agricultural economists have made major advancements to expand the tools and methodologies of economics.

Bruce Gardner

Agricultural economics has multiple fields of research, and agricultural policy is a major field that has evolved over the years. One of the field's giants was Willard Cochrane,[8] who argued that U.S. agricultural policy evolved from land policies to research policies to income support and environmental policies. He introduced the technological treadmill that has been used throughout economics, which emphasizes that most of the adopters of new technology may not gain much because of price effects, and most of the rent from new technologies goes to early adopters (Cochrane, 1979). Another leading scholar of agricultural economics

[8]https://www.aaea.org/trust/appreciation-clubs/willard-w-cochrane.

was Frederick Waugh,[9] a prolific microeconomist who developed a methodological approach to assess the economics of variability and unstable prices and evaluate the impact of stabilization policies. He identified conditions wherein certain groups may benefit from price instability (Waugh, 1944). Earl Heady[10] pioneered the use of mathematical programming for planning government policy, especially in agriculture, and was among the first to harness the power of computers to assess how alternative policies would affect distribution throughout the economy. Many have built on his approach. Bruce Gardner[11] analyzed the evolution of U.S. agricultural policy in the 20th century, recognizing that during this period, because of migration and technological change, farmers have ceased to be relatively disadvantaged groups and the support for policies reflects their political power. He suggested policy reform that would be as efficient as possible given the policy constraint (Gardner, 2009).

Agricultural economists also had a major impact on the economics of labor and community. Nobel laureate Theodore Schultz[12] introduced the notions of human capital and the ability to deal with disequilibrium, and his work revolutionized labor economics. Nobel laureate Eleanor Ostrom[13] introduced new insight to understand the important role of institutions and political arrangements in allocating resources, especially those shared by the community. Modern institutional economic research follows the path blazed by Ostrom. Agricultural economic research has addressed major labor issues that become prominent over time, including the economics of migration (Taylor, 1999) and the implication of technological innovation on workers (Schmitz and Seckler, 1970).

[9]https://www.aaea.org/trust/appreciation-clubs/frederick-v-waugh.
[10]https://www.aaea.org/trust/appreciation-clubs/earl-o-heady.
[11]https://prabook.com/web/bruce_l.gardner/1393823.
[12]https://www.nobelprize.org/prizes/economic-sciences/1979/schultz/facts/.
[13]https://en.wikipedia.org/wiki/Elinor_Ostrom.

Theodore Schultz

Eleanor Ostrom

Consumer economics has always been a major area of emphasis by agricultural economists. It evolved from a simple estimation of food demand to analyzing the economics of nutrition and product quality in agriculture, which led to the establishment of food stamps and other nutritional programs, where agricultural economists such as Sylvia Lane[14] played an important role. She was a scholar who contributed to the development and implementation of food and nutrition policies in the U.S. Over the years, research on consumer economics was expanded to understand the economics of local and organic food, the economics of food labeling, and the linkages between food nutrition and health. There is a large body of research on the global economics of food, addressing issues of global food security (Tweeten, 1999) and issues of food aid (Barrett, 2002). Agricultural economists, such as World Food Prize winner Per Pinstrup-Andersen,[15] developed a systematic way to assess the global food situation (Pinstrup-Andersen *et al.*, 1999), others developed programs to assess the impact of climate change on food security (Wheeler and von Braun, 2013).

[14]https://senate.universityofcalifornia.edu/_files/inmemoriam/html/SylviaLane.html.

[15]https://www.worldfoodprize.org/en/laureates/20002009_laureates/2001_pinstrupandersen/.

Sylvia Lane

Per Pinstrup-Andersen

Zvi Grilliches

Much of the emphasis in agricultural economics is on understanding agricultural production, technology, and innovation, where the data availability and demand from clientele groups afforded agricultural economists a head start compared to other disciplines. Agricultural economists were among the first to estimate the agricultural production function and use programming methods to improve production practices (Heady *et al.*, 1960). Several scholars have studied the evolution of agricultural systems from traditional to modern (Pingali, 1997; Antle, 1999; Chavas, 2008). With the advance of big data, improved monitoring and precision, agricultural economists have studied how information technology and this new capability will affect agriculture and food markets (Miao and Khanna, 2020; Finger *et al.*, 2019; Weersink *et al.*, 2018). Probably one of the most important contributions in this area to economics is the study of technology adoption. Grilliches's[16] (1957) seminal paper introduced a quantitative approach to estimating the factors that affect adoption, becoming a baseline for future papers, such as Feder *et al.* (1985).

Yujiro Hayami

Vernon Ruttan

Much of the research on the economics of innovation and the link between research, innovation, and technology has been done by agricultural economists (Evenson *et al.*, 1975). The notion of induced innovation, where differences in conditions and location result in differences in innovation, was articulated by agricultural economists Hayami[17] and Ruttan[18] (1971), and agricultural economists have developed measurements of research productivity and documented the high return rate and underinvestment in agricultural research (Huffman and Evenson, 2008; Alston and Pardey, 2021).

International trade is a key element of the agricultural economy, and agricultural trade issues were behind the development of comparative advantage by David Ricardo[19] (Ricardo, 1821). Agricultural

[16]https://nap.nationalacademies.org/read/10269/chapter/6#82.
[17]https://fukuoka-prize.org/en/laureates/detail/e28dfce3-1d2f-4b61-b739-666efa631e57.
[18]http://www.nasonline.org/member-directory/deceased-members/50953.html.
[19]https://www.econlib.org/library/Enc/bios/Ricardo.html.

economists documented how trade barriers and protectionism in developed countries harmed developing countries and advocated for freer trade that would assume affordable and healthy diets. Agricultural economists like D. Gale Johnson[20] adjusted and applied the ideas of Adam Smith and David Ricardo to a modern world and provided an empirical understanding of trade relationships needed for improved policy (Johnson, 1997). Study by Anderson *et al.* (2013) has found that, over time, agricultural markets have become more competitive, and many trade-distorted policies have been reduced.

Irma Adelman

Agriculture plays a much bigger role in developing economies. There is, therefore, an influential synchronization between agricultural and development economics. Irma Adleman[21] was a pioneer in developing computable general equilibrium models that assess the impact of proposed policies on the economy, as well as the efficiency and distributional allocation (Adelman *et al.*, 2014). Agricultural economists have used various quantitative methods to understand farmers' behavior and address poverty and malnourishment, enabling better decision-making for economic agents and promoting policy change (de Janvry and Sadoulet, 2022). Research in agricultural development also provides new insights into value chains and the mechanisms that lead to structural changes within economies and the emergence of modern value chains (Barrett *et al.*, 2022).

[20]https://nap.nationalacademies.org/read/11429/chapter/13.

[21]https://senate.universityofcalifornia.edu/in-memoriam/files/irma-adelman.html.

Oscar R. Burt

Agricultural economics gave rise to environmental and resource economics. Agriculture must deal with challenges of drought, dust bowls, and floods. Agricultural economists, such as Oscar Burt[22] developed dynamic models to address natural resource management over time (Burt, 1964). Similarly, there is a large body of literature on the economics of soil management (Stevens, 2018) and pest control (Sexton *et al.*, 2007). Siegfried von Ciriacy-Wantrup[23] was a pioneer of environmental economics and many of his concepts were modeled and estimated by economists over the years. Tony Fisher,[24] working with Kenneth Arrow,[25] developed a method to address concerns for irreversible damage in assessing new projects (Arrow and Fisher, 1974). Agricultural economists introduced multiple methods to assess the non-market benefits of environmental amenities and incorporate them into social decision-making (Hanemann *et al.*, 1991; Freeman III *et al.*, 2014; Randall *et al.*, 1974).

The development of agriculture depends on the availability of finance, and many financial institutions, including futures markets, originated in agriculture. Therefore, agricultural economists have made a great contribution to finance. Working (1961) was a major contributor to the economics of futures markets, and agricultural economists significantly contributed to this field (Carter, 1999). Agricultural economists were among the first to recognize that credit markets tend to be imperfect, and there is a role for different types of institutions to provide credit to agriculture and agribusiness. Barry and Robison (2001) provided an early survey of the literature on

[22]https://www.tributearchive.com/obituaries/664377/Oscar-Burt.
[23]https://en.wikipedia.org/wiki/Siegfried_von_Ciriacy-Wantrup.
[24]https://are.berkeley.edu/users/anthony-fisher.
[25]https://www.nobelprize.org/prizes/economic-sciences/1972/arrow/facts/.

agricultural finance mechanisms, policies, and institutions and their implications.

Ray Goldberg

Much of the production of agriculture is done outside farms, in processing, wholesaling, and retailing. The high rate of innovation in agriculture leads to new products and organizations that are implemented through modern supply chains (Zilberman *et al.*, 2022). Ray Goldberg[26] (1968) developed agribusiness research agenda that relies on case studies incorporating microeconomic concepts with economic reality. Michael Boehlje[27] (1999) documented and provided a framework to analyze the transition from traditional agriculture to modern agribusiness. Richard Sexton (2013) combined modern industrial economic thinking with a keen eye for economic reality to develop new approaches for analyses of agribusiness. Jeff Perloff and his collaborators wrote the classic text on industrial organization that serves the economic perspective (Carlton and Perloff, 2005).

Quantification has been a crucial element in agricultural economics, and agricultural economists developed and expanded new estimation and prediction methods. For instance, they developed advanced methods to assess the dynamics of supply and demand. Marc Nerlove[28] introduced the notion of adaptive expectation that allows for the assessment and prediction of supply response parameters over time (Nerlove, 1956). Shankar Subramanian collaborated

[26]https://www.hbs.edu/faculty/Pages/profile.aspx?facId=12285.

[27]https://agribusiness.purdue.edu/people/michael-boehlje/.

[28]https://www.aeaweb.org/about-aea/honors-awards/distinguished-fellows/marc-nerlove.

Marc Nerlove

George G. Judge

with Sir Agnus Deaton[29] to develop an applied system of equations for demand for food and calories (Subramanian and Deaton, 1996). Aigner *et al.* (1977) pioneered estimating stochastic frontiers of production functions. Mundlak (1978) developed creative methods to analyze pooled cross-section and time series data. George Judge's[30] research and writing integrated economic methods to make them approachable and coherent and introduced new methods (Judge, 1982; Judge and Mittelhammer, 2011).

The emphasis on applied policymaking in agriculture and the environment led agricultural economists to contribute to the development of an applied welfare analysis framework (Just *et al.*, 2005). The importance of political consideration led to the emergence of important contributions in political economy, which enables the assessment of complex issues; for example, attitudes toward biotechnology (Swinnen, 2010). Agricultural economists have developed many numerical systems over the years (e.g., McCarl and Spreen, 1997). Richard Howitt (1995) developed new, creative methods using constrained optimization for quantitative policy design. Agricultural economists have been crucial in developing an international trade model. Irma Adleman was crucial in developing the computer general equilibrium model, and Thomas Hertel[31] introduced the Global

[29]https://scholar.princeton.edu/deaton/home.
[30]https://are.berkeley.edu/users/george-g-judge.
[31]https://web.ics.purdue.edu/~hertel/.

Trade Analysis Project (GTAP), which includes both software and a database that allows the assessment of the economic impact of multiple policies (Hertel, 1997).

Because of the constant contact of agricultural economists with practitioners in the field, they recognized some of the limitations of neoclassical economics. They were pioneers in the development of models of "behavioral economics." Agricultural economics were among the first to use experiments to assess risk preferences, estimate imitation models of technology adoption, develop models of adaptive expectation, and introduce different *ad hoc* rules to resource allocation and risk management (Wuepper *et al.*, 2023). Consumer food choices have become an area with multiple applications of behavioral economics (Lusk and McClusky, 2018; Caputo and Just, 2022). Agricultural economists were among the first to apply the notion of social capital to economic choices (Schmid and Robison, 1995). Recent studies assess the impact of culture, beliefs, and self-efficacy on farmers' behavior and use methods from other social sciences to understand economic behavior.

The Present and the Future of Agricultural Economics

Agricultural economics is part of, but simultaneously distinct from, economics. It is inspired by reality, evolving over time; it is multi-disciplinary in the sense that it presents results of cross-pollination of economics and other disciplines, and therefore has its own applied theory and unique tools that have influenced economics and other disciplines; and it guides agricultural and environmental policies. Any discipline needs sources of financial support, and in the case of agricultural economics, it is the U.S. Department of Agriculture and other federal and state agencies that provide resources for research. Other international organizations, such as the Food and Agriculture Organization (FAO) and the World Bank, and other non-governmental organizations and private sector companies, have invested in agricultural research that they are interested in implementing. Agricultural economists have several associations, including the International Agricultural Economics Association, the Agricultural and Applied Economics Association, the European Agricultural Economics Association, and many national and regional associations. As the share of agriculture in the GDP and employment in agriculture declined, agricultural economists expanded their reach to address issues of natural resources, food, energy, and development. Today, the title "Agricultural and Applied Economics" is much more descriptive of the research activities by organizations that started as a narrowly defined agricultural economics unit.

We expect that these dynamics will continue, and the agricultural and applied economic discipline will expand to cover multiple areas, adapting to reality. There will be a larger emphasis beyond the farm gate, with more emphasis on agribusiness. With the new tools of biotechnology and the challenges of climate change, we expect that agriculture and natural resources will become a major part of a modern bioeconomy that applies tools of biotechnology and information technology with land and other natural resources to produce food, fuel, energy, and biochemicals. It is crucial to transition from a non-renewable to a renewable economy (Zilberman *et al.*, 2013). Agricultural and Applied Economics will continue to be an integrating discipline between economics and the natural sciences and will contribute to the emergence of more integrated social science tools. The capacity and approach of the discipline will be affected by the development of technology and computational capabilities, with enhanced utilization of expansive databases, modern analytical tools, and improved monitoring and interaction.

We hope that this book will provide a good introduction to some major issues and methods in agricultural and applied economics, and that it will be useful for graduate students and researchers who are studying, researching, or teaching agricultural economics and policy. Chapter 1 offers a brief history of U.S. agriculture and agricultural policy. Following it, we then present three chapters (i.e., Chapters 2–4) that summarize some core models related to production, demand, as well as decision-making under risk and uncertainty. Chapters 5 and 6 discuss welfare analysis and political economy of agricultural policies. Chapters 7 and 8 focus on technical innovation and adoption, respectively, on which Chapter 9 (Agricultural Supply Chain) is built. Chapter 10 examines food security and safety, and Chapter 11 studies the economics of pesticides. Chapter 12 investigates some major conservation policies and payments for ecosystem services in agriculture, followed by Chapter 13 in which the relationship between agriculture and climate change is discussed. Finally, the epilogue discusses the economics of sustainable development in agriculture.

The book has several advanced chapters that require some background in calculus, but we believe that much of the book is accessible to individuals with some quantitative background. The notes in this book do not cover all the fields of agricultural economics equally; it is based on classes that we actually taught and thus, for example, has a minimal discussion of agricultural trade, finance, labor, or nutrition. The text has evolved over time and is based on classes and knowledge that we obtained from our teachers (in particular, in the case of David Zilberman: Richard Just, Gordon Rausser, Andrew Schmitz, and Alain de Janvry) and many generations of students. We hope you will enjoy the book.

Acknowledgments

The book would not be possible without the help and support of many people. We thank Carlo Cafiero, who contributed to the early draft of the class note. We thank the late David Buschena for useful advice and comments. Comments and suggestions from Madhu Khanna, Jeff LeFrance, and from students in the course sequences at both University of California, Berkeley and Auburn University are deeply appreciated. We are particularly thankful for Benjamin Shapiro's thorough editing of the book. We thank Eugene Adjei, Nabin Bhandari, Brian Cornish, Bijesh Mishra, Pritam Mitra, Sadie Shoemaker, and Pathmanathan Sivashankar for reading some of the chapters in this book. Research assistance offered by Ngbede Musa, Sadie Shoemaker, and Azaz Zaman is deeply appreciated. The authors also thank Giannini Foundation at the University of California, Berkeley, Alabama Agricultural Experiment Station, and the Hatch program of the National Institute of Food and Agriculture within the USDA for financial support.

References

Adelman, I., D. Zilberman, and E. Kim. 2014. A Conversation with Irma Adelman. *Annual Review of Resource Economics* 6(1): 1–16.

Aigner, D., CA K. Lovell, and P. Schmidt. 1977. Formulation and Estimation of Stochastic Frontier Production Function Models. *Journal of Econometrics* 6(1): 21–37.

Alston, J.M. and P.G. Pardey. 2021. The Economics of Agricultural Innovation. *Handbook of Agricultural Economics* 5: 3895–3980.

Anderson, K., G. Rausser, and J. Swinnen. 2013. Political Economy of Public Policies: Insights from Distortions to Agricultural and Food Markets. *Journal of Economic Literature* 51(2): 423–477.

Antle, J.M. 1999. The New Economics of Agriculture. *American Journal of Agricultural Economics* 81(5): 993–1010.

Arrow, K.J. and A.C. Fisher. 1974. Environmental Preservation, Uncertainty, of Irreversibility. *The Quarterly Journal of Economics* 88(2): 312–319.

Barrett, C.B. 2002. Food Security and Food Assistance Programs. *Handbook of Agricultural Economics* 2: 2103–2190.

Barrett, C.B., T. Reardon, J. Swinnen, and D. Zilberman. 2022. Agri-Food Value Chain Revolutions in Low- and Middle-Income Countries. *Journal of Economic Literature* 60(4): 1316–1377.

Barry, P.J. and L.J. Robison. 2001. Agricultural Finance: Credit, Credit Constraints, and Consequences. *Handbook of Agricultural Economics* 1: 513–571.

Boehlje, M. 1999. Structural Changes in the Agricultural Industries: How Do We Measure, Analyze and Understand Them? *American Journal of Agricultural Economics* 81(5): 1028–1041.

Burt, O. 1964. The Economics of Conjunctive Use of Ground and Surface Water. *Hilgardia* 36(2): 31–111.

Caputo, V. and D. Just. 2022. The Economics of Food Related Policies: Considering Public Health and Malnutrition. *Handbook of Agricultural Economics* 6: 5117.

Carlton, D.W. and J.M. Perloff. 2005. *Modern Industrial Organization*, 4th Ed. Pearson Addison-Wesley, Boston.

Carter, C.A. 1999. Commodity Futures Markets: A Survey. *Australian Journal of Agricultural and Resource Economics* 43(2): 209–247.

Chavas, J.-P. 2008. On the Economics of Agricultural Production. *Australian Journal of Agricultural and Resource Economics* 52(4): 365–380.

Cochrane, W.W. 1979. *The Development of American Agriculture: A Historical Analysis.* University of Minnesota Press.

de Janvry, A. and E. Sadoulet. 2022. Agriculture for Development: Analytics and Action. *Annual Review of Resource Economics* 14: 1–16.

Evenson, R.E. and Y. Kislev. 1975. *Agricultural Research and Productivity.* Yale University Press.

Feder, G., R.E. Just, and D. Zilberman. 1985. Adoption of Agricultural Innovations in Developing Countries: A Survey. *Economic Development and Cultural Change* 33(2): 255–298.

Finger, R., S.M. Swinton, N. El Benni, and A. Walter. 2019. Precision Farming at the Nexus of Agricultural Production and the Environment. *Annual Review of Resource Economics* 11: 313–335.

Freeman III, A.M, J.A. Herriges, and C.L. Kling. 2014. *The Measurement of Environmental and Resource Values: Theory and Methods.* Routledge.

Galbraith, J.K. 1998. *The Affluent Society.* Houghton Mifflin Harcourt.

Gardner, B.L. 2009. *American Agriculture in the Twentieth Century: How It Flourished and What It Cost.* Harvard University Press.

Goldberg, R.A. 1968. Agribusiness Coordination: A Systems Approach to the Wheat, Soybean, and Florida Orange Economies. *Agribusiness Coordination: A Systems Approach to the Wheat, Soybean, and Florida Orange Economies* 50(3): 782–783.

Griliches, Z. 1957. Hybrid Corn: An Exploration in the Economics of Technological Change. *Econometrica, Journal of the Econometric Society* (1957): 501–522.

Hanemann, M., J. Loomis, and B. Kanninen. 1991. Statistical Efficiency of Double-Bounded Dichotomous Choice Contingent Valuation. *American Journal of Agricultural Economics* 73(4): 1255–1263.

Hayami, Y. and V.W. Ruttan. 1971. *Agricultural Development: An International Perspective.* Baltimore, Md/London: The Johns Hopkins Press.

Heady, E.O., C.F. Curtiss, and L.D. John. 1960. *Agricultural Production Functions.* Kalyani Publishers, Chennai.

Hertel, T.W. 1997. *Global Trade Analysis: Modeling and Applications.* Cambridge University Press.

Howitt, R.E. 1995. Positive Mathematical Programming. *American Journal of Agricultural Economics* 77(2): 329–342.

Huffman, W.E. and R.E. Evenson. 2008. *Science for Agriculture: A Long-Term Perspective.* John Wiley & Sons, Hoboken.

Johnson, D.G. 1997. Agriculture and the Wealth of Nations. *The American Economic Review* 87(2): 1–12.

Judge, G.G. 1982. *Introduction to the Theory and Practice of Econometrics.* Wiley, Hoboken.

Judge, G.G. and R.C. Mittelhammer. 2011. *An Information Theoretic Approach to Econometrics.* Cambridge University Press.

Just, R.E., D.L. Hueth, and A. Schmitz. 2005. *The Welfare Economics of Public Policy: A Practical Approach to Project and Policy Evaluation.* Edward Elgar Publishing.

Lusk, J.L. and J. McCluskey. 2018. Understanding the Impacts of Food Consumer Choice and Food Policy Outcomes. *Applied Economic Perspectives and Policy* 40(1): 5–21.

McCarl, B.A. and T.H. Spreen. 1997. *Applied Mathematical Programming Using Algebraic Systems.* Cambridge, MA.

Miao, R. and M. Khanna. 2020. Harnessing Advances in Agricultural Technologies to Optimize Resource Utilization in the Food-Energy-Water Nexus. *Annual Review of Resource Economics* 12: 65–85.

Mundlak, Y. 1978. On the Pooling of Time Series and Cross Section Data. *Econometrica: Journal of the Econometric Society* 46: 69–85.

Nerlove, M. 1956. Estimates of the Elasticities of Supply of Selected Agricultural Commodities. *American Journal of Agricultural Economics* 38(2): 496–509.

Pingali, P.L. 1997. From Subsistence to Commercial Production Systems: the Transformation of Asian Agriculture. *American Journal of Agricultural Economics* 79(2): 628–634.

Pinstrup-Andersen, P., R. Pandya-Lorch, and M.W. Rosegrant. 1999. *World Food Prospects: Critical Issues For the Early Twenty-First Century.* Food Policy Report.

Randall, A., B. Ives, and C. Eastman. 1974. Bidding Games for Valuation of Aesthetic Environmental Improvements. *Journal of Environmental Economics and Management* 1(2): 132–149.

Ricardo, D. 1821. *On the Principles of Political Economy.* J. Murray, London.

Schmid, A.A. and L.J. Robison. 1995. Applications of Social Capital Theory. *Journal of Agricultural and Applied Economics* 27(1): 59–66.

Schmitz, A. and D. Seckler. 1970. Mechanized Agriculture and Social Welfare: The Case of the Tomato Harvester. *American Journal of Agricultural Economics* 52(4): 569–577.

Schultz, T.W. 1961. Investment in Human Capital. *The American Economic Review* 51(1): 1–17.

Sexton, S.E., Z. Lei, and D. Zilberman. 2007. The Economics of Pesticides and Pest Control. *International Review of Environmental and Resource Economics* 1(3): 271–326.

Sexton, R.J. 2013. Market Power, Misconceptions, and Modern Agricultural Markets. *American Journal of Agricultural Economics* 95(2): 209–219.

Smith, A. 1776. *An Inquiry into the Nature and Causes of the Wealth of Nations.* W. Strahan and T. Cadell, London.

Stevens, A.W. 2018. The Economics of Soil Health. *Food Policy* 80: 1–9.

Subramanian, S. and A. Deaton. 1996. The Demand for Food and Calories. *Journal of Political Economy* 104(1): 133–162.

Swinnen, J.F.M. 2010. The Political Economy of Agricultural of Food Policies: Recent Contributions, New Insights, and Areas for Further Research. *Applied Economic Perspectives and Policy* 32(1): 33–58.

Taylor, E.J. 1999. The New Economics of Labour Migration and the Role of Remittances in the Migration Process. *International Migration* 37(1): 63–88.

Tweeten, L. 1999. The Economics of Global Food Security. *Applied Economic Perspectives and Policy* 21(2): 473–488.

Waugh, F.V. 1944. Does the Consumer Benefit from Price Instability? *The Quarterly Journal of Economics* 58(4): 602–614.

Weersink, A., E. Fraser, D. Pannell, E. Duncan, and S. Rotz. 2018. Opportunities and Challenges for Big Data in Agricultural and Environmental Analysis. *Annual Review of Resource Economics* 10: 19–37.

Wheeler, T. and J. von Braun. 2013. Climate Change Impacts on Global Food Security. *Science* 341(6145): 508–513.

Working, H. 1961. New Concepts Concerning Futures Markets and Prices. *The American Economic Review* 51(2): 160–163.

Wuepper, D., S. Bukchin-Peles, D. Just, and D. Zilberman. 2023. Behavioral Agricultural Economics. *Applied Economic Perspectives and Policy* 45: 2094–2105.

Zilberman, D. 2019. Agricultural Economics as a Poster Child of Applied Economics: Big Data & Big Issues. *American Journal of Agricultural Economics* 101(2): 353–364.

Zilberman, D., E. Kim, S. Kirschner, S. Kaplan, and J. Reeves. 2013. Technology and the Future Bioeconomy. *Agricultural Economics* 44(s1): 95–102.

Zilberman, D., T. Reardon, J. Silver, L. Lu, and A. Heiman. 2022. From the Laboratory to the Consumer: Innovation, Supply Chain, and Adoption with Applications to Natural Resources. *Proceedings of the National Academy of Sciences* 119(23): e2115880119.

Chapter 1

History of U.S. Agriculture: A Lesson in Development

The settlement of the United States and the evolution of U.S. agriculture offer unique case studies in economic development. In this chapter, we will discuss agricultural policies in the United States beginning around 1620 when settlers from Europe established new agricultural policies and systems. The discussion draws much from Cochrane (1979). Currently, when we speak about agricultural policies, we mostly speak about price supports, subsidies, as well as environmental regulations and payments, but agricultural policies evolved from land and settlement policies to farm support policies to landscape and environmental quality policies. We can distinguish between four stages in the U.S. agricultural development process: 1620–1740 (search for appropriate farming practices), 1740–1810 (establishment of viable production modes), 1810–1900 (the westward movement), and 1900–present (the intensification of farming practices). We now briefly describe some key evolvement in U.S. agriculture during these four stages.

1. Search for Appropriate Farming Practices — 1620–1740

In the early 1600s, groups of aspiring settlers migrated from Europe to find their luck in the new world. They brought farm animals, seeds, equipment, and some know-how, and started settling. But not many made it; the weather and soil conditions were not accommodating, and therefore many settlers perished. We mainly read about the success stories, though. To survive, the settlers became involved in fishing, hunting, and gathering, and their food production activities resembled those in the hunting-and-gathering stage of human development. Slowly, the early settlers learned how to farm in the New World. They adapted to the local conditions, borrowed practices and crops from Native Americans, and established some modes of operation that became successful.

The early settlers learned to plant quite a few crops from the Indigenous, including corn (or maize), pumpkins, squash, beans, and tobacco. With the exception of corn, crops during this period were specialized by geographic area and stage of settlement. In the early 1700s, New England had become the center of a sea-based fishing and whaling industry. In the middle colonies (New Jersey and Pennsylvania), settlers produced wheat, corn, rye, oats, and barley. In Maryland, Virginia, and North Carolina, the preeminent commercial crop was tobacco. Production of tobacco developed rapidly since the early settlement and provided an important cash crop for export (Cochrane, 1979). Rice was introduced in the late 1600s and became an established crop around Charleston, South Carolina by the early 1700s. In the 1600s, animal husbandry virtually did not exist. The livestock industry began to take shape in the 1700s due to the increased demand for higher-quality livestock.

Colonial agriculture was a hand-labor agriculture, and early settlers used little or no animal power. The basic tools were hoes, axes, and scythes. There was a continuing scarcity of human labor in the colonies. Farmers in New England depended almost entirely on family labor and sought to increase their labor supply by raising large families. Large farms imported indentured servants from Europe. Large tobacco or rice plantations in Maryland, Virginia, and South Carolina turned increasingly to the importation of slaves. The system of slavery was firmly institutionalized by the 1700s.

2. Establishment of Viable Production Modes — 1740–1810

By 1740, the older, settled areas became highly specialized in the production of agricultural commodities and food. In the New England states, farmers produced corn, wheat, hay, apples, and livestock. In Pennsylvania and New Jersey, farmers produced a surplus of wheat and potatoes, and developed a small livestock-producing and fattening industry. In the Southern states, tobacco, rice, cotton, and sugar cane were the major crops. The surplus of agricultural products was available for sale to the growing towns and export to Europe.

The modes of operation differed in the North and South of the New World. While the North attracted many migrants from Europe, who established relatively small farms and villages, the South established many large plantations that relied on slave labor. We must recall that the popular mode of settlement in South America, which attracted a relatively small number of European settlers, was also the plantation model. Brazil was a major importer of slaves in the production of sugar cane. The earlier slaves in the New World arrived in South Carolina for the production of sugar cane, but once the demand for cotton took off, the South transitioned to it. The division between the North and the South resulted in a continuous conflict that led to the U.S. Civil War.

During the American Revolution period, a freehold land tenure system was established, and the United States acquired the national public domain. The federal lands were sold in public auctions to private persons in cash initially, and then in both cash and credits through a series of Land Acts in 1785, 1796, 1800, and 1804. Purchases of the public domain were typically made by speculators who hoped to resell that land to settlers at higher prices. Pioneers who could not afford to buy land simply "squatted" on vacant public lands, which was a popular means of acquiring a farm during this period. In addition, large amounts of land were distributed as grants or bounties to people who had served in the Continental Army.

From 1775 to 1810, some pioneers started moving across the Appalachians. Hunters and woodsmen showed the way, followed by some small pioneer farmers who had a patch of corn and some livestock. Life for the pioneer farmers and their families was both hard and cruel as they traversed the Appalachian Mountains (Cochrane, 1979).

3. The Westward Movement — 1810–1900

While the early settlements were established on the East Coast, during the 1800s, the government promoted populating further west. After the Louisiana Purchase in 1803, the U.S. government controlled the majority of what we recognize as the continental U.S. today. While some people moved west and occupied land with no official rights (i.e., "squatters"), to attract people to move *en masse*, the government established a system of homesteading whereby a family was granted the rights to a parcel of land in a designated area of the west. The basic idea was that first arrivals ensured rights, but these rights were only held up when families occupied the land. Later this system was applied to water rights, where it is called the *prior appropriation* system based on the principle of "first in time, first in right," as well as "use it or lose it." These systems of land and resource allocation proved effective early on, but later became sources of inefficiency.

The government played a crucial role in the settlement processes because it owned much of the new land, allowing it to direct the processes. A series of land policies during this period promoted the westward movement. Under the provisions of the Preemption Act of 1841, a farmer could settle legally in the public domain before he purchased his land. Further, he could buy 160 acres of the land on which he had settled for $1.25 per acre once the land in that area was opened for sale. This was close to a policy of free land disposal. The government also granted land rights to farmers through homesteading. The Homestead Act was enacted on May 20, 1862, to distribute lands in the public domain to settlers free of charge under a few conditions. More and more people migrated west of the Mississippi River into the Great West. The final settlement and its linkage to the east through a railroad network occurred in the period of 1860–1897.

Moreover, due to its limited ability to collect taxes over this period, the U.S. government used land sales to finance the development of public goods. It also used land grants to incentivize the construction of the railroads, and the railroad companies owned a mile of land to each side of the tracks. As a result, to this day, the Southern Pacific Transportation Company is one of the biggest landowners in California. Adjacently, western land settlement was fueled by railroad construction. In each municipality, the government granted land to build schools and finance them through land sales. The establishment of rural schools was one of the major achievements of the U.S. Later, land grants were used to finance universities, and every state had a land grant university system.

The major rural ideology of the U.S., based on the reality of the North, was that family farms should be the main form of farming and that agriculture should be a competitive sector consisting of independent farmers instead of peasants. This ideology is called the Jeffersonian Vision, named after the renowned Thomas Jefferson. Within this ideology, the role of the government is to provide education, information, and technologies. Nobel Laureate Theodore Schultz, the father of the idea of human capital, emphasized the difference between a peasant and a farmer (Schultz, 1975). Peasants are traditional farmers who learn practices from their parents. Traditional agriculture has been in equilibrium, where yields and methods changed little, and therefore imitation was the best form of acquiring practices. A farmer, however, lives in a dynamic environment, requiring them to adjust to changes in economic conditions or technology. After the start of the Industrial Revolution, and the massive expansion of global trade, the importance of adapting to changes increased. Schultz distinguished between two types of human capital: worker ability and allocative ability. The former involves the physical capacity to conduct tasks, while the latter involves business and management decisions. He also used the term "the ability to deal with disequilibrium" to describe allocative ability. Allocative ability requires literacy and numeracy, and rural schools were introduced to train farmers with allocative ability.

Moreover, the thinkers behind the idea of family farms recognized that individual farms could not develop new technologies to address changing agricultural realities. Therefore, they later introduced land grant universities with experiment stations that developed new agricultural practices, and, later, Cooperative Extension, which transferred knowledge to farmers. The land grant colleges were established through the Morrill Act of 1862 during the Civil War. These colleges offered courses in agriculture and mechanical arts in addition to classical studies. The U.S. Department of Agriculture was established in 1862 as well, and one of its major roles was to provide price information to farmers to ensure competitive and fair trade. Agricultural experimentation stations were established by the Hatch Act of 1887 and Cooperative Extension through the Smith–Lever Act of 1914.

The idea of a competitive farm sector that is augmented by collective actions has prevailed throughout the history of U.S. agriculture. Farmers established the farm bureau, an organization that aimed to represent them politically and have the market muscle to obtain better terms of insurance and other products. In a history where buyers tended to have monopolistic power, there was a need for a countervailing power. Thus, agricultural cooperatives that were established to negotiate terms of trade for farmers helped balance the relationship by controlling supply. The other developments in agriculture during this period include farm mechanization, market expansion, and agribusiness development. The process of farm mechanization started in the 1830s, reached widespread proportions in the 1850s, and accelerated since 1860. The introduction of the steamboat, the construction of the Erie Canal, and the development of railroads in the early 1800s opened the market to western farmers. The later development of the refrigerator railroad car for shipping fresh meat, fruits, and vegetables also widened the markets for farm producers and increased their income-earning possibilities. Agribusiness was developed to produce farm inputs, and to store, process, and distribute farm products. Market centers such as Chicago, St. Louis, and New Orleans grew to handle and distribute the growing agricultural surpluses.

The specialization of agricultural production according to their comparative advantage by areas was largely completed in the period of 1860–1900. The Northeast specialized in fruit, truck crops, and dairy production. The Upper South specialized in tobacco production and produced a surplus of corn. The Deep South continued to specialize in the production and export of cotton even after the abolition of slavery. The Midwest specialized in corn production, and corn surplus was utilized to support a livestock-feeding industry. Grain farming on the Great Plains was firmly established by 1890. California agriculture developed rapidly in the 1850s, and fruit and vegetable production developed quickly. The production areas established during this period continued up to the present day.

Perhaps one of the reasons why U.S. citizens expect much from the government, but do not like to pay taxes, is that for much of its early history, the government acquired assets with little or no payment and used or sold them to provide essential services. One has to admit, though, that the investments made by the government have been effective and yielded fruits. At the beginning of the 20th century, the government realized that it now needed to raise taxes to continue expanding the services it could provide. This led to the establishment of various forms of taxation, including federal income tax and the Internal Revenue Service. The tax revenue would allow the government to establish safety nets that support agriculture.

4. The Intensification of Farming Practices — 1900–Present

Throughout the 19th century, agriculture expanded westward. Production per acre changed little, even though U.S. agriculture acquired the capacity to adapt production systems to various conditions. The U.S. is a large country, and adapting wheat, corn, cotton, and other products to various regions required significant efforts and innovation (Olmstead, 2008). But towards the end of the 19th century, it became clear that expansion of U.S. agricultural production would

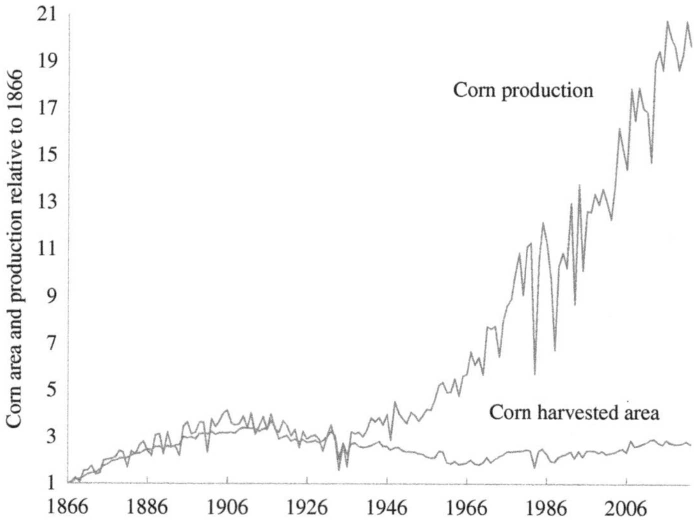

Figure 1. Area of corn harvested and production, U.S. 1866–2022 (indexed to 1866=1).

Source: The U.S. Census Bureau.

require increasing yields per acre, or intensification. The 20th century indeed has seen significant intensification as a result of breakthroughs such as the introduction of nitrogen fertilizer, modern breeding, and pest control. Some of these technologies were commercialized by the private sector, but their use was adapted to various locations by experimental stations and Cooperative Extension. The export market has played an important role in the development of U.S. agriculture. The level of agricultural exports reflected the demand for U.S. farm products and was critical to the economic well-being of U.S. farmers. While agricultural prices fluctuated — reflecting changes in market conditions — they reached a peak during the First World War. During the war, the U.S. was a food supplier for much of the world, and agricultural land use peaked between 1918 and 1925.

As Figure 1 demonstrates, corn production in the U.S. increased proportionally to acreage until the 1930s, and since then has risen more than 5-fold while acreage harvested declined. As the U.S. Department of Agriculture (USDA, 1969, Table 4) shows, crop acreage peaked in 1929 at 359.2 million acres, declined significantly

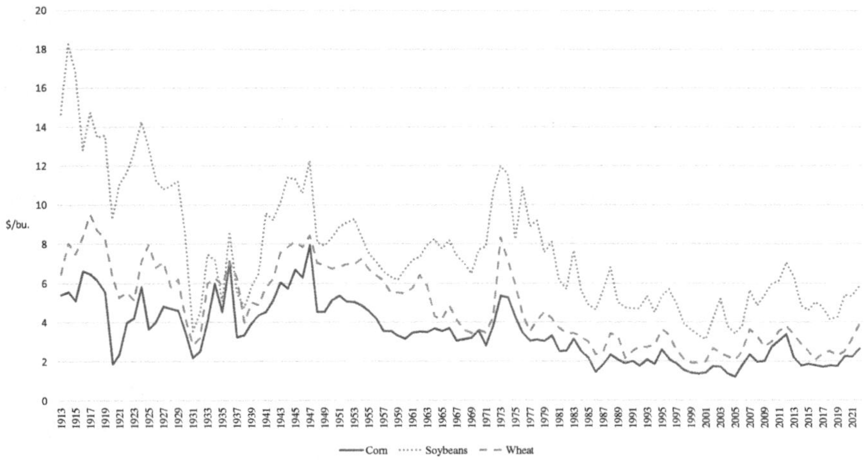

Figure 2. Major crop commodity prices in the United States, 1913–2022 ($/bushel, in 1982 dollars).

Source: National Agricultural Statistics Service of the USDA.

during the recession, rebounded almost to its peak during the Second World War, and then declined steadily to about 273 million acres in 1969. Since then, crop acreage has stabilized at around 310 million acres. In total, agricultural land, including cropland, rangeland, and woodland, is about 900 million acres. USDA (1969, Table 4) and USDA (2012, Table 8) also show that the number of farms has declined since 1935 when there were about 6.8 million farms in the U.S., and by 2012 there were around 2.1 million farms. At the same time, the size of the average farm increased and the productive resources of American agriculture had become concentrated in fewer and larger farms.

Figure 2 depicts the prices of major agricultural commodities over the 1912–2022 period. Inflation-adjusted prices reached their peak during the First World War (1914–1918), declined precipitously during the Great Depression (1929–1932), peaked again during the Second World War (1939–1945), declined afterward, but peaked briefly in 1973–1974 due to both the 1972 United States — Soviet Union Wheat Deal and the 1973–1974 Oil Embargo. In 1972, the U.S. government sold the Soviet Union a large volume of grains (about 10 million tons) at subsidized prices, not realizing that inventories were limited, and the net effect was a drastic increase in prices. President Nixon imposed price controls on foods and restricted exports in response. The government also established a more systematic monitoring process of grain inventories. Prices then declined until around 2005 and had risen as a result of the introduction of biofuels. Over 2013–2022, crop prices fluctuated due to supply, trade, and pandemic shocks.

5. Farm Problem and Agricultural Policies

The overall trends in the 20th century U.S. agriculture were declining prices and a reduction in acreage. Declining prices, resulting in declining farm income, were a dominating factor in U.S. agriculture policy. Thus, many policies sought to stabilize prices, assure income, and restrict acreage. Schultz (1964) and Cochrane (1979) developed a framework to analyze the major features of agriculture around the mid-20th century. They included:

(1) High rate of innovation.
(2) Many small farms.
(3) Homogenous product.
(4) Competitive markets.
(5) Inelastic demand.
(6) Randomness.
(7) Use of natural resources.
(8) Environmental and health side effects.
(9) Lack of mobility of inputs.
(10) Credit imperfection.

These features still apply today and encapsulate what people have called the "farm problem." This problem has several dimensions. The first dimension is that commodity prices tend to decline over time. The same may be true for the aggregate income of agricultural commodities. Inelastic demand for agricultural commodities, competition, and technological change lead to reduced farm prices and farm income. In particular, the adoption of new supply-enhancing technologies by competitive industries benefited consumers but reduced the overall income of the agricultural sector due to inelastic demand. Two factors contribute to increased demand for agricultural products and therefore agricultural income: One is increased non-farm income domestically, but this effect is declining because agricultural commodities have low-income elasticity in a country like the U.S.; the second factor is increased global demand. An increase in income in developing countries may result in increased international demand for food, and that may lead to increased export opportunities for U.S. farmers. Therefore, periods of low supply overseas, for example during the wars, and the opening of new markets like China and Russia tend to increase demand for and prices of U.S. crops.

The second dimension is the instability of prices. Randomness in supply and, sometimes, demand due to wars or changes in weather or economic conditions lead to fluctuating agricultural commodity prices. The third dimension is rural poverty. This is caused by the fact that agricultural assets, including human capital, are not mobile and cannot be easily reallocated to other uses. So, a reduction in farm prices leads to a reduction in farm income and farm assets, and sometimes causes significant bankruptcies and crises. The fourth dimension is the environmental side-effects of agriculture. Agricultural production may cause environmental and resource degradation, such as polluting groundwater, depleting soil resources, and harming wildlife. The great dust bowl of the 1930s was a wake-up call for the need for land stewardship. The publication of *Silent Spring* (Carson, 1962) raised awareness of the need for pesticide management.

Several policies were developed to address these different dimensions of the farm problem. Most of them were established by farm bills, such as price support, income support, supply control, inventory control, risk management, land conservation, environmental regulation, credit subsidies, and export support programs. Some other policies, such as biofuel policies and crop insurance policies, however, were not established by farm bills, but were still closely related to agriculture.

To address the problems of low income, the government established a series of price support and supply control policies. In the 1950s, price support policies served to increase supply and resulted in a high level of inventory, and the excess supply reduced prices even further. One solution to the excess supply problem was to send some of the excesses as foreign aid to countries that had food shortages but could not afford to import food. An unintended consequence was low prices in these countries that impeded the growth of their own agriculture sector. Recognition of this problem set a limit on food aid, and now the aim is to use it when it is justified. Another policy was deficiency payments, where the government allocated to farmers a certain quantity target (called payment yield), and prices were set based on the target. If the market price was below the target price, farmers would receive a payment that is equal to the price shortfall times the quantity target. This approach aimed to control supply and support farmer income. But what occurred was increased average prices and decline in risk, and thus supply increased. To deal with this problem, governments established *set-aside* requirements, where farmers were supposed to divert a certain percentage of their land to conservation or fallowing to qualify for deficiency payments. The establishment of some base yield and acreage that were entitled to deficiency payments was aimed to protect income, rather than price.

To address instabilities in agricultural prices, the government developed inventory control policies, which can be viewed as a break from supply control but still considered as direct intervention policies. The government established a price floor and ceiling — if the actual price was below the floor, the farmers were able to keep their crops in inventory while receiving a loan at the floor level. If the actual price went above the ceiling, the farmers were required to sell and pay the loan. In many cases, the government covered or subsidized the debt service on the loan. The idea behind this scheme was to keep the price within a range. Of course, there were periods when prices stayed low and inventory increased too much — indeed, there was one year (1983) when the government established a Payment-in-Kind program that paid farmers not to grow certain crops and instead sell crops from inventory.

Another approach to deal with instability is crop insurance which insures yields, and later, revenue. Farmers pay a premium and are assured a minimum level of income based on yield or revenue targets. The premium paid is based on several alternative levels of coverage. The program is subsidized heavily, so the premiums paid by farmers do not fully cover expected indemnity payments. The government also covers the administrative costs of this program. In addition to insurance, the government has disaster assistance programs in cases of catastrophes. Most of the government programs applied to major commodities, such as corn, wheat, and cotton. There are also programs for peanuts and others for dairy. Specialty crops, like vegetables, grown in specific states are not part of the major USDA programs, even though they were recently covered by crop insurance programs. But for these crops, growers may organize and vote on product quality standards enforceable through a *marketing order*. Because farmers are subject to credit constraints, the government instituted credit products provided by the Farm Credit Administration.

Agricultural policies include several environmental regulations. The initial set-aside program has become the payment for ecosystem services programs. The most notable is the Conservation Reserve Program under which farmers are paid to modify their production activities toward actions that provide ecological benefits. These benefits can be the protection of wildlife habitat and the reduction of soil erosion and wind erosion. Furthermore, the Environmental Protection Agency (EPA) was established in 1970 to protect people and the environment from significant health risks, to sponsor and conduct research, and to develop and enforce environmental regulations. Quotas and standards are the predominant approach to controlling agriculture-induced environmental and health risks. The Clean Air Act (1970), Clean Water Act (1972), Federal Insecticide, Fungicide & Rodenticide Act (FIFRA, 1947) and subsequent amendments are enforced by the EPA to protect air and water as well as regulate pesticide usage. The EPA has also issued rules to limit greenhouse gas emissions from various sources to address climate change issues.

One of the major issues of U.S. agriculture was labor shortages, especially in states such as California and Florida, where fruits and vegetables are a major agricultural output. The government developed programs to recruit inexpensive, international labor. One such program was the Bracero Program (1942–1964), where farm workers were recruited from Mexico to work in the U.S. at very low wage rates. The program was abolished in 1964, and afterward, farm workers unionized while migrants continued to enter the U.S., sometimes illegally, and work in farms at a higher rate than during the Bracero Program period.[1] Farmers were active in supporting policies to reduce immigration restrictions and allow illegal workers to become citizens. The 1986 Simpson–Mazzoli Act provided citizenship to a large number of previously illegal immigrants, legalized some illegal seasonal agriculture workers, and required only self-reporting of worker status by employers. To comply with some of the regulations, many farm owners used labor contractors to hire their seasonal workers.

6. Conclusion: Changes in Perspectives on Agriculture

Over time, the farm population decreased, and the average farm income increased. Farmers themselves have gained in wealth compared with the rest of the population (Gardner, 1992). In addition, international trade barriers have been reduced, allowing farmers to access more export markets, and farmers continue to develop differentiated products that enable higher income. In addition, the U.S. is part of the World Trade Organization, which aims to reduce barriers to trade, including decreased subsidies for agriculture. Deficiency payments were eliminated by the 1996 Farm Bill, but there was increased emphasis on crop insurance as well as green policies.

These new trends resulted in a reduction of policies focused on direct intervention strategies but an expansion of crop insurance programs that became the new carrier of subsidies, as well as a continuation of environmental policies. With growing awareness of

[1]See Clemens *et al.* (2018) for a study regarding the impact of Bracero Program's termination on wage rates for domestic farm workers.

climate change, there is an effort to reduce agricultural greenhouse gas emissions and, at the same time, to use agriculture to sequester carbon. One of the challenges is to incorporate credits from carbon sequestration in the various carbon reduction policies and markets. The concern about climate change, combined with concern over energy security, also led to the introduction of policies targeted at increasing the production of biofuels. Agricultural policies thus became meshed with energy policies. The introduction of biofuel policies was part of the growing emphasis on establishing the bioeconomy. Meanwhile, soil conservation has long been a concern and has been well supported through a host of conservation programs such as the Conservation Reserve Program. Moreover, technical innovation and adoption are viewed as major means to address many sustainable development issues in agriculture. Finally, to understand agricultural policies better, one must consider political economy issues. The remainder of this book will touch on many of these issues.

References

Carson, R. 1962. *Silent Spring.* Houghton Mifflin Harcourt.

Clemens, M.A., E.G. Lewis, and H.M. Postel. 2018. Immigration Restrictions as Active Labor Market Policy: Evidence from the Mexican Bracero Exclusion. *American Economic Review* 108(6): 1468–1487.

Cochrane, W.W. 1979. *The Development of American Agriculture: A Historical Analysis.* University of Minnesota Press.

Gardner, B.L. 1992. Changing Economic Perspectives on the Farm Problem. *Journal of Economic Literature* 30(1): 62–101.

Olmstead, A.L. and P.W. Rhode. 2008. *Creating Abundance.* Cambridge Books.

Schultz, T.W. 1964. *Transforming Traditional Agriculture.* Yale University Press, New Haven, CT.

Schultz, T.W. 1975. The Value of the Ability to Deal with Disequilibria. *Journal of Economic Literature* 13(3): 827–846.

The U.S. Department of Agriculture (USDA). 1969. Census of Agriculture, Part 1: Farms: Number, Use of Land. Available at: https://agcensus.library.cornell.edu/census_parts/1969-farms-number-use-of-land-size-of-farm/ (accessed January 2, 2023).

The U.S. Department of Agriculture (USDA). 2012. Census of Agriculture, Part 1: Farms: Number, Use of Land. Available at: https://agcensus.library.cornell.edu/wp-content/uploads/2012-United-States-st99_1_008_008.pdf (accessed January 2, 2023).

Chapter 2

Review of Production Economics

Production has long been a focus of agricultural economics. This is because not only food security relies on a stable supply of agricultural commodities but also agricultural production can impose considerable impacts on the environment. In this chapter, we first briefly review some basic properties of production functions. Centered on production, we then discuss economics of land-quality-augmenting input application technologies (e.g., drip irrigation). In the last section, we discuss aggregation issues associated with investments and production.

1. Production Function and Its Parameters

Production function is defined by the maximum output that can be produced with a given input combination. The basic element is technology. The detail and accuracy of a production function depend on its use. A production function is presented in more generic terms in a general theoretical context than in specific empirical applications.

Let y denote output and x denote input. The production function is $y = f(x)$, marginal product (MP) is $f_x = \partial f/\partial x$, and average

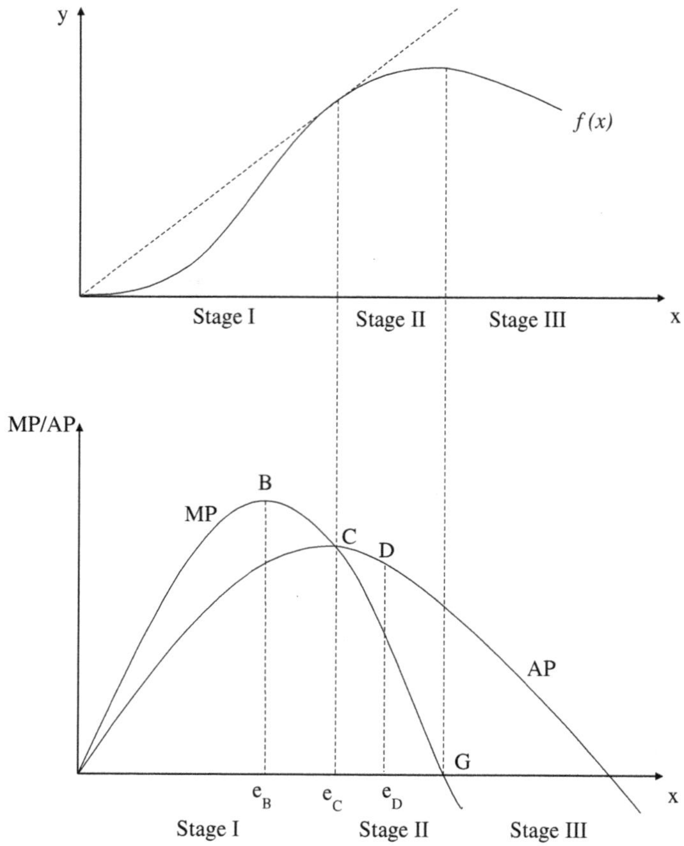

Figure 1. Three stages of production.

product (AP) is y/x. Recall that

$$\begin{cases} MP > AP > 0 & \text{at Stage I of production function} \\ AP > MP \geq 0 & \text{at Stage II of Production function} \\ MP < 0 & \text{at Stage III of production function.} \end{cases}$$

Figure 1 represents output as a function of input and introduces the three stages of production. The second stage is the economic region. This is the stage with positive but decreasing marginal product or concave production function. A competitive profit-maximizing firm is likely to operate at this stage of the production function.

Many mathematical specifications of production functions, such as the Cobb–Douglas function ($y = Ax^{\alpha}$, with $0 < \alpha < 1$), only represent situations when all outcomes are at the economic regions. Their use precludes identifying situations in which producers operate at the third stage of production and have negative marginal product. Quadratic production functions, $y = a + bx - cx^2$, allow outcomes at the second and third regions of production functions but not at the first. A simple and elegant production function which allows three regions of production is not easy to construct, so we often favor simplicity and use flawed production function specifications in many analyses.

A basic issue raised in Figure 1 is that of *economies of scale*, the relationship between average production cost and production scale. It presents that at Stage I of production, there is increasing returns to scale. This is because in this stage AP is increasing in input quantity, and thus the average cost is decreasing in input quantity. However, at the economic region (i.e., Stage II), there are constant or more likely decreasing returns to scale.

Figure 2 presents the relationships between inputs in the production process. The *isoquants* depicted in Graph A in the figure represents the different input level combinations producing the same level of output. Isoquants are useful to address issues, such as input intensity and input substitutability. If x_1 is capital and x_2 is labor, x_1/x_2 measures capital intensity relative to labor. Production at point A is capital intensive and at B is labor intensive.

Economists are also interested in assessing the ease of replacing one input for another while maintaining fixed output. When production function is of the Leontief type (i.e., with fixed proportion):

$$y = \min\left\{\frac{x_1}{a_1}, \frac{x_2}{a_2}\right\},$$

the isoquant for each production level is L-shaped, as shown in Graph B in Figure 2. For cost-minimizing firms, the isoquant is essentially one point,

$$(x_1 = a_1 \times y, x_2 = a_2 \times y)$$

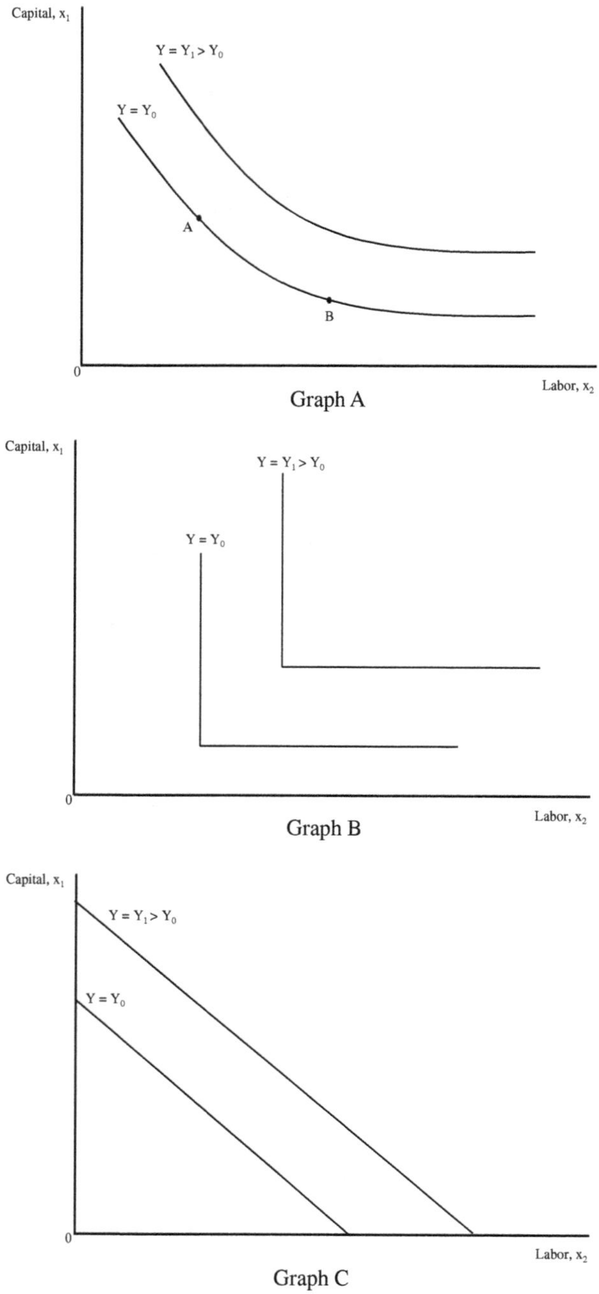

Figure 2. Isoquants and factor intensity.

and input intensity is constant at $x_1/x_2 = a_1/a_2$. If production function is linear, $y = a_1x_1 + a_2x_2$, the isoquant is a straight line (see Graph C in Figure 2), $x_1 = y/a_1 - a_2x_2/a_1$, and there are infinite substitution possibilities.

To allow quantification and comparison of production technologies, some key parameters of the production function are defined. They are as follows: the input elasticity, η_i; the scale elasticity, ε; and the elasticity of substitution, σ_{ij}. Let $y = f(x_1, x_2, \ldots, x_n)$ be a production function, where y indicates output and x_i the ith input. Then the following quantities can be defined:

- Marginal productivity: $f_i = \frac{\partial f}{\partial x_i}$.
- Input elasticity: $\eta_i = \frac{\partial f}{\partial x_i}\frac{x_i}{y} = f_i\frac{x_i}{y}$.
- Scale elasticity: $\varepsilon = \sum_{i=1}^{n} \eta_i$.
- The elasticity of substitution between input i and j:

$$\sigma_{ij} = -\frac{\partial(x_i/x_j)}{\partial(f_i/f_j)} \Big/ \frac{(x_i/x_j)}{(f_i/f_j)} = -\frac{d\ln(x_i/x_j)}{d\ln(f_i/f_j)}.$$

The elasticity of substitution measures the percentage change in x_i/x_j along an isoquant curve when the marginal rate of technical substitution (MRTS) between x_i and x_j (i.e., f_i/f_j) increases by one percent. Intuitively, it is a measure of the ease of change in input intensity. Note that if the production function is quasiconcave, then $\sigma_{ij} \geq 0$, with $\sigma_{ij} = 0$ implying fixed proportion production function and constant input intensity (e.g., the Leontief production function). At the opposite extreme, there is the linear production function ($y = a_1x_1 + a_2x_2$), where $\sigma = \infty$ and input intensity easily changes.

For Cobb–Douglas production functions, $y = Ax_1^{\alpha_1}x_2^{\alpha_2}$, where $\alpha_1 + \alpha_2 = 1$ and $\alpha_1, \alpha_2 \geq 0$, we have marginal product $f_i = \frac{\alpha_i y}{x_i}$, input elasticity $\eta_i = \alpha_i$, scale elasticity $\varepsilon = \alpha_1 + \alpha_2$, and elasticity of substitution $\sigma = 1$. The Cobb–Douglas production function is limited because it has constant elasticity of substitution with value at 1. Furthermore, they do not allow for negative marginal product.

Note that in the case of one input, $\varepsilon = \eta$, that is, input elasticity is equal to scale elasticity. Thus, at the first stage of the production function, we have $\varepsilon > 1$, at the economic stage, $1 > \varepsilon > 0$, and at the third stage, $\varepsilon < 0$.

1.1. *Production function under perfect competition*

The parameters of the production function have special interpretation under profit maximization and price taking. Under such conditions, the firm's optimization problem is

$$\max_{x_1,\ldots,x_n} Pf(x_1,\ldots,x_n) - \sum_{i=1}^{n} x_i W_i,$$

where W_i is the price of input i. The first-order condition for ith input is

$$Pf_i - W_i = 0,$$

and it can be interpreted as the value of marginal product of input i must equal its price. This condition can be expressed in terms of input elasticity: It becomes

$$Py\frac{f_i x_i}{y} - W_i x_i = 0 \Rightarrow Py\eta_i = W_i x_i \Rightarrow \eta_i = \frac{W_i x_i}{Py}, \tag{1}$$

that is, the input elasticity equals the share of revenue spent on input i. In the case of constant returns to scale, $\sum \eta_i = 1$ and $\eta_i =$ share of input i in all expenditures. Under perfect competition,

$$\frac{f_1}{f_2} = \frac{W_1}{W_2}.$$

1.2. *Duality and its implications*

The cost and profit functions are key relationships for deriving quantities demanded and supplied. The profit function is defined as

$$\Pi(P, W_1,\ldots,W_n) = \max_{y,x_1,\ldots,x_n} Py - \sum_{i=1}^{n} x_i W_i,$$

subject to $\quad y = f(x_1,\ldots,x_n).$

Hotelling's lemma states that the output supply and input demand are determined by

$$\frac{\partial \Pi}{\partial P} = y^*(P, W_1, \ldots, W_n),$$

$$-\frac{\partial \Pi}{\partial W_i} = x_i^*(P, W_1, \ldots, W_n).$$

We can use duality to present quantities as functions of monetary variables. This is particularly useful to estimate supply and demand for agricultural commodities and agricultural input. Furthermore, when data for output levels or input mix are not available, dual relationships can be used to estimate them. For example, one may have accounting data on the output of different firms and one may have price. Using duality, one can estimate output and input. In principle, one can use duality-based relationships to estimate even production function parameters from monetary data (see Chambers and Pope (1994) for an example).

One of the key challenges of applied economists is to estimate production parameters. Sometimes it is easier to obtain prices, expenditures or revenue data than quantity data. Duality and other relationships derived under profit maximization provide a basis for estimation of technology relationships without data on quantities. For example, if we know a farmer's revenue is 100, expenditure on input 1 (e.g., labor) is 20, and expenditure on input 2 (e.g., fertilizer) is 30, then based on Equation (1), the suggested labor elasticity is 0.2 and fertilizer elasticity is 0.3. If relative prices of labor increase by 10% and labor expenditures become 21 and fertilizer expenditures become 31, the implied elasticity of substitution under competition can be derived as follows. First, under the initial condition,

$$\frac{W_1^0 x_1^0}{W_2^0 x_2^0} = \frac{20}{30},$$

where W_i^0 and x_i^0 are the price and quantities under initial outcome. Let z be the rate of change in x_1/x_2. That is, $x_1^1/x_2^1 = (1+z)x_1^0/x_2^0$. Then, under the new outcome expenditures, the ratio $W_1^1 x_1^1/W_2^1 x_2^1$

can be written as

$$\frac{W_1^1 x_1^1}{W_2^1 x_2^1} = \frac{1.1 W_1^0 x_1^0}{W_2^0 x_2^0}(1+z) = \frac{2}{3}1.1(1+z) = \frac{21}{31}.$$

We can solve out $z = 63/(62 \times 1.1) - 1 = -0.0762$. Therefore, we have the elasticity of substitution as $\sigma = -(-0.0762/0.1) = 0.762$.

There are studies on the estimation of technological parameters from monetary data assuming profit maximization. However, it is clear that the estimated relationships are not necessarily the true technical parameters. Milton Friedman said that it is not clear that decision makers are profit maximizers, but the data are such that it seems "as if" decision makers are profit maximizers. Production function parameters that are estimated under the profit maximization assumptions are, in essence, "as if" production function parameters. One can separate between technological relationships and behavioral relationships. Behavioral relationships incorporate technological and behavioral assumptions. Production function parameters that are estimated under duality have a strong behavioral component. Even production theory recognizes that strict profit maximization is unrealistic; behavior has to adjust to risk and uncertainty, and there are new models of production behavior under uncertainty. Herbert Simon introduces a notion of bounded rationality. He suggested that the ability of humans to process and analyze data is limited. Therefore, choices are not perfect and reflect this limited ability. One of the challenges is to decipher the factor behind production decisions and to understand what leads producers to make choices. Choices under strict profit maximization may be different than under risk aversion and limited analytic capacities. The same technological relationships may result in different outcomes under different behavioral assumptions. However, it is difficult to untangle the behavioral and technological contributions to observed outcomes.

The previously discussed production functions are stylized into a metaphorical salad: All the components are put together and mixed instantaneously. Actual production relationships are more complex. Time plays an important role in production and production includes several stages. One of the challenges of production theory is to introduce the dimensions of time in the production process. Antle (1983) developed a model of a sequential production process, and there are several other attempts to look at the different stages of production in order to represent more realistic models of a production process.

However, modeling is an act of abstractism. For some purposes, we need a very simple representation of reality and in other uses we need a more realistic representation. In many aggregate analysis, a simple presentation of the production process associated with the traditional production function is sufficient. As the analysis become more aggregated, generic modeling is more relevant. For micro analysis, one may need more detailed modeling that takes into account specific biological and physical phenomena.

Before we proceed with explicit production modeling issues, we will discuss another issue, the measurements and nature of inputs used in the production process. Here we focus on capital, labor, land, pesticides, and water. Each input has unique features that may be essential in modeling behavior at the farm level.

Capital consists of all the equipment, structure, and machinery used for production. It represents outcomes of previous production activities that are embodied in some assets relating to present production activities. Generally, capital is utilized with viable inputs — labor, energy, and fertilizers — that are consumed by the production process. Producers may purchase services of capital goods or they may own capital assets that would be reflected differently in their accounting documents. In each period, there is a cost associated with the use of capital goods, which includes the cost of physical depreciation as well as the periodical costs for the resources that were used in the capital investment (e.g., interest costs). One difficulty in measuring labor comes from the differences in quality between different individuals. Generally, there can be different wage rates according to the quality of labor services provided. Knowledge acquired through training and education in the past is a determinant of productivity in the present. Compensation for workers combines payment for the raw labor services as well as a return for their human capital. Similar to labor, land is not a homogeneous input. Land quality varies depending on location and physical characteristics. There are different mechanisms for payment of land services including rental fee and sharecropping. Moreover, quality of land may affect the effectiveness of new technologies. Pesticides are damage control agents. Their productivity depends on the environment, the pest situation, and the product. The value of water depends on its use, quality, and location.

In the following section, we develop models to analyze problems of water. The modeling will demonstrate how some of the basic biological or physical properties of water affect the specifics of the modeling of the production process, the nature of choices that are applied, and the type of outcome that we observe.

2. The Economics of Land-Quality-Augmenting Input Application Technology

In this section, we model how adoption of an input application technology that augments land quality may affect the use of the corresponding input. We focus specifically on drip irrigation technology and water use in the model, but the framework and insight developed here can be applied to understanding the impact of many other input application technologies on input uses, even including the relationship between fuel efficiency enhancing technology and gasoline use by automobiles.

Let y denote output per acre and e effective input per acre. Applied input per acre is a. The output price is P and the water input price is W. Let i be application technology indicator, where $i = 0$ stands for the traditional technology and $i = 1$ for the modern technology. Land quality is denoted by $\alpha \in (0, 1)$. We can view α as a measure of input use efficiency of the land, which can be enhanced by technologies. Suppose the production function is $y = f(e)$, with $f' > 0$ and $f'' < 0$. Let $h_i(\alpha)$ be the input efficiency function, reflecting the fraction of input consumed by crop with technology i and land quality α. Therefore, we have $e_i = h_i(\alpha)a_i$. For simplicity, we assume $h_0(\alpha) = \alpha$. We further assume that $0 \leq \alpha \leq h_1(\alpha) \leq 1$, $h_i' > 0$, and $h_i'' < 0$. The cost of technology i per acre of land is k_i, with $k_1 > k_0$. Let δ_i be a technology selection indicator. If technology i is chosen, then $\delta_i = 1$; otherwise, $\delta_i = 0$.

The optimization problem that a farmer faces when choosing the technology is

$$\max_{\delta_i, a_i} \sum_{i=0}^{1} \delta_i \left(Pf(h_i(\alpha)a_i) - Wa_i - k_i\right) \tag{2}$$

subject to

$$\delta_i \in \{0,1\}, \quad 0 \leq \sum_{i=0}^{1} \delta_i \leq 1, \quad \text{and} \quad a_i \geq 0.$$

The search for an optimal solution is conducted in two stages. First, the optimal continuous choice is analyzed for each of the alternative technologies:

$$\pi_i = \max_{a_i} Pf(h_i(\alpha)a_i) - Wa_i - k_i, \tag{3}$$

with the first-order condition:

$$Pf'h_i(\alpha) = W, \tag{4}$$

indicating that at the optimal water input level, the value of the marginal product of input is equal to the price of water. Rearranging Equation (4), we obtain $Pf' = W/h_i(\alpha)$, which states that at the optimal water use level, the value of marginal product of effective input is equal to the price of effective input.

Once the optimal quantity of input to be used under each technology, a_i, is found, the *discrete choice* problem is solved, by choosing

$$\delta_1 = 1 \text{ if } \pi_1 > \pi_0 \text{ and } \pi_1 > 0,$$

$$\delta_0 = 1 \text{ if } \pi_0 > \pi_1 \text{ and } \pi_0 > 0,$$

$$\delta_1 = \delta_0 = 0 \text{ if } \pi_1 < 0 \text{ and } \pi_0 < 0.$$

The second-order condition of optimization problem (3) is $Pf_i''h_i^2 < 0$. Total differentiation of (4) yields

$$Pf''h_i^2 da_i + f'h_i dP + [Pf''h_i h_i' a_i + Pf'h_i']d\alpha - dW = 0. \tag{5}$$

Let $\Psi(e) = f'(e)e/f(e)$ be the *output elasticity of effective water*, $\phi(e) = -f''(e)e/f'(e)$ be the *elasticity of marginal product* (EMP) of e, and $\eta(\alpha) = h_i'(\alpha)\alpha/h_i(\alpha)$ be the *elasticity of input use efficiency* with respect to land quality.

From Equation (5), we can obtain

$$\frac{da_i^*}{dP} = \frac{-f'h_i}{Pf''h_i^2} = -\frac{a_i f'}{Pf''e} = \frac{a_i}{P\phi} > 0, \tag{6}$$

$$\frac{da_i^*}{dW} = \frac{1}{Pf''h_i^2} = \frac{f'}{Pf'h_i f''h_i} = -\frac{a_i}{W\phi} < 0, \tag{7}$$

$$\begin{aligned}\frac{da_i^*}{d\alpha} &= -\frac{[Pf''h_i h_i' a_i + Pf'h_i']}{Pf''h_i^2} = -\frac{a_i h_i'}{h_i} - \frac{f'h_i'}{f''h_i^2}\\ &= -\frac{a_i\eta_i(\alpha)}{\alpha}\left[1 - \frac{1}{\phi_i(h_i(\alpha)a_i)}\right] \lesseqqgtr 0 \quad \text{if } \phi_i(h_i(\alpha)a_i) \gtreqqless 1,\end{aligned} \tag{8}$$

$$\frac{dy_i^*}{dP} = f'h_i\frac{da_i}{dP} = \frac{f'h_i a_i}{P\phi} = \frac{y_i f'e}{f\cdot P\phi} = \frac{y_i\Psi}{P\phi} > 0, \tag{9}$$

$$\frac{dy_i^*}{dW} = -\frac{y_i\Psi}{W\phi} < 0, \tag{10}$$

$$\begin{aligned}\frac{dy^*}{d\alpha} &= f'h_i(\alpha)\frac{da_i}{d\alpha} + f'a_i h_i'(\alpha) = f'h_i(\alpha)\left[\frac{da_i}{d\alpha} + \frac{a_i\eta_i}{\alpha}\right]\\ &= \frac{f'h_i a_i\eta}{\phi\alpha} = \frac{y_i\Psi\eta}{\phi\alpha} > 0.\end{aligned} \tag{11}$$

Equations (6)–(11) have intuitive interpretations. Equations (6) and (7) state that optimal input use under technology i increases in output price and decreases in input price. Equations (9) and (10) indicate the opposite is true regarding the optimal output. Although an enhancement in land quality or input use efficiency (i.e., an increase in α) will increase the optimal output (see Equation (11)), its impact on input use depends on the elasticity of marginal product of effective input per acre (i.e., $e_i = h_i(\alpha)a_i$) (see Equation (8)). Particularly, if the elasticity of marginal product of effective input is equal to 1, then an increase in land quality or input use efficiency will not affect the optimal input use. However, if the elasticity is less than 1, then an increase in input use efficiency will drive up input use. In other words, the input use outcomes under an improved, more efficient technology could be opposite to what is originally expected (e.g., using drip irrigation to save water). This rebound effect exists commonly in conservation and resource-saving practices. For example, the adoption of fuel-efficient cars might actually increase gasoline consumption, instead of decreasing it, because driving would be less expensive and people would drive more and thus, perhaps, use more fuel.

2.1. *Comparison of input use and output under the two technologies*

Technology switch from $i = 0$ to $i = 1$ is equivalent to land quality improvement from α to $h_1(\alpha)$ (recall that for simplicity we set $h_0(\alpha) = \alpha$). View optimal input use as a function of land quality. Therefore, by the first-order Taylor expansion, we have $a_1 \approx a_0 + \frac{\partial a_0}{\partial \alpha}(h_1(\alpha) - \alpha)$. Define $\Delta a \equiv a_1 - a_0$. Then, based on Equation (8) and the assumption $h_0(\alpha) = \alpha$, it is readily checked that

$$\begin{aligned}\Delta a \equiv a_1 - a_0 &\approx \frac{\partial a_0}{\partial \alpha}(h_1(\alpha) - \alpha)\\ &= -\frac{a_0}{\alpha}\left[1 - \frac{1}{\phi}\right](h_1(\alpha) - \alpha) \lesseqgtr 0 \text{ when } \phi \gtreqless 1.\end{aligned} \tag{12}$$

Similarly, we have

$$\Delta y \equiv y_1 - y_0 \approx \frac{\partial y_0}{\partial \alpha}(h_1(\alpha) - \alpha) = \frac{y_0 \Psi}{\alpha \phi}(h_1(\alpha) - \alpha) > 0. \tag{13}$$

Thus, we can see that the adoption of modern technology always increases output but saves water only when $\phi > 1$. Intuitively, when marginal product is sensitive to effective input use (i.e., $\phi > 1$), then an increase in effective input use will decrease the marginal product significantly. The first-order condition in Equation (4) will then ensure less water would be used in the optimal solution.

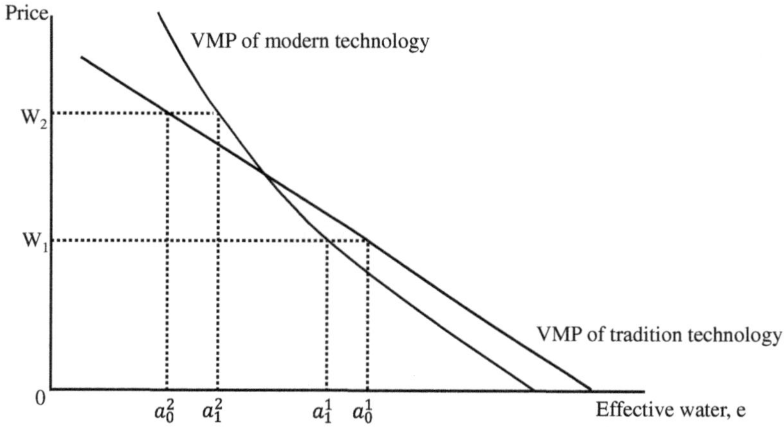

Figure 3. Technology adoption and input use.

Alternatively, based on Equation (13), we can say that when the yield effect (i.e., Δy) is small (i.e., large ϕ), then $\Delta a < 0$; and that when the yield effect is large (i.e., small ϕ), then $\Delta a > 0$. Figure 3 provides a visual presentation of the impact of the new technology on output and water use. The two curves in this figure stand for the value of marginal product (VMP) of water under the two technologies, respectively. When water price is W_1, switching from the traditional to modern technology would save water use. When water price is W_2, however, switching to the modern technology would increase water use. Since the areas under the VMP curves approximate output (or yield), we can see that the yield effect of the switching under price W_2 is larger than that under price W_1.

What do we know about the elasticity of marginal product (EMP) of e, ϕ? Assuming that $f(\cdot)$ has three regions of production, its marginal and average productivity (MP and AP) are depicted in the lower panel of Figure 1. The economic region ($MP < AP$ and $MP > 0$) is between C and G, and MP is negative to the right of G. The MP reaches its peak at B, where $f''(e_b) = 0$. Hence, at point B, the EMP is $\phi(e_B) = -f''(e_B)(e_B)/f'(e_B) = 0$; at point G, the EMP is $+\infty$. Thus, between points B and G, the EMP increases from 0 to ∞. Assuming continuity, there is a point D with $\phi(e) \gtreqless 1$ if $e \gtreqless e_D$ and if $e < e_G$.

2.2. *Implication for Cobb–Douglas production function*

The Cobb–Douglas production function is quite popular because of its ease of use. We argue here that it is not very realistic to apply it to micro-level studies. Suppose $y = Ae^{\psi_0}$, with $(1 - \psi_0) < 1$. In this case, the two elasticities of interest are constant: the output elasticity of effective water, $\Psi(e) = \psi_0$, the EMP, $\phi(e) = 1 - \psi_0 < 1$. As stated previously, Cobb–Douglas functions do not allow a region with negative marginal product. Furthermore, consider the case with $i = 0$, where $h_0(\alpha) = \alpha$, and thus $e = \alpha a$: The first-order condition is $\psi_0 PAe^{\psi_0 - 1} = W/\alpha$ (see Equation (4)). Hence, it is readily to check that the first-order condition implies $Wa/Py = \psi_0$. However, the share of water cost per acre is rarely constant in reality; it is likely to increase with W. Furthermore, water prices vary radically in places like California and water use per acre does not respond as drastically as predicted by Cobb–Douglas. Supposing $\phi_0 = 0.5$ and $W_A = 10W_B$, we are unlikely to observe that $a_A^* = a_B^*/100$. Therefore, production functions like the quadratic may be more realistic for depicting micro-level behavior.

2.3. *Quality and technology choices*

In this subsection, we show that there are segments of lower quality lands that adopt the new technology. Note first that

$$\begin{aligned}\frac{d\pi_i}{d\alpha} &= \frac{\partial[Pf(h_i(\alpha)a_i) - Wa_i - k_i]}{\partial\alpha} \\ &= (Pf'h_i - W)\frac{\partial a_i^*}{\partial\alpha} + Pf'h_i'a_i^* \\ &= Pf'h_i a_i \frac{\eta_i}{\alpha} = \frac{Wa_i\eta_i}{\alpha} > 0,\end{aligned}$$

where the last equality holds because of Equation (4). Thus, profits increase in land quality. Furthermore,

$$\frac{d\Delta\pi}{d\alpha} \equiv \frac{d(\pi_1 - \pi_0)}{d\alpha} = W\left[\frac{a_1^*\eta_1 - a_0^*}{\alpha}\right].$$

For $\alpha = 1$, we have $a_1^*(1) = a_0^*(1)$, $\pi_o(1) = \pi_1(1) + k_1 - k_0$. Since $0 \leq \alpha \leq h_1(\alpha) \leq 1$, we know that when evaluated at $\alpha = 1$, then $\eta_1(1) < 1$. Therefore,

$$\frac{d\Delta\pi}{d\alpha}(1) = Wa_1^*(\eta_1(1) - 1) < 0.$$

The modern technology is less profitable for $\alpha = 1$, but the profitability gaps decline as α becomes smaller, and at $\alpha = \alpha_1^s$ their profits per acre are equal. There may be many feasible patterns of technology adoption as functions of quality, but the highest quality land is much less likely to adopt. The pattern we analyze is depicted in Figure 4. For land with quality better than α^s, profit under the conventional technology is higher than that under the modern technology ($\pi_0 > \pi_1 > 0$), suggesting that producers will stick to the conventional technology (i.e., $\delta_0 = 1$). On the other hand, for land with quality between α_1^m and α^s, profit under the modern technology is higher than that under the conventional technology (i.e., $\pi_1 > \pi_0$),

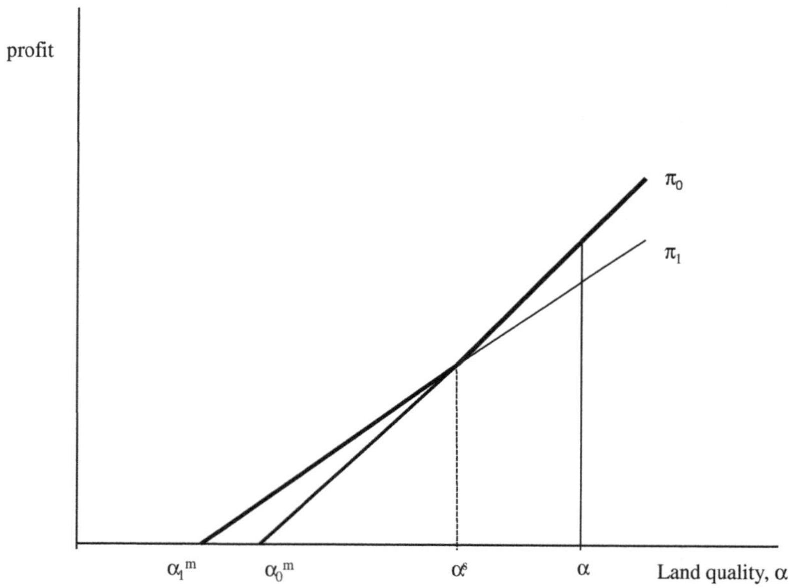

Figure 4. Switching land quality.

and thus adoption of modern technology will occur (i.e., $\delta_1 = 1$). Note that α_i^m is land quality such that $\pi_i(\alpha_i^m) = 0$. In other words, it is the minimum land quality for the profit to be non-negative under technology i. The value α^s is switching land quality. At this quality, $\pi_1(\alpha^S) = \pi_0(\alpha^S)$. That is,

$$Pf[h_1(\alpha^S)a_1^*(\alpha^S)] - Wa_1^*(\alpha^S) - k_1 = Pf[\alpha^S a_0^*(\alpha^S)] - Wa_0^*(\alpha^S) - k_0. \tag{14}$$

The introduction of the new technology will lead to production at the extensive margin (i.e., land with quality between α_1^m and α_0^m) operating under the modern technology. Therefore, the profits of land with different quality can be summarized as

$$r = \begin{cases} \pi_1(\alpha) & \text{for } \alpha_1^m < \alpha < \alpha^s \\ \pi_0(\alpha) & \text{for } \alpha_1^S \leq \alpha \leq 1. \end{cases}$$

The switching quality α^S and marginal qualities are functions of prices. Total differentiation equation (14) yields

$$\begin{aligned} &[Pf_1'h_1 - W]da_1^* + Pf_1'h_1'a_1^*d\alpha^S + f_1dP - a_1^*dW - dk_1 \\ &\quad = [Pf_0'h_1 - W]da_0^* + Pf_0'a_0^*d\alpha^S + f_0dP - a_0^*dW - dk_0. \end{aligned}$$

Rearranging terms, we have

$$\frac{W[a_1^*\eta_1 - a_0^*]}{\alpha^S}d\alpha^S + (y_1 - y_0)dP - (a_1^* - a_0^*)dW - dk_1 + dk_0 = 0.$$

Therefore, we have

$$\frac{d\alpha^S}{dP} = -\frac{(y_1 - y_0)\alpha^S}{W[a_1^*\eta_1 - a_0^*]} > 0 \text{ and } \frac{d\alpha^S}{dW} = \frac{(a_1^* - a_0^*)\alpha^S}{W[a_1^*\eta_1 - a_0^*]} > 0$$
$$\text{if } \phi > 1 \text{ and } \eta_1 < 1.$$

Similarly, total differentiation of $Pf[h_1(\alpha_1^m)a_1^*(\alpha_1^m)] - Wa_1^*(\alpha_1^m) - k_1 = 0$ yields

$$[Pf_1'h_1 - W]da_1^* + Pf_1'h_1'a_1^*d\alpha_1^m + y_1dP - a_1^*dW - dk_1 = 0,$$

which implies

$$\begin{cases} \dfrac{d\alpha_1^m}{dP} = -\dfrac{y_1}{Pf_1'h_1'a_1^*} < 0 \\ \dfrac{d\alpha_1^m}{dW} = \dfrac{a_1^*}{Pf_1'h_1'a_1^*} > 0. \end{cases}$$

From the above expressions, we can conclude that a higher output price will trigger the existence of the rent-efficient firms (i.e., $d\alpha_1^m/dP < 0$). When $\phi > 1$, it will trigger adoption of modern technologies by firms around α^s (i.e., $d\alpha^S/dP > 0$). Higher input prices will trigger technology switching toward the modern one at $\alpha = \alpha^s$ (i.e., $d\alpha^S/dW > 0$), and entry of producers with marginal quality which will adopt the modern technology (i.e., $d\alpha_1^m/dW > 0$).

2.4. *Aggregation*

Suppose the distribution of land quality is described by a probability distribution function $g(\alpha)$, so the total land area is $A = \int_0^\infty g(\alpha)d\alpha$. The area of land with quality in the range of $\left(\alpha - \frac{\Delta\alpha}{2}, \alpha + \frac{\Delta\alpha}{2}\right)$ is $g(\alpha)\Delta\alpha$. Aggregate supply is

$$Y^S = \int_{\alpha_1^m}^{\alpha^s} y_1 g(\alpha)d\alpha + \int_{\alpha^s}^{1} y_0 g(\alpha)d\alpha.$$

The marginal change in supply with respect to price is given by

$$\begin{aligned} Y_P^S &= \int_{\alpha_1^m}^{\alpha^S} \frac{\partial y_1}{\partial P} g(\alpha)d\alpha + \int_{\alpha^S}^{1} \frac{\partial y_0}{\partial P} g(\alpha)d\alpha \\ &\quad + g(\alpha^S)\left[y_1(\alpha^S) - y_0(\alpha^S)\right]\frac{\partial \alpha^S}{\partial P} - y_1(\alpha_1^m)g(\alpha_1^m)\frac{\partial \alpha_1^m}{\partial P} > 0 \end{aligned} \tag{15}$$

and

$$\begin{aligned} Y_W^S &= \int_{\alpha_1^m}^{\alpha^S} \frac{\partial y_1}{\partial W} g(\alpha)d\alpha + \int_{\alpha^S}^{1} \frac{\partial y_0}{\partial W} g(\alpha)d\alpha - y(\alpha_1^m)g(\alpha_1^m)\frac{\partial \alpha_1^m}{\partial W} \\ &\quad + \frac{\partial \alpha^S}{\partial W}\left[y_1(\alpha^S) - y_0(\alpha^S)\right] g(\alpha^S) \gtreqless 0. \end{aligned} \tag{16}$$

For Equation (16), the first three items are negative, but the fourth item (i.e., the switching effect of higher W on supply) may be positive, leaving the sign of Y_W^S undetermined.

2.5. *Impact of pollution tax*

The model can be readily expanded to examine the impact of some environmental policies, such as pollution tax, on agricultural production. Recall that $e = h_i(\alpha)a_i$ is the effective input consumed by the crop. Then $Z = [1 - h_i(\alpha)]a_i$ is the unused input that causes pollution (e.g., irrigation water runoff or chemical runoff). Suppose pollution tax rate is V, the maximization problem for technology i becomes

$$\max_{a_i} Pf(h_i(\alpha)a_i) - Wa_i - [1 - h_i(\alpha)]a_i V - k_i \tag{17}$$

with first-order condition

$$Pf'h_i = W + V(1 - h_i(\alpha)) \quad \Rightarrow \quad Pf' = \tfrac{W}{h_i} + V\left[\tfrac{1-h_i(\alpha)}{h_i(\alpha)}\right].$$

By following the approach in this section, one can derive the impact of the tax on technology adoption, output, and resource uses. We leave this to readers as an exercise.

3. Economic Analysis of Investments and Production Aggregation

Modeling production processes is essential for developing realistic policy analysis frameworks. In all of the modeling, one needs to investigate the implications of the approach for policy purposes. In this section, we study the putty-clay framework, which is a general framework to view production choices and their outcomes. Before beginning, we emphasize a few points. First, some decision variables are discrete. For instance, decisions made about the nature of technology to be adopted (e.g., drip vs. sprinkler irrigation or biological vs. chemical pest control approaches) can be dichotomous choices, assuming binary values of 0 and 1. Other decision variables, such as the amount of water that should be applied, are continuous and observed in a total amount. Second, producers operate under varying sets of circumstances that may result in different outcomes, creating heterogeneity in production. The causes for variability may be differences in environmental conditions, land quality, human capital, and physical capital. Third, decisions are often time-dependent: Short-run choices entail much less flexibility but are easier to predict than long-run choices. Fourth, aggregation is a challenge in both short-run and long-run analysis. To obtain meaningful predictions of production choices and market outcomes under heterogeneity, meaningful aggregation procedures are essential.

3.1. *The Cambridge controversy*

The notion of production function is applied for different levels of aggregation. We can speak about the production function of an individual process (e.g., a production function of wheat in one field), of producers (e.g., a production function of wheat producers with several fields), of an industry producing the same product, of a sector that includes several industries, and, finally, of the aggregate economy.

Aggregation may require a redefinition of input and output, especially for conceptual analysis, as one has to reduce the number of variables to a bare minimum to illustrate some concept without having an extremely complicated analysis. Even empirical analysis may require reducing the dimensionality and aggregation. One question is as follows: "Under what condition would aggregation become meaningless and the results not useful?" The biggest controversy has been related to economy-wide production functions. One of the most important areas of research after Word War II was attempts to understand the process of economic growth. Kuznets established a national accounting data on output, capital, and aggregate labor. Many researchers, most notably Robert Solow, developed a neoclassical growth theory to analyze these data. The growth literature that Solow developed was very important during the 1960s and early 1970s, and it spawned another body of literature that attempted to explain the process of innovation. The earliest seminal article in the literature on innovation and growth was Kenneth Arrow's (1962) writing on learning-by-doing. There has been a resurrection in the mid-1980s from the works of Robert Lucas Jr. and, in particular, Paul Romer, who introduced a new concept: endogenous growth. Romer's work has become an important element of macroeconomics, but we return to our discussion of production and, in particular, the Cambridge controversy that led to the putty-clay model which is our subject of interest.

The Cambridge controversy was a debate between economists in Cambridge, Massachusetts, headed by Robert Solow and Paul Samuelson, proponents of the neoclassical production function and neoclassical growth theory, and economists in Cambridge, England, headed by Joan Robinson, Piero Sraffa, and Luigi Pasinetti. Neoclassical growth theory assumes the existence of an aggregate production function where national output is produced by aggregate labor and aggregate capital stock. It also assumes that there is an endogenous process of technological change that increases input productivity over time. Solow estimated an aggregate model of economic growth of the form

$$Y_t = AL_t^{\alpha} K_t^{\beta} e^{\eta t},$$

where Y_t, L_t, and K_t stand for aggregate output, aggregate labor, and aggregate capital, respectively.

His model has had a good statistical fit, and η, the time coefficient, was found to be quite substantial, indicating the importance of technological change. The model assumes that the economy has a stock of capital, K_t, which is augmented by investment I_t, but may decline due to depreciation. This approach suggests measuring capital by dollar units and assumes that capital goods are malleable.

The malleability of capital seemed unreasonable to economists in Cambridge, England. The English economists argued that there is much specialization of capital goods — a tractor cannot print books. Therefore, the notion of aggregate capital is meaningless, and policies based on assumption of smooth substitution between capital and labor are misleading.

In this macroeconomic debate on the formulation of production, both groups had valid points. The basic idea of assessing aggregate productivity in the economy — taken by the Cambridge, Massachusetts, scholars — was viable. The effort they started led to important results, and growth theory is a very important area of research. However, the England group was correct that higher capital expenditures do not necessarily mean more flexibility in production because capital goods are limited in their uses. One of the important elements in Romer's new model is the explicit recognition of the role of specialized capital goods and the limited extent of malleability that capital goods have. The Cambridge controversy can be summarized succinctly as the argument about the magnitude of the elasticity of substitution between capital and labor. The neoclassical economists assume that the elasticity of substitution is quite high and the English economists assume that it is very low and relationships are converging to a fixed proportion production function. The compromise within the Cambridge controversy was presented in "putty-clay" models.

3.2. *Putty-clay models*

Putty-clay models were introduced by Johansen (1959) and Salter (1960). They separated between micro and macro as well as *ex ante* and *ex post* production functions. A micro production function is the production function of an individual producer. A macro production function is a production function of an industry. One challenge is to develop aggregation procedures to move from micro to macro relationships. The *ex ante* choices are the putty stage, before the shape of the final machine is determined. *Ex post* choices are at the clay stage where the equipment is well formed and limits the flexibility of choices. The *ex ante* production function is used for long-run choices before investment takes place where the capital level is flexible. An *ex post* production function reflects choices when capital outlay is completed and capital is less flexible. Putty-clay models assume that, at the microlevel, *ex ante* production functions are neoclassical and have positive elasticities between capital and other inputs, but *ex post* functions have fixed proportions and zero elasticity of substitution. Thus, the putty-clay models separate between micro *ex ante* production function, micro *ex post* production function, aggregate *ex ante* production function, and aggregate *ex post* production function.

3.2.1. *The Salter model*

Salter (1960) introduced a graphical presentation that is useful for explaining the putty-clay model. His model is dynamic, and he looks at the determination of prices and investment at a given period. At the start of the period, the industry has a distribution of existing production units that were built in previous years. Every year entrepreneurs make *ex ante* decisions about new capital. Here we make some general assumptions about the trend in capital costs and variable costs over time. Every year entrepreneurs determine the cost of a new capital good, its production technology, and its production capacity. Salter assumes that technology has constant returns to scale, and the cost of variable inputs such as labor increases over time relative to capital.[1] Technological change and the relative price of labor result in new technology with lower variable costs but may have slightly higher annualized fixed costs.

Suppose we are at the beginning of period t. The industry inherits capital that was built in previous periods. Let C_{t-j} be the productive capacity of facilities that were built j years before t. We can refer to these machines as vintage $t-j$, and C_{t-j} is the productive capacity of vintage $t-j$. Productive capacity is the maximum output that these machines can produce if they are utilized. Let V_{t-j} be the variable input cost per unit of output of machines of vintage $t-j$. Thus, at the beginning of the period, the industry has output supply of an existing plant that is a step function such as the one depicted in Figure 5.

If output price P is smaller than V_{t-j}, then the capacity of vintage $t-j$ would not be utilized. If output price is greater than V_{t-j}, then

[1]The reason that capital becomes cheaper overtime is that technological change results in improved machinery. Labor cost may decline only when population growth is very drastic, but in most developed countries, capital cost has declined relative to labor costs.

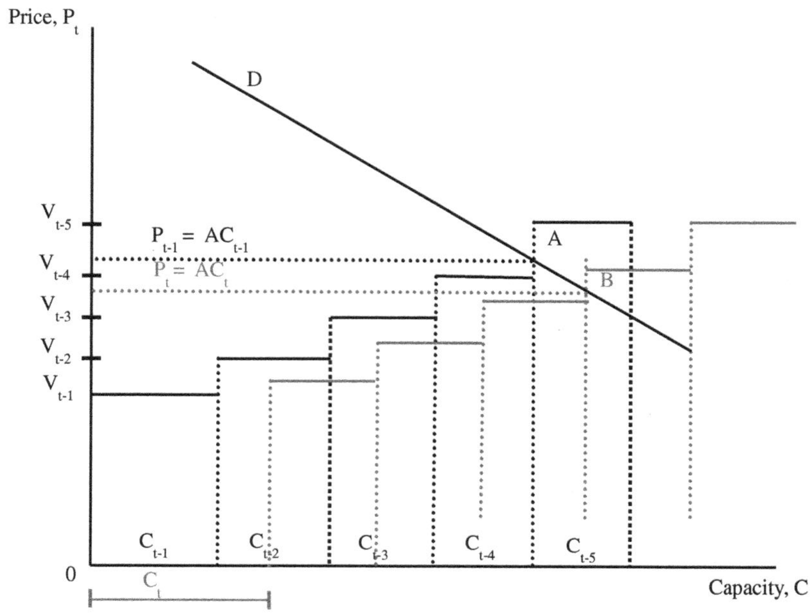

Figure 5. Total capacity and price in the Salter model.

the output capacity of vintage $t-j$ will be utilized. Part or all of the capacity of vintage $t-j$ will be utilized if the price is equal to V_{t-j}. Let AC_t be the average cost per period (total cost divided by output) of a machine of vintage t. AC includes both variable cost and annualized fixed cost.[2] New productive capacity is introduced in period t as long as price is greater than average cost. Thus, in equilibrium, output price has to be equal to average cost of the current vintage.

Figure 5 helps us to understand the determination of the equilibrium of time t, assuming that the industry is facing negative sloped demand curve D. Suppose that the equilibrium at period $t-1$ was at point A. During period $t-1$, the industry produced q_{t-1} units of output using the productive capacity of vintage $t-1$, $t-2$, $t-3$, and $t-4$. The productive capacity of vintage $t-5$ was idle because the variable cost of this vintage, V_{t-5}, was higher than the price. The price at period $t-1$ is equal to the average cost of vintage $t-1$,

[2]The assumption of constant returns to scale allows us to present average cost regardless of size.

which is AC_{t-1}. Now, suppose that the average cost of vintage t is AC_t, which is smaller than AC_{t-1}, and that AC_t is between V_{t-3} and V_{t-4}. The new output price P_t will be equal to AC_t. The capacity of vintage C_{t-4} will not be utilized. The new capacity of vintage t, C_t, introduced at time t will be equal to C_{t-4} plus the increase in quantity demanded because of lower prices. This can be represented by a shift to the right of the supply step function. The new equilibrium is at point B in the figure. Thus, Salter's analysis suggests that old capital equipment continues to operate as long as revenues can cover its variable cost. However, at a certain time, this capital will be out of production because its variable costs are too high. In his model, capital is not being destroyed, it is only becoming obsolete. At the same time, new capital is introduced reflecting the fact that there is a technological change that reduces average cost below the previous prices. When a firm makes *ex ante* investment decisions, it has to recognize that the economic life of capital is limited and it has to compute the cost of capital accordingly. Furthermore, when computing the cost of capital, it has to recognize that variable costs may increase over time and may reduce both the economic life of capital and its future earning capacity. The following section addresses the investment choice taking into account changes in prices over time and final economic life.

The Salter model provides the framework for long-term decisions when investments in new capital is incorporated explicitly into the analysis. In the shorter run, choices are limited to existing equipment. Therefore, if one wants to know the immediate effect of changes in policies, she may ignore the possibility of developing new equipment but consider the impact given existing vintages.

3.2.2. *A quantitative analysis of investments*

An investment involves an initial outlay of capital and results in a stream of benefits. To analyze an investment, one needs to know the stream of costs and benefits over time. Let x_0, $x_1, \ldots,$ and x_T denote the net benefit from a project at period $0, \ldots, T$. When $x_t < 0$, it represents a cost. For example, x_0 may be the initial investment, x_t,

$t = 1, \ldots, T$, are the returns. In some cases, there may be several periods of negative outlay. The interest or discount rate, denoted by r, is a fee for the use of \$1.00 for one period. The interest rate can provide a base for comparing an income stream at different time periods. A dollar earned next year is worth $\left(\frac{1}{1+r}\right)$ today and a dollar earned five years from now is worth $\left(\frac{1}{1+r}\right)^5$ dollars today. The net present value (NPV) of an investment is $NPV = \sum_{t=0}^{T} \frac{x_t}{(1+r)^t}$. When time is continuous, one can use $NPV = \int_0^T e^{-rt} x_t dt$.

A project is worthwhile if $NPV > 0$. One way to compare projects is to compare their *internal rate of return* (IRR). It is defined by z which solves

$$\sum_{t=0}^{T} \frac{x_t}{(1+z)^t} = 0 \quad \text{or} \quad \int_0^T e^{-zt} x_t dt = 0.$$

One can think of IRR as a return rate of the investment. If IRR is larger than the actual interest rate (i.e., return of the investment is larger than the opportunity cost of the investment), then the project will be profitable. Suppose a project requires an investment of K to be paid in T equal payments with an interest rate of r. The annual payment required to break even will be Y, where

$$\int_0^T e^{-rt} Y dt = K \quad \text{or} \quad Y = \frac{r}{1 - e^{-rT}} K.$$

When a project is of infinite length, then it is simply $Y = rK$.

When capital equipment worth K dollars is used in the production process, the capital expenditure during period t includes interest cost rK (or $rK/(1-e^{-rT})$ if the total number of period is T) and depreciation (the loss of value because of utilization). If depreciation is assumed to be proportional to the value of the stock, it can be denoted as δK, with δ as a fixed depreciation coefficient. Investment choices, purchases, and the use of capital goods are the results of choices over time.

Consider a long-run micro model under which, once established, the capital will be used for a long period. This involves the choice of capital at the beginning period and the choice of labor at each period. The information available is output prices, P_t, and labor prices, W_t, for $t = 0, \ldots, \infty$. The production function is $f(K, L)$, where K is the capital and L is the labor. The objective function is

$$\max_{K,L_t} \int_0^{\infty} e^{-rt} \left[P_t f(K, L_t) - W_t L_t\right] dt - K,$$

subject to

$$K \geq 0 \text{ and } L_t \geq 0.$$

The *ex post* choice problem given K is

$$\max_{L_t} P_t f(K, L_t) - W_t L_t, \quad \text{for } t = 1, \ldots, T,$$

and the *ex post* decision rules are to choose L_t such that

$$P_t \frac{\partial f}{\partial L} - W_t = 0, \quad \text{for all } t,$$

and

$$P_t f(K, L_t) - W_t L_t \geq 0.$$

For every K, there is a function $L_t(K)$ denoting labor use over time. Once the optimal *ex post* decision rules are determined, the *ex ante* choice is to choose K to

$$\max_{K} \int_0^{\infty} \left\{e^{-rt} P_t f(K, L_t(K)) - W_t L_t(K)\right\} dt - K.$$

If P_t grows faster than W_t, then L_t will be positive forever. However, when the labor price grows faster than the price of output, there may be a period T_1 where maximum short-term profit is zero. Beyond this period, no output is produced. T_1 is therefore the economic life of capital. That is, capital stops operation because of obsolescence in period T_1 and beyond. When prices fluctuate a lot, the firm may shut down, then operate, then shut down, and so on.

Consider a simpler case where the *ex post* technology is a fixed proportion. Then, at time zero, both capital and labor are determined and the ratios are followed thereafter. The objective function is

$$\max_{K,L} \int_0^\infty e^{-rt} \{P_t f(K,L) - W_t L\} \, dt - K$$

subject to

$$P_t f(K,L) - W_t L > 0.$$

Consider the case when output and labor prices grow exponentially, $P_t = P_0 e^{\gamma t}$ and $W_t = W_0 e^{\theta t}$. Suppose that the rate of growth of output price is smaller than that of labor price, $\gamma < \theta$, and further, $\gamma < \theta < r$. Assume that $P_0 f(K,L) > W_0 L$. In this case, production occurs between $t = 0$ and $t = T_1$, and the optimization problem is

$$\max_{T_1,K,L} \frac{P_0 f(K,L)}{r-\gamma}\left(1 - e^{-(r-\gamma)T_1}\right) - \frac{W_0 L}{r-\theta}\left(1 - e^{-(r-\theta)T_1}\right) - K. \quad (18)$$

The economic life of capital is determined by solving

$$P_0 e^{\gamma T_1} f(K,L) = W_0 e^{\theta T_1} L.$$

When $\theta = \gamma$, the dynamic problem becomes the classical static problem. Once T_1 is solved for, the *ex ante* optimal levels of K and L are derived solving Equation (18). In this case, the dynamic optimization looks like a standard static optimization with labor and capital costs adjusted to deal with different growth rates and economic lives of capital.

3.3. *Aggregation from micro to macro*

3.3.1. *Short-run derivation in putty-clay models*

Following the putty-clay assumption, each production unit has a fixed-proportion, *ex post* production function. Production coefficients vary among production units to reflect their vintages and other variables that affect the *ex ante* choices. Note that each production unit has only one unit of production capacity. Suppose we have one input. Let y denote the productivity of a unit expressed as output/input ratio, P the output price, and W the input price. Production units (machines or plants) with $y > W/P$ will operate

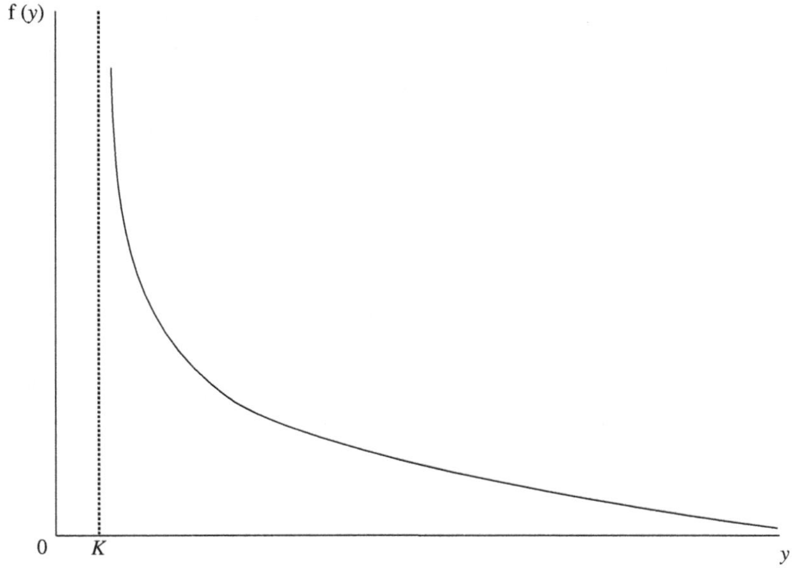

Figure 6. The pareto distribution.

with full capacity, while production units with $y < W/P$ will be idle. Let the density of the distribution of output capacity as a function of output/input ratio be denoted by $f(y)$, which means that the output capacity of firms with $y' - \frac{\Delta y}{2} < y < y' + \frac{\Delta y}{2}$ for a very small Δy is $f(y')\Delta y$, and that total output capacity of the industry is $C = \int_0^\infty f(y)dy$. The output supply of industry is given by

$$Y(P, W) = \int_{W/P}^{\infty} f(y)dy, \tag{19}$$

and the input demand is given by

$$X(P, W) = \int_{W/P}^{\infty} \frac{f(y)}{y} dy. \tag{20}$$

Suppose y has a Pareto distribution (see Figure 6). This distribution is found to be useful describing income distribution and farm size distribution:

$$f(y) = \begin{cases} Ay^{-(\alpha+1)}, & \text{for } y \geq K \\ 0, & \text{for } y < K, \end{cases}$$

with $\alpha > 0$ and K is the output/input ratio of the least efficient machine. What is A? We know that total productive capacity is C, and

$$C = \int_K^{\infty} Ay^{-(\alpha+1)}dy = \left[\frac{A}{-\alpha}y^{-\alpha}\right]_K^{\infty} = \frac{A}{\alpha K^{\alpha}}. \tag{21}$$

From (21), we have $A = \alpha C K^{\alpha}$, hence,

$$f(y) = \frac{\alpha C}{K}\left(\frac{y}{K}\right)^{-(\alpha+1)}.$$

Under the Pareto distribution, productive capacity declines as efficiency (measured by y) increases. Note that

$$(\alpha + 1) = -\frac{\partial f(y)}{\partial y}\frac{y}{f(y)}$$

is the rate of decline in productive capacity associated with increased efficiency. Higher α assures more skewed capacity distribution. The Pareto distribution, like the log normal and exponential distributions, is approximated with the empirical distribution of income but not necessarily distribution of output capacity.

From (19), the supply when capacity is distributed as a Pareto function of output/input ratio is

$$Y(P,W) = \int_{W/P}^{\infty} Ay^{-(\alpha+1)}dy = \left[-\frac{A}{\alpha}y^{-\alpha}\right]_{W/P}^{\infty} = \frac{A}{\alpha}\left(\frac{P}{W}\right)^{\alpha}, \tag{22}$$

and from (20), we have

$$\begin{aligned} X(P,W) &= \int_{W/P}^{\infty} \frac{Ay^{-(\alpha+1)}}{y}dy = \left[-\frac{A}{(\alpha+1)}y^{-(\alpha+1)}\right]_{W/P}^{\infty} \\ &= \frac{A}{\alpha+1}\left(\frac{P}{W}\right)^{\alpha+1}. \end{aligned} \tag{23}$$

From (23), we obtain

$$\frac{P}{W} = \left[\frac{\alpha+1}{A}X\right]^{\frac{1}{\alpha+1}}.$$

Substituting it to (22) yields

$$Y = \frac{A}{\alpha}\left[\frac{\alpha+1}{A}X\right]^{\frac{\alpha}{\alpha+1}}$$

or

$$Y = BX^{\frac{\alpha}{\alpha+1}}, \tag{24}$$

where

$$B = \frac{A}{\alpha}\left[\frac{\alpha+1}{A}\right]^{\frac{\alpha}{\alpha+1}}.$$

Equation (24) provides what seems to be an aggregate production function, but this is not a "technological" relationship. It is a hybrid incorporating both technological (micro production function) and behavioral (profit maximization) elements and relating aggregate output and inputs under profit maximization.

The above analysis suggests that the input elasticity of the aggregate production function, $\alpha/(\alpha+1)$, reflects the productive capacity distribution and not a "technical" coefficient. Instead, $\alpha/(\alpha+1)$ is an outcome of investment decisions of the past that have resulted in the distribution of productive capacity. The Pareto distribution used here is not realistic for cases where we have growing industries and where there are relatively more capacity in newer vintages than older ones. It is reasonable in describing declining industries. When the input is land, it describes situations where higher quality lands (with higher y) are growing scarce and the mode of the productivity capacity distribution is at lower land qualities. The reservation we have regarding the Pareto distribution raises doubt on the appropriateness of aggregate Cobb–Douglas production functions.

3.3.2. *A simple model of aggregation with some variability*

The putty-clay framework does not allow short-term flexibility. However, existing plants may change variable inputs to affect output. Thus, let us assume that production function is of constant returns to scale, but plants vary in quality. Let q be a variable measuring the quality of the capacity unit. Higher q represents, say, higher human capital of plant managers. Let production per capacity unit be

$$y = f(q, x),$$

where x is the variable input per capacity unit. Assume

$$f_x > 0, \quad f_{xx} < 0, \quad f_{qx} > 0, \quad f_{qxx} < 0.$$

For example,

$$f(q, x) = q^\gamma x^\beta, \quad 1 > \gamma > 0, \quad 1 > \beta > 0.$$

Let us also assume when a capacity unit operates, a fixed-cost C is required. For a micro unit, the two choices are (i) whether to operate or not and (ii) if operate, then how much input per capacity unit to use.

Let P indicate the output price and W the input price. The decision problem is

$$\max_x Pf(q, x) - Wx - C.$$

The first-order condition is

$$Pf_x - W = 0.$$

The capacity unit operates if

$$Pf(q, x) - Wx - C > 0.$$

For the case $f(q, x) = q^\gamma x^\beta$, at the optimal solution,

$$P\beta q^\gamma x^{\beta-1} = W, \tag{25}$$

or the micro-level input demand is

$$x(P, W, q) = \left[\frac{P\beta q^\gamma}{W}\right]^{\frac{1}{1-\beta}},$$

and the micro-level supply is

$$y(P, W, q) = q^\gamma \left[\frac{P\beta q^\gamma}{W}\right]^{\frac{\beta}{1-\beta}}.$$

In this case, x increases with quality and output price and declines with input price. Profit per capacity unit is

$$\pi(P, W, q, C) = Pq^\gamma \left[\frac{P\beta q^\gamma}{W}\right]^{\frac{\beta}{1-\beta}} - W\left[\frac{P\beta q^\gamma}{W}\right]^{\frac{1}{1-\beta}} - C.$$

Setting this expression equal to zero and solving for q, the marginal producing quality, q^m, can be found; it is a function of P, W, and C:

$$q^m(P, W, C) = \left(\frac{W}{\beta P}\right)^{\frac{1}{\gamma}} \left[\frac{C\beta}{(1-\beta)W}\right]^{\frac{1-\beta}{\gamma}}.$$

Let the distribution of capacity be denoted by $g(q)$, where $g(q)\Delta q$ denotes the number of capacity unit between $q - \frac{\Delta q}{2}$ and $q + \frac{\Delta q}{2}$. Let

$$\int_0^\infty g(q)d(q) = M,$$

where M is the number of capacity units, then the aggregate supply is

$$Y(P, W, q) = \int_{q^m(P,W)}^\infty y(P, W, q)g(q)dq.$$

To find the supply slope, we need to differentiate $Y(P, W, q)$. The Leibnitz rule is used for differentiating integrals. For a function

$$F(x) = \int_{a(x)}^{b(x)} g(x, z)dz,$$

the Leibnitz rule states that $F_x(x) = b_x g(x, b(x)) - a_x g(x, a(x)) + \int_{a(x)}^{b(x)} g_x(x, z)dz$. Using this rule, the slope of the supply curve is

$$Y_P(P, W) = \underbrace{\int_{q^m}^\infty y_P(P, W, q)g(q)dq}_{(1)} - \underbrace{\frac{\partial q^m(P, W)}{\partial P} y(P, W, q^m)g(q^m)}_{(2)},$$

from which we can see that marginal change in supply includes change in intensive margin (i.e., term (1)) and change in extensive margin (i.e., term (2)). A lower price will reduce marginally output of every operating production unit, and it will cause closure of some borderline capacity units.

3.3.3. *Determination of aggregate relationship in cases with varying input quality*

In this section, we use the irrigation model that was presented in Section 2 as a base for aggregation. Just a recap of that model is presented here. Suppose we have a constant returns to scale technology, in which agricultural product is produced using land and E, effective input. Given constant returns to scale, output and input use can be expressed on a per-acre basis. Let $y = f(e)$ be the yield per acre, e be the effective input per acre (input used in production process), a be the total applied input per acre, and finally, α be the quality of land, a continuous variable from 0 to 1.

The amount of effective input is a function of the amount applied, of land quality, and of the kind of technology: $e = h(i, \alpha)a$, where i is a technology index, assuming value 2 for modern technology and value 1 for traditional ones. When no technology is used, $i = 0$. $h(i, \alpha) = e/a$ is input-use efficiency. When input is water, it is irrigation efficiency. Let α be an index of land quality with respect to input use (e.g., water-holding capacity). Assume $1 \geq h(2, \alpha) \geq h(1, \alpha) = \alpha > 0$. Let us also assume that production requires fixed cost per acre, C_i with $C_2 > C_1$. Assuming profit maximization for each α, there is an optimal a (applied water) and an optimal i (technology) determined by solving

$$\max_i \begin{cases} \Pi(i) = \max_a Pf(h(i,\alpha)a) - Wa - C_i, & i = 1, 2 \\ \Pi(0) = 0, \end{cases}$$

where P is the output price, W is the input price, and C_i is the cost of adopting technology i. The optimization is solved in two steps: First, we solve for optimal a given $i = 1, 2$, and the first-order condition is

$$Pf_e h(i, \alpha) = W,$$

or $Pf_e = W/h(i, \alpha)$, where $W/h(i, a)$ is price of effective water. Then we compute optimal i according to

$$i = \begin{cases} 2 & \text{if} \quad \Pi(2) > \Pi(1) \quad \text{and} \quad \Pi(2) > 0 \\ 1 & \text{if} \quad \Pi(1) > \Pi(2) \quad \text{and} \quad \Pi(1) > 0 \\ 0 & \text{if} \quad \Pi(1), \Pi(2) < 0. \end{cases}$$

When land quality is the highest (i.e., $\alpha = 1$), $a(2) = a(1)$ and $\Pi(1) > \Pi(2)$ because $C_2 > C_1$. It can be easily shown that $\Pi_\alpha(i) > 0$, for $i = 1, 2$ (i.e., profit increases with land quality), and that, for high-quality lands, the marginal effects of quality ($\Pi_\alpha(1) > \Pi_\alpha(2)$) hold that loss in profit as land quality declines is larger under traditional technology. This is reasonable since modern technology tends to *augment* land quality, especially if we assume that the ratio $\frac{h(2,\alpha)-h(1,\alpha)}{h(1,\alpha)}$ becomes bigger as α declines. This assumption is true with respect to sprinkler or drip irrigation because their impact on water-use efficiency compared to furrow irrigation is stronger in locations with low water-holding capacity. This assumption suggests the following technology-use pattern:

$$\begin{aligned} i &= 0 \ \text{ for } \alpha \leq \alpha^m, \\ i &= 2 \ \text{ for } \alpha^m < q < \alpha^s, \\ i &= 1 \ \text{ for } \alpha > \alpha^s, \end{aligned}$$

where α^m is the marginal quality under technology 2 and α^s is the switching quality. Recall that α^m is determined by solving $\Pi(2, P, \alpha^m, a^*(P, \alpha^m)) = 0$ or

$$\max_a \{Pf[h(2, \alpha^m)a] - Wa - C_2\} = 0, \tag{26}$$

and that α^s is determined by solving $\Pi(1, \alpha^s) = \Pi(2, \alpha^s)$, or

$$\max_a Pf[h(2, \alpha^s)a] - Wa - C_2 = \max_a Pf[h(1, \alpha^s)a] - Wa - C_1. \tag{27}$$

To see how changes in price will affect marginal or switching quality, we need to perform a comparative static analysis based on

(26) and (27). Differentiation of (26) with respect to α and P yields

$$\frac{d\alpha^m}{dP} = -\frac{\Pi_P(2) + \Pi_a(2)a_P}{\Pi_\alpha(2) + \Pi_a(2)a_\alpha}.$$

Since first-order conditions are met at α^m, $\Pi_a(2) = 0$, and

$$\frac{d\alpha^m}{dP} = -\frac{\Pi_P(2)}{\Pi_\alpha(2)} = -\frac{y(2)}{Pf_e h_\alpha(2)a(2)} < 0. \tag{28}$$

Note that the second equality in (28) holds because $Pf_e h = W$ based on the first-order condition. Define $\Psi(i) \equiv \frac{h_\alpha(i)}{h(i)}\alpha$ as the elasticity of irrigation efficiency with respect to land quality. Therefore, (28) becomes

$$\frac{d\alpha^m}{dP} = -\frac{\alpha^m}{W}\frac{y(2)}{\Psi(2)a(2)}.$$

Similarly, differentiation of (27) with respect to α and P yields

$$\frac{d\alpha^S}{dP} = -\frac{\Pi_P(2) - \Pi_P(1)}{\Pi_\alpha(2) - \Pi_\alpha(1)}.$$

Note that, since $h(\alpha, 1) = \alpha$, $\Psi(1) = 1$, we get

$$\frac{d\alpha^S}{dP} = -\frac{(y(2) - y(1))\alpha^s}{W[\Psi(2)a(2) - a(1)]}. \tag{29}$$

It can be argued that $\Psi(2) < 1$, and we know that $y(2) > y(1)$. In most cases, $a(1) > a(2)$; therefore, $\frac{d\alpha^s}{dP} > 0$. Namely, increase in output price will increase adoption by increasing the switching land quality. Now, let us assume that $g(\alpha)$ is the land quality density function; $g(\alpha)\Delta\alpha$ denotes the amount of land with qualities between $\alpha - \frac{\Delta\alpha}{2}$ and $\alpha + \frac{\Delta\alpha}{2}$ for a small $\Delta\alpha$. Thus, aggregate output supply and input demand are given by

$$Y[P, W, c_1, c_2] = \int_{\alpha^m}^{\alpha^s} y(2, \alpha) g(\alpha) d\alpha + \int_{\alpha^s}^{1} y(1, \alpha) g(\alpha) d\alpha, \quad (30)$$

$$A[P, W, c_1, c_2] = \int_{\alpha^m}^{\alpha^s} a(2, \alpha) g(\alpha) d\alpha + \int_{\alpha^s}^{1} a(1, \alpha) g(\alpha) d\alpha. \quad (31)$$

The Leibnitz rule is useful in analyzing the properties of the aggregate supply response. Using this rule,

$$\frac{dY[P, W, c_1, c_2]}{dP} = \underbrace{\frac{\partial \alpha^S}{\partial P}[y(2, \alpha^s) - y(1, \alpha^s)]\, g(\alpha^s)}_{\text{term 1: +}} \underbrace{- \frac{\partial \alpha^m}{\partial P} g(\alpha^m) y(2, \alpha^m)}_{\text{term 2: +}}$$
$$\underbrace{+ \int_{\alpha^m}^{\alpha^s} \frac{\partial y(2, \alpha)}{\partial P} g(\alpha) d\alpha}_{\text{term 3: +}} \underbrace{+ \int_{\alpha^s}^{1} \frac{\partial y(1, \alpha)}{\partial P} g(\alpha) d\alpha.}_{\text{term 4: +}} \quad (32)$$

The first two terms reflect changes in the extensive margin, and the last two reflect changes in the intensive margin. All elements are positive which means that supply curve slopes upward. The extensive margins are especially important when there is a relatively large amount of land having switching or marginal qualities. One can use similar procedures to evaluate Y_W, A_P, and A_W.

4. Conclusion

In this chapter, we have discussed some basic properties of production functions, emphasizing on duality and its implications. By using drip irrigation as an example, we have analyzed the economics of input-quality-augmenting technology. A key insight is that the impact of such technology on input use depends on the elasticity of marginal product with respect to effective input: If the elasticity is less than one, then the adoption of this technology will increase the optimal input use. This rebound effect has wide applications in understanding conservation and resource-saving technologies. This chapter has also covered basic economic analysis of investments and production aggregation. Putty-clay models were introduced as a general framework for understanding production choices, technology adoption, and investment decisions. The production functions and related analyses introduced in this chapter establish the basis for the analyses in many other chapters within this book, particularly the chapters regarding risk and uncertainty, welfare analysis, as well as technology innovation and adoption. Before we move onto those chapters, let us first discuss a field that is closely related to production economics: consumer demand.

References

Antle, J.M. 1983. Sequential Decision Making in Production Models. *American Journal of Agricultural Economics* 65(2): 282–290.

Arrow, K.J. 1962. The Economic Implications of Learning by Doing. *The Review of Economic Studies* 29(3): 155–173.

Chambers, R.G. and D.R. Pope. 1994. A Virtually Ideal Production System; Specifying and Estimating the VIPS Model. *American Journal of Agricultural Economics*, 76(1): 105–113.

Johansen, L. 1959. Substitution versus Fixed Production Coefficients in the Theory of Economic Growth: A Synthesis. *Econometrica* 27(2): 157–176.

Salter, W.E.G. 1960. *Productivity and Technological Change* (2nd edition). Cambridge: Cambridge University Press.

Chapter 3

Consumer Demand

Consumer demand for a product reflects consumers' evaluation of the product and is thus critical for assessing consumer's welfare associated with the product. Moreover, understanding consumer demand is critical for firms to set their optimal prices and quantities, and to estimate the degree of substitution between differentiated products. For market analysts, knowing consumer demand of a product is an important component to evaluate the extent of market power. In this chapter, we will first briefly review the key results of the standard neoclassical demand theory, and then introduce several demand estimation models that have been widely used in the literature, including the Almost Ideal Demand System (AIDS) model developed by Deaton and Muellbauer (1980a,b) and the Exact Affine Stone Index (EASI) model developed by Lewbel and Pendakur (2009). We then discuss the critiques of the standard theory and corresponding models, and introduce demand theory and models that are based on product characteristics, which originate from the seminal work by Lancaster (1966).

1. Key Results of Standard Consumer Demand Theory

Standard consumer demand theory analyzes consumer demand in the space of products. Assume there are n products to be considered by a consumer, whose disposable income is denoted by I. Taking product prices, p_i, $\forall i \in \{1, \ldots, n\}$, as given, the consumer maximizes her utility by optimally choosing the quantity of each product, q_i, $\forall i \in \{1, \ldots, n\}$, under her budget constraint. The consumer's decision problem can be written as

$$v(\boldsymbol{p}, I) \equiv \max_{q \in R_+^n} U(\boldsymbol{q}), \quad \text{s.t. } \boldsymbol{p} \cdot \boldsymbol{q} \leq I, \tag{1}$$

where $\boldsymbol{p} \equiv (p_1, \ldots, p_n)$ and $\boldsymbol{q} \equiv (q_1, \ldots, q_n)$ are respectively price and quantity vectors of the n products, and $U(\cdot)$ is the consumer's utility function such that $U' > 0 > U''$. Here $v(\boldsymbol{p}, I)$ is defined as an indirect utility function given product prices and consumer income.

The Lagrangian equation of problem (1) can be written as

$$\max_{q \in R_+^n} (U(\boldsymbol{q}) + \lambda(I - \boldsymbol{p} \cdot \boldsymbol{q})), \tag{2}$$

where λ is the Lagrangian multiplier. The first order conditions of the maximization problem in Equation (2) can be written as

$$\frac{\partial U'(\boldsymbol{q})}{\partial q_i} - \lambda p_i = 0 \quad \text{for } i \in \{1, \ldots, n\}, \text{ and} \tag{3}$$

$$I - \boldsymbol{p} \cdot \boldsymbol{q} = 0. \tag{4}$$

Here the Lagrangian multiplier λ can be interpreted as the marginal utility of disposable income. Equation (3) states that in the optimal solution, the marginal utility of product i (i.e. $\partial U'(\boldsymbol{q})/\partial q_i$) is equal to the marginal utility of income spent on one additional unit of this product (i.e. λp_i). If $\partial U'(\boldsymbol{q})/\partial q_i > \lambda p_i$ then the consumer should buy more of product i; and if $\partial U'(\boldsymbol{q})/\partial q_i < \lambda p_i$ then the consumer should buy less.

By solving the $n + 1$ equations in (3) and (4) we can obtain the optimal consumption levels of each product, denoted by $\boldsymbol{q}^*(\boldsymbol{p}, I)$, and the optimal Lagrangian multiplier, denoted by λ^*. Here $\boldsymbol{q}^*(\boldsymbol{p}, I)$ is termed Marshallian demand, and it can also be thought of as uncompensated demand because a rise in product price is not compensated by any rise in the consumer's nominal disposable income. Based on Equation (1), the indirect utility function can be written as

$$v(\boldsymbol{p}, I) = U(\boldsymbol{q}^*). \tag{5}$$

One can readily check that $\partial v(\boldsymbol{p}, I)/\partial p_i \leq 0$, $\partial v(\boldsymbol{p}, I)/\partial I > 0$ and that $v(\boldsymbol{p}, I)$ is homogeneous of degree zero in (p, I). Moreover, once we obtain $\boldsymbol{q}^*(\boldsymbol{p}, I)$, we can calculate demand elasticity with respect to own price and income for product j as $\eta_j \equiv (d\boldsymbol{q}_j^*(\boldsymbol{p}, I)/dp_j)p_j/\boldsymbol{q}_j^*(\boldsymbol{p}, I)$ and $\eta_j^I \equiv (d\boldsymbol{q}_j^*(\boldsymbol{p}, I)/dI)I/\boldsymbol{q}_j^*(\boldsymbol{p}, I)$, respectively. When $\eta_j > 0$ product j is called Giffen good. In contrast, when $\eta_j < 0$, project j is called ordinary good. Particularly, when $\eta_j \in (-1, 0)$, we say the demand is inelastic; when $\eta_j < -1$, the demand is elastic. Moreover, product j is called luxury (respectively, normal and inferior) good if $\eta_j^I > 1$ (respectively, $\eta_j^I \in (0, 1)$ and $\eta_j^I < 0$). One takeaway is that a Giffen good must be an inferior good, but an inferior good is not necessarily a Giffen good.

An alternate way to model demand is to minimize expenditure for a given utility level target. The optimization problem can be written as

$$e(\boldsymbol{p}, u) \equiv \min_{q \in R_+^n} \boldsymbol{p} \cdot \boldsymbol{q}, \quad \text{s.t. } U(\boldsymbol{q}) \geq u, \tag{6}$$

where $e(\boldsymbol{p}, u)$ is termed the expenditure function for a given price vector $\boldsymbol{p}$ and utility level u. The Lagrangian for optimization problem (6) is

$$\min_{q \in R_+^n} [\boldsymbol{p} \cdot \boldsymbol{q} + \eta(u - U(q))], \tag{7}$$

where η is the Lagrangian multiplier, which reflects the increase in the minimized expenditure if the fixed utility level u were to be increased by one unit. Assuming a binding constraint, the first-order conditions of problem (7) are

$$p_i = \eta \frac{\partial U'(\boldsymbol{q})}{\partial q_i} \quad \text{for } i \in \{1, \ldots, n\}, \text{ and} \tag{8}$$

$$U(\boldsymbol{q}) = u. \tag{9}$$

By solving these $n + 1$ equations, we can obtain the optimal consumption levels, $\boldsymbol{q}^h(\boldsymbol{p}, u)$, for each product given the price and target utility level. The solution $\boldsymbol{q}^h(\boldsymbol{p}, u)$ here is called Hicksian demand, denoted by superscript h. In contrast to Marshallian demand, Hicksian demand can be termed compensated demand because when the price of a product increases, the consumer will behave like her income is compensated to guarantee a minimum utility level u. Once we obtain $\boldsymbol{q}^*(u, \boldsymbol{p})$, the expenditure function is simply $e(\boldsymbol{p}, u) = \boldsymbol{p} \cdot \boldsymbol{q}^*(u, \boldsymbol{p})$. One can readily check that $\partial e(\boldsymbol{p}, u)/\partial p_i \geq 0$, $\partial e(\boldsymbol{p}, u)/\partial u > 0$, and $e(\alpha \boldsymbol{p}, u) = \alpha e(\boldsymbol{p}, u)$ (i.e., homogenous of degree one in $\boldsymbol{p}$).

Several important properties regarding the Marshallian demand and Hicksian demand are discussed in almost every advanced microeconomics textbook. Because they are critical for understanding the demand models to be discussed further in the chapter, here we provide a brief recap of these properties.

1.1. *Roy's identity and Shephard's lemma*

Based on the envelope theorem, we can obtain two important results for the Marshallian demand and Hicksian demand: Roy's identity and Shephard's lemma[1]:

$$\text{Roy's identity: } q_i^*(\boldsymbol{p}, I) = -\frac{\partial v(\boldsymbol{p}, I)/\partial p_i}{\partial v(\boldsymbol{p}, I)/\partial I}, \tag{10}$$

$$\text{Shephard's lemma: } q_i^h(\boldsymbol{p}, u) = \frac{\partial e(\boldsymbol{p}, u)}{\partial p_i}. \tag{11}$$

Roy's identity shows that the Marshallian demand can be obtained from the indirect utility function. It states that the Marshallian demand is the ratio between the marginal impact of product price on the indirect utility and the marginal impact of income on the indirect utility. The intuition of Roy's identity can be better illustrated if we rewrite Equation (10) as

$$-\partial v(\boldsymbol{p}, I)/\partial p_i = q_i^*(\boldsymbol{p}, I) \cdot \partial v(\boldsymbol{p}, I)/\partial I. \tag{12}$$

---

[1]Readers can find the proofs in advanced microeconomics textbooks such as Mas-Colell *et al.* (1995) and Jehle and Reny (2001).

Equation (12) indicates that at optimum, utility increase caused by one-unit reduction in price p_i (i.e., the left-hand side of the equation) is equal to the expenditure freed up by the price reduction (i.e., $q_i^*(\boldsymbol{p}, I)$) times the marginal impact of expenditure on the maximized utility (i.e., $\partial v(\boldsymbol{p}, I)/\partial I$).

Shephard's lemma shows that the Hicksian demand can be readily obtained from the expenditure function: The Hicksian demand for product i is simply the partial derivative of the expenditure function with respect to price p_i. Because $e(\boldsymbol{p}, u) = \boldsymbol{p} \cdot \boldsymbol{q}^h(u, \boldsymbol{p})$, we have $\partial e(\boldsymbol{p}, u)/\partial p_i = q_i^h(\boldsymbol{p}, u) + \boldsymbol{p} \cdot (\partial \boldsymbol{q^h}(\boldsymbol{p}, u)/\partial p_i)$. Note that the second term on the right-hand side of this equation (i.e., $\boldsymbol{p} \cdot (\partial \boldsymbol{q^h}(\boldsymbol{p}, u)/\partial p_i)$) is the impact of price change of product i on the minimized expenditure through affecting demand for each product. Shephard's lemma states that $\boldsymbol{p} \cdot (\partial \boldsymbol{q^h}(\boldsymbol{p}, u)/\partial p_i) = 0$, indicating that overall this *indirect* expenditure effect (i.e., influencing expenditure by affecting demand quantity) of price change of a product is 0 due to changes in the expenditure on each product caused by demand quantity changes canceling out each other in the optimum. Combined with Young's theorem, the Shephard's lemma implies $\partial q_i^h(\boldsymbol{p}, u)/\partial p_j = \partial q_j^h(\boldsymbol{p}, u)/\partial p_i$ (i.e., symmetric substitution terms).

1.2. *Slutsky equation*

Before we discuss Slutsky equation, it is helpful to consider a few relations between Marshallian demand and Hicksian demand as well as between indirect utility function and expenditure function. These relations are

$$\begin{cases} \boldsymbol{q}^*(\boldsymbol{p}, I) = \boldsymbol{q}^h(\boldsymbol{p}, v(\boldsymbol{p}, I)) \\ \boldsymbol{q}^h(\boldsymbol{p}, u) = q^*(\boldsymbol{p}, e(\boldsymbol{p}, u)) \\ e(\boldsymbol{p}, v(\boldsymbol{p}, I)) = I \\ v(\boldsymbol{p}, e(\boldsymbol{p}, u)) = u. \end{cases} \tag{13}$$

The first two equations in (13) show the duality between Marshallian and Hicksian demand. The first equation indicates that at price vector $\boldsymbol{p}$, the Marshallian demand under budget constraint I is the same as the Hicksian demand under the utility constraint that is the highest possible the consumer can reach at price $\boldsymbol{p}$ and income I, i.e., $v(\boldsymbol{p}, I)$. The last two equations in (13) show that given price $\boldsymbol{p}$, the minimum expenditure to achieve the maximized utility under income I is I, and that given price $\boldsymbol{p}$, the maximum utility the consumer can reach under the minimum expenditure to reach utility level u is u.

The Slutsky equation can be written as

$$\frac{\partial q_i^*(\boldsymbol{p}, I)}{\partial p_j} = \frac{\partial q_i^h(\boldsymbol{p}, v(\boldsymbol{p}, I))}{\partial p_j} - q_j^*(\boldsymbol{p}, I)\frac{\partial q_i^*(\boldsymbol{p}, I)}{\partial I}, \quad \forall i,\ j \in \{1, \ldots, n\}. \tag{14}$$

To better interpret the Slutsky equation, note that at optimum $q_j^*(\boldsymbol{p}, I) = q_j^h(\boldsymbol{p}, v(\boldsymbol{p}, I)) = \partial e(\boldsymbol{p}, v(\boldsymbol{p}, I))/\partial p_j$ based on Equations (11) and (13). As a result, Equation (14) can be re-written as

$$\frac{\partial q_i^*(\boldsymbol{p}, I)}{\partial p_j} = \frac{\partial q_i^h(\boldsymbol{p}, v(\boldsymbol{p}, I))}{\partial p_j} - \frac{\partial e(\boldsymbol{p}, v(\boldsymbol{p}, I))}{\partial p_j}\frac{\partial q_i^*(\boldsymbol{p}, I)}{\partial I}, \quad \forall i, j \in \{1, \ldots, n\}, \tag{15}$$

where the first term on the right-hand side of Equation (15) is the substitution effect of price change and the second term is the income effect caused by the price change. The price effect on Marshallian demand is the sum of the substitution effect and the income effect.

2. Popular Demand Models Based on the Standard Consumer Demand Theory

Based on the neoclassical demand theory illustrated above, economists have developed some popular demand models for empirical analyses. In this section we discuss three of them: (1) constant elasticity of substitution demand model, (2) the Almost Ideal Demand System (AIDS) model, and (3) the Exact Affine Stone Index (EASI) model.[2]

[2]Some other popular demand models in the product space include Linear Expenditure System models, Rotterdam demand model, and translog demand models. We refer readers to Stone (1954), Christensen *et al.* (1975), and Clements and Gao (2015) for details about these models.

2.1. *Constant elasticity of substitution (CES) demand model*

The CES functions are popular in both consumer theory and production theory due to their convenient properties such as monotonicity and concavity. Moreover, Cobb–Douglas functions and Leontief functions are special cases of the CES function family. A CES utility function on n goods can take the following form:

$$U(q_1, \ldots, q_n) = \left(\sum_{i=1}^{n} q_i^{\rho}\right)^{1/\rho}, \tag{16}$$

where parameter $\rho < 1$ and $\rho \neq 0$. Under price vector $\boldsymbol{p}$ and income I, a utility maximization problem like in optimization problem (1) with the CES utility function can be solved as

$$\boldsymbol{q}_i^*(\boldsymbol{p}, I) = I \cdot (p_i)^{\frac{1}{\rho-1}} \cdot P^{\frac{\rho}{1-\rho}}, \tag{17}$$

where $P \equiv (\sum_{i=1}^{n} p_i^{\frac{\rho}{\rho-1}})^{(\rho-1)/\rho}$ can be viewed as a price index. Taking natural logarithm of Equation (17), we obtain

$$\ln \boldsymbol{q}_i^*(\boldsymbol{p}, I) = \ln I + \frac{1}{\rho - 1} \ln p_i + \frac{\rho}{1-\rho} \ln P. \tag{18}$$

If we have data for prices and quantity demanded of a group of products over a period of time, then we can estimate a regression model based on Equation (18),

$$\ln \boldsymbol{q}_{it}^* = \beta_0 + \beta_1 \ln p_{it} + \beta_2 \ln P_t + \epsilon_t, \tag{19}$$

where t stands for time period. One might have noticed that the price index P contains the unknown parameter ρ, and, therefore, the values of P_t are unknown for the regression. In practice, researchers can get around this issue by using time period dummies to replace $\ln P_t$.

The estimate of β_1 can be interpreted as the demand elasticity of product i with respect to its own price. The demand model offers simplicity, but it imposes strict restrictions on price elasticity and the elasticity of substitution between products. Specifically, within this demand model, any product's demand elasticity with respect to its own price is the same, and the elasticity of substitution between any pair of products is the same as well. This is certainly not true in reality. Therefore, some demand models that can relax these restrictions are in order. We will discuss two such models for the remainder of this section.

2.2. *The AIDS model*

Unlike the aforementioned CES demand model that is built on an arbitrary utility function, the AIDS model starts with expenditure function. In their seminal paper that introduces the AIDS model, Deaton and Muellbauer (1980a) assume the expenditure function takes the following form:

$$\ln e(\boldsymbol{p}, u) = (1-u)\ln a(\boldsymbol{p}) + u \ln b(\boldsymbol{p}), \tag{20}$$

where $u \in [0, 1]$, with $u = 0$ indicating subsistence and $u = 1$ bliss. Furthermore,

$$\ln a(\boldsymbol{p}) = a_0 + \Sigma_k \alpha_k \ln p_k + \frac{1}{2}\Sigma_k \Sigma_j \gamma^*_{kj} \ln p_k \ln p_j, \tag{21}$$

$$\ln b(\boldsymbol{p}) = \ln a(\boldsymbol{p}) + \beta_0 \prod_k p_k^{\beta_k}, \tag{22}$$

where α, β, and γ are parameters.

Plugging Equations (21) and (22) into Equation (20), we obtain the AIDS expenditure function

$$\ln e(\boldsymbol{p}, u) = \alpha_0 + \Sigma_k \alpha_k \ln p_k + \frac{1}{2}\Sigma_k \Sigma_j \gamma^*_{kj} \ln p_k \ln p_j + u\beta_0 \prod_k p_k^{\beta_k}. \tag{23}$$

Based on Shephard's lemma, we know that

$$\frac{\partial \ln e(\boldsymbol{p}, u)}{\partial \ln p_i} = \frac{p_i q_i}{e(\boldsymbol{p}, u)} \equiv w_i, \tag{24}$$

where w_i is expenditure share of good i among the group of studied goods. Therefore, taking the derivative of Equation (23) with respect to $\ln p_i$, we obtain

$$w_i = \alpha_i + \Sigma_j \gamma_{ij} \ln p_j + \beta_i u \beta_0 \prod_k p_k^{\beta_k}, \tag{25}$$

where $\gamma_{ij} \equiv 1/2 \cdot (\gamma_{ij}^* + \gamma_{ji}^*)$.

As we discussed earlier, for a utility maximization consumer, the indirect utility can be expressed as a function of prices and disposable income, which is equal to the minimum expenditure needed to obtain the maximized utility conditional on prices and income (see Equation (13)). Therefore, based on Equation (23), we have

$$u = \left[\ln I - \left(\alpha_0 + \Sigma_k \alpha_k \ln p_k + \frac{1}{2} \Sigma_k \Sigma_j \gamma_{kj}^* \ln p_k \ln p_j\right)\right] \Big/ \beta_0 \prod_k p_k^{\beta_k}, \tag{26}$$

where I is disposable income (or, equivalently, total expenditure) of the consumer. Plugging Equation (26) into Equation (25), we have

$$w_i = \alpha_i + \Sigma_j \gamma_{ij} \ln p_j + \beta_i \ln (I/P), \tag{27}$$

where P is a price index such that

$$\ln P = a_0 + \Sigma_k \alpha_k \ln p_k + \frac{1}{2} \Sigma_k \Sigma_j \gamma_{kj} \ln p_k \ln p_j. \qquad (28)^3$$

The restrictions of the parameters in Equation (27) include

$$\Sigma_i \alpha_i = 1, \quad \Sigma_i \beta_i = 0, \quad \Sigma_i \gamma_{ij} = 0, \quad \Sigma_j \gamma_{ij} = 0, \text{ and } \gamma_{ij} = \gamma_{ji}. \tag{29}$$

With the restrictions in Equation (29), one can check that $\Sigma_i w_i = 1$, w_i is homogeneous of degree zero in prices and total expenditure, and that $e(\boldsymbol{p}, u)$ is homogeneous of degree one in $\boldsymbol{p}$.

[3]We obtain Equation (28) by using the fact that $\Sigma_k \Sigma_j \gamma_{kj} = \Sigma_k \Sigma_j \gamma_{kj}^*$.

Based on $w_i = p_i q_i^*(\boldsymbol{p}, I)/I$ and Equation (27), the Marshallian demand elasticity with respect to price can be written as

$$\eta_{ij} = \frac{\partial \ln q_i^*(\boldsymbol{p}, I)}{\partial \ln p_j} = -\delta_{ij} + \frac{\partial \ln w_i}{\partial \ln p_j} = -\delta_{ij} + \left\{\gamma_{ij} - \beta_i \frac{\partial \ln P}{\partial \ln p_j}\right\} \Big/ w_i, \tag{30}$$

where δ_{ij} is the Kronecker delta equal to 1 if $i = j$ and 0 otherwise.

If we have data for product prices and expenditure on each product, then we can estimate Equation (27) and, thereby, price elasticities in Equation (30). By comparing Equation (30) with Equation (18), we can see that, unlike the CES demand models, the own price elasticities across products are not necessarily the same, indicating that the AIDS models are more flexible than the CES models. For practical considerations of estimating the AIDS demand system, we refer readers to Deaton and Muellbauer (1980a) and Green and Alston (1990).

2.3. *The EASI model*

Although simple, relatively flexible, and widely applied, the AIDS models nevertheless have some significant drawbacks. First, Engel curves (expenditure on a good as a function of total disposable income) derived from the AIDS models can only take quite restrictive forms (e.g., linear-log form, see Deaton and Muellbauer (1980a)), and Engel curves across all goods within the AIDS model assume the same form. Second, the AIDS models cannot accommodate observed and unobserved preference heterogeneity across consumers, while, in reality, one would expect that the Engel curves for different products may differ from one another (e.g., normal goods vs. inferior goods). Moreover, studies have documented that preference heterogeneity is prevalent in consumer choices and that it is important to consider the heterogeneity in demand analysis (e.g., Beckert and Blundell 2008).

The EASI model proposed by Lewbel and Pendakur (2009) aims to address the foregoing two issues. Similar to the AIDS models, the EASI model also starts from an expenditure function, although the expenditure function under the EASI model is quite different from that under the AIDS model. The tricks employed by the two demand models to derive the Marshallian demand share equations are also quite similar. Following Pendakur (2009), we first introduce the simplest version of the expenditure function used by Lewbel and Pendakur (2009), and then add on features to accommodate preference heterogeneity. Continuing with the notation above, the simplest expenditure function in the EASI models is

$$\ln e(\boldsymbol{p}, u) = u + \Sigma_i m_i(u) \ln p_i, \tag{31}$$

where $m_i(u)$ is a function of u such that $\Sigma_i m_i(u) = 1$. By taking derivative of this equation with respect to $\ln p_i$ we obtain

$$w_i(\boldsymbol{p}, u) = m_i(u). \tag{32}$$

We make two observations from Equation (32) (the Hicksian expenditure share function). First, each good can have a completely different expenditure function form than that of another good.[4] This feature will allow different Engel curves across all goods. Second, the expenditure share function is unrelated to prices, which is a drawback that needs to be overcome.

Similar to what we have done to derive the AIDS models, we can obtain an expression of utility, u, based on Equations (31) and (32) with the help of Equation (13),

$$u = \ln I - \Sigma_i w_i \ln p_i. \tag{33}$$

Plugging Equation (33) into Equation (32), we obtain

$$w_i = m_i(\ln I - \Sigma_i w_i \ln p_i), \tag{34}$$

which is termed implicit Marshallian demand because the Marshallian expenditure share, w_i, appears on both sides of the equation. However, all the variables in Equation (34) are now observables.

[4]Note that in the AIDS models, the Hicksian expenditure share functions differ across goods only by parameters α_i and β_i (see Equation (27)).

Define implicit utility as

$$y \equiv \ln I - \Sigma_i w_i \ln p_i, \tag{35}$$

which can be interpreted as disposable income I deflated by price index $\Sigma_i w_i \ln p_i$. For a given functional form of $m_i(\cdot)$, (say, polynomials), Equation (34) can be readily estimated by regressing w_i on y instrumented by $\ln I$ and $\ln p_j$, $j \in \{1, \ldots, n\}$.

To add on unobserved preference heterogeneity, we simply assume that the expenditure function takes the form

$$\ln e(\boldsymbol{p}, u, \boldsymbol{\epsilon}) = u + \Sigma_i m_i(u) \ln p_i + \Sigma_i \epsilon_i \ln p_i, \tag{36}$$

where $\epsilon = [\epsilon_1, \ldots, \epsilon_n]$ represents unobserved preference characteristics of consumers associated with good $i \in \{1, \ldots, n\}$, and $E(\epsilon) = 0$. Again, taking derivative of Equation (36) with respect to $\ln p_i$, we obtain the Hicksian expenditure share function

$$w_i(\boldsymbol{p}, u, \boldsymbol{\epsilon}) = m_i(u) + \epsilon_i. \tag{37}$$

Furthermore, by plugging $m_i(u) = w_i(\boldsymbol{p}, u, \boldsymbol{\epsilon}) - \epsilon_i$ obtained from Equation (37) into Equation (36), and rearranging, we again have $y = u = \ln I - \Sigma_i w_i \ln p_i$ as in Equation (35). Plugging this result into Equation (37), we obtain the implicit Marshallian budget share equation

$$w_i = m_i(y) + \epsilon_i. \tag{38}$$

Again, these budget share equations can be estimated separately by using instrumental variables as discussed above. Lewbel and Pendakur (2009) term Equation (38) the Exact Stone Index (ESI) demand because the nominal disposable income I is deflated exactly by the Stone index defined by $\prod_i p_i^{w_i}$. One should note that even though the demand models in Equation (38) can accommodate the unobserved preference heterogeneity and allow for arbitrary form of Engel curves for each good, prices do not directly enter the Hicksian or Marshallian expenditure functions in Equations (37) and (38). To address this issue, Lewbel and Pendakur (2009) employ the following expenditure function form

$$\ln e(\boldsymbol{p}, u, \boldsymbol{z}, \boldsymbol{\epsilon}) = u + \Sigma_i m_i(u, \boldsymbol{z}) \ln p_i + \frac{1}{2}\Sigma_i\Sigma_j[\alpha_{ij}(\boldsymbol{z}) \ln p_i \ln p_j] + \Sigma_i \epsilon_i \ln p_i, \tag{39}$$

where vector $z = [z_1, \ldots, z_T]$ stands for observable demographics of consumers. Taking the derivative of Equation (39) with respect to $\ln p_i$, we obtain the Hicksian expenditure share function as

$$w_i(\boldsymbol{p}, u, \boldsymbol{z}, \boldsymbol{\epsilon}) = m_i(u, \boldsymbol{z}) + \Sigma_j \alpha_{ij}(\boldsymbol{z}) \ln p_j + \epsilon_i, \tag{40}$$

where $\alpha_{ij} = \alpha_{ji} \forall i, j \in \{1, \ldots, n\}$. Multiplying $\ln p_i$ to both sides of Equation (40) and sum across all goods, we obtain

$$\Sigma_i(w_i \ln p_i) = \Sigma_i(m_i(u, \boldsymbol{z}) \ln p_i) + \Sigma_i\Sigma_j \left[\alpha_{ij}(\boldsymbol{z}) \ln p_i \ln p_j\right] + \Sigma_i(\epsilon_i \ln p_i). \tag{41}$$

By solving out $\Sigma_i(m_i(u, \boldsymbol{z}) \ln p_i)$ from Equation (41) and plug it in Equation (39), we obtain

$$y = u = \ln I - \Sigma_i(w_i \ln p_i) + \frac{1}{2}\Sigma_i\Sigma_j[\alpha_{ij}(\boldsymbol{z}) \ln p_i \ln p_j]. \tag{42}$$

Note that in Equation (42) the nominal disposable income I is deflated by an affine transformation of Stone price index, $\Sigma_i(w_i \ln p_i) - \frac{1}{2}\Sigma_i\Sigma_j[\alpha_{ij}(\boldsymbol{z}) \ln p_i \ln p_j]$, given the name of EASI (Exact Affine Stone Index) demand models. Plugging Equation (42) into Equation (40), we then obtain the implicit Marshallian budget share

$$w_i = m_i(y, \boldsymbol{z}) + \Sigma_j(\alpha_{ij}(\boldsymbol{z}) \ln p_j) + \epsilon_i, \tag{43}$$

where $\alpha_{ij} = \alpha_{ji} \forall i, j \in \{1, \ldots, n\}$. Note that Equation (43) remains the features that the Engel curves can have any shapes for good i. Moreover, it now accommodates observable and non-observable preference heterogeneity, as well as a linear price effect on expenditure share. Assuming a functional form for $m_i(y, \boldsymbol{z})$, we can estimate the EASI demand model in (43) by using instrumental variables as discussed above.

3. Critiques of Standard Demand Theory and Models

Perhaps the strongest critiques of the standard demand theory and models were from Kelvin Lancaster (1924–1999) and Gary Becker (1930–2014).[5] Lancaster (1966) criticized that although the standard demand theory is elegant, it is also too general and vacuous. He argued that the pursuit of generality resulted in a minimal set of assumptions (i.e., utility maximization, income constraint, and quasi-concave utility function), but a minimal set of results (i.e., Hicksian demand curves are negatively sloped). Because of the pursuit of generality, all goods in the standard demand theory are treated alike. Anything that people want more of are goods. No attention is given to the intrinsic properties of goods that separate bread from bicycles. The standard demand theory assumes that preferences are given and does not try to explain variation in preferences. Although the theory can explain observed patterns in a static primitive economy, it cannot deal with modern interesting issues such as prediction of demand for new products and understanding the effects of product quality differences.

Is Lancaster right? Almost, but his criticisms are somewhat harsh. The notions of substitutes and complements and the notions of separability were all attempts to enrich the power of standard demand theory.[6] These attempts, however, are weak. They do not consider intrinsic properties, and therefore, they are not useful for explaining product innovation and quality changes.

On the other hand, Michael and Becker (1973) argued that the standard demand theories use income and prices as the main explanatory variables for consumption patterns, and whatever is not

[5]Becker was a student of Theodore W. Schultz (1902–1998). Schultz coined the term "human capital" and started the literature on economics of education and learning. He emphasizes the study of behavior outside the market and in situations of disequilibrium. Another student of Schultz, Zvi Griliches (1930–1999), started formal economic research on technology adoption. We will cover some of Griliches' work in the chapter on technology adoption.

[6]See Nevo (2011) for a brief discussion about separability.

explained by income and prices is attributed to tastes. However, income and price variations are found to explain only a small part of the variation in family consumption patterns. Although taste has an important role, there is no consideration of the formation of taste in the standard demand theory. Moreover, a standard demand theory explains consumption patterns of goods purchased in the market, and that imposes an important limitation on phenomenon investigation. In other words, applications of the standard demand theory are restricted to market segments or monetary segments in the economy, therefore, non-market activities are ignored. This limits the usefulness of the theory to developed nations and reduces its effectiveness in developing nations, in which markets are incomplete or absent.

According to Becker, economics is a science that explains behavioral choices with limited resources among competing needs. These choices include both market and non-market decisions. Some examples of non-market decisions include choices on family size, lifestyle, occupation, political party, marriage, crime, migration, suicides, and so on. Becker expanded the range of issues analyzed by economists to include some of these non-market decisions. His works are insightful but show the limitation of the notion of "economic man." A better understanding of choices and behavior may need to incorporate more from psychology and sociology into economic models.

Overall, the critiques from Lancaster and Becker revealed that the standard demand theory ignored intrinsic properties of goods, left too much explanation to "taste", and cannot deal with important phenomenon such as product innovation, product quality differences, and non-market activities. Lancaster's critiques originated an important alternative demand theory that focuses on the characteristics space, while Becker's critiques were followed by family production models, another alternative of the standard demand theory. Both alternatives incorporate production activities into demand: a consumption unit contains a production process that transforms goods and other inputs into sources of utility. We now discuss these two alternatives in the following two sections.

4. Consumer Demand Based on Product Characteristics

4.1. *Lancaster's approach*

Unlike the standard demand theory discussed in Sections 1 and 2, which assumes that consumers derive utility directly from goods, Lancaster (1966) assumes that consumers derive utility directly from the characteristics of goods, not from the goods themselves. In Lancaster's approach, consumers purchase goods from markets as "inputs" for "activities" that convert goods to characteristics. Assume that one unit of activity k will consume a_{jk} units of good j. Let x_j denote the total quantity of good j consumed, and y_k denote the level of activity k. We then have

$$x_j = \Sigma_k a_{jk} y_k. \tag{44}$$

We further assume that one unit of activity k will produce b_{ik} units of characteristics i. Therefore, the total amount of characteristics i produced by all activities is

$$z_i = \Sigma_k b_{ik} y_k. \tag{45}$$

In matrix format, Equations (44) and (45) can be written as $x = Ay$ and $z = By$, respectively. Suppose the dimensions of x, y, and z are $n \times 1$, $m \times 1$, and $r \times 1$, respectively. Then the size of matrices A and B are $n \times m$ and $r \times m$, respectively. B is called consumption technology. In Lancaster's model, consumers derive utility directly from characteristics, which is reflected by utility function $U(z)$. Based on the foregoing model setup, the consumer's optimization problem can be written as

$$\text{Max}\, U(z), \quad \text{s.t. } z = By,\ x = Ay,\ p'x \leq I, \quad \text{and} \quad x, y, z \geq 0, \tag{46}$$

where p is the price vector and I is disposable income.

Note that when $m = n = r$, we will have a one-to-one relationship between goods and characteristics, i.e., $z = BA^{-1}x$ and $U(z) = U(BA^{-1}x) = V(x)$. In this case, the consumer's demand problem becomes the standard demand model, which shows that the standard model can be a special case of Lancaster's model.

Generally, however, we do not have $m = n = r$, so we have to take a different path connecting goods to characteristics. Fortunately, many such paths exist. For simplicity, let us assume that goods and activities are identical. Thus, optimization problem in (46) can be simplified as

$$\max U(z), \quad \text{s.t. } z = Bx, \quad px \leq I, \quad \text{and} \quad x, z \geq 0. \tag{47}$$

If $r > n$ (i.e., the number of characteristics is greater than the number of goods), then we have a primitive society. In this case, not all consumption combinations are reachable. There is a relatively small number of goods that cannot meet many needs, independent of income constraints.

For advanced economies, we will have $n > r$ (i.e., there are more goods than characteristics). Consumers can attain any characteristic combination in many ways. In this case, the consumer has to make two types of choices. First, the efficiency choices to determine the least costly way to produce a characteristic combination for a given price vector p and characteristic vector z^*. This is a linear programming decision problem that can be written as

$$\min px, \quad \text{s.t. } z^* = Bx \quad \text{and} \quad x \geq 0. \tag{48}$$

Repetition of this choice can yield a characteristic frontier such that the cost of obtaining any z^* on the frontier is exactly I. Figure 1 shows an example of such characteristic frontier when the consumption technology involves two characteristics and four goods (see curve $E_1E_2E_3E_4$ in the figure). Note that problem (48) does not involve any utility function, which indicates that the characteristic frontiers are the same for all consumers with the same budget constraint. Given the consumption technology B, the characteristic frontiers will expand or shrink parallelly when budget increases or decreases. It is also readily checked that the characteristic frontier is concave.

After making the efficiency choices, the second type of choices that the consumer will make is the private consumption

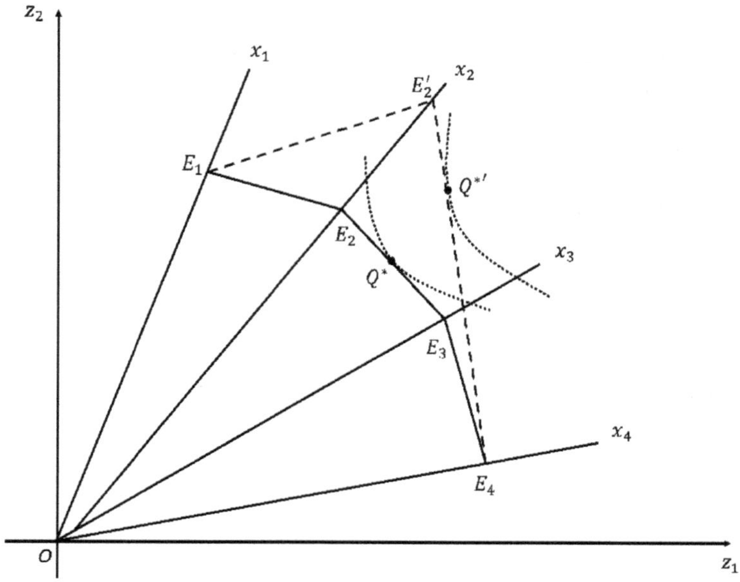

Figure 1. An example of Lancaster (1966) model.

choice—a selection of consumption points on the characteristic frontier. This choice depends on the consumer's utility function and is therefore subjective.

Let us continue with the 2-characteristic and 4-good example. Suppose the relationship between the two characteristics and the four goods are described as follows:

$$\begin{cases} z_1 = b_{11}x_1 + b_{12}x_2 + b_{13}x_3 + b_{14}x_4 \\ z_2 = b_{21}x_1 + b_{22}x_2 + b_{23}x_3 + b_{24}x_4. \end{cases} \tag{49}$$

If the consumer spends all her income on good 1, then the amount of good she can purchase is $E_1 \equiv I/p_1$. In this case, the quantity of characteristics 1 and 2 obtained will be such that $z_1/z_2 = b_{11}/b_{21}$. This relationship is depicted by ray OE_1 in Figure 1. Similarly, we have ray OE_2 to OE_4 in the figure. For example, point E_2 indicates the maximum amount of good 2 that can be obtained by the consumer, and ray OE_2 has a slope of b_{12}/b_{22}, indicating the ratio between z_1 and z_2 when only good 2 is available to the consumer. Note that the shape of the curve $E_1E_2E_3E_4$ indicates that the prices of the four goods and the consumption technology B happen to make the combinations of goods 1 and 2, 2 and 3, and 3 and 4 efficient. When prices or consumption technology changes, then the shape of the curve $E_1E_2E_3E_4$ may change as well. Moreover, a point on segment E_1E_2 indicates a linear combination of E_1 and E_2 (i.e., $\lambda E_1 + (1-\lambda)E_2$ where $\lambda \in [0,1]$). One can readily check that all points on the curve $E_1E_2E_3E_4$ have the same cost.

Under the setup associated with Figure 1 we can study the impact of a change in price. Suppose good 2 becomes cheaper. Then the characteristic frontier moves from $E_1E_2E_3E_4$ to $E_1E_2'E_4$, and the optimal choice changes from Q^* to $Q^{*\prime}$ in the figure, which is determined by the characteristic frontiers and the indifference curves (i.e., the dotted curves in the figure). Before the reduction in price of good 2, good 3 was consumed; now good 3 is not in the optimal solution and it is not used. As a result, the efficient substitution effect eliminates the consumption of good 3 in our case and causes a switch. Thus, negatively sloped demand is not only a result of concave utility function but also of a certain consumption and production technology set. It is not only justified by one's taste but by all the people's consumption technology.

To summarize, one has to distinguish between efficiency substitution and private substitution. The former is an objective substitution where a bundle of characteristics may be produced better by a different set of goods after price changes. The latter is a subjective substitution where a change in prices changes the characteristic frontier and then there is a change in consumption within a given technology reflecting utility and preference. These substitutions are complementing one another, and they strengthen the notion of negatively sloped demand.

We now explore more about a specific version of the Lancaster model where $m = n = r = N$. In this case, both matrices A and B are $N \times N$ matrix. Specifically, we have

$$z = BA^{-1}x = \begin{pmatrix} b_{11} & \cdots & b_{1N} \\ \vdots & \ddots & \vdots \\ b_{N1} & \cdots & b_{NN} \end{pmatrix} \begin{pmatrix} a_{11} & \cdots & a_{1N} \\ \vdots & \ddots & \vdots \\ a_{N1} & \cdots & a_{NN} \end{pmatrix}^{-1} \begin{pmatrix} x_1 \\ \vdots \\ x_N \end{pmatrix}, \quad \text{or}$$

$$z_j = \Sigma_k \Sigma_l b_{jl} a_{lk}^{-1} x_k, \tag{50}$$

where a_{lk}^{-1} is the element in the lth row and kth column of matrix A^{-1}, and $j, k, l \in \{1, \ldots, N\}$. The optimal demand choice problem is

$$\max_x U(BA^{-1}x), \quad \text{s.t. } p'x = I. \tag{51}$$

It can be presented in Lagrangian form

$$L = \max_x U(BA^{-1}x) + \lambda[I - p'x], \tag{52}$$

where λ is the shadow price of the income constraint. The first-order conditions are

$$\frac{\partial L}{\partial x_l} = \Sigma_k \left(\frac{\partial U}{\partial z_k}\frac{\partial z_k}{\partial x_l}\right) - \lambda p_l = 0, \quad l \in \{1, \ldots, N\}, \text{ and} \tag{53}$$

$$\frac{\partial L}{\partial \lambda} = I - p'x = 0. \tag{54}$$

Based on Equation (50), we have $(\partial z_k)/(\partial x_l) = \Sigma_j b_{kj} a_{jl}^{-1}$. Therefore, Equation (53) can be re-written as

$$\frac{\partial L}{\partial x_l} = \Sigma_k \left(\frac{\partial U}{\partial z_k}\Sigma_j\, b_{kj}\, a_{jl}^{-1}\right) - \lambda p_l = 0, \quad l \in \{1, \ldots, N\}. \tag{55}$$

Rearranging terms in Equation (55), we have

$$\Sigma_k \left(\frac{1}{\lambda}\frac{\partial U}{\partial z_k} \times \Sigma_j\, b_{kj}\, a_{jl}^{-1}\right) = p_l. \tag{56}$$

Terms in Equation (56) have an intuitive interpretation. Clearly, the right-hand side of the equation is the cost of one more unit of good l, price p_l. The term on the left-hand side of the equation is the marginal value to the consumer, represented in monetary form (because it is divided by λ), caused by one unit increase in good l. More specifically, the term $(1/\lambda)\partial U/(\partial z_k)$ is the marginal value of characteristic k and the term $\Sigma_j\, b_{kj}\, a_{jl}^{-1}$ is the marginal productivity of good l summed in producing characteristic k in all activities.

The model has originated a new branch of demand system models that are different from the AIDS and EASI models discussed above. Here, we introduce demand models in characteristic space, which are a derivation of econometric models based on the Lancaster model.

4.2. *Demand models in the characteristic space*

For simplicity, let us continue with the assumption that there is a one-to-one relationship between goods and activities (i.e., A is an identity matrix). Also, maintaining the notation above, we have n goods and each good $j \in \{1, \ldots, n\}$ has r characteristics, labeled as $z_j = (z_{j1}, \ldots, z_{jr})'$. One example is a local housing market where the number of goods is the number of houses available in the local market and the characteristics include the number of bedrooms, bathrooms, stories, and so on. Let i be the index of a consumer. We assume that there is a continuum of consumers so that the total number of consumers sums up to 1. We further assume that consumer i's utility function on characteristics is $U_i(z, \epsilon, e_i)$, where ϵ stands for unobservable characteristics of goods and e_i for consumer attributes. Lastly, we assume that a consumer only purchases at most one good (e.g., one house). Consumer i's decision problem is then

$$\max_{d_{i1},\ldots,d_{in}} u_i(I_i - \Sigma_j(d_j p_j), e_i) + \Sigma_j(d_j U_i(z_j, \epsilon_j, e_i)),$$
$$\text{s.t. } I_i - \Sigma_j(d_j p_j) \geq 0,\ d_{ij} \in \{0, 1\}, \quad \text{and} \quad \Sigma_j d_j \leq 1, \tag{57}$$

where $u_i(\cdot)$ indicates consumer i's utility from income or all other goods; z_j is defined by equation (50); $d_j = 0$ indicates that good j is not purchased and $d_j = 1$ indicates the opposite. Denote the optimal solutions of problem (57) as $\{d^*_{i1}(p, z, I_i, e_i), \ldots, d^*_{in}(p, z, I_i, e_i)\}$. If $d^*_{i1} = d^*_{i2} = \cdots = d^*_{in} = 0$, then the consumer will not buy any of the n goods. Aggregating individual demand for good j across all consumers, we have the market demand for the good as

$$Q_j(p, z) = \int d^*_{ij}(p, z, I_i, e_i) f(I_i, e_i) dI_i de_i, \tag{58}$$

where $f(I_i, e_i)$ is the probability density function of individual income and attributes. Here $Q_j(p, z)$ can also be viewed as market share of good j because the total amount of consumers is normalized to 1. Based on individual or market level of data about quantity demanded, prices, expenditure, characteristics, as well as assumption on the probability density function, we can estimate the marginal impact of characteristics on consumer demand.[7] This model can be used to forecast the demand for a new product that has different levels of characteristics, but it fails if the new product's characteristics do not appear in any existing good.

5. Family Production Model

Michael and Becker (1973) emphasized on the time allocated to activities processing goods at the household level. They distinguished between goods and commodities (analogous to characteristics in Lancaster's model). The household spends time to convert goods into commodities, and household utility is derived from commodities and leisure. According to Michael and Becker (1973), "The consumer's demand for these market goods is a derived demand analogous to the derived demand by a firm for any factor of production."

Following the notation in the Lancaster model discussed above, we again assume that the consumer's utility function is $U(z)$, where $z = (z_1, \ldots, z_r)$ is a vector of commodities (or characteristics). For simplicity, we assume there are r goods available, and each is used to produce a unique commodity. The household allocates its time to convert the r goods, $x = (x_1, \ldots, x_r)$, into commodities, with a production function

$$z_j = g_j(x_j, t_j; E), \tag{59}$$

where $g_j(\cdot)$ is the production function, t_j is time used to produce commodity z_j, and E stands for the production environment. Note that leisure decision is also covered in the model. For example, one can view x_1 as the amount of goods consumed during leisure time (e.g., movie theater tickets) and t_1 as the time spent on leisure.

Assume the time that the household supplies in the labor market is t_w, earning wage rate at w. Therefore, the total time constraint of the household is $t_w + \Sigma_j t_j = T$, where T is the total amount of time that the household has. Let V be the non-wage income of

[7]We refer readers to Nevo (2011) for a detailed discussion about estimation for demand models in characteristic space.

the household. Therefore, the budget constraint of the household is $\Sigma_j p_j x_j = wt_w + V$. Merging the time and budget constraint, we obtain $S = wT + V = \Sigma_j(wt_j + p_j x_j)$. The household's demand problem can be written as

$$\max_{x,t} U(g_1(x_1, t_1; E), \ldots, g_r(x_r, t_r; E)) \quad \text{s.t. } \Sigma_j(wt_j + p_j x_j) = S, \tag{60}$$

whose Lagrangian is

$$L = U(g_1(x_1, t_1; E), \ldots, g_r(x_r, t_r; E)) - \lambda[\Sigma_j(wt_j + p_j x_j) - S]. \tag{61}$$

The first order conditions include

$$\frac{\partial L}{\partial x_j} = \frac{\partial U}{\partial z_j}\frac{\partial g_j}{\partial x_j} - \lambda p_j = 0, \quad \forall j \in \{1, \ldots, r\}, \text{ and} \tag{62}$$

$$\frac{\partial L}{\partial t_j} = \frac{\partial U}{\partial z_j}\frac{\partial g_j}{\partial t_j} - \lambda w = 0, \quad \forall j \in \{1, \ldots, r\}. \tag{63}$$

These first order conditions imply that, at the optimum, the marginal utility of a factor (good or time) is equal to its marginal cost (price or wage rate).

Solution of the system provides the demands for goods, leisure, and supply of labor in the market. Specifically, demand for goods are functions of prices, income level, wage rate, and household production environment. Total demand for a good (an input in commodity production) is the sum of induced demands from all demand for commodities. The demand for goods depends on the decomposition of income between wage and non-wage income. Wage affects the demand of goods which are substitutes or complements of labor in production of commodities. The model can be expanded to include several family members with different wage rates and to address labor allocations within the family.

There are several differences between the models proposed by Lancaster (1966) and by Michael and Becker (1973). First, the sources of utility are treated and defined differently. On the one hand, Lancaster's (1966) *characteristics* (e.g., brightness, sweetness, beauty) are abstract. On the other hand, Michael and Becker's *commodities* are more concrete and physical, but they distinguish between an omelet cooked at home and an omelet at a restaurant, or a salad vs. just tomato and lettuce. Second, the models are different in the nature of production technology. In Lancaster (1966), the production process, with linear technology, includes three elements: *activities* which combine *goods* to yield *characteristics*. In Michael and Becker (1973), the production process assumes a neoclassical production function in two stages: *time* plus *goods* produce *commodities*. Lancaster (1966) emphasizes intrinsic, atomistic elements in goods and actual enjoyment of production, while Michael and Becker (1973) emphasize the role of time in family production.

6. Conclusion

In this chapter, we have summarized some key results of the standard demand theory and introduced a few demand system models that are widely used in the literature. The AIDS model is quite flexible and easy to estimate, however, its limitations lie in that it puts restrictions on Engel curves that can be derived from the estimates. Moreover, the AIDS model cannot accommodate consumers' preference heterogeneity. The EASI model addresses these issues by starting from a different expenditure function than that used by the AIDS model. Both the AIDS model and the EASI model are models in the product space. These models suffer from high dimensionality issue because there are numerous products in the market, which requires estimates of large amount of parameters. They also have difficulties to predict the demand for new products. Demand models in the characteristic space originated from Lancaster (1966) aim to address these issues. Another line of enrichment of the demand theory comes from Becker who emphasizes on household time allocation and household production. Overall, we have an array of working models to choose from when estimating demand. However, which model to choose will eventually be determined by the specific research question and focus. For instance, if the research purpose is to predict the demand of some new products, then demand models in the characteristic space should be considered.

References

Beckert, W. and R. Blundell. 2008. Heterogeneity and the Non-Parametric Analysis of Consumer Choice: Conditions for Invertibility. *The Review of Economic Studies* 75(4): 1069–1080.

Christensen, L.R., D.W. Jorgenson, and L.J. Lau. 1975. Transcendental Logarithmic Utility Functions. *American Economic Review* 65(3): 367–383.

Clements, K.W. and G. Gao. 2015. The Rotterdam Demand Model Half a Century On. *Economic Modeling* 49: 91–103.

Deaton, A. and J. Muellbauer. 1980a. An Almost Ideal Demand System. *American Economic Review* 70(3): 312–326.

Deaton, A. and J. Muellbauer. 1980b. *Economics and Consumer Behavior.* Cambridge University Press, Cambridge, UK.

Green, R. and J.M. Alston. 1990. Elasticities in AIDS Models. *American Journal of Agricultural Economics* 72(2): 442–445.

Jehle, G.A. and P.J. Reny. 2001. *Advance Microeconomic Theory* (2nd edition). Addison-Wesley, Boston, MA.

Lancaster, K.J. 1966. A New Approach to Consumer Theory. *Journal of Political Economy* 74(2): 132–157.

Lewbel, A. and K. Pendakur. 2009. Tricks with Hicks: The EASI Demand System. *American Economic Review* 99(3): 827–863.

Mas-Colell, A., M.D. Whinston, and J.R. Green. 1995. *Microeconomic Theory.* Oxford University Press, Inc., Oxford.

Michael, R.T. and G.S. Becker. 1973. On the New Theory of Consumer Behavior. *The Swedish Journal of Economics* 75(4): 378–396.

Nevo, A. 2011. Empirical Models of Consumer Behavior. *Annual Review of Economics* 3: 51–75.

Pendakur, K. (2009), Chapter 7: EASI Made Easier, Slottje, D.J. (Ed.), *Quantifying Consumer Preferences (Contributions to Economic Analysis, Vol. 288)*, Emerald Group Publishing Limited, Bingley, pp. 179–206. https://doi.org/10.1108/S0573-8555(2009)0000288010.

Stone, R. 1954. Linear Expenditure Systems and Demand Analysis: An Application to the Pattern of British Demand. *The Economic Journal* 64(255): 511–527.

Chapter 4

Economic Analysis of Behavior under Risk and Uncertainty

Risk and uncertainty are prevalent in agriculture. This chapter presents economic modeling of decision-making under risk and uncertainty. Choices under *risk* occur when the probability distribution of the outcomes is objectively known to the decision maker. Choices under *uncertainty* occur when no objective probability distribution is given to the agent.

The expected utility model, introduced by von Neumann and Morgenstern in *The Theory of Games and Economic Behavior* (1944), represents the traditional approach to modeling behavior under risk. It describes the relationship between an individual's scale of preferences for a set of acts and their associated consequences. Given certain postulates about rational choice, von Neumann and Morgenstern developed a set of axioms about the ordering, continuity, and independence of individual choice and used this as a base to derive the properties of the expected utility function, thus describing the conditions under which an individual's preferences under random choices correspond to maximization under the expected utility model.

Friedman and Savage's paper (1948) is perhaps the first where the expected utility approach is applied to explaining economic behavior. The utility function is defined on wealth, where diversification and general risk aversion are explained by the function's concavity. Moreover, an S-shaped specification for the utility function explains why an individual may be risk-averse for some choices but risk-loving for other choices.

Arrow (1971) and Pratt (1964) introduced measures of risk aversion. They defined a measure of *absolute risk aversion*, $R_A = -U''/U'$, and a measure of *relative risk aversion*, $R_R = -wU''/U'$, where U'' and U' indicate, respectively, the second and first derivatives of the von Neumann–Morgenstern utility function, and w is the wealth. It was established that, under the expected utility hypothesis, there exists a one-to-one relationship between preferences over random income (or wealth) and the measures of risk aversion. Additionally, as income grows, one cares less about one "unit" of risk — the measure of absolute risk aversion is declining but cares equally about the risk involving a given share of his wealth — the measure of relative risk aversion may be constant and perhaps even equal to 1.

The next step in the theory of decision-making under risk was the development of models and concepts for measuring risk. The first efforts in this direction used statistical indexes such as mean and variance of the random outcome as arguments of the utility functions. Recognizing that variance is not always a good measure of risk, Hadar and Russell (1969) and Rothschild and Stiglitz (1970) developed models and concepts that are useful for a more general comparison of risky prospects. These approaches use probability distributions and are independent of the decision maker's utility function. Concepts such as the *mean-preserving spread* and *stochastic dominance* fall under this rubric and have been used in agricultural economic research.

Although widely used in agricultural economics, expected utility theory has been criticized for not being able to predict well people's behavior under risk. Prospect theory, developed by Kahneman and Tversky (1979), has emerged as an alternative of expected utility theory and has been recently applied in agricultural economic studies. Different from expected utility theory, prospect theory differentiates gains and losses from a reference point while considering people's biased reactions to large probabilities and small probabilities (i.e., under-weighting large probabilities and over-weighting small probabilities). Moreover, assuming that decision makers know distributions of outcomes is, in many cases, unrealistic. Relaxing this assumption involves modeling decision-making under uncertainty, where no objective probability distribution is given.

In the following sections, we first discuss some of the main approaches currently used to measure risk and risk aversion and then introduce some models that are used to analyze decision-making under risk and uncertainty.

1. Measures of Risk Aversion and Their Interpretation

What does it mean to say that an individual is risk averse in the context of expected utility? How can we measure people's attitudes toward risk? Arrow (1971) developed answers to these questions. Working from the definition of a risk-averse individual as one who "starting from a position of certainty, is unwilling to take a bet which is actuarially fair", Arrow derived a series of quantitative measures of risk attitudes. The most important of these are the *absolute* and *relative risk-aversion coefficients*, which can be derived from the von Neumann–Morgenstern utility function. Arrow also hypothesized that individuals would exhibit decreasing absolute risk aversion and increasing relative risk aversion under most circumstances. These hypotheses have critical implications for the empirical specification of utility functions. Some of the most simply formulated utility functions, however, do not exhibit the risk preference structure postulated by Arrow.

1.1. *Absolute risk aversion*

Suppose $U(w)$ is a von Neumann–Morgenstern utility function which is bounded and twice differentiable, where w is the wealth. Let U' be the marginal utility of wealth, and U'' be the rate of change of marginal utility with respect to wealth. Absolute risk aversion, R_a, is then defined as

$$R_A = -\frac{U''(w)}{U'(w)}.$$

1.1.1. *Absolute risk aversion with a discrete probability distribution*

Suppose a risk-averse individual is offered, for a small amount h, the following gamble: win h with probability P or lose h with probability $1 - P$. When will the individual be indifferent to the gamble? With an initial wealth level of w_0, equalizing the expected utility of taking the gamble to the utility achieved with no gamble, we obtain

$$PU(w_0 + h) + (1 - P)U(w_0 - h) = U(w_0). \tag{1}$$

Estimating a Taylor series approximation around w_0,

$$U(w_0 + h) \approx U(w_0) + U'(w_0)h + \frac{1}{2}U''(w_0)h^2,$$

$$U(w_0 - h) \approx U(w_0) - U'(w_0)h + \frac{1}{2}U''(w_0)h^2.$$

Substituting these approximations into (1), we get

$$\begin{aligned} &PU(w_0 + h) + (1 - P)U(w_0 - h) \\ &\quad \approx U(w_0) + (2P - 1)U'(w_0)h + \frac{1}{2}U''(w_0)h^2. \end{aligned}$$

Canceling like terms and rearranging terms, we obtain

$$\begin{aligned} (2P - 1)U'(w_0)h &= -\frac{1}{2}U''(w_0)h^2 \\ \Rightarrow (2P - 1) &= \frac{1}{2}R_A(w_0)h \\ \Rightarrow P &= \frac{1}{2} + \frac{1}{4}R_A(w_0)h \\ \Rightarrow \frac{dP}{dh} &= \frac{1}{4}R_A(w_0). \end{aligned}$$

Therefore, the coefficient of absolute risk aversion R_A indicates the odds of winning (i.e., P) have to be affected to induce a risk-averse individual to take a constant sum gamble. For a risk-averse individual, this coefficient should be positive. Thus, the coefficient of absolute risk aversion directly measures how much over fair odds an individual requires before accepting a bet. As the amount gambled increases, a higher probability of winning is needed in order for an individual to be indifferent between gambling and certainty.

1.1.2. *Absolute risk aversion with a continuous probability distribution*

Consider a small gamble x with mean μ and variance σ^2. If we express this gamble in terms of the first two moments of the distribution and use a Taylor series approximation around the mean, we get

$$EU(w_0 + x) \approx E\left\{U(w_0 + \mu) + U'(w_0 + \mu)(x - \mu) + \frac{1}{2}U''(w_0 + \mu)(x - \mu)^2\right\}. \quad (2)$$

Defining a constant z as the certainty equivalent of x such that

$$EU(w_0 + x) = U(w_0 + z),$$

and taking the expectations operator through (2), we obtain

$$EU(w_0 + x) = U(w_0 + z) \approx U(w_0 + \mu) + \frac{1}{2}U''(w_0 + \mu)\sigma^2. \quad (3)$$

Since both μ and z are small, we can make the following approximations:

$$U'(w_0) \approx U'(w_0 + \mu) \approx U'(w_0 + z)$$

and

$$U''(w_0) \approx U''(w_0 + \mu).$$

Therefore, based on Equation (3), we can have the following approximations:

$$EU(w_0 + x) \approx U(w_0) + U'(w_0)\mu + \frac{1}{2}U''(w_0)\sigma^2 \approx U(w_0) + U'(w_0)z.$$

Solving for z:

$$U'(w_0)\mu + \frac{1}{2}U''(w_0)\sigma^2 = U'(w_0)z,$$

$$z = \mu - \frac{1}{2}R_A\sigma^2.$$

Finally, expressing the risk-aversion coefficient in terms of the moments of the distribution:

$$R_A = \frac{\mu - z}{\frac{1}{2}\sigma^2}.$$

We conclude the following: (*i*) if $\mu > z$, then $R_A > 0$, indicating that the individual is risk-averse; (*ii*) if $\mu = z$, then $R_A = 0$, indicating risk neutral; and (*iii*) if $\mu < z$, then $R_A < 0$, indicating risk loving.

1.2. *Relative risk aversion*

Based on the notation above regarding utility function and wealth, we further define relative risk aversion, R_R, as

$$R_R = -\frac{U''}{U'}w = R_A(w) \cdot w.$$

Relative risk aversion is a measure of risk proportional to the level of wealth. It is the elasticity of marginal utility with respect to wealth and can be thought of as the sensitivity of risk aversion to changes in wealth. Consider a discrete probability distribution with a gamble to win a fraction of t of wealth with probability P or lose it with probability $1 - P$. When an individual is indifferent to the gamble, then we have

$$PU[w(1+t)] + (1-P)U[w(1-t)] = U(w).$$

Following a similar procedure as with the absolute risk aversion coefficient, we can derive the following equation:

$$U(w) + (2P-1)U'(w)tw + \frac{1}{2}U''(w)t^2w^2 \approx U(w).$$

Dividing both sides by $U'(w)tw$ and canceling like terms, we obtain

$$2P - 1 \approx -\frac{1}{2}\frac{U''}{U'}tw = \frac{1}{2}R_Rt.$$

The higher the relative risk aversion coefficient, R_R, the higher must be the probability of winning for the individual to be indifferent, for a given share of wealth at stake, t.

1.3. *Hypotheses about risk preferences*

In his 1971 essay, Kenneth Arrow put forward two hypotheses about the behavior of the measures of risk aversion. These are decreasing absolute risk aversion (DARA) and increasing relative risk aversion (IRRA). Decreasing absolute risk aversion implies that the willingness of individuals to take small bets of fixed size increases with wealth. Increasing relative risk aversion implies that, as wealth increases, the proportion of wealth that the individual is willing to risk declines. For example, Elon Musk will be more likely to accept a $100 bet than a PhD student (assuming no obscenely rich PhD student!), but he will be less likely to wager 10% of his wealth.

Going back to the derivations above in Section 1.1.1, note that the assumption of *decreasing absolute risk aversion* is associated with

$$\frac{dP}{dw} = \frac{1}{4}\frac{\partial R_A}{\partial w}h < 0,$$

indicating that as wealth level increases, a lower winning probability is needed for an individual to be indifferent between gambling and certainty. From the derivation of the measure of relative risk aversion, if we assume $\frac{\partial R_R}{\partial w} > 0$, then we have $\frac{\partial P}{\partial w} > 0$. This implies that for individuals with increasing relative risk aversion, as wealth level increases, a higher winning probability is needed for an individual to be indifferent between gambling and certainty.

1.4. *The implications of risk preferences for empirical specification of utility functions*

Empirical applications of the expected utility framework may require specification of the utility function. In order to achieve a reasonable depiction of reality with a tractable form, it is desirable that the specific utility function $U(w)$, where w is the wealth (or income), will have some of the following characteristics: (a) simplicity; (b) positive and decreasing marginal utility ($U' > 0$ and $U'' < 0$); (c) decreasing (or at least non-increasing) absolute risk aversion (i.e., $\partial R_A/\partial w \leq 0$, where $R_A = -U''(w)/U'(w)$); and (d) non-decreasing relative risk aversion ($\partial R_R/\partial w \geq 0$, where $R_R = -wU''(w)/U'(w)$), and if R_R is constant, it is preferably near 1. A few specific cases of utility functions are discussed as follows:

Quadratic Utility Functions: $U(w) = a + bw - \frac{1}{2}cw^2$, for $w < b/c$, where a, b, and c are positive parameters. This utility function may be objectionable because it implies increasing absolute risk aversion ($R_A = c/(b - cw)$, and $\frac{\partial R_A}{\partial w} = cR_A/(b - cw) > 0$).

Cobb–Douglas Utility Functions: $U(w) = Aw^{\alpha}$, $0 < \alpha < 1$. This utility implies constant relative risk aversion and decreasing absolute risk aversion with $R_R(w) = 1 - a$ and $R_A(w) = (1 - a)/w$. The deficiencies of this function include the following: (*i*) $R_R = 1$ when $\alpha = 0$, and (*ii*) the expectation of utility under this function, $E(Aw^{\alpha})$, may result in complex expressions.

Logarithmic Utility Function: $U(w) = \ln w$. Defined only for $w > 0$, this function implies constant relative risk aversion with $R_R(w) = 1$ and decreasing absolute risk aversion. The expected value of this utility, $E(\ln w)$, may be cumbersome in problems where w is a linear function of decision variables.

Exponential Utility Functions: $U(w) = 1 - e^{-rw}$. This utility function implies constant absolute risk aversion with $R_A(w) = r$. It is easy to apply with distributions which can be defined by their moment-generating functions. Moment-generating functions are functions of the parameters of the distribution associated with random variables. Specifically, for a random variable, z, its moment-generating function can be written as $M_z(t) = E(e^{zt})$. Therefore, one can see that for the exponential utility function, $EU(w) = 1 - E[e^{-rw}]$ and $E[e^{-rw}]$ is a moment-generating function. When w is a normally distributed random variable with $E(w) = \mu$ and $\text{var}(w) = \sigma^2$, the moment-generating function to the second-order gives[1]

$$EU(w) = 1 - e^{-r\left[\mu - \frac{1}{2}r\sigma^2\right]}. \tag{4}$$

Since any solution that maximizes $\mu - (1/2)r\sigma^2$ also maximizes $EU(w)$ in this case, when utility is exponential and the random variable is normally distributed, maximization of a linear function

[1]Chavas (2004, p. 39) presents a direct way to obtain Equation (4).

of the mean and variance of income is equivalent to expected utility maximization. That is,

$$\arg\max_X EU(w) = \arg\max_X \left\{\mu - \frac{1}{2}r\sigma^2\right\}.$$

Let us see an example. Suppose $w = w_0 + \bar{P}X\varepsilon - C(X)$, where X stands for output quantity; $\bar{P}$ for average price; ε for random price variability, $\varepsilon \sim N(1, \sigma^2)$; and $C(X)$ for cost function with $C' > 0$ and $C'' > 0$. Expected utility maximizing outcome in this case can be obtained by solving

$$\max_X \bar{P}X - C(X) - \frac{1}{2}r\sigma^2\bar{P}^2X^2.$$

The optimal solution is obtained by solving the first-order condition:

$$\bar{P} - C'(X) - r\sigma^2\bar{P}^2X = 0.$$

Suppose $C(X) = cX$. The first-order condition becomes

$$\bar{P} - c - r\sigma^2\bar{P}^2X = 0,$$

which gives

$$X = \frac{\bar{P} - c}{r\sigma^2\bar{P}^2}.$$

Readers may want to check if the supply (X as a function of $\bar{P}$) can be negatively sloped in this case and think about the reasons. Furthermore, readers may try to obtain the supply assuming that price P follows a gamma distribution. We leave this as exercises for readers. Hints can be found in Yassour *et al.* (1981).

1.5. *Estimation of risk aversion coefficient*

The Arrow–Pratt measures of risk aversion and conceptual models, such as Sandmo (1971), have established a very rich theory of decision-making under risk in agricultural production and resource use. However, one of the challenges of applied economics and agricultural economics research is to develop an empirical base to test the theory. This subsection identifies some of the problems and alternative approaches to address them.

The most difficult problem in assessing empirical expected utility models is the unobservable nature of an individual's evaluation of utility levels and the probabilities associated with them. Expected utility models assume that choices under risk result from a mental process where the utility of many wealth levels is assessed and multiplied with the right probabilities, resulting in the expected utility of each prospect. Expected utilities are then compared to obtain the optimal choice. Unfortunately, these evaluations of utility levels are not observable, but, for standard economic analysis, we have to rely on observable variables. These include choices, for example, to adopt or not to adopt a technology, as well as characteristics of decision makers, such as farm size, age, and education. Information about the subjective probabilities of different outcomes is also not readily available, which makes the estimation of decision makers' parameters even more difficult.

One approach for empirical estimation of expected utility is to reduce the uncertainty of the researcher by conducting experiments where the decision maker is presented with rewards and the probabilities of rewards is specified. The decision maker has to make choices between outcomes. In these cases, the researcher does not know the utility functions but supposedly knows everything else associated with the decision. Such experiments can be used to assess empirically to what extent the expected utility model is realistic, and in the case where it is a realistic description of reality, what the values of key parameters are (i.e., the measures of absolute and relative risk aversion).

In later sections, we discuss some of the experiments and tests of expected utility hypothesis. In this subsection, we concentrate on models that try to estimate risk aversion parameters and, in particular, to test whether there is decreasing absolute risk aversion, increasing relative risk aversion, and if relative risk aversion is around one.

Binswanger (1980) used experiments where farmers in India were given actual monetary rewards as part of different gambles, eliciting risk-aversion parameters from his subjects' individual choices.

Since the income level of the individuals involved was relatively low, with a reasonable amount of money, he was able to collect a large set of data. He found substantial variability in the measures of risk aversion between individuals, who demonstrate heterogeneity in risk preferences. He also found that, for any given individual, the measure of relative risk aversion did not change much with different gambles.

Other experimental studies, especially ones conducted in the United States, were largely not done with actual rewards but instead with hypothetical choices. These studies were mostly intended to identify paradoxes in risk choice patterns that contradict expected utility and not to elicit the parameters of the utility function.

Popular approaches to estimate the parameters of the utility function were ones using programming models and econometric models. The following subsection describes how one can use econometric models such as the Just–Zilberman model to elicit risk aversion coefficients.

1.5.1. *Estimation*

Let us consider a simple model where a farmer allocates her total land, $\bar{L}$, between two crops, 1 and 2. Assume that the net returns from crop $i \in \{1, 2\}$ are $\pi_i = \mu_i + \epsilon_i$, where μ_i is a constant and ϵ_i is a random variable with mean at 0 and variance at σ_i^2. The covariance between ϵ_1 and ϵ_2 is σ_{12}. Based on equation (7) in Just and Zilberman (1983), the amount of land allocated for crop 1, L_1, can be written as

$$L_1 = \frac{\mu_1 - \mu_2}{(\sigma_1^2 + \sigma_2^2 - 2\sigma_{12})\phi(\bar{W})} + \frac{\sigma_2 - \sigma_{12}}{(\sigma_1^2 + \sigma_2^2 - 2\sigma_{12})}\bar{L} \equiv \frac{A_1}{\phi(\bar{W})} + A_2\bar{L}, \tag{5}$$

where the function $\phi(\bar{W})$ is a measure of absolute risk aversion as a function of average wealth, $\bar{W}$, which is determined by the farmer's initial wealth and returns from land use.

This model, which is based on a Taylor series as an approximation of the first-order condition, allows us to get a quantitative assessment of the behavior of risk aversion measures. Since one cannot observe the utility function changing with wealth for one individual, we try to estimate how the measure of risk aversion is changing between individuals where we tried to estimate the measure of risk aversion as a function of average wealth, $\bar{W}$, using our results derived by our approximation. Several relationships which can be derived using these models depend on the data available and the degree of statistical sophistication.

Now, consider the simplest case. One assumes constant absolute risk aversion and has only data on acre and land allocation with two crops. In this case, the estimated models will be $L_1 = A_1 + A_2\bar{L} + \varepsilon$, where ε is a random variable. Such a model can be estimated using a simple linear regression to test some simple empirical hypotheses. For example, if crop 1 returns have a higher mean and higher variance, and the correlation of returns between the two crops is not large, one can test hypotheses that A_1 is positive and A_2 is negative. If one ran such models in different regions and obtained an A_1 estimate for the two regions, then one could test a hypothesis that a region where the correlation between yield is larger has a larger A_1.

One can use this land allocation equation and incorporate it with other elements that determine land allocation, for example, fixed costs of different technologies as well as credit constraints. Marra and Carlson (1990) have a nice application of this approach to allocate assessment of adoption of double cropping in the United States.

If one assumes that ϕ varies with $\bar{W}$ instead of being constant and if a more sophisticated econometric model is used, then data on L_1 and L can lead to more insightful results. Furthermore, if one assumes a constant ratio between farm size and expected wealth $\bar{W} \approx \alpha\bar{L}$, then risk aversion can be approximated and estimated as a function of farm size. Suppose

$$\phi(\bar{W}) = C \cdot \bar{W}^{-\eta},$$

where η is the elasticity of absolute risk aversion with respect to wealth,

$$\eta = -\frac{\partial\phi}{\partial\bar{W}}\frac{\bar{W}}{\phi}$$

and C is a scaling constant. In the case of constant absolute risk aversion, $\eta = 0$. In the case of decreasing absolute risk aversion, however, $\eta > 0$. Let $r = \phi w$ be a measure of relative risk aversion. Note that if we define the elasticity of relative risk aversion as δ, it is

$$\delta = \frac{\partial r}{\partial \bar{W}} \frac{\bar{W}}{r} = \left[\frac{\partial \phi}{\partial \bar{W}} \frac{\bar{W}}{\phi} + 1 \right] = 1 - \eta.$$

We can see that in the case of constant relative risk aversion, $\eta = 1$, and that in the case of increasing relative risk aversion, $\eta < 1$. Thus, assuming decreasing absolute and increasing relative risk aversion implies $0 < \eta < 1$ (or $0 < \delta < 1$).

Moreover, when $\phi(\bar{W}) = C\bar{W}^{-\eta}$ and $\bar{W} = \alpha \bar{L}$, the absolute risk aversion coefficient, ϕ, is $\phi = C\alpha^{-\eta}\bar{L}^{-\eta}$ and the estimatable model that corresponds to these assumption is

$$L_1 = A_3/\bar{L}^{-\eta} + A_2\bar{L} = A_3\bar{L}^{\eta} + A_2\bar{L},$$

where $A_3 = A_1/(C\alpha^{-\eta})$. An alternative formulation is

$$\frac{L_1}{\bar{L}} = A_2 + A_3 L^{-\delta}.$$

Estimation of these models provides $\hat{A}_2$, $\hat{A}_3$, and $\hat{\delta}$ or $\hat{\eta}$, which allows testing when absolute risk aversion is decreasing in wealth (approximated by size) and relative risk aversion is increasing in wealth.

This formulation can be extended to identify other factors affecting risk aversion. If socioeconomic data (denoted by S) are available (e.g., age, gender, and education), one may replace C in the expression of ϕ with $g(S)$, a function of socioeconomic variable. One plausible specification is $\phi(\bar{W}) = g(S)\bar{W}^{-\eta}$. This specification can lead to an estimatable relationship which is a function of farm size and socioeconomic variables. More detailed data on profit and wealth may allow all estimation of the Just and Zilberman (1983) model with less approximation. Even then, one may need to use bold assumptions. Data on the subjective values of mean at the individual farm levels are not easily obtainable. Thus, one may need to estimate these variables as well and introduce them to an estimatable form. Similarly, average wealth of individual farmers is needed to be computed from other accounting data. In essence, estimation of risk aversion coefficient from a simple specification such as (5) requires much compromise and ingenuity. We also have to recognize that the decision maker has the same problem of data assembly as the researcher: None of the farmers know their μ_1, μ_2, and σ_2. A more complete model should recognize this.

Chalfant *et al.* (1990) developed an approach for when risk-aversion parameters are utilized by farmers who recognize the uncertainty of their estimates of the key profit distribution parameters. The model is complex, but the optimal L_1 depends not only on the estimated means or variance of profits and the measures of risk aversion but also on measures of the estimators' reliability and the moments of farmers' profits.

2. Risk in Production

Risk occurs in several aspects of the production process. Various institutional mechanisms for reducing risk have been developed. Table 1 includes a partial list of these mechanisms and the type of production risk they address. Many other institutions were developed to address risks faced by firms. In this section, we focus on the building blocks of modeling production risk.

2.1. *Risk specification*

Production risk is generally modeled through alternative specifications of the production function. Several examples of production functions and their implications for risk analysis are discussed in

Table 1. Types of risks faced by producers and mechanisms to remedy.

Risks	Remedies
Output price risk	Future markets, forward contracts, crop insurance
Yield risk	Crop insurance
Labor supply availability	Mechanization, long-term labor contract
Input reliability	Product warranty
Input price uncertainty	Forward contacts

this subsection. Let Y be output quantity, X input quantity, and ε a random variable in each of the following models:

Model 1. Additive risk

$$Y = f(X) + \varepsilon, \qquad E(\varepsilon) = 0.$$

In this case, input use does not affect risk and the only type of risk considered is output risk.

Model 2. Multiplicative risk

$$Y = f(X) \cdot \varepsilon, \qquad E(\varepsilon) = 1.$$

In this case, any input that increases mean yield also increases risks associated with yields.

Model 3. Linear risk (Just and Pope production function)

$$Y = f(X) + g(X)\varepsilon, \qquad E(\varepsilon) = 0.$$

Under this specification, impacts of inputs on yield mean and risk can be differentiated. For example, some inputs may be yield increasing (i.e., $f' > 0$) and risk reducing (i.e., $g' < 0$); others may increase both yield and risk (i.e., $f' > 0$, $g' > 0$).

2.2. *Sandmo's model*

How will a firm behave when output price is a random variable as opposed to when it is a constant? Sandmo (1971) used a multiplicative risk specification to develop a model of a competitive firm facing output price uncertainty. Specifically, price P is a random variable with mean value at $\bar{P}$. Firms maximize expected utility with cost function $C(Y)$, where $C' > 0$, $C'' > 0$. The decision problem is

$$L = \max_{Y} EU(PY - C(Y) + w_0),$$

where w_0 is initial wealth. The first-order condition is

$$\frac{\partial L}{\partial Y} = E\{U'(PY - C(Y) + w_0)[P - C'(Y)]\} = 0. \tag{6}$$

By using the statistical theorem concerning the expected value of the product of two random variables which states

$$E(XZ) = E(X)E(Z) + \text{Cov}(X, Z),$$

we can rewrite (6) as

$$E[P - C'(Y)] + \frac{\text{Cov}[U'(w), P - C'(Y)]}{EU'(w)} = 0, \tag{7}$$

where $w = PY - C(Y) + w_0$.

In order to determine the impact of risk on output, we need to determine the signs of each element in this expression. The steps are as follows:

(1) By definition, $w = PY - C(Y) + w_0$ and $E(w) = \bar{P}Y - C(Y) + w_0$. Therefore, $w - E(w) = (P - \bar{P})Y$ and $w = E(w) + (P - \bar{P})Y$.
(2) If $P \geq \bar{P}$, then from step 1 we know that $w \geq E(w)$, and therefore, that $U'(w) \leq U'[E(w)]$. Similarly, if $P < \bar{P}$, then $w < E(w)$ and $U'(w) > U'[E(w)]$.
(3) If we multiply $(P - \bar{P})$ to both $U'(w)$ and $U'[E(w)]$, then, based on step 2, we can conclude that $(P - \bar{P})U'(w) \leq (P - \bar{P})U'[E(w)]$ whether or not $P \geq \bar{P}$. Take the expectation of both sides, we get

$$E((P - \bar{P})U'(w)) \leq U'[E(w)]E(P - \bar{P}) = 0.$$

(4) Since $\text{Cov}[U'(w), P - C'(Y)] = E[(P - \bar{P})U'(w)]$, from Equation (7) and the results in step 3, we have $E(P - C'(Y)) \geq 0$, which indicates $C'(Y) \leq \bar{P}$.

Based on the above steps, it is readily checked that under risk neutrality, $C'(Y) = \bar{P}$. With risk-averse behavior, however, $C'(Y) \leq \bar{P}$. Since $C''(Y) > 0$, we can conclude that risk-averse firms will produce less than risk-neutral firms (see Figure 1). This finding implies that price stabilization policies will lead to an increase in output.

Suppose utility depends on wealth and $w = PY - C(Y) + w_0$. What will be the impact of higher wealth on the optimal Y?

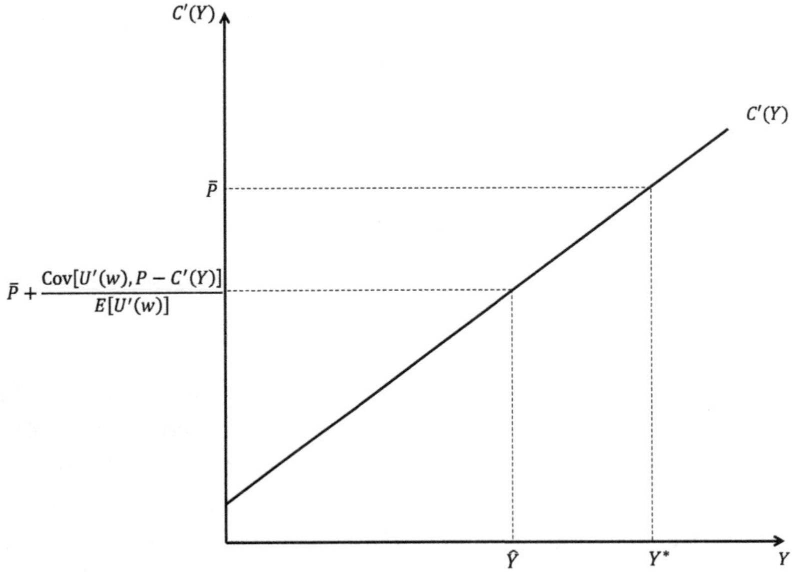

Figure 1. Production level in Sandmo's model.

Note: Y^* indicates optimal production level under risk neutrality, and $\hat{Y}$ indicates optimal production level under risk aversion.

Based on the first-order condition in Equation (6), the second-order condition is

$$\begin{aligned}\frac{\partial^2 L}{\partial Y^2} &= E[U''(PY - C(Y) + w_0)(P - C'(Y))^2] \\ &\quad - E[U'(PY - C(Y) + w_0)C''(Y)] < 0.\end{aligned}$$

Total differentiation of the first-order condition with respect to w_0 yields

$$\frac{dY}{dw_0} = -\frac{E[U''(PY - C(Y) + w_0)(P - C'(Y))]}{\frac{\partial^2 L}{\partial Y^2}}. \tag{8}$$

Let us first assume decreasing absolute risk aversion (DARA). Let $\tilde{W}$ be the level of wealth associated with $\tilde{P}$, and $\tilde{P} = C'(Y)$.

Therefore, if $P < \tilde{P}$, then $-\frac{U''(w)}{U'(w)} > R_A(\tilde{W})$, and if $P > \tilde{P}$, then $-\frac{U''(w)}{U'(w)} < R_A(\tilde{W})$. As a result, we have

$$\begin{aligned}
&-\frac{U''(w)}{U'(w)}[P - C'(Y)] < R_A(\tilde{W})[P - C'(Y)] \\
&\Rightarrow -U''(w)[P - C'(Y)] < R_A(\tilde{W})U'(w)[P - C'(Y)] \\
&\Rightarrow -E\{U''(w)[P - C'(Y)]\} < R_A(\tilde{W})E\{U'(w)[P - C'(Y)]\} = 0 \\
&\Rightarrow E\{U''(w)[P - C'(Y)]\} > 0.
\end{aligned}$$

The third line in the above four lines of equations holds because of the first-order condition. In other words, when evaluated at the optimal output level, $E\{U'(w)[P - C'(Y)]\} = 0$. Together with Equation (8), $E\{U''(w)[P - C'(Y)]\} > 0$ indicates that under decreasing absolute risk aversion, we have $dY/dw_0 > 0$. This result states that under DARA, more affluent risk-averse producers will provide more output, and wealth has a positive effect on supply. Following similar steps, readers can readily check that, under constant absolute risk aversion (CARA), $dY/dw_0 = 0$; under increasing absolute risk aversion (IARA), $dY/dw_0 < 0$.

Sandmo also shows that increasing relative risk aversion may lead to a reduction in supply as income taxes increase. He was able to partially show that increase in riskiness (measured by a mean-preserving spread) reduces supply. His technique has been used to obtain conceptual results in many problems with multiplicative risk.

We can also examine the impact of price risk on optimal output level by following the same approach. Let $P_1 = \gamma P + (1-\gamma)\bar{P}$, where $\bar{P} = E(P)$. Note that here $\gamma \in [0, 1]$ can be viewed as a measure of price risk with $\gamma = 0$ indicating a fixed price, $\bar{P}$. Replacing P with P_1 in the firm's profit maximization problem, we obtain

$$L = \max_Y EU((\gamma P + (1 - \gamma)\bar{P})Y - C(Y) + w_0).$$

One can show that under DARA, we have $\frac{\partial Y}{\partial \gamma}|_{\gamma=1} < 0$. To see this, note that

$$\frac{dY}{d\gamma} = -\frac{E[U''(w)(P - C'(Y))(P - \bar{P})Y + U'(w)(P - \bar{P})]}{\frac{\partial^2 L}{\partial Y^2}}$$

$$= -\frac{\begin{array}{c} E[U''(w)(P - C'(Y))^2 Y] + Y(C'(Y) - \bar{P})\times \\ E[U''(w)(P - C'(Y))] + E[U'(w)(P - \bar{P})] \end{array}}{\frac{\partial^2 L}{\partial Y^2}}.$$

Under risk aversion, $U''(w)(P - C'(Y))^2 Y < 0$. In this subsection, we also have shown that under risk aversion $C'(Y) - \bar{P} < 0$ and $E[U'(w)(P - \bar{P})] < 0$ (see steps 1 to 4 above). Furthermore, we have shown that under DARA, $E[U''(w)(P - C'(Y))] > 0$. Based on these results, we can conclude that $dY/d\gamma < 0$, indicating that under DARA an increase in risk (measured by γ) will decrease the optimal output. We can draw the same conclusion under CARA but not under IARA.[2]

If DARA reflects the risk preferences of general decision makers, then this subsection demonstrates that less output will be produced under risk than under no risk; that an increase in risk aversion will reduce output; and that optimal resource allocation by a risk-averse firm requires that the value of the expected marginal product of a resource exceeds its rental value (i.e., $\bar{P} > C'(Y)$). Moreover, under DARA, reductions in fixed cost will increase output. Thus, financial conditions may affect production decisions. Expected profit will be the highest for firms which are closest to being risk neutral and have the highest output.

Sandmo's approach, while general, cannot be applied to situations with multiple and correlated risks. One may need to specify utility functions in more detail to address these problems. The model, focusing on price risk, does not allow for the analysis of the differential impacts of an input on output and production risk. Further, it is only possible to handle one random variable at a time.

[2]Chavas (2004, Chapter 8) provides a detailed discussion on production under risk.

The advantage of the model is its generalized form, allowing for the use of less restrictive utility forms, in contrast with specific functional forms. Sandmo's approach was extended by Feder (1977) to model situations where multiplicative risk arises, and in particular, the adoption of new technologies in less-developed countries. The Sandmo approach was also used by Batra and Ullah (1974) for input demand, Feder (1980) for technological adoption, Feder, Just, and Schmitz (1980) for futures market behavior, and Chavas (1993) for land allocation.

2.3. *The mean–variance approach*

The mean–variance approach was introduced by Tobin (1958) and Markovitz (1959). It plays a key role in finance — being used as a base for capital asset pricing. The basic idea of this model is that utility from random prospects, $EU(y) = \int U(y)f(y)dy$, can be described as a function of the moments of the distribution around a mean outcome $\bar{y}$ through a Taylor series expansion. Here, y is the random returns from a prospect and $f(y)$ is the probability density function of y. Let $\bar{y}$ denote the mean of y. Based on Taylor series expansion, we have

$$U(y) = U(\bar{y}) + U'(\bar{y})(y - \bar{y}) + U''(\bar{y})\frac{(y - \bar{y})^2}{2} + \sum_{n=3}^{\infty} U^n \frac{(y - \bar{y})^n}{n!},$$

from which, taking the expectations of both sides, we have

$$EU(y) = U(\bar{y}) + \sum_{n=2}^{\infty} \frac{U^n(\bar{y})}{n!} E(y - \bar{y})^n = g(M_1, M_2, M_3, \ldots),$$

where M_1, M_2, ... denote the first and second moment, and so on. If a distribution can be completely defined by n moments, then the expected utility is a function of these moments. If a distribution is defined by its first two moments, then the expected utility is a function of the distribution's mean and variance. For example, in the case of financial assets, the price of any asset is determined by its mean return and its variance with the market portfolio.

Certain restrictive conditions on the utility functions and the distribution of the random outcome variable are required in order to be able to express expected utility as a function of the mean and variance. These are (i) the utility function must be quadratic or exponential in form and (ii) the outcome variable should be normally distributed. Given these conditions, the expected utility can be expressed as

$$EU(y) = \alpha\bar{y} + \beta\frac{\sigma^2}{2},$$

where σ^2 is the variance and α and β are parameters.

Freund (1956) proved the linearity of the expected utility function under the condition of normality and exponential utility. The linear mean–variance approach has one big advantage: It is easy to work with and it allows the consideration of behavior under risk with a large number of random variables. It is used very frequently (see Just and Zilberman (1983) for an early application and Miao and Khanna (2017) for a recent application). However, the model is objectionable on three grounds. First, quadratic utility implies increasing absolute risk aversion. Second, exponential utility implies constant absolute risk aversion. Third, normality of the outcome variable may be unreasonable (e.g., crop yields have a negative gamma distribution as Day (1965) has shown).

Despite these shortcomings, the linear mean–variance approach is popular since it results in models useful for dynamic programming. In the following section, some examples of how this approach has been applied are discussed.

2.3.1. *Applications of the mean–variance approach*

The mean–variance approach can be useful in modeling a typical farmer's land allocation problem among M crops or uses. Let l_m denote total acreage for crop $m = 1, \ldots, M$. Define $L \equiv (l_1, \ldots, l_M)'$. Using the mean-variance approach, the farmer's problem can be stated as

$$\max(U' - V')L - rL'\Sigma L,$$

where $U = (u_1, \ldots, u_M)'$ is the average revenue vector for all M crops, V is the variable cost vector, r is a measure of risk aversion, and Σ is the variance–covariance matrix of net returns per acre across the M crops.

One way to apply the mean–variance approach is to construct an efficiency locus of mean–variance (or standard deviation) tradeoffs. This is done through a quadratic programming problem where the land allocation that minimizes variance is computed to attain expected profit from the land,

$$\min_{L} L'\Sigma L,$$

subject to a mean income constraint:

$$(U' - V')L = \bar{Z},$$

where $\bar{Z}$ is a mean income. Solving this minimization problem will map each income level to a land-use choice which minimizes the income variance. Then, the next step is to optimally choose a $\bar{Z}$ and corresponding variance to maximize the decision maker's utility.

2.3.2. *Mean–variance models*

When the distribution of wealth (or profit) has two parameters, expected utility can be expressed as function of the mean and variance of wealth (or profit). With the negative exponential utility function and normal distribution, utility maximization can be expressed as a linear function of mean and variance of wealth (or profit). These assumptions have been used extensively, especially in agricultural economics and in finance. They are used primarily in conceptual analysis when decision makers are affected by several *correlated* random variables when more general frameworks, such as Sandmo's (1971), cannot be easily applied.

The linear mean–variance formulation has been extensively used in modeling land allocation by farmers. Assume that a farmer has $\bar{L}$ acres of land which can be divided among n crops. The profit of the ith crop per unit of land, π_i, is normally distributed with mean

μ_i, variance σ_i^2, and covariance $cov(\pi_i, \pi_j) = \sigma_{ij}$. The land allocation problem is a constrained quadratic programming problem

$$\max_{L_i} \sum_{i=1}^{N} L_i\mu_i - \frac{r}{2}\left[\sum_{i=1}^{N}(L_i^2\sigma_i^2) + \sum_{j\neq i} L_iL_j\sigma_{ij}\right],$$

subject to

$$\sum_{i=1}^{n} L_i \leq \bar{L},$$

where r is a measure of risk aversion. Let λ be the shadow price of land. The Lagrangian formulation of this problem is

$$L = \max_{L_i} \sum_{i=1}^{N} L_i\mu_i - \frac{r}{2}\left[\sum_{i=1}^{N}(L_i^2\sigma_i^2) + \sum_{j\neq i} L_iL_j\sigma_{ij}\right] + \lambda\left[\bar{L} - \sum_{i=1}^{N} L_i\right].$$

The optimality conditions, when there is an interior solution, are

$$\frac{\partial L}{\partial L_i} = \mu_i - r\left[L_i\sigma_i^2 + \frac{1}{2}\sum_{j\neq i} L_j\sigma_{ij}\right] - \lambda = 0, \qquad i = 1, \ldots, N, \quad (9)$$

$$\frac{\partial L}{\partial \lambda} = \bar{L} - \sum_{i=1}^{N} L_i \geq 0.$$

At the optimal solution, λ equals the marginal contribution of land to expected net benefits. For the ith crop, this marginal value is equal to the mean of net profit per acres, μ_i, minus marginal contribution to risk cost $\left(MV_i \equiv r\left[L_i\sigma_i^2 + \frac{1}{2}\sum_{j\neq i} L_j\sigma_{ij}\right]\right)$. Note that the marginal contribution to overall risk depends on the inherent risk of the crop and correlation of its profits with those from other crops. A crop whose profits are negatively correlated to those of other crops may *reduce* the overall cost of risk. Such a crop may have substantial acreage even if it is less profitable on average than other crops. By averaging all the first-order conditions, the marginal value of land λ can be expressed as

$$\lambda = \bar{\mu} - \overline{MV},$$

where

$$\bar{\mu} = \frac{1}{N}\sum_{i=1}^{N}\mu_i \qquad \text{and} \qquad \overline{MV} = \frac{1}{N}\sum_{i=1}^{N} MV_i.$$

The first-order condition (9) can be rewritten as

$$\mu_i - \bar{\mu} - (MV_i - \overline{MV}) = 0.$$

A crop will be grown if it is either more profitable or less risky than average. Lower risk may not reflect less variability but, rather, negative correlation of profit with other crops.

2.3.3. *Linking mean–variance and general EU models*

There have been many attempts to generalize the linear mean–variance framework. One such attempt is presented in Just and Zilberman (1983). Consider the case when two crops are grown and each has a constant return-to-scale technology. Suppose profits per acre, Π_i, is a random variable with mean μ_i. Land devoted to crop $i = 1, 2$ is L_i. When all land is used (i.e., $L_1 + L_2 = \bar{L}$), the expected utility problem becomes

$$\max_{L_1} EU[\Pi_1 L_1 + \Pi_2(\bar{L} - L_1) + w_0], \tag{10}$$

where w_0 is initial wealth. The first-order condition is

$$E\{U'(w)(\Pi_1 - \Pi_2)\} = 0. \tag{11}$$

Marginal utility at w can be approximated by

$$U'(w) = U'(\bar{w}) + U''(w)\left[L_1(\Pi_1 - \mu_1) + (\bar{L} - L_1)(\Pi_2 - \mu_2)\right], \tag{12}$$

where $\bar{w} = w_0 + \mu_1 L_1 + \mu_2(\bar{L} - L_1)$. By introducing this approximation to the first-order condition, (11) becomes

$$\begin{aligned} E\{&U'(\bar{w})(\Pi_1 - \Pi_2) + U''(\bar{w}) \\ &\times \left[L_1(\Pi_1 - \mu_1) + (\bar{L} - L_1)(\Pi_2 - \mu_2)\right](\Pi_1 - \Pi_2)\} \\ &= U'(\bar{w})\{\mu_1 - \mu_2 - R_A(\bar{w})\left[L_1(\sigma_1^2 - \sigma_{12}) + (\bar{L} - L_1)(\sigma_{12} - \sigma_2^2)\right]\} \\ &= 0, \end{aligned} \tag{13}$$

which suggests that

$$L_1 = \frac{\mu_1 - \mu_2}{V(\Pi_1 - \Pi_2)R_A(\bar{w})} + \frac{\sigma_2^2 - \sigma_{12}}{V(\Pi_1 - \Pi_2)}\bar{L}, \tag{14}$$

where $V(\Pi_1 - \Pi_2) = \sigma_1^2 + \sigma_2^2 - 2\sigma_{12}$.

Under risk neutrality, a producer will specialize in the crop with higher mean profit. With risk aversion, consideration of riskiness is added to those of average profitability, and the weight of the expected profit differential in determining L_1 declines as $V(\Pi_1 - \Pi_2)$ increases. Suppose crop 1 has a higher profit and higher risk than crop 2. For example, it maybe a modern export crop that is sensitive to weather and economic conditions, while crop 2 may be a traditional crop. It may be of interest to understand the impact of farm size on the acreage of each crop. Differentiation of (14) yields

$$\frac{dL_1}{d\bar{L}} = -\frac{\mu_1 - \mu_2}{V(\Pi_1 - \Pi_2)R_A(\bar{w})} \cdot \frac{dR_A(w)}{d\bar{w}} \cdot \frac{\bar{w}}{R_A(w)} \cdot \frac{d\bar{w}}{d\bar{L}} \cdot \frac{1}{\bar{w}} + \frac{\sigma_2^2 - \sigma_{12}}{V(\Pi_1 - \Pi_2)}. \tag{15}$$

Substituting (14) into the equation gives us

$$\begin{aligned}\frac{dL_1}{d\bar{L}} &= \left[\frac{\sigma_2^2 - \sigma_{12}}{V(\Pi_1 - \Pi_2)}\bar{L} - L_1\right]\frac{dR_A(w)}{d\bar{w}} \cdot \frac{\bar{w}}{R_A(w)} \cdot \frac{d\bar{w}}{d\bar{L}} \cdot \frac{1}{\bar{w}} + \frac{\sigma_2^2 - \sigma_{12}}{V(\Pi_1 - \Pi_2)} \\ &= \frac{\sigma_2^2 - \sigma_{12}}{V(\Pi_1 - \Pi_2)}\left[1 + \bar{L}\frac{dR_A}{d\bar{w}} \cdot \frac{\bar{w}}{R_A(w)} \cdot \frac{d\bar{w}}{d\bar{L}} \cdot \frac{1}{\bar{w}}\right] \\ &\quad - L_1\frac{dR_A(w)}{d\bar{w}} \cdot \frac{\bar{w}}{R_A(w)} \cdot \frac{d\bar{w}}{d\bar{L}} \cdot \frac{1}{\bar{w}}.\end{aligned} \tag{16}$$

Let $\eta_R = -\frac{dR_A}{dW}\frac{\bar{W}}{R_A}$ be the elasticity of absolute risk aversion with respect to wealth. Assume decreasing absolute risk aversion, thus, $\eta_R > 0$. With this definition, the change in crop 1's acreage with respect to size can be presented as

$$\frac{dL_1}{d\bar{L}} = \frac{\sigma_2^2 - \sigma_{12}}{V(\Pi_1 - \Pi_2)}\left[1 - \eta_R\frac{\bar{L}}{\bar{w}}\frac{d\bar{w}}{d\bar{L}}\right] + \eta_R\frac{L_1}{\bar{L}}\frac{\bar{L}}{\bar{w}}\frac{d\bar{w}}{d\bar{L}}.$$

As we discussed earlier in this chapter, decreasing absolute and increasing relative risk aversion implies $0 < \eta_R < 1$. It is reasonable to argue that $(d\bar{w}/d\bar{L}) \cdot (\bar{L}/\bar{w})$ is also likely to be smaller than 1. If we examine the case of constant absolute risk aversion where $\eta_R = 0$, then

$$\text{sign}\left(\frac{dL_1}{d\bar{L}}\right) = \text{sign}\left(\frac{\sigma_2^2 - \sigma_{12}}{V(\Pi_1 - \Pi_2)}\right). \tag{17}$$

Note that $\sigma_2^2 - \sigma_{12} = \sigma_2[\sigma_2 - \rho\sigma_1]$, where $\rho \equiv \sigma_{12}/(\sigma_1\sigma_2)$ is the correlation coefficient between the two crops' profits and σ_i is the standard deviation of crop i's profits. Equation (17) suggests that, if crop 2 is much less risky than crop 1 and the correlation between their profit is high (so that $\sigma_2 < \rho\sigma_1$), risk consideration will cause larger farmers to grow less of the risky crop than the smaller farmers. When $0 < \eta_R < 1$, the land share of the more risky technology *declines* with farm size. Since risk costs increase more than proportionally with farm size, *larger formers* are likely to grow *relatively* less of the risky crops. The optimization problem (10) is not a constrained one, but we have to realize that $0 \leq L_1 \leq \bar{L}$. Therefore, letting the result of this optimization problem be denoted as L_1^*, ultimately

$$L_1 = \begin{cases} \bar{L} & \text{if } L_1^* > \bar{L} \\ L_1^* & \text{if } 0 \leq L_1^* \leq \bar{L} \\ 0 & \text{if } L_1^* < 0. \end{cases}$$

Suppose $\mu_1 > \mu_2$ and $\rho < \sigma_2/\sigma_1$. One can readily check that if σ_1 is not very high, then $L_1^* > \bar{L}$ may hold. This means that the higher profits of crop 1 may lead to specialization of small farms if its risk is not so high. Larger farms may grow both crops (note that farm size affects $R_A(\bar{w})$). However, when the profit correlation is not sufficiently large and when $0 < \eta_R < 1$, then the production of crop 1 will grow absolutely and its land share will decline with size.

Now, let us suppose $\mu_1 > \mu_2$ and $\rho > \sigma_2/\sigma_1$. In this case, correlation is so large that, beyond a certain size, acreage of crop 1 declines with size. When $\mu_2 > \mu_1$ but $\sigma_1^2 < \sigma_2^2$ (i.e., when crop 1 is less risky but less profitable on average), it may not be grown by small farmers but may be added to the portfolio of larger ones. It may become the major crop of some very big operators.

In this analysis, risk was the only reason for diversification, and we ignored other constraints facing farmers. There are many situations when other factors (e.g., labor or equipment scarcity) cause diversification. Growers may grow several crops to spread the harvesting season, thus overcoming labor or capital constraints. Credit limitation may provide another reason. The high value crop may require more credits and that may limit a farmer. Economists have a tendency to attribute too much to risk considerations and to ignore those other factors. In a more realistic analysis, one has to study local conditions in detail to incorporate relevant constraints before investigating land allocation.

The framework presented here can be extended to other choices. It is a variation of financial portfolio analysis which is used to investigate distribution of wealth among assets and analysis of financial investments. Similarly, it applies to time allocation analysis including land diversification between on-farm and off-farm activities and migration decisions (time allocation between locations).

3. Measuring Risk: Mean-Preserving Spread and Stochastic Dominance

Given a set of choices, which will a risk-averse individual prefer and how will the degree of risk affect her choices? To address these questions, economists have made many attempts to define a good measurement for the riskiness of a prospect. Several general measures were developed within the context of expected utility. Rothschild and Stiglitz (1970) provided a methodology for the ranking of prospects which have the same mean outcome but different levels of risk. In addition, their method provides comparative statics results describing the impact of risk on key parameters. Hadar and Russell (1969) developed a method for ranking prospects with differing mean outcomes. Both of these methods are set within the framework of expected utility, ranking prospects derived from a von Neumann–Morgenstern concave utility function to imply risk-averse behavior. Moreover, the stochastic dominance rule is useful for the comparison of risky prospects because it allows us to compare the risk associated with each of two probability distributions and to determine which is preferable under an expected utility framework (Whitmore and Findlay, 1978).

3.1. *Mean-preserving spread*

Rothschild and Stiglitz (1970) put forth four possible ways to compare two prospects, namely, X and Y, with equal means. They are as follows:

(1) For any X, Y with $E(X) = E(Y)$, if $EU(X) \geq EU(Y)$ for every U with $U' > 0$, and $U'' < 0$, then Y is riskier than X. In other words, if every risk-averse individual prefers X to Y, then Y is riskier than X.
(2) If $Y \overset{d}{\rightarrow} X + Z$ (i.e., Y is equivalent in distribution to X plus Z) where Z is a random variable with $E(Z|x) = 0$, then Y is riskier than X. In other words, if Y is the sum of X and another random variable Z and the conditional expectation of Z for every X is zero, then Y is riskier than X.
(3) If Y can be constructed from X through the use of a *mean-preserving spread* (i.e., "spread" some probability weight from the center to the tails), then Y is riskier than X.
(4) A conventional approach: Variance of X is smaller than that of Y.

Rothschild and Stiglitz (1970) showed that the first three ways are equivalent to each other in terms of ranking the riskiness of X and Y but different from the fourth one. Regarding the fourth way, they pointed out that it is possible that some risk-averse decision makers may still prefer Y even if X and Y have the same mean and X has smaller variance. A numerical example of how a mean-preserving spread works may help shed some light. Given a random variable X, we establish the following probability distribution:

x	$P(X = x)$
1	1/8
2	1/8
3	1/2
4	1/8
5	1/8

A new random variable Y is generated from X through the use of a mean-preserving spread such that increasing the probability weight assigned to 1 and 5 by 1/8, respectively, and decreasing the probability weight assigned to 2 and 4 by 1/8, respectively. Y would then have the following probability distribution:

y	$P(Y = y)$
1	1/4
3	1/2
5	1/4

According to Rothschild and Stiglitz (1970), if and only if Y is constructed by a sequence of a mean-preserving spread from X, then $EU(X) > EU(Y)$ for any utility function U such that $U' > 0$ and $U'' < 0$. To illustrate the last point, consider the above example where we moved from X to Y by a mean-preserving spread. In that case,

$$EU(X) = \left\{\frac{1}{8}U(1) + \frac{1}{8}U(2) + \frac{1}{2}U(3) + \frac{1}{8}U(4) + \frac{1}{8}U(5),\right\}$$

$$EU(Y) = \left\{\frac{1}{4}U(1) + \frac{1}{2}U(3) + \frac{1}{4}U(5),\right\}$$

$$EU(X) - EU(Y) = \frac{1}{8}[U(2) - U(1) + U(4) - U(5)],$$

which is positive due to a decreasing marginal utility under risk-averse behavior (thus, $U(2) - U(1) > U(5) - U(4)$), and the alternative X is preferred to Y.

The concept of mean-preserving spread is important because it allows for an analysis of the marginal impact of risk. For example, given a production system such that

$$\Pi = PY - wX.$$

We can use the mean-preserving spread to manipulate P and create a new variable with the same mean but different variance:

$$P_1 = \gamma P + Z,$$

where $\gamma \in [0, 1]$ is a constant and Z is a random variable with mean $E(Z) = (1 - \gamma)E(P)$. We can then calculate $dY^*/d\gamma$ to determine the impact of price risk on the optimal output.

3.2. *Stochastic dominance*

Hadar and Russell (1969) developed the concept of stochastic dominance which allows for the comparison of outcomes with differing means. This method also allows for the ranking of uncertain prospects without assuming a specific utility function. This approach can be used for comparisons of both discrete and continuous risky choices. However, its usefulness is limited since not all distributions can be ordered through second-order stochastic dominance.

3.2.1. *First-order stochastic dominance (FOSD)*

Let X denote the value of a variable (e.g., wealth and income) which can assume values in the range $(-\infty, \infty)$. Let the function $F_i^X(x)$ be defined recursively where

$$F_i^X(x) = \int_{-\infty}^{x} F_{i-1}^X(Z)dZ$$

and where $F_0^X(x)$ is the probability density function of X.

Under this definition, $F_1^X(x)$ is the cumulative distribution function (CDF) of X. Consider two random prospects, X and Y. There is a first-order stochastic dominance of Y by X (i.e., X FOSD Y) if

$$F_1^X(m) \leq F_1^Y(m) \quad \text{for } -\infty < m < \infty,$$

with at least one point of strong inequality. Figure 2 illustrates FOSD graphically. In other words, X is first-order stochastic dominant to Y if the cumulative distribution of X is below that of Y for every m, indicating that $\text{Prob}(X \geq m) > \text{Prob}(Y \geq m)$ for every m.

It is easy to argue that if X FOSD Y, then every individual with positive marginal utility will prefer X to Y. That is, if X and Y represent income, then every individual will prefer X over Y since X represents a higher probability of achieving a high income.

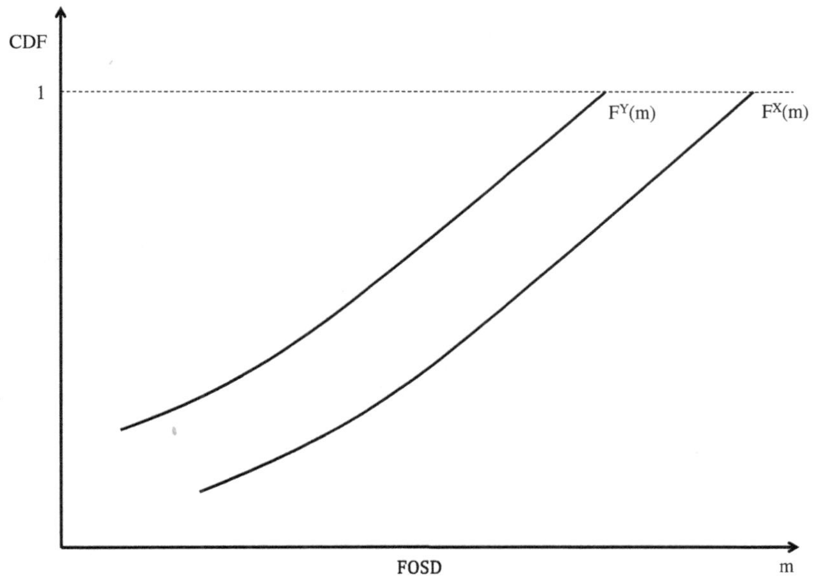

Figure 2. First-order stochastic dominance (FOSD).
Note: In this figure, $F^X(m)$ first-order stochastically dominates $F^Y(m)$.

3.2.2. *Second-order stochastic dominance (SOSD)*

SOSD is a weaker domination concept than FOSD. We define that X second-order stochastically dominates Y if and only if

$$\int_{-\infty}^{m} F_1^X(z)dz \leq \int_{-\infty}^{m} F_1^Y(z)dz.$$

One can check that if X SOSD Y, then risk-averse individuals will prefer X to Y and that if X FOSD Y, then X SOSD Y. SOSD is useful when the decision makers are risk-averse. Figure 3 depicts cumulative distributions under SOSD, from which we can see that there is some cross-over between the CDFs of the two prospects, but the area under F^Y is greater than that under F^X. The cumulative functions in this case intersect twice, with $F_1^Y(m) < F_1^X(m)$ in the range between the intersection points.

Beyond FOSD and SOSD, stochastic dominance is much less useful as a concept. It is unclear what choices a risk-averse individual will make in the presence of third- or greater-order stochastic

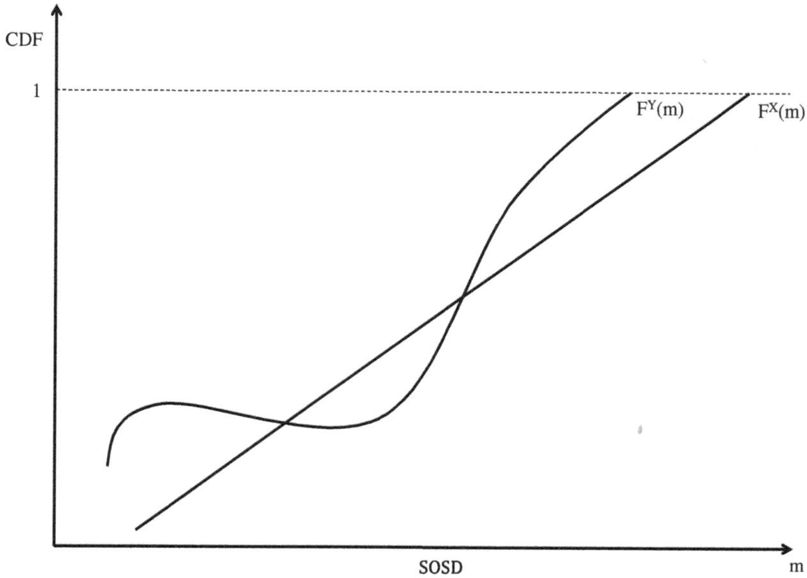

Figure 3. Second-order stochastic dominance (FOSD).
Note: In this figure, $F^X(m)$ second-order stochastically dominates $F^Y(m)$.

dominance. Very restrictive assumptions about behavior are required in order to derive results from higher orders of stochastic dominance. When FOSD or SOSD is applicable, they are useful, but they are not applicable in every situation. They only present a "partial" ordering, ranking only some of the prospects while leaving others out. In particular, stochastic dominance may not capture the tradeoffs between risks and returns.

3.3. *Variance as a measure of risk*

Is variance a good measure of risk? Consider two variables with the following probability distributions:

$$X = \begin{cases} \frac{n+1}{n} & \text{with probability } \frac{n-1}{n} \\ \frac{1}{n} & \text{with probability } \frac{1}{n} \end{cases}$$

$$Y = \begin{cases} \frac{n-1}{n} & \text{with probability } \frac{n-1}{n} \\ \frac{2n-1}{n} & \text{with probability } \frac{1}{n}. \end{cases}$$

The means and variances of the two distributions will be as follows:

$$E(X) = U(Y) = 1 \qquad \text{and} \qquad V(X) = V(Y) = \frac{n-1}{n^2}.$$

However, even though the means and variances are the same, many risk-averse individuals will prefer Y to X. For this reason, variance is *not* a good measure of risk, although it is often used as a proxy because it is easy to calculate and the data necessary are usually available.

3.4. *Just and Pope production model*

Just and Pope (1978) developed general models for analyzing cases of production risk econometrically. Before their work, one had the option of assuming either:

Additive risk: $y = f(x) + \varepsilon$, with $E(\varepsilon) = 0$ or
Multiplicative risk: $y = f(x)\varepsilon$, with $E(\varepsilon) = 1$.

Risk in the production function causes difficulties in the use of linear programming estimation procedures since an investigation into the properties of the random variables is required. Both the additive and the multiplicative models are criticized heavily by Just and Pope. The additive specification does not allow the uncertainty effect to be correlated with the input mix, while the multiplicative specification does not allow for inputs that have differing impacts on mean and variance, such as fertilizer (yield increasing and risk decreasing).

To offer greater flexibility when describing stochastic technological processes and related behavior, Just and Pope (1978) suggest

$$y = f_1(x) + f_2(x)\varepsilon, \qquad \text{with } E(\varepsilon) = 0.$$

By including two components in the production function, one relating to output level and the other to output variability, the Just and Pope production model allows for the differential impacts of an input on output and risk. The shortcomings of this model are that it only allows for the consideration of one random variable, and that it requires a large number of estimations, including the production function, the risk element, and the behavioral element.

3.5. *Exponential utility*

Another approach to estimating behavior under risk calls for the use of a utility function that is applicable to any distribution. Yassour *et al.* (1981) adopted this approach and used an exponential utility function in order to look at farm technology adoption decisions. This utility function can be applied conveniently in conjunction with all distributions which have moment-generating functions. The utility function is written as

$$U(x) = -e^{-rx},$$

and the expected utility function as

$$E[U(x)] = -E[e^{-rx}] = -M(-r),$$

where M is a moment-generating function and $E[\cdot]$ is the expectation operator. Since the moment-generating function is a function of the parameters, the utility function can be expressed in terms of this function. One shortcoming of this approach is that it implies constant rather than decreasing absolute risk aversion.

Saha (1993) proposed a new utility function, the expo-power function, which allows for flexibility in the modeling of risk preference structures. This form allows the data to reveal both the degree and structure (i.e., increasing, constant, or decreasing) of risk aversion. Use of this utility function means that no *a priori* assumptions about risk preferences are necessary. The expo-power function is

$$U(w) = \theta - \exp\{-\beta w^{\alpha}\},$$

where

$$\theta > 1, \quad \alpha \neq 0, \quad \beta \neq 0, \quad \alpha\beta > 0.$$

The properties of the expo-power utility function are as follows: (1) It is unique up to an affine transformation; (2) $-\frac{U''}{U'} = \frac{1-\alpha+\alpha\beta w^{\alpha}}{w}$ and $-\frac{U''}{U'}w = 1 - \alpha + \alpha\beta w^{\alpha}$; (3) when $\alpha < 1$ ($= 1$, or > 1), there is decreasing (constant, or increasing) absolute risk aversion; (4) when $\beta < 0$ ($= 0$, or > 0), there is decreasing (constant, or increasing) relative risk aversion; and finally, (5) the utility function is quasi-concave for all $w > 0$.

The parameters, α and β, are the key determinants of the risk preference structure. The effect of α on $A(w)$ and $R(w)$ — the coefficients of absolute and relative risk aversion — depends on the relative magnitude of w and the parameters.

In sum, expected utility has theoretical usefulness — such as in Sandmo's results and in the mean variance model — and practical usefulness in applications through either the mean variance model or the Just–Pope production function. Some of the shortcomings of these models have been addressed by the work of Yassour *et al.* (1981) and Saha (1993). The former allows for the consideration of non-normal yield distributions in an easy-to-manipulate format. The latter proposes a flexible utility form with no *a priori* assumptions about risk preferences specified. A major problem is that, up to now, only one variable (either yield or price) is considered random. Many times, both are random. In this case, only the log-normal distribution yields analytic results.

4. Safety Rules

The main appeal of the expected-utility approach to modeling decisions under risk is that it is derived rigorously from a well-defined and reasonable set of assumptions about preferences. One disadvantage of this approach is the assumption that individuals know the probabilities associated with each possible outcome of a prospect and have based their decision upon this knowledge. In many cases, the degree of information and computation required may make his assumption unrealistic. An alternative approach for modeling choices under risk and uncertainty is embodied by the various "safety rules".

Safety rules correspond to expected utility in the same way that classical statistics relate to Bayesian. Safety rules are simple, reasonable, but somewhat arbitrary. They imply lexicographic rules and an objective function that is linear in mean and variance, reflecting a "behavioristic" approach to modeling behavior. The models are based upon simple decision criteria economists believe people use in making day-to-day decisions. One common element of these rules is that they reflect "satisfying" behavior, where people make choices to meet some objective. Thus, under this approach, people do not "maximize", rather they aim to meet a target. A major proponent of this approach was Herbert Simon, a Nobel Prize winner in Economics. Simon introduced the notion of "bounded rationality", where people are constrained by high computation information and competition costs, and therefore, they develop simple decision rules. Simon saw these behavioristic rules as outcomes of optimization subject to all computation and data costs and constraints, and his views pose a challenge to economists to identify the constrained optimization problems that have resulted in the behavioristic rules whose existence is supported statistically.

The safety rules have multiple advantages. First, they can be used with programming techniques. Second, they follow the logic of conventional statistics, avoiding the Bayesian style of expected utility theory. Third, they can provide a satisfying model of behavior in many circumstances. Lastly, these models are useful both in positive and normative analyses. Safety rules are frequently used by engineers and regulators in constructing nuclear power plants and devising earthquake regulations.

When economists identify persistent behavioral rules, they can be used for prediction and analysis of appropriate policy. They can be particularly relevant in setting government regulations. The safety rules that we present here are intuitively appealing and are likely to represent the behavior of at least some people. They correspond in their structure to decision rules of "classical" statistics, and in particular, they resemble the use of statistical significance in classical "hypothesis testing."

4.1. *Roy's minimum probability rule*

Let π, denoting profit, be a random variable whose distribution depends on a decision variable, X. For example, $\pi = PX - C(X)$, where P is a random variable. One safety rule is the Safety First approach introduced by Roy (1952). Under this approach, decision makers will choose the decision variable to minimizing the probability of π falling below a threshold level D. The objective function is

$$\min_X Prob\{\pi(X) \leq D\} \text{ or } \max_X Prob\{\pi(X) \geq D\}.$$

Under this approach, decision makers' choices are dominated by the desire to minimize the probability of falling under the threshold level. This approach corresponds to a lexicographic utility model, and is useful in modeling subsistence agriculture. If $P \sim N(\bar{P}, \sigma^2)$, then Roy's safety rule suggests setting the X that minimizes the probability that a standard-normal random variable is smaller than $\frac{D-\bar{P}X+C(X)}{\sigma X}$. If the cumulative distribution of the standard normal random variable is denoted by $\Phi(Z)$, then Roy's rule is

$$X^* = \arg\min_X \Phi\left(\frac{D - \bar{P}X + C(X)}{\sigma X}\right).$$

4.2. *Telser's safety-first rule*

An alternative approach is provided by Telser (1955). In his case, the decision maker's objective is to maximize expected profit subject to a bound on the probability of profit falling below the threshold level D. This model can be written as

$$\max_X E[\pi(X)] \quad \text{s.t. Prob}\{\pi(x) \leq D\} \leq \alpha,$$

where α is a tolerance level of profit lower than the threshold.

For our previous example with a normal distribution, the Telser rule is

$$\max_X PX - C(X) \quad \text{s.t. Prob}\left\{Z \leq \frac{D - \bar{P}X + C(X)}{\sigma X}\right\} \leq \alpha,$$

where $Z \sim N(0, 1)$ is a standardized normally distributed random variable.

This rule has application in the development of many engineering and health codes and is based on the concept of an onerous event in a manner much like the use of critical levels in classical statistics.

4.3. *Kataoka's safety-fixed rule*

Kataoka (1963) developed the safety rule that maximizes a minimum profit level (threshold level) where the random profit is higher than this minimum profit with a probability of at least $1 - \alpha$. Mathematically, the safety-fixed rule can be presented as

$$\max_{X} D \quad \text{s.t. } \text{Prob}\{\pi(X) \geq D\} \geq 1 - \alpha.$$

This safety-fixed rule and the safety-first rule are inversely related. The statistical significance level α is the parameter of the safety fixed rule, and its objective is to find the profit distribution which has the highest level of minimum profit where the cumulative distribution value is α. The disaster level D is the parameter of Roy's safety-first rule, and its objective is to select the profit distribution with the lowest level of cumulative distribution when profit is equal to D. Figure 4 demonstrates the two rules graphically.

Suppose we have to choose among three activities. The cumulative distributions of profits of the three activities are denoted by the

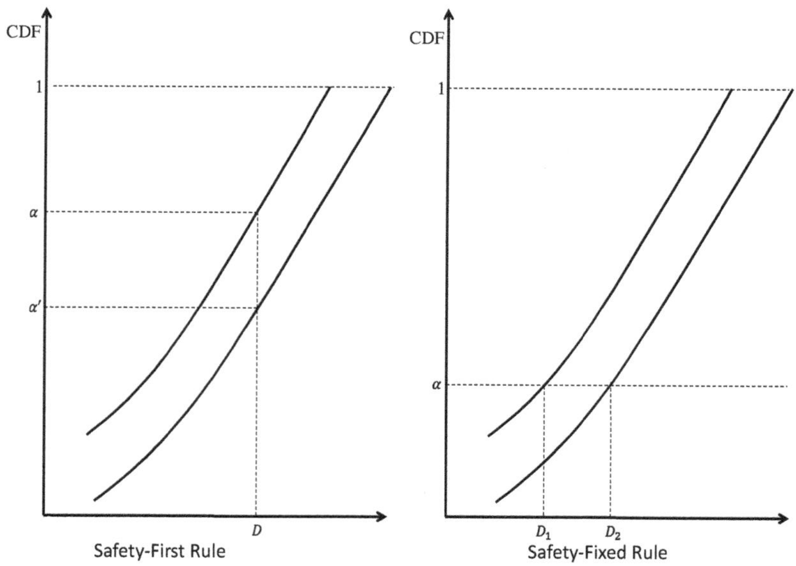

Figure 4. Safety-first rule and safety-fixed rule.

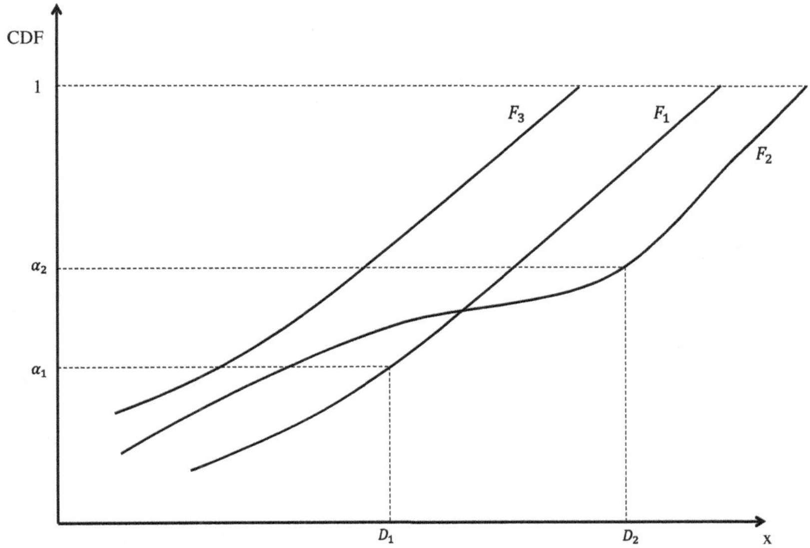

Figure 5. Choices among three activities based on safety-first and safety-fixed rules.

F_i functions in Figure 5. Activity 1 is selected under the safety-fixed rule when α is α_1 and under the safety-first rule when D is D_1. When the safety-fixed rule is not as restrictive and α is α_2, then activity 2 is selected. Activity 2 is also selected under the safety-first rule when D is D_2.

Continuing with the normality example, we choose a line of actions to maximize D subject to the constraint:

$$\text{Prob}\left(\frac{\Pi(x)-\bar{\Pi}}{\sigma}<\frac{D-\bar{\Pi}}{\sigma}\right)\leq\alpha.$$

If the constraint is binding, this amounts to choose D such that

$$\frac{D-\bar{\Pi}}{\sigma}=Z_{\alpha},$$

where Z_α is such that $\text{Prob}(x<Z_\alpha)=\alpha$ under the standard normal distribution. Thus, $D=\bar{\Pi}+Z_\alpha\sigma$, and maximizing D, in the case of the normal distribution, amounts to maximize the sum of the mean and a multiple of the standard deviation. If α is small (i.e., $\alpha<0.5$), then Z_α is negative and we have some form of risk aversion. We can see the link between this safety rule and the mean–variance utility function.

4.4. *Safety rules and expected utility*

Safety rules can be expressed as special cases of the expected utility framework. The safety-first rule can be expressed as the outcome of the expected utility framework when the utility function is lexicographic. The objective of the safety-first rule is to minimize the probability of profits below the disaster level D, which is equivalent to the expected utility maximization when the utility function is

$$U(\pi) = \begin{cases} 1 & \text{when } \pi \geq D \\ 0 & \text{when } \pi < D. \end{cases}$$

With this utility function, the probability that profit is greater than D is maximized under Roy's minimum probability rule. The main criticism of this minimum probability rule is that lexicographic utility functions are unreasonable and individuals prefer making more money than less once their profits are above the disaster level. However, there are likely to be situations where the safety rules are good approximations of reality, and their use is justified. Note that one major flaw of the standard expected utility models is that they put too much emphasis on income within utility functions, ignoring other variables, such as social status (e.g., landlord vs. landless peasant; hired vs. self-employed). If social status is lost when profits are below a threshold level, and if such a status loss entails a drastic reduction in welfare, then the use of safety first rule may provide a good approximation of expected utility outcomes.

5. The Validity of the Expected Utility (EU) Model

The attractive feature of expected utility (EU) theory is that it is derived from a set of axioms about human behavior, creating a reasonable, rational, and desirable basis for normative analysis. The EU model has been widely embraced by economists for modeling decisions under risk because of its ease of use, normative appeal

Table 2. Four choice pairs.

	Choice pair 1			Choice pair 2		
	X	$P(X)$	chosen	X	$P(X)$	chosen
Option A	4,000	.80	20%	4,000	.20	65%
Option B	3,000	1	80%	3,000	.25	35%
	Choice pair 3			**Choice pair 4**		
	X	$P(X)$	chosen	X	$P(X)$	chosen
Option A	−4,000	.80	92%	−4,000	.20	42%
Option B	−3,000	1	8%	−3,000	.25	58%

and, arguably, for its reasonable accuracy in predicting behavior under risk for many economic activities. However, the EU model has repeatedly been shown to lack descriptive and predictive validity in experimental settings. These empirical violations of EU have given rise to the formulation of a large number of alternative Generalized-EU models, even though not much is known about the underlying reasons for the occurrence of EU violations. The following experimental examples show some instances of where individuals violate expected utility.

5.1. *Kahneman and Tversky experiments*

Kahneman and Tversky (1979) conducted experiments to test the validity of the expected utility model. Individuals were asked to select one of two options (Option A vs. Option B) from the following choice pairs:

In Table 2, X stands for a random return under Option A or B, $P(X)$ is the probability of X taking a value under an option, and "chosen" stands for the percentage of experiment participant chose an option. For instance, in choice pair 1, Option A offers a \$4,000 return at probability 0.8 (and, implicitly, a zero return at probability 0.2). Option B offers a sure \$3,000 return. For choice pair 1, 20% participants chose Option A and 80% chose Option B.

Assume that the utility function is $U(\cdot)$. Then the choice outcome under pair 1 indicates that $U(3000) > 0.8U(4000)$. Choice pair 2 indicates that $.25U(3,000) < .2U(4,000)$, or $U(3,000) < .8U(4,000)$. We can see that the choices for the pairs 1 and 2 are inconsistent with each other. Similarly, choice pair 3 indicates that $.8U(-4,000) > U(-3,000)$, and choice pair 4 indicates that $.2U(-4,000) < .25U(-3,000)$, or $.8U(-4,000) < U(-3,000)$. Again, inconsistency arises between outcomes in choice pairs 3 and 4. Therefore, the validity or expected utility theory is cast into doubt. Two major explanations for the apparent failure of the expected utility model to correctly predict human behavior have been advanced. First, people under-weigh outcomes that are probable in comparison to certain outcomes, even when they both have the same expected utility, which is known as the *certainty effect*. Second, people are risk-averse when they gain and risk-loving when they lose; known as the *reflection effect*.

Applied economists face a dilemma when choosing between models of decision-making under risk. They must choose between either (1) the EU model that has normative appeal but has been shown to be systematically violated by behavior or (2) one of a number of generalized models that lack normative appeal and allow for some behavioral violations of EU. Here, we offer a brief discussion of the EU model's implications for behavior, the experimental violations of EU, the approach of the generalized-EU models, and an explanation for the occurrence of choices violating EU which offers direction to applied economists for model selection in risky choice environments.

5.2. *Background: The EU model's critical implications for behavior*

There are three main axioms in the EU framework. They are defined over a binary relation where $\succeq$ denotes weak preference, $\succ$ denotes strong preference, and $\sim$ denotes indifference for preferences over probability distributions $p, q \in P$ that are defined over a common (discrete or continuous) outcome vector $\mathbf{x}$. The three axioms that are necessary and sufficient for the EU representation $u(\cdot)$ over preferences are as follows:

Axiom O (Order): The preference ordering is complete (all distributions $p, q \in P$ are comparable via the ordering $\succeq$) and transitive (if $p \succeq q$ and $q \succeq r$, then $p \succeq r$).

Axiom I (Independence): For all $p, q, r \in P$, and for all $\alpha \in (0, 1)$, if $p \succeq q$, then $\alpha p + (1 - \alpha)r \succeq \alpha q + (1 - \alpha)r$. This axiom holds that preferences over probability distributions should only depend on the portions of the distributions that differ (p and q), not on their common elements (r). This independence of preference with respect to r holds regardless of r and of the level of α that defines the linear combination.

Axiom C (Continuity): For all $p, q, r \in P$ with $p \succeq q$ and $q \succeq r$, there exist $\alpha, \beta \in (0, 1)$ such that

$$\alpha p + (1 - \alpha)r \succeq q \text{ and } q \succeq \beta p + (1 - \beta)r.$$

This axiom gives a degree of continuity to the preferences.

Axioms **O**, **I**, and **C** can be shown to be necessary and sufficient (Fishburn, 1983) for the existence of a function $u(\cdot)$ on the outcomes $x \in \mathbf{x}$ that represents preferences through $\succeq$. In the discrete case where $p = \{p_1, p_2, \ldots, p_n\}$, it gives the probabilities of occurrence for $x = \{x_1, x_2, \ldots, x_n\}$:

$$p \succeq q \Leftrightarrow \sum_{i=1}^{n} u(x_i)p_i \geq \sum_{i=1}^{n} u(x_i)q_i.$$

Most of the violations of EU hinge on an implication stemming primarily from the Independence Axiom.

A useful diagram for viewing the implications for models of behavior under risk was developed by Marschak (1950) and reintroduced by Machina (1982). Let us call it Machina–Marschak triangle (see Figure 6). This triangle in two dimensions has boundaries from 0 to 1 (a simplex) consistent with rules of probability.

Probability distributions defining gambles over three (low, medium, and high) discrete outcomes are represented by points inside or on the boundaries of this triangle. The distribution's probability for the occurrence of the lowest outcome (x_L) is given on the horizontal axis, the probability of occurrence for the highest outcome (x_H) is given on the vertical axis, and the probability of the medium

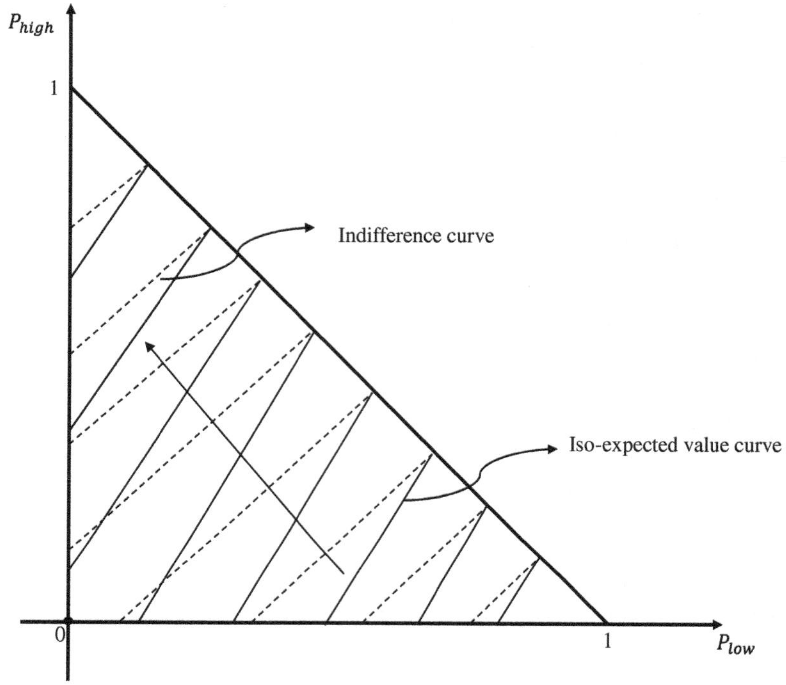

Figure 6. Machina-Marschak triangle.

outcome (x_M) is given implicitly by 1 less the sum of the probabilities for the high and low outcomes.

To further explain, points on the hypotenuse represent gambles with no choice of occurrence for the middle outcome (the sum of the probabilities for the low and the high outcomes is one), while the point on the vertex of the triangle opposite to the hypotenuse represents a gamble giving the middle outcome with certainty.

Preferences over gambles can be illustrated by indifference curves within the triangle; the EU model holds that these indifference curves must be parallel as in Figure 6. These indifference curves can be compared with the iso-expected value curves in the figure, where the gambles have the same expected values (note: not the expected utility). The indifference curves shown in Figure 6 indicate that the individual is risk loving, as increased risk (movements along an indifference curve to the "Northeast") require a lower expected value for indifference to hold. Individuals prefer movements toward the "Northwest" of the triangle, as the probability of the highest outcome increases while that of the lowest outcome decreases.

5.2.1. *Violations of EU*

There have been many advances in the economic analysis of decisions under risk using the EU model. However, the majority of these papers take the validity of the EU model as given. A serious challenge to the use of EU was made by the Nobel Prize winner (in economics) Maurice Allais soon after its introduction. His work and that of others following him elicited choices between hypothetical risky alternatives to show that EU lacked complete predictive, and hence descriptive, validity.

Some well-known risky choice examples are given in a paper by Kahneman and Tversky (1979) and that synthesizes work by Allais and by others who have shown experimental violations of EU. Kahneman and Tversky (1979) also present a model of choice which strives for only descriptive (not normative) validity. Their paper remains a standard in this subject of modeling choice under risk; in particular, their experimental results have had a great deal of influence on the literature. The first of Kahneman and Tversky's examples showing EU violations discussed here asks individuals to select between two gambles as shown in Table 3. Note that gamble A (respectively, C) is less risky than gamble B (respectively, D). On the other hand, gamble A (respectively, C) has lower expected value than does gamble B (respectively, D).

The EU model requires that the choice between A and B must be compatible with the choice between C and D; i.e., if the more risky alternative B is selected in the first choice, the more risky alternative D must be selected in the second choice, and vice versa. One of these choice patterns is required due to the Independence Axiom, since the probability vectors $\{p_C = (.75, .25, 0), p_D = (.8, 0, .2)\}$ over the outcome vector $x = (\$0, \$3000, \$4000)$ defining alternatives C and D, respectively, can be viewed as a linear combination of the probability distributions $\{p_A = (0, 1.0, 0), p_B = (.2, 0, .8)\}$ that define

Table 3. Kahneman and Tversky's experiments.

Choice 1: Select between Gambles A and B	
Gamble A	Gamble B
\$3000 with probability 1.0	\$4000 with probability .8, \$0 with probability .2
Choice 2: Select between Gambles C and D	
Gamble C	Gamble D
\$3000 with probability .25, \$0 with probability .75	\$4000 with probability .2 \$0 with probability .8
Choice 3: Select between Gambles E and F.	
Gamble E	Gamble F
\$3000 with probability .9, \$ 0 with probability .1	\$6000 with probability .45, \$ 0 with probability .55
Choice 4: Select between Gambles G and H.	
Gamble G	Gamble H
\$3000 with probability .002, \$ 0 with probability .998	\$6000 with probability .001, \$ 0 with probability .999

A and B, respectively. To see this, first let us define a distribution carrying a certain outcome of \$0 based on the outcome vector $x = (\$0, \$3000, \$4000)$ as $(1.0, 0, 0)$. Then we have,

$$.25 \cdot p_A + .75 \cdot (1.0, 0, 0) = (.75, .25, 0) = p_C,$$

$$.25 \cdot p_B + .75 \cdot (1.0, 0, 0) = (.80, 0, .20) = p_D.$$

In this case, the Independence Axiom implies that if $p_A \succeq p_B$ then $p_C \succeq p_D$. In their experiment using hypothetical payoff outcomes, many (about 65%) of Kahneman and Tversky's subjects selected A over B in the first pair but selected D over C in the second pair of choice, a choice pattern that violates EU. Figure 7 illustrates this pattern of choice. This inconsistency between expected utility theory predictions is termed "Certainty Effect" as Gamble A presents a sure return.

The gamble pairs (A,B) and (C,D) are depicted in a Machina–Marschak triangle (see Figure 7). One can readily check that lines

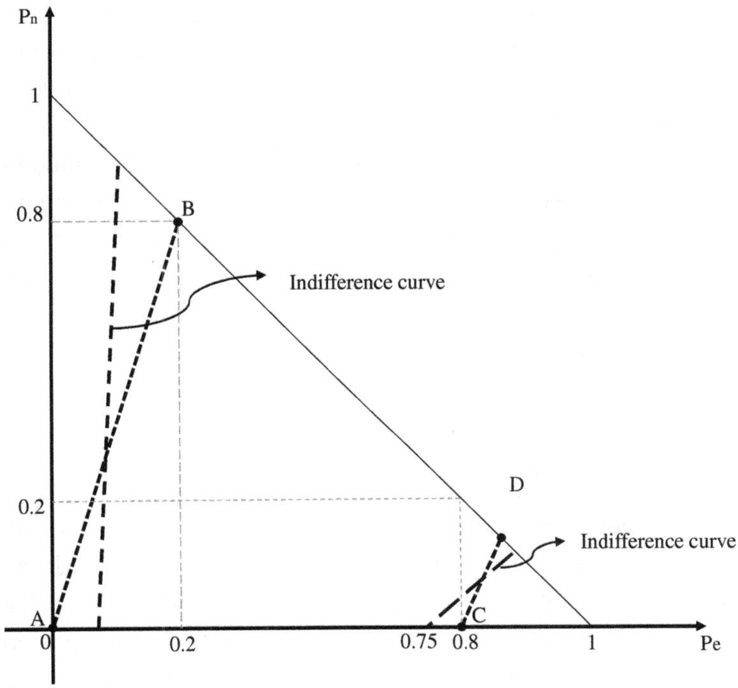

Figure 7. Gamble pairs (A, B) and (C, D) in a Machina-Marschak triangle.

AB and CD are parallel. These parallel lines are important for the analysis of choice with respect to the EU model. If the majority of subjects prefer gamble A to gamble B and prefer gamble D to gamble C, then some indifference curves must be unparallel, which contradicts the property under EU that indifference curves are parallel.

Another well-known EU violation was found by Kahneman and Tversky where they asked respondents to select between hypothetical risky alternatives that have equal expected values (see choice pairs 3 and 4 in Table 3). The probabilities defining G and H can also be written as a linear combination of the probabilities that define E and F, with $(1.0, 0, 0)$ defining a distribution giving a sure outcome of \$0 (we leave this as an exercise to readers). The EU model requires consistency of choice: If E is selected in the first pair, G must be selected in the second. On the other hand, if F is selected in the first choice, H must be selected in the second. However, respondents also violated the EU model in their choices over these two pairs, with most respondents selecting E over F and H over G. The choice of the riskier H over G also violates second-degree stochastic dominance predictions for risk averse decision makers as G second-order stochastically dominates H. Note that the inconsistency of expected utility predictions illustrated by choice pairs 3 and 4 is termed "Common Ratio Effect" because the ratio of the winning probabilities in Gambles E and G ((i.e., .9 to .002)) is the same as that in Gambles F and H (i.e., .45 to .001).

5.2.2. *The generalized-EU models*

A number of models have been set forth as alternatives to EU in light of the behavioral violations of EU such as those developed by Kahneman and Tversky described above. These models weaken the Independence Axiom of EU in order to allow for observed behavioral violations. The upshot of these models is that preferences are represented through both a function $u(x)$ over the outcomes and a nonlinear function $g(s)$ for $s \in \{p, q\}$ over the probability distributions, giving the representation:

$$p \succeq q \Leftrightarrow \sum_{i=1}^{n} u(x_i)g_i(p) \geq \sum_{i=1}^{n} u(x_i)g_i(q).$$

The function $u(x)$ has similar structure as in the EU model; the interesting part of these models is the function $g(\cdot)$. Quiggin (1982) proposed a model where $g(\cdot)$ overweighted extremely small probabilities when defined over either very low ($0 in the examples) or relatively high ($4000, $6000 in the examples) outcomes. Later work by Tversky and Kahneman (1992) incorporated Quiggin's structure of this function $g(\cdot)$ and developed the cumulative prospect theory, which are discussed in the following section.

Another early, well known, and simple to illustrate form of the generalized-EU models was developed by Machina (1982). In his model, preferences locally correspond with EU in the same manner as Taylor's series approximations for non-stochastic functional forms.

Machina further specified the behavior of the preferences in order to allow for the empirical violations of EU through a curvature change in the Machina–Marschak triangle known as "fanning out," where the indifference curves become steeper with increases in the expected values of the gamble (movements toward the northwest) (see graph (b) in Figure 5 of Machina 1982). This fanning out notion has been used for other generalized-EU models but is neither strongly motivated nor predictively accurate.

5.2.3. *The similarity model: Alternative explanation for the paradoxes*

An appealing explanation of the patterns of choices showing inconsistencies with what EU proposes is that individuals evaluate risky alternatives differently, dependent on the similarity of the alternatives. This similarity has both objective and subjective connotations. In risky choice, selection between the more similar alternatives would likely be both (1) more difficult or (mentally) costly and (2) less beneficial or important because the alternatives differ little in an objective sense. As a result, comparisons between two sets of choice pairs that differ considerably in their degree of similarity (such as those used to show violations of EU) may give misleading implications about preferences in the nature of model misspecification, since both preferences and perceptions are reflected in choices.

To illustrate the application of this similarity idea, consider the pairs of risky alternatives in the certainty effect and the common ratio effect examples discussed above respectively. In both of these examples, one of the choice pairs (Gambles A and B in choice pair 1 as well as E and F in choice pair 3) is quite "dissimilar" as defined by the Euclidean distance over the probability space:

$$d(p,q) = \left[\sum_{i=1}^{n}(p_i - q_i)^2\right]^{\frac{1}{2}}.$$

In addition to distance differences, the pair A and B is qualitatively different because A gives \$3000 with certainty (i.e., no risk at all).

Choices between these dissimilar pairs are compared with choices between similar pairs (Gambles C and D in choice pair 2 as well as G and H in choice pair 4). Kahneman and Tversky's results can be explained if individuals are more likely to select the riskier (Gambles D and H) alternative when the alternatives are similar.

Work by Rubinstein (1988) and Leland (1994) has explored some of the implications of various models of similarity on risky choice, although the models suggested by these authors are quite limited in their applications. Buschena and Zilberman (1999) have developed and tested more general models for the similarity of risky choice and have found considerable effects of similarity on both the pattern of choice and on the occurrence of EU violations. The tests show two primary results. First, as the risky choice pair becomes more similar (the choice is less critical and the evaluation is more costly), the riskier alternative is much more likely to be selected. Second, violations of EU are much more likely to occur when the differences in the dissimilarity between the two sets of risky choice pairs is large, i.e., when there is a good deal of dichotomy between the dissimilarity of the pairs.

The results of the similarity tests in Buschena and Zilberman (1999) show some results that should be of significant interest to general and applied economists, namely, the following:

(1) There is an operational and intuitively appealing explanation for the occurrence of choice patterns that violate EU.
(2) There are a significant number of decisions over risky alternatives for which the EU model is descriptively accurate. EU works well for dissimilar choice pairs.
(3) Statistical analysis shows significant violations of the models set forth as alternatives to EU (generalized-EU and others); moreover, these violations were in the direction predicted by the similarity model.

There remain a number of unanswered questions regarding the effects of similarity on risky choice. Of particular note are those concerning the effects of using real, rather than hypothetical, payoffs on the influence of similarity on choice. Further questions of interest that are quite unexplored are the occurrence of EU violations themselves and also the effects of similarity on the occurrence of violations, for non-experimental choices (e.g., agricultural production decisions and risky resource protection issues). There is some evidence (e.g., Bar–Shira, 1992) that the EU model works well for modeling crop portfolio choices.

Research modeling and testing the robustness of the findings of experiments to risky decisions made in "everyday life" is a very fertile one. This line of research, however, will likely be quite difficult to carry out given data availability and calls for a good deal of creativity in experimental design. Some of the recent findings to be discussed in the following within this chapter indicate promise for models of behavior incorporating factors reflective of more comprehensive models of decision-making.

6. Prospect Theory

In recent years, prospect theory has attracted increasing attention among agricultural economists, with applications for understanding farmers' decision-making under risk in various contexts. For instance, Liu (2013) used prospect theory to explain Chinese farmers' biotechnology adoption decisions, Babcock (2015) applied prospect theory to understand US farmers' crop insurance take-up decisions, and Bocquého *et al.* (2015) and Anand *et al.* (2019) employed prospect theory to study farmers' adoption decision toward bioenergy crops in France and the United States, respectively. Recently, Wilson and Miao (in press) applied prospect theory to interpreting consumers' food waste behavior. In this section we briefly discuss this theory. Barberis (2013) provides an outstanding review of prospect theory, including its applications in finance, insurance, behavioral economics, labor supply, and industrial organization.

The original prospect theory was developed by Kahneman and Tversky (1979) in their seminal paper "Prospect Theory: An Analysis of Decision under Risk" published in *Econometrica*, where, as we discussed in the previous section, the authors documented quite a few examples that predictions from expected utility theory contradicted experimental results. Although focusing on prospects with only no more than two non-zero outcomes, Kahneman and Tversky established the key features of prospect theory: reference point, loss aversion, and probability weighting. The reference point reflects the phenomenon that people's utility is largely determined by the change in their incomes relative to a benchmark value (i.e., the reference point). Incomes higher than the reference point are viewed as gains, whereas incomes lower than the reference point are viewed as losses. Loss aversion indicates that, for losses and gains with the same absolute value (e.g., a loss of \$100 and a gain of \$100), people are more sensitive to the former than the latter. In other words, the \$100 loss would bring in much larger disutility to a decision maker than the utility brought to her by the \$100 gain. Probability weighting reflects the idea that people tend to overweight small probabilities but underweight large probabilities. Kahneman and Tversky (1979) argue that probability weighting can help explain why people buy both lotteries and insurance. Lotteries bring in gains with extremely small probability and insurance covers low-chance losses. Then tendency to overweight small probabilities makes both lotteries and insurance appealing. A typical value function of prospect theory that reflects the idea of reference point and loss aversion is depicted in Figure 8. Probability weighting is depicted in Figure 9.

Let $v(\cdot)$ denote the value function for outcomes under prospect theory. We normalize the reference to be 0. Suppose that a prospect yields income x with probability p and income y with probability q, where $p+q=1$. The utility function defined on the prospect can be written as

$$U(x,p;y,q) = \begin{cases} w(p)v(x) + w(q)v(y) & x \geq 0 \geq y \text{ or } y \geq 0 \geq x \\ v(y) + w(p)[v(x) - v(y)] & x > y > 0 \text{ or } x < y < 0, \end{cases} \quad (18)$$

where $w(\cdot)$ is a probability weighting function. In applications (e.g., Liu 2013), one can set

$$w(p) = \exp[-(-\ln p)^{\alpha}] \text{ and} \quad (19)$$

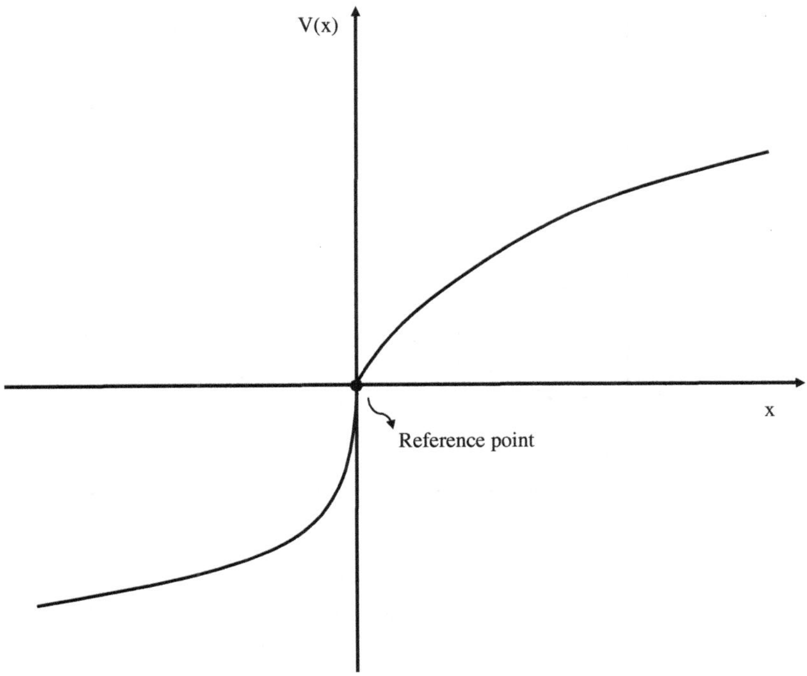

Figure 8. Value function of prospect theory.

$$v(x) = \begin{cases} x^{1-\sigma} & \text{for } x > 0 \\ 0 & \text{for } x = 0 \\ -\lambda(-x)^{1-\sigma} & \text{for } x < 0, \end{cases} \tag{20}$$

where $\alpha > 0$ is a probability weighting measure, $\lambda > 0$ is the loss aversion parameter, and $\sigma \leq 1$ is the risk aversion parameter. When $\alpha \in (0, 1)$, the probability weighting curve, $w(p)$, is inverted S-shaped (see Figure 9). When $\lambda > 1$ (respectively, $\lambda = 1$ or $\lambda \in (0, 1)$), the decision maker is loss averse (respectively, loss neutral or loss loving). Finally, when $\sigma < 0$ (respectively, $\sigma = 0$ or $\sigma \in (0, 1)$), the decision maker is risk loving (respectively, risk neutral or risk-averse).

The original prospect theory was further modified by Tversky and Kahneman (1992) to accommodate prospects with more than two outcomes and to avoid some implausible predictions (Barberis, 2013). The new version of prospect theory was called

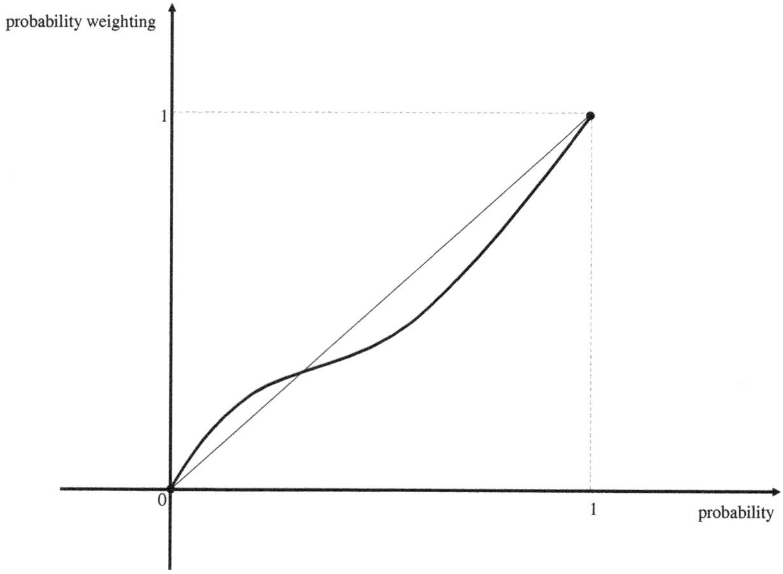

Figure 9. Probability weighting function of prospect theory.

"cumulative prospect theory," where probability weights were assigned to cumulative probabilities instead of probabilities of individual events. However, the feature of overweighting small (cumulative) probabilities and underweighting large (cumulative) probabilities remained in the new version. We now discuss cumulative prospect theory.

Suppose a prospect has $m + n$ possible outcomes, denoted by

$$(x_{-m}, q_{-m}; x_{-m+1}, q_{-m+1}; \ldots; x_{-1}, q_{-1}; x_1, q_1; \ldots; x_n, q_n),$$

where $m \geq 1$, $n \geq 1$, $x_i \leq x_j$ $\forall i \leq j$, and q_k is the probability of x_k occurring, $k \in \{-m, \ldots, -1, 1, \ldots, n\}$. Here we still assume that the reference point value is 0. Leaving the value function (20) unchanged, the probability weighting function under cumulative prospect theory is written as

$$\begin{cases} w^+(\phi_k) = \frac{\phi_k^\gamma}{(\phi_k^\gamma + (1-\phi_k)^\gamma)^{1/\gamma}} \text{ for gains} \\ w^-(\phi_k) = \frac{\phi_k^\delta}{(\phi_k^\delta + (1-\phi_k)^\delta)^{1/\delta}} \text{ for losses,} \end{cases} \tag{21}$$

where γ and δ are non-stochastic parameters, and ϕ_k is the cumulative probability of outcome x_k. This cumulative probability differs from the usual cumulative distribution function (CDF). If $x_k > 0$, then $\phi_k = \Pr\{x \geq x_k\}$ (i.e., probability of having a gain no less than x_k). If $x_k < 0$, then $\phi_k = \Pr\{x \leq x_k\}$ (i.e., probability of having a loss no less than x_k). One can check that $w^+(\phi_k)$ and $w^-(\phi_k)$ are both increasing in ϕ_k and with range $[0, 1]$. Particularly, $w^+(0) = w^-(0) = 0$ and $w^+(1) = w^-(1) = 1$. The decision weight assigned to outcome x_k is defined as

$$d_k = \begin{cases} w^+(q_n) & \text{if } k = n \\ w^+(\phi_k) - w^+(\phi_{k+1}) & \text{if } 1 \leq k < n \\ w^-(\phi_k) - w^-(\phi_{k-1}) & \text{if } -m < k \leq -1 \\ w^-(q_{-m}) & \text{if } k = -m. \end{cases} \tag{22}$$

Based on equations (20) and (22), the prospect's expected value is

$$\sum_{k=-m}^{n} d_k v(x_k). \tag{23}$$

The decision maker will choose prospect that generates the largest expected value based on Equation (23).

A strand of literature pertains to using experimental methods to elicit participants' risk and loss aversion parameters based on prospect theory. In the realm of agricultural economics and development economics, examples include Tanaka *et al.* (2010), Liu (2013), and Wilson and Miao (2023). These studies typically present three series of choice experiments between two options with actual monetary payments to participants (see Table 2 in Liu (2013) for an example). Within a series of choice experiments, researchers usually fix one option and increase the attractiveness of the other option. Here one choice experiment can be something like the following:

Option A	Option B
win \$20 with pr. 0.3 and \$5 with prob. 0.7	win \$40 with pr. 0.1 and \$3 with prob. 0.9

A series could include 7 to 14 choice experiments like this. The researchers record the chosen option in each choice experiment of each series. The switching point, the choice experiment where the participant switches their choices between Options A and B when compared with the immediate previous choice experiment is of critical importance as it reveals much information about a participant's preferences. Based on the choices made, the researcher can estimate a set of parameters (i.e., λ, σ, α) in Equations (19) and (20) for each participant. It is worth noting that the average values of λ, the loss aversion parameter, are around 2 across Tanaka *et al.* (2010), Liu (2013), and Wilson and Miao (2023), indicating that participants in their experiments are generally loss averse. Once the individual parameters about loss aversion, risk aversion, and probability weighting are obtained, one can associate participants' risk and loss preferences to some economic variables (e.g., household income, technology adoption decision, or willingness to pay for a food item) of the participants. For details about the experiment design and applications, we refer readers to Tanaka *et al.* (2010), Liu (2013), and Wilson and Miao (2023).

Although being able to offer more reasonable predictions than does expected utility theory for decision-making under risk, prospect theory, including its modified version (cumulative prospect theory), still have not replaced expected utility theory as a workhorse in modeling people's behaviors under risk. One obvious reason is that, as one can see, the weighting function and decision weight in Equations (21) and (22) are quite complex, which makes it almost impossible to obtain analytical solutions for a model built upon cumulative prospect theory. Anand *et al.* (2019) provide an example of using numerical simulation approach to analyze US farmers' bioenergy crop adoption decisions under a prospect theory framework. Another reason is that it is difficult for researchers to determine the reference point for a prospect theory model (Barberis, 2013). A common practice is to select multiple reference point for the model and examine the robustness of results to these reference points. Babcock (2015) provides an excellent example in this regard.

7. Decision-Making Under Ambiguity

When modeling decision-making under risk, we assume that decision makers know the probability distribution of prospect outcomes. This is a strong assumption and often unrealistic. For instance, it is difficult for farmers to come up with a precise distribution of net returns from adopting a new technology (e.g., advanced irrigation system, drought-tolerant seeds, or a new harvester), perhaps because the new technology in question may become obsolete at an unknown probability. When we relax this assumption (i.e., known probability distribution), we encounter decision-making under ambiguity. Uncertainty can be viewed as a combination of risk and ambiguity (Klibanoff *et al.*, 2005; Barham *et al.*, 2014). In what follows, we discuss some models that have been used to depict decision-making under ambiguity.

7.1. *MaxMin, MaxMax, and α-MaxMin models*

Let us start with the MaxMin model, which assumes that people are pessimistic when viewing probabilities of prospect outcomes. In other words, under this model, decision makers will always use the worst possible probability distribution to evaluate the prospect (i.e., Min) and then select the prospect with the highest minimum value (i.e., MaxMin). Suppose a decision maker is facing two options: Option A that provides a sure return at \$10, and Option B that provides a \$20 return with probability p and nothing with probability $1 - p$. However, the decision maker does not know the specific value of p. She only knows the range of p, which is $[\underline{p}, \bar{p}]$. Let $U(\cdot)$ denote the utility function of the decision maker. Under the MaxMin model, the decision maker's choice problem can be written as

$$\max\left\{\min_{p\in[\underline{p},\bar{p}]}\{pU(20) + (1-p)U(0)\}, \quad U(10)\right\}.$$

The decision maker will choose Option B if and only if $\min_{p\in[\underline{p},\bar{p}]}\{pU(20) + (1-p)U(0)\} \geq U(10)$.

Due to the underlying pessimism of the MaxMin model, it naturally reflects ambiguity aversion. In contrast, MaxMax assumes optimistic decision-makers, who always use the best possible probability distribution when evaluating a prospect. Continuing with the above example, the decision maker's choice problem under the MaxMax model can be written as

$$\max\left\{\max_{p\in[\underline{p},\bar{p}]}\{pU(20)+(1-p)U(0)\},\quad U(10)\right\}.$$

The decision maker will choose Option B if and only if $\max_{p\in[\underline{p},\bar{p}]}\{pU(20)+(1-p)U(0)\}\geq U(10)$. It is not surprising that the MaxMax model predicts ambiguity seeking behaviors.

The MaxMin model and the MaxMax model are two extremes, and none of them can accommodate both ambiguity averse and ambiguity seeking behaviors. A combination of the two models, termed $\alpha-$MaxMin model, overcomes this limitation. Continuing with the above example with Options A and B, we can write the $\alpha-$MaxMin model as

$$\begin{aligned} V_{\alpha\text{MaxMin}}(B) \equiv \alpha\cdot \min_{p\in[\underline{p},\bar{p}]}\{pU(20)+(1-p)U(0)\} \\ +(1-\alpha)\cdot \max_{p\in[\underline{p},\bar{p}]}\{pU(20)+(1-p)U(0)\}, \end{aligned} \tag{24}$$

where $\alpha\in[0,1]$ can be viewed as a weight assigned to the MaxMin model. Its value reflects the magnitude of ambiguity aversion of the decision maker. One can readily check that when $\alpha=1$, then the α-MaxMin model degenerates into the MaxMin model, and when $\alpha=0$, then the α-MaxMin model degenerates into the MaxMax model. Under the α-MaxMin model, the decision maker will choose Option B if and only if $V_{\alpha\text{MaxMin}}(B)\geq U(10)$. Dimmock *et al.* (2015) demonstrate that the α-MaxMin model can predict both ambiguity averse and seeking behaviors.

7.2. *Impact of partial insurance under ambiguity: A MaxMin model*

By using a MaxMin model, Bryan (2019) shows that partial insurance, whose indemnity payments are not directly related to a farmer's actual indemnity (e.g., rainfall index insurance), may hinder farmers' adoption of new crop varieties. Here we briefly summarize the model.

Suppose farmers in a region originally plant a traditional crop, from which they gain utility $V^T = \alpha + A + \epsilon_i$, where α is the average utility from growing the traditional crop, A is disutility caused by ambiguity aversion for ambiguity averse farmers, and ϵ_i is a uniformly distributed error term associated with each farmer i. Now, suppose that the local government or an organization promotes a modern crop variety. Their strategy is to offer rainfall index insurance to farmers who adopt the modern variety. Note that the utility of growing the traditional crop is not affected by the rainfall index insurance because the insurance is unavailable to farmers who grow the traditional crop.

Consider a rainfall index insurance policy that generates a *net* payment (i.e., indemnity payment minus premium) with value I when rainfall is low (i.e., rainfall state R_L) and costs the policyholder a premium with value P when rainfall is high (i.e., rainfall state R_H). Assume that only two crop yield stats exist: low yield, y_L, and high yield, y_H. Therefore, in total we have four states to consider in the model, namely, (y_H, R_H), (y_H, R_L), (y_L, R_H), and (y_L, R_L). Let λ_H and p_H denote the probability of high yield and high rainfall, respectively. The probability of high rainfall and low yield (i.e., state (y_L, R_H)) is denoted by q. Therefore, we can readily check that the probability of state (y_H, R_H) is $p_H - q$, (y_H, R_L) is $\lambda_H - p_H + q$, and (y_L, R_L) is $1 - \lambda_H - q$. We assume that the policyholder knows the exact values of λ_H and p_H and that she is uncertain about the value of q, just knowing that $q \in [\underline{q}, \bar{q}]$. Here the justification is that farmers have good sense about the chance of having high yield or high rainfall in a typical year; however, it is a bit difficult to have an accurate estimate about the chance of having a low yield in a high rainfall year. Also note that state (y_L, R_H) is the worst state to the policyholder because, under this state, she suffers from low yield but will not receive any indemnity payment.

If there is no rainfall index insurance at all, the expected utility from growing the modern crop variety is simply $V^M_{\text{NoInsu}} \equiv \lambda_H U(y_H) + (1 - \lambda_H)U(y_L)$, from which we can see that q does not appear in the expected utility. Farmers will adopt the modern crop variety if and only if $V^M_{\text{NoInsu}} \geq V^T$.

With the rainfall index insurance, for a given probability of state (y_L, R_H), q, and net payment under low rainfall state, I, the expected utility from growing the modern variety is

$$\begin{aligned} V^M_{\text{Insu}}(q, I) \equiv\ & qU(y_L - P) + (1 - \lambda_H - q)U(y_L + I) \\ & + (p_H - q)U(y_H - P) + (\lambda_H - p_H + q)U(y_H + I). \end{aligned}$$

Under the assumption that $U''(\cdot) < 0 < U'(\cdot)$ and $y_L < y_H$, one can readily check that $\partial V^M_{\text{Insu}}(q, I)/\partial q < 0$. This indicates that, with a MaxMin preference, a decision maker's expected utility from growing the modern crop variety is $V^M_{\text{Insu}}(\bar{q}, I)$ and she will adopt the modern crop variety if and only if

$$V^M_{\text{Insu}}(\bar{q}, I) \geq \alpha + A + \epsilon.$$

Bryan (2019) compares the impact of the rainfall index insurance on an ambiguity-averse farmer's incentive to adopt the modern crop variety and that on an ambiguity neutral farmer's. The ambiguity-neutral farmer is assumed to have a belief of q at $q^{\text{SEU}} \in [\underline{q}, \bar{q}]$, and hence her expected utility from growing the modern crop variety is $V^M_{\text{Insu}}(q^{\text{SEU}}, I)$. Clearly, because $\partial V^M_{\text{Insu}}(q, I)/\partial q < 0$, we have $V^M_{\text{Insu}}(\bar{q}, I) \leq V^M_{\text{Insu}}(q^{\text{SEU}}, I)$. Therefore, one can draw the conclusion that the impact of the rainfall index insurance on an ambiguity averse farmer's incentive to adopt the modern crop variety is smaller than that on an ambiguity neutral farmer's incentive (see Prediction 1 in Bryan, 2019).

One can further explore whether a mandatory rainfall index insurance will reduce ambiguity averse farmers' incentive to adopt the modern crop variety. Note that, unlike complete insurance, partial insurance, even if actuarially fair, may make policyholders worse off if the basis risk is high (e.g., q is large in the above example). This is because if the probability of high rainfall but low yield is large, then the policyholders will often not get indemnity payment when crop yield is low but still need to pay the insurance premium. Consequently, the rainfall index insurance is actually make the policyholder's farming returns riskier than the returns without insurance. Given the pessimistic nature of decision-makers under the MaxMin model, an ambiguity averse farmer's expected utility from growing the modern crop variety in the presence of rainfall index insurance may be lower than that from growing the modern variety in the *absence* of the insurance. Therefore, the rainfall index insurance may actually disincentivize the adoption of the new crop variety, even though its intent is to increase the adoption.

7.3. *Technology adoption under ambiguity: An α-MaxMin model*

As we have discussed in Section 7.1, the MaxMin model is inconsistent with ambiguity-seeking behaviors and the MaxMax model cannot accommodate ambiguity averse behaviors. The α-MaxMin model is a hybrid of the MaxMin and MaxMax models and can predict both risk averse and risk-seeking behaviors (Dimmock *et al.*, 2015). In this section, we present a simple α-MaxMin model in the context of technology adoption based on the model specification illustrated in Dimmock *et al.* (2015).

Suppose a farmer is facing two technologies: a traditional technology and a new technology. For simplicity, we assume that the traditional technology will provide a sure return at \$1,000. The new technology will provide a \$2,000 return with probability p and a \$800 return with probability $1-p$. Further assume that the farmer's utility function is $U(\cdot)$ such that $U'' < 0 < U'$. If probability p were known, the expected utility theory would predict the farmer's choice by comparing $U(1000)$ and $pU(2000) + (1 - p)U(800)$. When p is unknown to the farmer, however, the usual expected utility theory framework discussed in early sections in this chapter that is used to model decision-making under risk does not apply.

The α-MaxMin model offers a useful framework when p is unknown to the farmer. Define $C_\delta \equiv [(1-\delta)\pi, (1-\delta)\pi + \delta]$ as the prior probability distribution set for the farmer, where $\pi \in [0,1]$ is the reference probability for having the \$2000 return, and $\delta \in [0,1]$ is the perceived level of ambiguity (or, $1-\delta$ can be viewed as a degree of confidence in π). Under the α-MaxMin model, a farmer with prior probability distribution set C_δ will evaluate the new technology as

$$V(\text{NewTech}) = \alpha \cdot \min_{p \in C_\delta} \{pU(2000) + (1-p)U(800)\} + (1-\alpha) \cdot \max_{p \in C_\delta} \{pU(2000) + (1-p)U(800)\}. \quad (25)$$

The farmer will then compare $V(\text{NewTech})$ with $U(1000)$ (the utility from the traditional technology) and make technology adoption decisions. One can readily check that, when $\delta = 0$ (i.e., no perceived ambiguity), the prior distribution set $C_\delta = \pi$ and the α-MaxMin model in Equation (25) degenerates into an expected utility theory model under risk: $V(\text{NewTech})|_{\delta=0} = pU(2000) + (1-p)U(800)$.

One challenge of applying the α-MaxMin model is parameterization (i.e., obtaining values for α, δ, and π). Dimmock *et al.* (2015) present an experimental approach to elicit and estimate people's ambiguity aversion parameter (i.e., α) and ambiguity perception parameter (i.e., δ). The approach has been applied by Mitra *et al.* (2023) to studying the roles of date labels in determining food waste. Based on a representative sample of U.S. population, Dimmock *et al.* (2015) estimate that the values of α and δ are about 0.56 and 0.4, respectively. Certainly, the values of the two parameters would vary across sub-samples of the population and specific prospects in question. Particularly, similar to determining the reference point in prospect theory, the reference probability value in the α-MaxMin model highly depends on decision-makers' experience and decision-making context for each research project. There is no unique "correct" value for π. Thus, we may want to examine the sensitivity of α-MaxMin model results to the values of π.

7.4. *Technology adoption under ambiguity: A different approach*

Sometimes, the decision environment involves both risk and ambiguity. Barham *et al.* (2014) define this combination of risk and ambiguity as "uncertainty" and present a model that can be used to differentiate the roles of risk and ambiguity. In this section, we present a simplified version of this model.

Let us continue with the previous example of technology adoption. However, we will add a slight twist: Instead of assuming a prior probability distribution set as under the α-MaxMin model, here we assume that p, the probability of \$2,000 occurring, is random and has cumulative distribution function $F(p)$. In addition to the von Neumann–Morgenstern utility function $U(\cdot)$, the model introduces ambiguity preference function $h(\cdot)$ with $h' > 0 > h''$.[3] The model evaluates the new technology as

$$W(\text{NewTech}) \equiv E_p\left[h(pU(2000) + (1-p)U(800))\right]. \qquad (26)$$

By comparing the values of $W(\text{NewTech})$ and $h(U(1000))$, the model can predict the decision maker's choice between the new and old technologies.

Following the idea of certainty equivalence, Barham *et al.* (2014) define uncertainty premium and decompose it into risk premium and ambiguity premium. First, one calculates the *ex ante* mean return of new technology as $M(\text{NewTech}) \equiv E_p[p \cdot 2000 + (1-p) \cdot 800]$. The uncertainty premium is then define as a fixed amount of returns R such that

$$W(\text{NewTech}) = h(U(M(\text{NewTech}) - R)), \qquad (27)$$

where $W(\text{NewTech})$ is defined in equation (26). Intuitively, the uncertainty premium R can be viewed as the decision maker's

[3]Klibanoff *et al.* (2005) show that when the curvature of $h(\cdot)$ is large enough, then the model reduces to the MaxMin model.

willingness to pay to exchange the uncertain returns from the new technology with the certain, mean payment M(NewTech).

Second, one identifies the ambiguity premium, R_a. Let μ_p be the mean value of p, i.e., $\mu_p = \int_0^1 pdF(p)$. Then R_a is a fixed amount of returns such that

$$W(\text{NewTech}) = h(\mu_p U(2000 - R_a) + (1 - \mu_p)U(800 - R_a)), \quad (28)$$

where W(NewTech) is defined in equation (26). Intuitively, the ambiguity premium R_a can be understood as the decision maker's willingness to pay to eliminate the ambiguity of p and to fix the p value at μ_p. The risk premium is defined as $R_r \equiv R - R_a$. Therefore, Equation (27) can be rewritten as

$$W(\text{NewTech}) = h(U(M(\text{NewTech}) - R_a - R_r)), \quad (29)$$

from which we can see that for prospects with the same *ex ante* mean returns and risk premium, the ones with smaller ambiguity premium (R_a) provide the farmer with higher expected utility. Based on field experiments and survey data collected in Minnesota and Wisconsin, Barham *et al.* (2014) find that ambiguity aversion promotes the adoption of genetically modified (GM) corn. They argue that GM corn reduces return ambiguity due to their insect-resistance trait.

One can see that the model in Barham *et al.* (2014) interpret ambiguity as "risk of risk," assigning a (known) probability distribution to the distribution of prospect returns. The MaxMin and MaxMax models can be viewed as special cases of the Barham *et al.* (2014) model, where the MaxMin model assigns probability 1 to the worst probability distribution and the MaxMax model assigns probability 1 to the best probability distribution.

8. Conclusion

Risk is crucial in agricultural production and marketing. Research on risk is work in progress and it is critical for policy design (e.g., crop insurance and investment incentives) and policy welfare analysis. In this chapter, we have reviewed some common tools to measure and model risks in agriculture, as well as to estimate risk parameters.

These tools are important for developing risk management policies and for future research work on risk. Traditional risk analysis based on rational and standard neoclassical models fails to predict people's behaviors under risk and uncertainty in many occasions. New insights from behavioral economics (e.g., loss aversion and decision-making under ambiguity) should be incorporated when modeling policy and developing analytical tools (Wuepper *et al.* 2023).

References

Anand, M., R. Miao, and M. Khanna. 2019. Adopting Bioenergy Crops: Does Farmers' Attitude toward Loss Matter? *Agricultural Economics* 50(4): 435–450.

Arrow, K. J. 1971. *Essays in the Theory of Risk Bearing*, Chapter 3 (pp. 90–133). Chicago: Markham Publishing Company.

Babcock, B. 2015. Using Cumulative Prospect Theory to Explain Anomalous Crop Insurance Coverage Choice. *American Journal of Agricultural Economics* 97(5): 1371–1384.

Bar-Shira, Ziv. 1992. Nonparametric Test of the Expected Utility Hypothesis. *American Journal of Agricultural Economics* 74(3): 523–533.

Barham, B. L., C. Jean-Paul, D. Fitz, Vanessa Ríos Salas, and L. Schechter. 2014. The Roles of Risk and Ambiguity in Technology Adoption. *Journal of Economic Behavior & Organization* 97: 204–218.

Barberis, N. C. 2013. Thirty Years of Prospect Theory in Economics: A Review and Assessment. *Journal of Economic Perspectives*, 27(1): 173–96.

Batra, R. N. and A. Ullah. 1974. Competitive Firm and the Theory of Input Demand under Price Uncertainty. *Journal of Political Economy* 82(3): 537–548.

Binswanger, H. P. 1980. Attitudes Toward Risk: Experimental Measurement in Rural India. *American Journal of Agricultural Economics* 62(3): 395–407.

Bocquého, G., Jacquet, F., and Reynaud, A. 2015. Adoption of Perennial Crops and Behavioral Risk Preferences. An Empirical Investigation among French Farmers. Paper presented in the "Risk and Environment" Session at Journées de Recherche en Sciences Sociales, SFER, Nancy, France. December 11–12.

Bryan, G. 2019. Ambiguity Aversion Decreases the Impact of Partial Insurance: Evidence from African Farmers. *Journal of the European Economic Association* 17(5): 1428–1469.

Buschena, D. E. and D. Zilberman. 1999. Testing the Effects of Similarity on Risky Choice: Implications for Violations of Expected Utility. *Theory and Decision Volume* 46(3): 253–280.

Chalfant, J. A., R. N. Collender, and S. Subramanian. 1990. The Mean and Variance of the Mean-Variance Decision Rule. *American Journal of Agricultural Economics* 72(4): 966–974.

Chavas, J. 1993. The Ricardian Rent and the Allocation of Land Under Uncertainty. *European Review of Agricultural Economics* 20(4): 451–469.

Chavas, J. 2004. *Risk Analysis in Theory and Practice.* Elsevier Academic Press, San Diego, California.

Day, R. H. 1965. Probability Distributions of Field Crop Yields. *American Journal of Agricultural Economics* 47(3): 713–741.

Dimmock, S. G., R. Kouwenberg, O. S. Mitchell, and K. Peijnenburg. 2015. Estimating Ambiguity Preferences and Perceptions in Multiple Prior Models: Evidence from the Field. *Journal of Risk and Uncertainty* 51(3): 219–244.

Feder, G. 1977. The Impact of Uncertainty in a Class of Objective Functions. *Journal of Economic Theory* 16(2): 504–512.

Feder, G. 1980. Farm Size, Risk Aversion and the Adoption of New Technology under Uncertainty. *Oxford Economic Papers* 32(2): 263–283.

Feder, G., R. E. Just, and A. Schmitz. 1980. Futures Markets and the Theory of the Firm under Price Uncertainty. *The Quarterly Journal of Economics* 94(2): 317–328.

Fishburn, P. C. 1983. Transitive Measurable Utility. *Journal of Economic Theory* 31(2): 293–317.

Freund, R. J. 1956. The Introduction of Risk into a Programming Model. *Econometrica* 24(3): 253–263.

Friedman, M. and L. J. Savage. 1948. The Utility Analysis of Choices Involving Risk. *Journal of Political Economy* 56(4): 279–304.

Hadar, J. and W. R. Russell. 1969. Rules for Ordering Uncertain Prospects. *The American Economic Review* 59(1): 25–34.

Just, R. E. and D. Zilberman. 1983. Stochastic Structure, Farm Size and Technology Adoption in Developing Agriculture. *Oxford Economic Papers* 35(2): 307–328.

Just, R. E. and R. D. Pope. 1978. Stochastic Specification of Production Functions and Economic Implications. *Journal of Econometrics* 7(1): 67–86.

Kahneman, D. and A. Tversky. 1979. Prospect Theory: An Analysis of Decision under Risk. *Econometrica* 47(2): 263–291.

Kataoka, S. 1963. A Stochastic Programming Model. *Econometrica* 31(1/2): 181–196.

Klibanoff, P., M. Marinacci, S. Mukerji. 2005. A Smooth Model of Decision Making Under Ambiguity. *Econometrica* 73(6): 1849–1892.

Leland, J. W. 1994. Generalized Similarity Judgments: An Alternative Explanation for Choice Anomalies. *Journal of Risk and Uncertainty* 9(2): 151–172.

Liu, E. 2013. Time to Change What to Sow: Risk Preferences and Technology Adoption Decisions of Cotton Farmers in China. *The Review of Economics and Statistics*, 95(4), 1386–1403.

Machina, M. J. 1982. "Expected Utility" Analysis Without the Independence Axiom. *Econometrica* 50(2): 227–323.

Markowitz, H. 1959. *Portfolio Section*, New York: Wiley.

Marra, M. C. and G. A. Carlson. 1990. The Decision to Double Crop: An Application of Expected Utility Theory Using Stein's Theorem. *American Journal of Agricultural Economics* 72(2): 337–345.

Marschak, J. 1950. Rational Behavior, Uncertain Prospects, and Measurable Utility. *Econometrica* 18(2): 111–141.

Miao, R. and M. Khanna. 2017. Costs of Meeting a Cellulosic Biofuel Mandate with Perennial Energy Crops: Implications for Policy. *Energy Economics* 64: 321–334.

Mitra, P., R. Miao, and N. L. W. Wilson. 2023. Ambiguity, Date Labels, and Food Waste. *Working paper.* Department of Agricultural Economics and Rural Sociology, Auburn University.

Pratt, J. W. Risk Aversion in the Small and in the Large. *Econometrica* 32(1/2): 122–136.

Quiggin, J. 1982. A Theory of Anticipated Utility. *Journal of Economic Behavior and Organization* 3(4): 323–343.

Rothschild, M. and J. E. Stiglitz. 1970. Increasing Risk: I. A Definition. *Journal of Economic Theory* 2(3): 225–243.

Roy, A. D. 1952. Safety First and the Holding of Assets. *Econometrica* 20(3): 431–449.

Rubinstein, A. 1988. Similarity and Decision Making Under Risk: Is there a Utility Theory Resolution to the Allais Paradox? *Journal of Economic Theory* 46(1): 145–153.

Saha, A. 1993. Expo-Power Utility: A 'Flexible' Form for Absolute and Relative Risk Aversion. *American Journal of Agricultural Economics* 75(4): 905–913.

Sandmo, A. 1971. On the Theory of the Competitive Firm under Price Uncertainty. *American Economic Review* 61(1): 65–73.

Tanaka, T., C. F. Camerer, and Q. Nguyen. 2010. Risk and Time Preferences: Linking Experimental and Household Survey Data from Vietnam. *American Economic Review*, 100(1): 557–571.

Telser, L. G. 1955. Safety First and Hedging. *The Review of Economic Studies* 23(1): 1–16.

Tobin, J. E. 1958. Liquidity Preference as Behaviour towards Risk. *Review of Economic Studies* 25(2): 65–86.

Tversky, A. and D. Kahneman. 1992. Advances in Prospect Theory: Cumulative Representation of Uncertainty. *Journal of Risk and Uncertainty* 5(4): 297–323.

von Neumann, J. and O. Morgenstern. 1944. *Theory of Games and Economic Behavior.* Princeton University Press, Princeton, New Jersey.

Wuepper, D., S. Bukchin-Peles, D. Just, D. Zilberman. 2023. Behavioral Agricultural Economics. *Applied Economic Perspectives and Policy* 45(4): 2094–2105, https://doi.org/10.1002/aepp.13343.

Whitmore, G. A. and M. C. Findlay. 1978. *Stochastic Dominance: An Approach to Decision-Making under Risk.* Lexington Books, D.C. Heath and Co., Lexington, MA.

Wilson, N. L. W. and R. Miao. in press. Food Waste, Date Labels, and Lost Aversion: An Experimental Exploration. *Applied Economic Perspectives and Policy.* doi: https://doi.org/10.1002/aepp.13507

Yassour, J., D. Zilberman, and G. C. Rausser. 1981. Optimal Choices among Alternative Technologies with Stochastic Yield. *American Journal of Agricultural Economics* 63(4): 718–723.

Chapter 5

Welfare Analysis of Agricultural Policies

Once an economic policy is implemented, it has the potential to create a large impact on a society through affecting the decisions of consumers and producers in the economy. One way to quantify the policy impact is to conduct welfare analysis, whereby the policy impact on consumers, producers, and government is examined, and the efficiency of resource allocation is evaluated. The net welfare impact of a policy in question is the sum of the welfare impact on these three economic entities. Due to the prevalence of agricultural policies (e.g., price support, acreage control, risk management interventions, and input use regulations) in the United States and many other countries, agricultural economics research has a long tradition to conduct welfare analysis. In this chapter, we first outline the basics of welfare analysis of some common agricultural policies and then discuss a few advanced applications pertaining to some major agricultural policies in the United States, such as price support, input regulations, crop insurance, and biofuel policies. For a comprehensive treatment of welfare analysis, we refer readers to Just *et al.* (2004). Atkinson (2011) makes an appealing argument that economists should resume their focus on welfare analysis in teaching and research.

1. Basic Welfare Analysis

Two groups of participants are essential for almost any markets of goods: consumers and suppliers. We use the demand curve to measure consumers' willingness to pay (WTP) for a specific good (e.g., corn) and the supply curve to measure suppliers' willingness to sell (WTS) of such a good. WTP of a consumer for a good is the maximum price under which this consumer would buy, and WTS of a supplier is the minimum price under which this supplier would sell. Imagine that we have numerous consumers and suppliers in a market with a range of WTP and WTS values. By plotting out these WTP and WTS values we obtain the demand and supply curves of this market. Based on these two curves we can construct consumer surplus and producer surplus, two key concepts in welfare analysis. Consumer surplus is defined as the area below the demand curve but above a price paid by consumers (i.e., the aggregate of the difference between price paid and WTP across all consumers), whereas producer surplus is defined as the area above the supply curve but below the price received by the producer (i.e., the aggregate of the difference between price received and WTS across all suppliers).

Government may often intervene the market as another important player. With various policies, government intervention alters consumer and producer surplus, creating government revenue or expenditure. The total social welfare is the sum of consumer surplus, producer surplus, and government revenue (or negative expenditure).

Figure 1 provides an example of the definition of consumer surplus and producer surplus. Without policy intervention in the market, the demand curve and supply curves intersect at point (Q^*, P^*) where the market clears. In this case, the consumer surplus is area $a + b + d$ and the producer surplus is area $c + e + l$. The total social welfare is, therefore, $a + b + c + d + e + l$. Government policies that causes the market to deviate from (Q^*, P^*) will create social welfare losses (i.e., deadweight loss). Next, we will focus on some major agricultural policies and analyze their welfare impact.

In developed countries, governments often implement policies such as price support and supply controls. A price support sets a

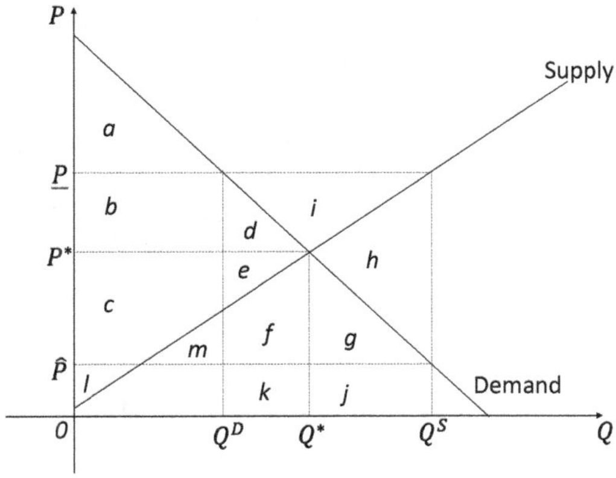

Figure 1. Welfare analysis of price support and quantitative restriction.

minimum price that is higher than the market equilibrium price so that producers' surplus can be increased. In contrast, supply controls aim to increase commodity prices by reducing the supply, thereby increasing producer surplus. In this section, we briefly discuss the welfare analysis of these two types of policies. In Section 2 we analyze crop insurance program's welfare impact. In Section 3 we explore welfare analysis of overlapped policies. Section 4 concludes.

1.1. *Price support*

The first price support programs in the United States were implemented during the Great Depression with the creation of the Commodity Credit Corporation (CCC). Although the specific price support programs evolved over time (e.g., from loan support to deficiency payment), the essence of these programs was to guarantee a minimum price for covered commodities. Intuitively, price support would increase the quantity supplied and decrease the quantity demanded in the market, and, therefore, would initiate a supply surplus in the market, which the federal government would purchase in the early period of the price support programs (e.g., loan support). However, due to the high costs of storage the government had to pay for the surplus, later the government shifted to deficiency payments wherein farmers sold their products at market prices but could get the price difference from the government if the market price is lower than the support price (i.e., deficiency payment).

We now show an example about the welfare analysis of price support. Suppose that Figure 1 depicts the supply and demand in corn market. When there is no policy intervention, the market equilibrium quantity and price are Q^* and P^*, respectively. The consumer surplus is area $a + b + d$, and the producer surplus is $c + e + l$. The total social welfare is,

$$S^0 = a + b + c + d + e + l. \tag{1}$$

Now the government introduces a price support program that sets the price of corn at $\underline{P}$ which is higher than P^*. Due to the increased price, the new quantity demanded Q^D is lower than the new quantity supplied Q^s (i.e., $Q^S > Q^D$), and the consumer surplus shrinks to area a. If the government purchases the overproduced quantity $Q^S - Q^D$ at price $\underline{P}$, then the producer surplus would become area $b+c+d+e+i+l$. The government outlay is area $d+e+f+g+h+i+j+k$. Therefore, the total social welfare under the price support program is

$$\begin{aligned} S^1 &= a+b+c+d+e+i+l-(d+e+f+g+h+i+j+k) \\ &= a+b+c+l-(f+g+h+j+k)\,. \end{aligned} \tag{2}$$

By comparing S^0 and S^1, we can see the deadweight loss of the price support policy is

$$S^0 - S^1 = d+e+f+g+h+j+k. \tag{3}$$

Note that the deadweight loss would remain the same regardless of whether the government purchases the overproduced quantity $(Q^S - Q^D)$. To illustrate, when the government does not purchase the overproduced quantity, the cost of overproduction falls on the producer, whose surplus is area $b + c + l - (f + g + h + j + k)$. The total social welfare is $S^{1'} = a + b + c + l - (f + g + h + j + k)$. By comparing S^0 and $S^{1'}$ we have

$$S^0 - S^{1'} = d+e+f+g+h+j+k, \tag{4}$$

which is the same as $S^0 - S^1$. When the government purchases overproduced quantity $Q^S - Q^D$, then the cost of overproduction falls on taxpayers, but the net total social welfare change is the same.

Let us now consider how the overproduction is disposed. If the government redistributes the purchased overproduction to consumers for free, then consumer surplus will increase by $d+e+f+g+j+k$, and the total social welfare change will be $-h$, the deadweight loss. Under deficiency payment, a more realistic scenario could be this: Knowing that the government will guarantee a price at $\underline{P}$, farmers will produce at quantity Q^S. The overproduction will drive market price down to $\hat{P}$. Farmers sell their commodity at price $\hat{P}$ in the market, and get price difference $\underline{P} - \hat{P}$ from the government. Therefore, with the deficiency payment, the consumer surplus will be the area below the demand curve but above price $\hat{P}$ (i.e., area $a + b + c + d + e + f + g + m$), the producer surplus will be the area above the supply curve but below price $\underline{P}$ (i.e., area $b + c + d + e + i + l$), and government expenditure will be $(\underline{P} - \hat{P})Q^S = b + c + d + e + f + g + h + i + m$. As opposed to the surpluses without any policy interventions, under deficiency payment consumer surplus increases by $c+e+f+g+m$, and producer surplus increases by $b+d+i$. Considering government expenditure, the change in total social welfare is still $-h$, the deadweight loss. This social welfare analysis under deficiency payment will be used in the next section when we discuss welfare analysis of overlapped policies.

1.2. *Supply controls*

Another policy instrument that can increase commodity price is quantitative restriction. Let us continue with Figure 1. Instead of setting a target price for corn, the government can set a maximum quantity of corn that can be produced, e.g., Q^D. In this case, the price of corn will be $\underline{P}$. The consumer surplus and producer surplus become area a and area $b + c + l$, respectively. Therefore, the total social welfare under the quantity restriction is

$$S^2 = a + b + c + l. \tag{5}$$

By comparing S^0 and S^2 we have

$$S^0 - S^2 = d + e. \tag{6}$$

However, in reality it is difficult to put an effective quantitative restriction as it is often politically challenged by both consumers and producers and motivates black market (think about Prohibition in the U.S.). An alternative way to implement supply controls is for the government to pay farmers to idle part of their land, which is often called set-aside programs. A prominent example is the Conservation Reserve Program in the United States, where the government pays an annual rent to have farmers keep their land out of crop production for 10–15 years. Figure 2 presents welfare effects of such set-aside programs. After the program is implemented, the supply curve will be shifted upward because for any given price, less land will be used for production and therefore less quantity will be produced. The consumer surplus will shift from area $a+b+c$ to area a, with the net loss equal to area $b+c$. The producer surplus will be changed from area $d+e$ to area $b+e$. Denote ΔG as the government outlay under the program. Now, the net total social welfare loss is $c+d+\Delta G$. However, the set-aside program often generates environmental benefits because keeping cropland out of production reduces fertilizer and pesticide uses which are some major pollutants nowadays. From this, with ΔE denoting environmental benefits from the set-aside

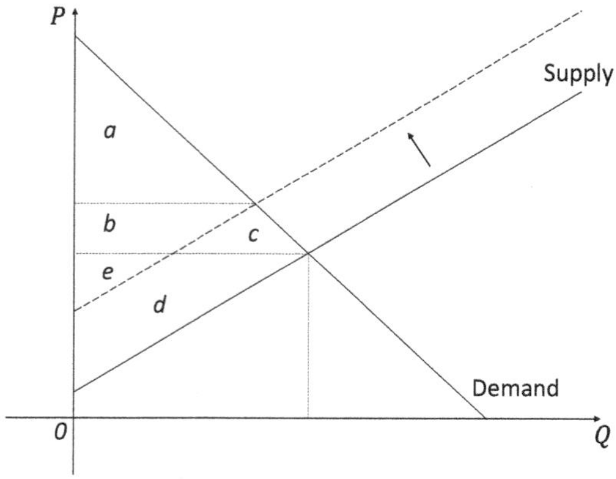

Figure 2. Welfare impact of set aside programs.

program, the net total social welfare loss caused by the set-aside program is $c + d + \Delta G - \Delta E$.

2. Crop Insurance

Since the passage of the Federal Crop Insurance Act (FCIA) of 1980, the federal crop insurance program has developed into a major pillar of agricultural policy in U.S. agriculture. Neo-classical economics predicts that a risk averse farmer would purchase crop insurance if it is actuarially fair, but crop insurance take-up rate had been low, even with a moderate premium subsidy rate (e.g., 30% of insurance premium) as specified in the FCIA of 1980. Later legislations further increased the take-up rate by significantly increasing premium subsidy levels. Whether or not the government should subsidize crop insurance has been debated by agricultural economists since 1980. We refer readers to the U.S. Government Accountability Office (USGAO) (2023), Coble and Barnett (2013), and Goodwin and Smith (2013) for further discussions about premium subsidies.

In this section, we discuss the welfare impact of crop insurance and of its associated policy (namely, premium subsidy), by following a framework documented in Chetty and Finkelstein (2013). Assume that there is a continuum of farmers that differ from each other in terms of unobserved characteristics, ϵ. Let $G(\epsilon)$ denote the cumulative distribution function of ϵ. Assume that all farmers are facing one type of crop insurance with premium p and are considering whether or not they will purchase the insurance. Denote the expected utility of farmer i with crop insurance by $u^1(\epsilon_i, p)$, and without insurance by $u^0(\epsilon_i)$. Farmer i will purchase the insurance if and only if $u^1(\epsilon_i, p) \geq u^0(\epsilon_i)$. Define $\pi(\epsilon_i)$ as the maximum willingness to pay of farmer i for crop insurance, i.e., $\pi(\epsilon_i) \equiv \max\left\{p : u^1(\epsilon_i, p) \geq u^0(\epsilon_i)\right\}$. The demand for crop insurance can be written as,

$$D(p) = \int 1\left(\pi(\epsilon) \geq p\right) dG(\epsilon), \tag{7}$$

where $1(\cdot)$ is an indicator function.

Here we further assume that the cost of providing crop insurance only includes the expected indemnity payment to farmers. In other words, there is no cost to administrate the insurance program (i.e., no loading factors). Denote the expected indemnity payment for farmer i by $c(\epsilon_i)$. Therefore, the average cost and marginal cost of the insurance program are

$$AC(p) = \frac{1}{D(p)} \int c(\epsilon) 1\left(\pi(\epsilon) \geq p\right) dG(\epsilon) = E\left(c(\epsilon) \mid \pi(\epsilon) \geq p\right), \text{ and} \tag{8}$$

$$MC(p) = E(c(\epsilon) \mid \pi(\epsilon) = p), \tag{9}$$

where $E(\cdot)$ is the expectation operator. Chetty and Finkelstein (2013) further assume that the marginal cost curve and the demand curve intersect no more than once, which guarantees the existence and uniqueness of the insurance market equilibrium.

Due to adverse selection, the marginal cost curve of providing crop insurance is downward sloping: farmers who expect to have larger indemnity payment (i.e., cost for insurance providers) will be more willing to pay for the insurance. Furthermore, the downward sloping marginal curve implies a downward sloping average cost curve. Figure 3 depicts curves of demand, average cost, and marginal cost associated with this insurance contract. Because the risk factor ϵ_i is unobservable to the insurer, the insurer cannot charge a differentiated price based on the risk factor, they can only charge a

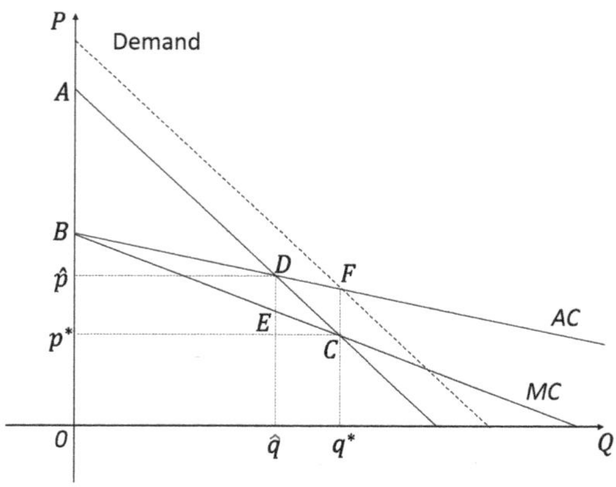

Figure 3. Adverse selection in crop insurance market.
Source: Adapted from Figure 2 in Chetty and Finkelstein (2013).

uniform price to all buyers of this insurance contract. In the insurance market, the competitive equilibrium is reached at $(\hat{q}, \hat{p})$, where the average cost curve intersects the demand curve (see Figure 3). It is readily checked that, assuming no loading factors, the insurer's profit is zero in the competitive equilibrium.

Following Chetty and Finkelstein (2013), we use certainty equivalence to measure welfare. Recall that certainty equivalence of a random return is a sure payment that equates the utility from this sure payment with the expected utility from the random return. Let $e^1(\epsilon_i)$ and $e^0(\epsilon_i)$ be the certainty equivalence of farmer i's returns with and without crop insurance, respectively. Specifically, if we assume that farmers' utility function is $U(\cdot)$, then we have $U(e^1(\epsilon_i)) = u^1(\epsilon_i, p)$ and $U(e^0(\epsilon_i)) = u^0(\epsilon_i)$. The willingness to pay for crop insurance is then $\pi(\epsilon_i) = e^1(\epsilon_i) - e^0(\epsilon_i)$. For risk averse farmers, we expect that $\pi(\epsilon_i) > 0$. According to Chetty and Finkelstein (2013), the consumer surplus, producer surplus, and total social welfare in the presence of crop insurance can be written as,

$$CS = \int \left[\left(e^1(\epsilon) - p\right) 1\left(\pi(\epsilon) \geq p\right) + e^0(\epsilon) 1\left(\pi(\epsilon) < p\right) \right] dG(\epsilon), \quad (10)$$

$$PS = \int \left(p - c(\epsilon)\right) 1\left(\pi(\epsilon) \geq p\right) dG(\epsilon), \text{ and} \quad (11)$$

$$\begin{aligned} TS &= CS + PS \\ &= \int \left[\left(e^1(\epsilon) - c(\epsilon)\right) 1\left(\pi(\epsilon) \geq p\right) + e^0(\epsilon) 1\left(\pi(\epsilon) < p\right) \right] dG(\epsilon). \end{aligned} \quad (12)$$

Notice that in the absence of crop insurance, farmers' welfare is simply $\int e^0(\epsilon) dG(\epsilon)$. For farmers, the welfare increase due to crop insurance is $CS - \int e^0(\epsilon) dG(\epsilon)$.

Moreover, based on Equation (12), to maximize total social welfare, each farmer who has the willingness to pay for the insurance larger than the insurance cost (i.e., expected indemnity payment) should purchase the insurance. In Figure 3, the market equilibrium is reached at $(\hat{q}, \hat{p})$, point D, where the marginal farmer's willingness to pay is equal to the average insurance cost. However, the efficient equilibrium should be at point C (i.e., (q^*, p^*)) where the marginal farmer's willingness to pay is equal to the marginal cost of providing the insurance. We can see that the total social welfare under crop insurance outcome ($\hat{q}$, $\hat{p}$) and (q^*, p^*) are area *ADEB* and area *ABC*, respectively. Clearly, the welfare loss due to adverse selection is area *CDE*.

Policy instruments can be implemented to reduce this welfare loss. One approach is to simply set insurance premium at p^* via government regulation. Because p^* is lower than $\hat{p}$, setting the premium at p^* will increase the quantity demanded for the insurance to q^*, reaching the efficient equilibrium. In the case that the total farmer population is smaller than q^*, the government can also mandate that all farmers purchase crop insurance.[1] Another policy instrument that is most common in the case of crop insurance is premium subsidy. Nowadays the U.S. federal government covers about 65% of the crop insurance premium. Figure 3 shows that a premium subsidy shifts insurance demand curve upward. If the shifted demand curve intersects the average cost curve at point F, then the insurance program can reach its efficient outcome (q^*, p^*). Because subsidizing premium requires government expenditure, whether or not premium subsidy will generate net welfare gains is an empirical question. A recent working paper by Yu *et al.* (2023) examines the welfare impact of premium subsidies in the context of U.S. crop insurance. Its findings suggest that the current subsidy rate is higher than the social optimal rate.

3. Welfare Analysis of Overlapped Policies

The welfare analyses above implicitly assume that the market is in competitive equilibrium before the policy instrument in question is implemented. However, in reality, it is often the case that one policy instrument is implemented in the presence of some other

[1]Note that if all farmers are risk averse and if there are no loading factors, the marginal cost curve will be always below the demand curve. That is, the expected indemnity payment is always smaller than the willingness to pay for the insurance. In this case, (q^*, p^*), the intersect point of the marginal cost curve and the demand curve, does not exist (see Figure 2 in Chetty and Finkelstein (2013)).

existing policies. This is particularly true for U.S. agriculture because various policy instruments had been introduced in the 20th century. New instruments often have to take previous policies as "given" and cannot do anything to those pre-existing policies. As a result, Lichtenberg and Zilberman (1986) argue that policymakers are often "policy takers". For instance, although the EPA can regulate pesticide uses, it has no legislative power on the deficiency payment that may have affected pesticide uses in the first place. Therefore, EPA's regulation on pesticide use has to take place in the presence of the deficiency payment, instead of a *laissez-fair* market. As to be discussed in this section, ignoring the existence of other relevant policies when conducting the welfare analysis of a policy instrument may result in biased conclusions.

3.1. *Production regulation in the presence of deficiency payment*

Lichtenberg and Zilberman (1986) analyze the potential biases of welfare analysis when ignoring co-existing policies by using production regulation in the presence of deficiency payment as an example. The production regulation in question can be restrictions on pesticide use, fertilizer use, or uses of genetically engineered seeds, which is expected to reduce supply if implemented.

Figure 4 is used to illustrate the conceptual framework developed in Lichtenberg and Zilberman (1986). In this figure, the demand curve is denoted by the downward sloping line D, and the true supply curve before the implementation of the production regulation is labeled as S_1. Due to the existence of deficiency payment with target price P_T, without the production regulation, the quantity supplied is Q_1, price paid by consumers is P_1, and the effective price received by farmers is P_T. Let CS^0, PS^0, and G^0 denote consumer surplus, producer surplus, and government expenditure *without* production regulation. Then we have

$$CS^0 = \Delta ACP_1,\ PS^0 = \Delta P_T DG,\ \text{and}\ G^0 = P_T DCP_1. \tag{13}$$

With production regulation, the supply curve will shift to S_2. Due to the deficiency payment, the quantity supplied will become Q_2.

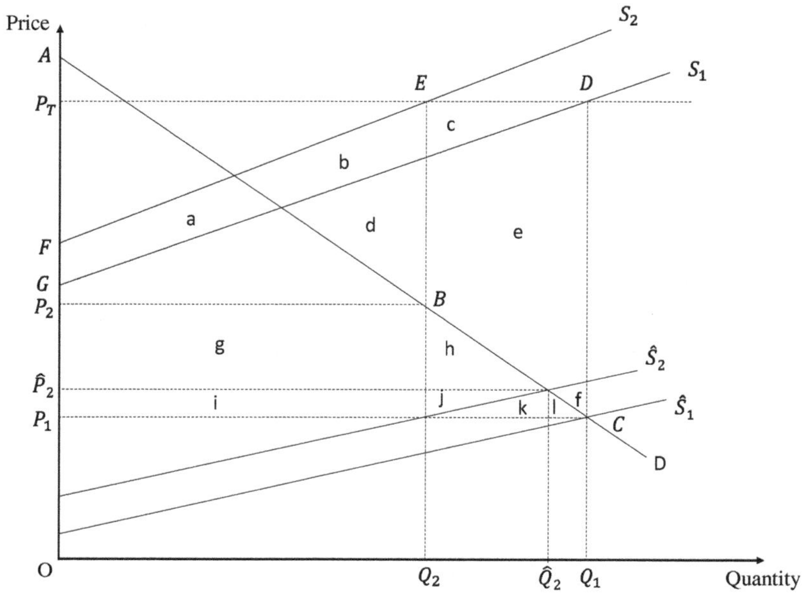

Figure 4. Welfare impacts of regulation in the presence of price support.
Source: Reproduced from Lichtenberg and Zilberman (1986). Permission obtained from the authors and the American Economic Association.

Because the demand curve is unaffected, price paid by consumers becomes P_2. The effective price received by farmers is still at P_T. Let CS^1, PS^1, and G^1 denote consumer surplus, producer surplus, and government expenditure *with* production regulation. Then we have

$$CS^1 = \Delta ABP_2, \; PS^1 = \Delta P_T EF, \text{ and } G^1 = P_T EBP_2. \tag{14}$$

By comparing Equations (13) and (14), we can obtain the welfare changes of consumers and producers, as well as changes in government expenditure. Specifically,

$$\Delta CS = CS^1 - CS^0 = \Delta ABP_2 - \Delta ACP_1$$
$$= -(g + h + i + j + k + l), \tag{15}$$
$$\Delta PS = PS^1 - PS^0 = \Delta P_T EF - \Delta P_T DG = -(a + b + c) \tag{16}$$
$$\Delta G = G^1 - G^0 = P_T EBP_2 - P_T DCP_1$$
$$= -(c + e + f + g + h + i + j + k + l). \tag{17}$$

From Equation (17) we can see that a portion of government expenditure reduction is represented by consumer surplus decrease, $-(g + h + i + j + k + l)$. Another portion is represented by the loss in producer surplus, $-c$. These transfers do not affect total social welfare, and the total welfare change caused by the production regulation is therefore,

$$\Delta TS = \Delta CS + \Delta PS - \Delta G = e + f - a - b. \tag{18}$$

Following Harberger (1971), Lichtenberg and Zilberman (1986) decomposed $e + f - a - b$ into two components. The first component is $-a$, which is interpreted as the net social welfare loss caused by the production regulation when deficiency payment does not exist. The second component is $e + f - b$, which is the reduction in deadweight loss when supply shifts from S_1 to S_2 while hold the deficiency payment policy unchanged. Note that following the discussion in Section 1.1 of this chapter, we know that the deadweight loss caused by the deficiency payment is $d + e + f$ when supply is S_1 and is $b + d$ when supply is S_2. Therefore, the change in deadweight loss when supply shifts from S_1 to S_2 is $(d + e + f) - (b + d) = e + f - b$. In sum, the net social welfare change caused by the production regulation in the presence of deficiency payment is $e + f - a - b$.

The discussion above shows that, in the presence of price support, P_T, the production regulation has negative impact on producer surplus. However, for consumers, due to their dual role as consumers and taxpayers, the net effect of the production regulation on them is positive (i.e., savings in government expenditure is larger than consumer surplus reduction). Without price support, the same production regulation is likely to have net negative impact on consumers (i.e., reducing consumer surplus without savings in government expenditure) but perhaps negligible or even positive impact on producer surplus because of low elasticities of demand for agricultural commodities. Therefore, Lichtenberg and Zilberman (1986) conclude that price supports are "to strengthen producers' opposition to and consumers' support for regulation."

What if price supports are ignored when conducting the welfare analysis of production regulation? Lichtenberg and Zilberman (1986) illustrate that the consequence is a biased welfare estimate of the regulation. They argue that if price supports are ignored, then the supply curve will likely be estimated at $\hat{S}_1$ instead of at S_1 because the commodity is traded at quantity Q_1 and price P_1 in the market. Suppose that the regulation will shift the supply curve from $\hat{S}_1$ to $\hat{S}_2$, and that the production regulation in question has the same effect on the supply curve with and without considering price support (i.e., $\hat{S}_2 - \hat{S}_1 = S_2 - S_1$). Figure 4 shows that when supply curve shifts from $\hat{S}_1$ to $\hat{S}_2$, consumer surplus will reduce by area $i + j + k + l$. From Equation (15), we can see that the true consumer surplus change is $-(g + h + i + j + k + l)$. Therefore, ignoring price support will underestimate consumer surplus reduction by $g + h$. Similarly, assuming that all supply curves in Figure 4 are parallel, it will underestimate producer surplus reduction by area $i + j$. Moreover, ignoring price support overlooks savings in government expenditure (i.e., $c+e+f+g+h+i+j+k+l$), and overestimates net social welfare losses of production regulation by $c + e + f + k + l$ when compared with the approach without ignoring price support. When calibrated using U.S. corn, cotton, and rice data, Lichtenberg and Zilberman (1986) find that the overestimation can be as high as 30%–50%, thus conclude that welfare analysis of production regulation ignoring price support will "be biased against regulation" (Lichtenberg and Zilberman, 1986).

Lichtenberg and Zilberman (1986) provide a classic example of welfare analysis in the presence of an overlapped policy instrument. In the next subsection we discuss one example that uses their approach to analyze the welfare effect of biofuel tax credit.

3.2. *Welfare effect of biofuel tax credit in the presence of deficiency payment*

The ethanol boom over the last two decades in the United States gave rise to a great deal of research on the economics of ethanol and biofuels in general. By using around one third of corn grain produced in the U.S., ethanol production links the gasoline market with the agricultural commodity market. Moreover, policy instruments supporting biofuel development, such as Renewable Fuel Standard (RFS) originated from the Energy Policy Act of 2005 and RFS2 specified in the Energy Independence and Security Act of 2007, may interact with existing farm policies such as deficiency payment described above. Numerous studies have examined the welfare impacts of these biofuel policy instruments (e.g., de Gorter and Just, 2009a,b; de Gorter and Just, 2010; Lapan and Moschini, 2012; Khanna *et al.*, 2016; and Moschini *et al.*, 2017). In this subsection, we focus on de Gorter and Just (2009a) as it offers an intuitive example examining how biofuel tax credit may interact with deficiency payment when studying the welfare impacts of the two.

The key ideas of de Gorter and Just (2009a) can be illustrated through Figures 5–7. Figure 5 shows the impact of an ethanol tax credit on the market equilibrium of the corn and fuel markets. In panel (a) of Figure 5, line S_C stands for U.S. corn supply and line D_{NE} stands for non-ethanol demand for corn (including both domestic demand and international demand for U.S. corn). If there is no ethanol production, the intersection of lines S_C and D_{NE} determines corn price, P_{NE}. In panel (b) of Figure 5, ethanol supply curve is denoted by S_E. The intercept of S_E is assumed to be at a level equivalent to P_{NE} in panel (a).[2] Furthermore, domestic supply of gasoline is denoted by line S_d, and total fuel supply (including domestic gasoline supply, imported gasoline, and any ethanol) is represented by line S_F. Without tax credit for ethanol, the equilibrium fuel price is P_G, determined by total fuel supply S_F and total fuel demand D_F. We can see that P_G is lower than the intercept of S_E, indicating that there is no ethanol production at P_G if there is no tax credit for ethanol, so P_G is just the price for gasoline.

Now assume that the government introduces a tax credit, t_c (51 cents per gallon as in de Gorter and Just (2009a)) for refiners or blenders who mix ethanol with gasoline. In a competitive market, this policy will increase ethanol price by the amount that is equal to the tax credit (i.e., increasing the price to P_G+t_c). This tax credit policy shifts ethanol supply curve downward to $S_E^{'}$. As a result, the total

[2]Equation (1) in Gorter and Just (2009a) shows how to convert ethanol price from dollar per gallon to dollar per bushel.

fuel supply curve will be shifted downward to S_F' (note that there is a kink on S_F' when fuel price is equal to the intercept of S_E'). The new equilibrium fuel price is P_G', and ethanol price is $P_E = P_G' + t_c$. At fuel price P_G' and ethanol tax credit t_c, quantity of domestic gasoline supplied is OG, imported gasoline is GH, and the quality of ethanol produced is HJ (or, equivalently, OF).

The tax-credit-caused production of ethanol will increase the total demand for U.S. corn and increase corn price. Note that the non-ethanol demand curve for corn is not shifted by the tax credit. Reflected in corn market illustrated in panel (a) of Figure 5, corn price increases to P_C, which is equal to ethanol price measured in dollars per bushel. Due to the increased corn price, the quantity demanded by non-ethanol uses shrinks from OC to OA, and the quantity supplied of corn increases from OC to OB. The amount AB is used for ethanol production. de Gorter and Just (2009a) define water in tax credit as $w = P_{NE} - P_{Gb}'$, where P_{Gb}' is fuel

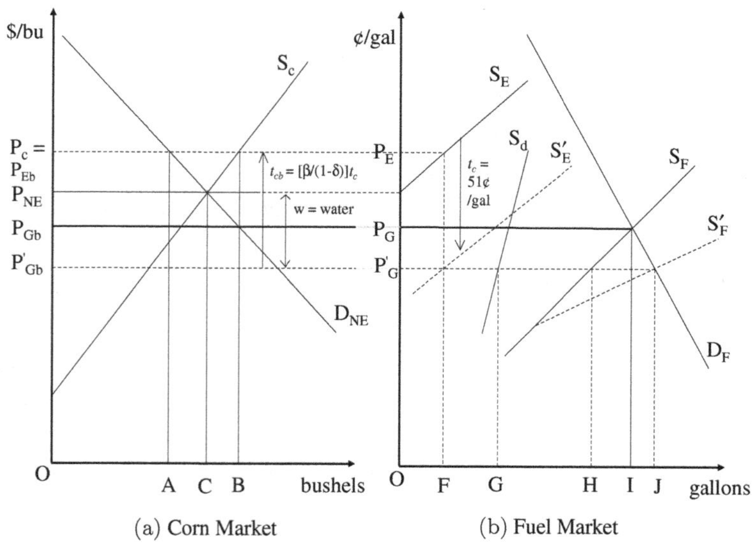

Figure 5. Equilibrium in corn and fuel markets under an ethanol tax credit.
Source: Reproduced from Figure 1 in de Gorter and Just (2009a). Permission obtained from the authors and the Agricultural and Applied Economics Association.

price measured in dollars per bushel considering the conversion rate between corn and ethanol (see footnote 2). From panel (a) of Figure 5, one can see that within tax credit t_{cb}, only the portion "above" the water can increase corn price. If the water is "deep" enough (e.g., fuel price very low), the tax credit may not increase corn price at all.

Now let us see the welfare impact of the tax credit on fuel and corn markets in the absence of deficiency payment. Panel (a) in Figure 6 depicts the welfare changes in the fuel market. Note that de Gorter and Just (2009a) assume that profits of ethanol producers are zero and, therefore, do not include producer surplus of ethanol in the discussion.[3] The tax credit decreases fuel price from P_G to $P_G^{'}$, resulting in a gain in consumer surplus equal to area $e+f+g+h+i+j$. Domestic gasoline producers and international gasoline producers lose producer surplus of areas $e+f$ and $g+h+i$, respectively. Area $i+j+k$ can be interpreted as transfer of funds from taxpayers to fuel consumers through increased ethanol production. Overall, the deadweight loss in the fuel market is area $i+k$, which has the same size as area j.

Panel (b) in Figure 6 depicts the welfare impact of the tax credit on corn market. Line D_d stands for domestic non-ethanol demand for corn, and recall that, D_{NE} stands for total non-ethanol demand for corn (including international demand). As discussed above, the tax credit will increase corn price from P_{NE} to P_c. Non-ethanol corn consumers lose consumer surplus at a magnitude represented by area $l+n+q+a$. Corn producers gain producer surplus of area $l+n+q+a+b$. Taxpayers' fund transferred to corn producers is represented by area $a+b+c$, where area a is the deadweight cost of underconsumption of non-ethanol corn and area c is the deadweight cost of overproduction of corn. Area b is transferred to corn producers as producer surplus. What is unique in panel (b) is that the authors identify a rectangular area, the hatched area, that is pure deadweight loss. Note that taxpayers' fund denoted by this area is not transferred to any party in the corn or fuel market.

[3]We thank David Just for pointing this out to us.

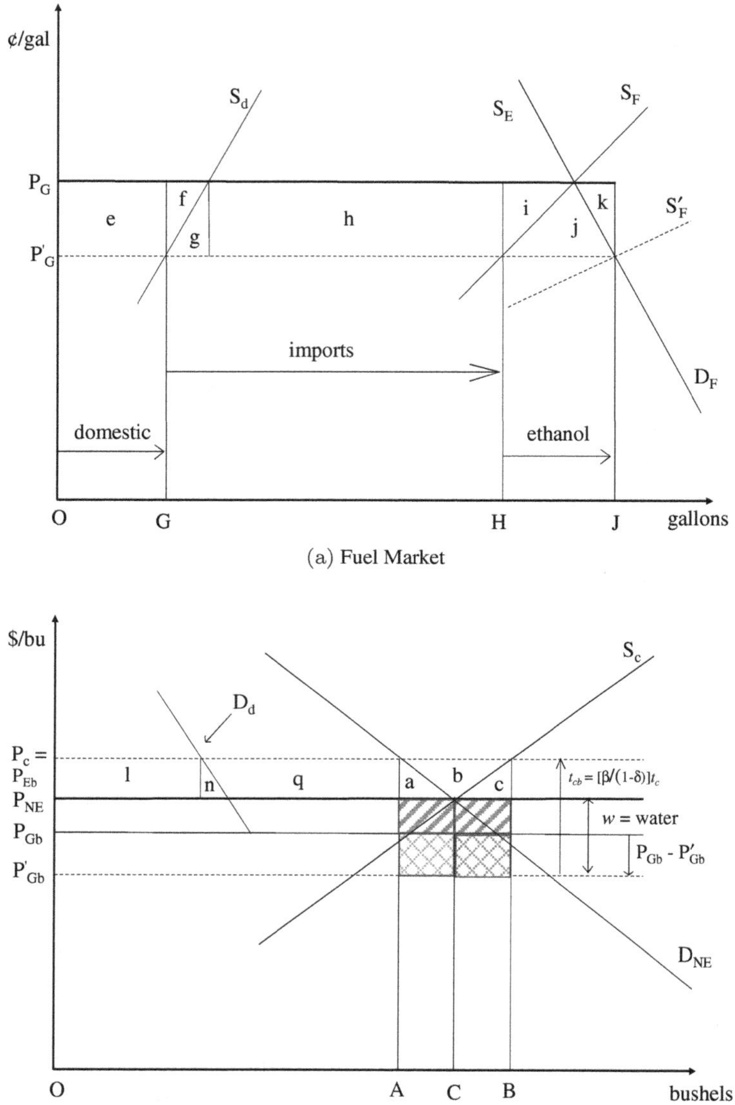

(a) Fuel Market

(b) Corn Market

Figure 6. Welfare impact of an ethanol tax credit on fuel and corn markets.
Source: Reproduced from Figure 2 in de Gorter and Just (2009a). Permission obtained from the authors and the Agricultural and Applied Economics Association.

Even though the upper left corner of this hatched area overlaps with part of producer surplus, one should note that this part of producer surplus is already there before the implementation of tax credit. Therefore, the upper left corner of this hatched area is not new surplus, while it is an additional expense to taxpayers. Therefore, the whole hatched rectangular is a deadweight loss. The numerical simulation in de Gorter and Just (2009a) shows that the magnitude of this rectangular deadweight loss can be as large as $2.3 billion, much higher than the triangular deadweight loss (e.g., areas a and c in panel (b) of Figure 6). Finally, the cross-hatched rectangular area stands for taxpayers' funds transferred to fuel consumers. It is corresponding to area $i + j + k$ in panel (a) of Figure 6, with areas i and k are deadweight losses.

How does the ethanol tax credit interact with deficiency payment for corn? In contrast to Lichtenberg and Zilberman (1986), in the framework developed by de Gorter and Just (2009a), the deficiency payment may be dormant, depending on the relative size of the deficiency payment rate and corn price under the tax credit. de Gorter and Just (2009a) specified all possible scenarios of market equilibrium when both tax credit and deficiency payment are considered. Here we only focus on one scenario that de Gorter and Just (2009a) discuss in detail. Under this scenario, the deficiency payment rate, L, is greater than corn price under tax credit only, P_C, which is in turn greater than non-ethanol corn price, P_{NE}, which is in turn greater than corn market price under deficiency payment only, P_L, and in turn P_{Gb}. That is, $L > P_C > P_{NE} > P_L > P_{Gb}$. Figure 7 depicts the relationship between these prices.

Under the setup in Figure 7, if the tax credit is the only policy instrument in place, then the government expenditure is $t_{cb} \cdot (Q_C - C_{NE})$, where t_{cb} is the tax credit measured in dollar per bushel, Q_C is corn production under tax credit, and C_{NE} is non-ethanol corn consumption. If the deficiency payment is the only policy instrument, then the government expenditure is $(L - P_L) \cdot Q_L$, where Q_L is corn production under deficiency payment only. When we consider both tax credit, t_{cb}, and deficiency payment, L,

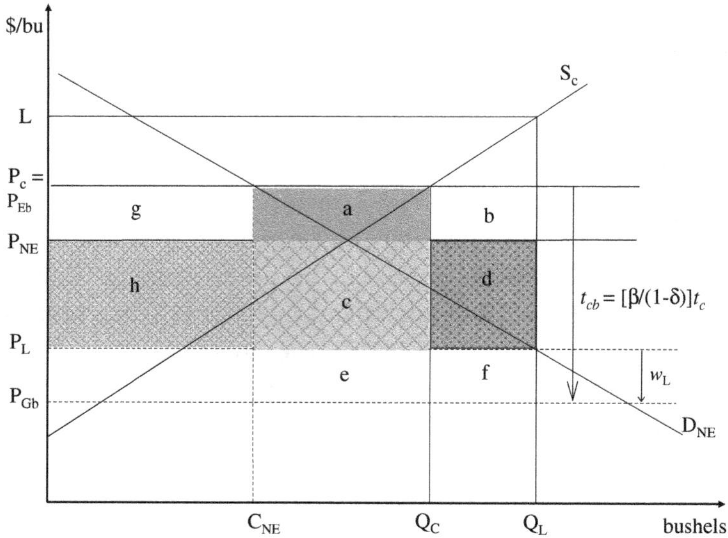

Figure 7. Impact of co-existence of the tax credit and deficiency payment. *Source*: Reproduced from Figure 3 in de Gorter and Just (2009a). Permission obtained from the authors and the Agricultural and Applied Economics Association.

the government expenditure is,

$$(L - P_C) \cdot Q_L + t_{cb}(Q_L - C_{NE}). \tag{19}$$

Clearly, the tax credit saves government expenditure on deficiency payment by the amount of $(P_C - P_L) \cdot Q_L$, and the deficiency payment increases government expenditure on tax credit by amount $t_{cb} \cdot (Q_L - Q_C)$. However, the sizes of the two amounts are ambiguous without further information. We therefore cannot determine whether the total government expenditure is increased or decreased by the co-existence of the two policy instruments when compared with the expenditure under a single policy instrument.

Because $Q_L = C_{NE} + (Q_C - C_{NE}) + (Q_L - Q_C)$, the government expenditure savings in deficiency payment caused by the tax credit, $(P_C - P_L) \cdot Q_L$, can be decomposed into three parts. They are: (1) $(P_C - P_L) \cdot C_{NE}$, represented by area $g + h$ in Figure 7, which can be interpreted as the consumer surplus reduction of non-ethanol corn consumers; (2) $(P_C - P_L) \cdot (Q_C - C_{NE})$, represented by area

$a + c$, which is part of tax credit cost that cancels the same amount of deficiency payment; (3) $(P_C - P_L) \cdot (Q_L - Q_C)$, represented by area $b + d$, which is another part of tax credit payment canceling the same amount of deficiency payment. Note that areas e and f, parts of tax credit payment, do not offset any deficiency payment or are transferred to any parties. Therefore, they are deadweight loss. Specifically, area e is rectangular deadweight loss of tax credit in the absence of deficiency payment, and area f is the deadweight loss of tax credit caused by the existence of deficiency payment.

4. Conclusion

Welfare analysis is a key component in agricultural economics and policy. In this chapter, we have provided a few examples of welfare analysis on some major agricultural policies such as crop insurance, deficiency payment, and biofuel policies. We emphasize considering the interactions between policy instruments when conducting welfare analysis. As crop insurance is gaining importance in the realm of agricultural policy in the U.S., examining the interaction between crop insurance and other policy instruments may yield meaningful insights to understand the impact of these policies. Miao *et al.* (2016) offer an example studying the interaction between crop insurance and the Conservation Reserve Program (CRP), showing that were saved insurance premium subsidy from enrolled CRP land to be considered, then the CRP enrollment efficiency would be enhanced significantly. Miao (2020) investigates how crop insurance may interact with agricultural innovation in the context of climate change. Further research is needed to understand how crop insurance may interact with other agricultural policies related to renewable energy, organic agriculture, rural development, and even nutrition.

References

Atkinson, A.B. 2011. The Restoration of Welfare Economics. *American Economic Review: Papers and Proceedings* 101(3): 157–161.

Chetty, R. and A. Finkelstein. 2013. Social Insurance: Connecting Theory to Data, Alan J. Auerbach, R.C., Feldstein, M., and E. Saez (Eds.), *Handbook of Public Economics*, Vol. 5. Elsevier, Amsterdam.

Coble, K.H. and B.J. Barnett. 2013. Why Do We Subsidize Crop Insurance? *American Journal of Agricultural Economics* 95(2): 498–504.

de Gorter, H. and D.R. Just. 2009a. The Welfare Economics of a Biofuel Tax Credit and the Interaction Effects with Price Contingent Farm Subsidies. *American Journal of Agricultural Economics* 91(2): 477–478.

de Gorter, H. and D.R. Just. 2009b. The Economics of a Blend Mandate for Biofuels. *American Journal of Agricultural Economics* 91(3): 738–750.

de Gorter, H. and D.R. Just. 2010. The Social Costs and Benefits of Biofuels: The Intersection of Environmental, Energy and Agricultural Policy. *Applied Economic Perspectives and Policy* 32(1): 4–32.

Goodwin, B.K. and V.H. Smith. 2013. What Harm Is Done by Subsidizing Crop Insurance? *American Journal of Agricultural Economics* 95(2): 489–497.

Harberger, A.C. 1971. Three Basic Postulates for Applied Welfare Economics: An Interpretive Essay. *Journal of Economic Literature* 9: 785–797.

Khanna, M., H.M. Nuñez, and D. Zilberman. 2016. Who Pays and Who Gains from Fuel Policies in Brazil? *Energy Economics* 54: 133–143.

Just, R.E., D.L. Hueth, and A. Schmitz. 2004. *The Welfare Economics of Public Policy: A Practical Approach to Project and Policy Evaluation.* Edward Elgar Publishing, Inc. Northampton, MA.

Lapan, H. and G.C. Moschini. 2012. Second-Best Biofuel Policies and the Welfare Effects of Quantity Mandates and Subsidies. *Journal of Environmental Economics and Management* 63(2): 224–241.

Lichtenberg, E. and D. Zilberman. 1986. The Welfare Economics of Price Supports in U.S. Agriculture. *The American Economic Review* 76(5): 1135–1141.

Miao, R., H. Feng, D.A. Hennessy, and X. Du. 2016. Assessing Cost-effectiveness of the Conservation Reserve Program and Its Interaction with Crop Insurance Subsidies. *Land Economics* 92(4): 593–617.

Miao, R. 2020. Climate, Insurance, and Innovation: The Case of Drought and Innovations in Drought-Tolerant Traits in U.S. Agriculture. *European Review of Agricultural Economics* 47(5): 1826–1860.

Moschini, G.C., H. Lapan, and H. Kim. 2017. The Renewable Fuel Standard in Competitive Equilibrium: Market and Welfare Effects. *American Journal of Agricultural Economics* 99(5): 1117–1142.

U.S. Government Accountability Office (USGAO). 2023. Farm Bill: Reducing Crop Insurance Costs Could Fund Other Priorities. GAO-23-106228.

Yu, J., J.J. Wu, and R. Miao. 2023. Welfare Effects of the U.S. Federal Crop Insurance Program: The Sufficient Statistics Approach. Working Paper, Department of Agricultural Economics and Rural Sociology, Auburn University.

Chapter 6

The Political Economy of Agricultural Policies

Economists do not run the world. In principle, there are at least two mechanisms for resource allocation. One is the economic system (e.g., markets and prices) and the other is the political system. In some cases, there is a hierarchy wherein the political system dominates the economic system, but in most cases, the relationship is symbiotic. So, economic analysis needs to incorporate political considerations to realistically understand resource allocation.

There are several lines of analysis in political economy. The first is a model by Black (1948), who developed the median voter theorem. For every choice, we have a distribution of preferences, and the evaluation of the median voter would result in an outcome where a majority rule governs. It can be used to assess voters' responses to propositions, for example, whether to vote for or against GMOs. Zilberman *et al.* (2014) address this issue and show how the parties aim to affect the vote through expenditures and other activities. A more sophisticated paper on the same topic is by Waterfield *et al.* (2020), which distinguishes between willingness to vote, to ban, and to pay for GMOs. It emphasizes the different considerations that affect voting vs. buying. The model is elegant, and the two papers are complementary.

The median voter model is important for democracy or voting. Still, in many cases, policymakers make regulatory choices, and they have an objective function that considers their likelihood of being re-elected and their gain from certain economic activities. Becker (1983) had an interesting model. There are other models by Besley and Coate (1997). Another important model is Grossman and Helpman (1994), which started a big literature with a lot of following. In all these models, a common element is that the different groups have varying power. Groups with a lot of political power can influence the political system. One approach to the political system maximizes the sum of weighted consumer, producer, and international consumer surplus. Because different groups have different weights, the outcome may be biased towards a particular group. An important author is Mancur Olson (1965), who wrote a wonderful book on collective action that emphasizes the notion that small, coherent groups with common objectives may have more power than dispersed groups. That is the reason why grower groups are successful in influencing agricultural policies. The book by Rausser *et al.* (2011) uses cooperative game theory to reach this conclusion. Groups build coalitions, and the relative power of different groups depends on their ability to operate independently; groups that can survive without the coalition may have more weight than others.

A strand of political economy studies focuses on agriculture in particular. A strong paper is Rausser's (1982) study on PESTs (political economic-seeking transfers) vs. PERTs (political economic resource transactions). A related model is presented in Rausser and Foster (1990). Another nice application studying PESTs and PERTs in agriculture is documented by Rausser (1992). The survey by Swinnen and Vans der Zee (1993) is a good way to start studying the evolution of agricultural policies from the perspective of political economy. A more recent survey paper on the political economy of agricultural policies is Anderson *et al.* (2013). Zilberman (1984) examines the dynamics of agricultural policy, showing that technological change may lead to what we see today, which is a reduction in the prices of agricultural commodities. Since farmers know they lose from innovation, they need to be subsidized to accept it. Zilberman *et al.* (2014) discuss the politics of biotechnology and why political consideration results in some of the industry's challenges.

In the remaining part of this chapter, we will first speak about political economy in general and then the political economy in agriculture, emphasizing modeling that deals with resource allocation in the political system and agricultural issues.

1. Basic Models in Political Economy

In this section, we will discuss three basic models in the literature on political economy. They are the median voter model, pressure group competition model, and a Nash bargaining model for various interest groups.

1.1. *Median voter theorem*

As discussed in the introduction, the median voter theory predicts that two competing political parties or candidates will tailor their political proposals to appeal to the median voter and try to win their vote. The theory was perhaps first postulated by Harold Hotelling in his famous 1929 paper "Stability in Competition," and then developed and formalized by later studies such as Black (1948) and Downs (1957). We present a simplified model with only two political candidates here, but readers can refer to Black (1948) for a more intricate model with n candidates.

Suppose there are an odd number of I voters.[1] Let V_{ij} denote the voting behavior of individual i, with $V_{ij} = 1$ if voter i votes for candidate j and $V_{ij} = 0$ if voter i does not vote for candidate j. We further assume that voter i will select candidate j^* if and only if her utility from selecting candidate j^* is greater than that from

[1]When I is an even number, then we need a mechanism that can break a possible tie. Black (1948) shows that the median voter theorem still holds in such a case.

Table 1. A simple numerical example for the median voter model.

Voter	1	2	3	4 (median)	5	6	7
ΔU_i	−53	−36	−7	6	8	22	30
Vote for Candidate	2	2	2	1	1	1	1

any other candidates (i.e., $V_{ij^*} = 1$ if and only if $U_{ij^*} > U_{ij}$ for all $j \neq j^*$). The winner, denoted by $\hat{j}$, will be the candidate who has the most votes (i.e., $\sum_{i=1}^{I} V_{i\hat{j}} > \sum_{i=1}^{I} V_{ij}$ for all $j \neq \hat{j}$). For simplicity, let us assume there are only two candidates, 1 and 2. Then, for voter i, the difference in utility from choosing the two candidates is $\Delta U_i = U_{i1} - U_{i2}$. We ascendingly order the voters according to the value of this utility difference. It is readily checked that the winning candidate will be the one whom the median voter selects. Table 1 presents a simple numerical example, where the winner is Candidate 1, and the median voter is pivotal for the winning candidate to obtain the majority.

The median voter theorem is helpful for understanding why the priorities of median voters shape campaigns and influence policies. In many countries, where regional or tribal considerations affect political alliances, policies and campaigning are often targeted to switchable regions or groups. This is perhaps why the "swing states" attract so much attention during presidential elections in the United States.

1.2. *Rent and rent-seeking*

Rent, the amount paid for a factor of production above what it needs to be economically viable, is one of the most important concepts in economics. The economic rent is what people would consider above "normal" profit. Textbook models suggest that at the equilibrium firms operate with normal profit, but some agents will obtain rents for unique capacities. For example, farmers operating at the margin will make zero profit with prices equaling average total cost; other farmers who have higher productivity, however, will gain additional surplus, i.e., rent. So, we can relate the notion of rent to that of producer surplus, and one can even expand it and interpret consumer surplus as the rent for the consumer who is not at the margin, where the price paid is smaller than the marginal utility.

Rent-seeking involves activities that aim to increase one's rent. Numerous examples exist. For instance, domestic producers may lobby to set or increase import tariffs so that they can enjoy protected prices and markets. They may share the gains from tariffs with politicians explicitly or implicitly. International groups such as the World Trade Organization attempt to reduce this type of behavior. Further, regulators can provide an exemption from environmental laws, regulations, or zoning to some groups of producers under their requests. For example, the mandates for advanced biofuels established in the Energy Independence and Security Act of 2007 had been continuously waived. Another example is that the EPA waived some small refineries' obligation to blend a certain amount of biofuels into gasoline via Small Refinery Exemptions.

Social welfare under perfect competition is typically higher than that under monopoly. Monopoly causes deadweight loss with producer surplus increasing but consumer supply decreasing (see Figure 1). If a government provides a company with monopoly power,

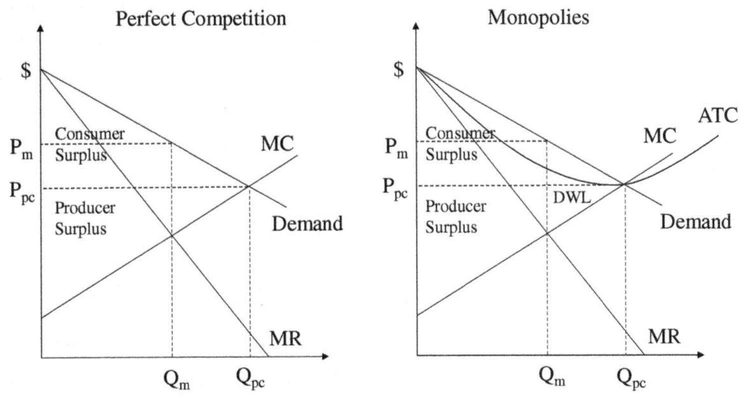

Figure 1. Consumer surplus and producer surplus under perfect competition and monopoly.

say, through regulation, it creates rent, reducing social welfare but generating profits for the monopolist. In many cases, the politician gets a kickback, but they do have to take political accountability into consideration. Suppose that the regulation moves output from the competitive outcome, Q_{pc}, to a lower regulation output, Q_r. The gain to the industry is the increased producer surplus: $\Delta PS(Q_r) = PS(Q_r) - PS(Q_{pc})$, where $PS(Q)$ stands for producer surplus at output Q. Note that $\Delta PS(Q_r)$ reaches its maximum when $Q_r = Q_m$, where Q_m is the optimal output for the monopolist. Under the regulation, consumers lose $\Delta CS(Q_r) = CS(Q_{pc}) - CS(Q_r)$. Assume that the industry pays X dollars to the politician. The regulation, owing to its welfare-reducing nature, may cause the politician to lose re-election, say, at probability $f(Q_r)$. Let us assume $f(Q_{pc}) = 0$ and $f_{Q_r}(Q_r) = df/dQ_r \leq 0$. Finally, let C_p denote the politician's gain from staying in power (excluding any kickback money).

With the above notation, the optimization problem of the two parties (i.e., the industry and the politician) can be written as

$$\text{Max}_{\{Q_r\}}\ NG = (1 - f(Q_r))\, \Delta PS(Q_r) - f\,(Q_r)\, C_P, \tag{1}$$

subject to $Q_m \leq Q_r \leq Q_{pc}$.

The first term on the right-hand side of Equation (1) is the expected gain from the regulation (i.e., $(1 - f(Q_r))\, \Delta PS(Q_r)$) and the second term is the expected loss from the regulation (i.e., loss from losing power, $-f(Q_r)C_P$). Suppose there is an interior solution. Then the first-order condition that determines the optimal Q_r is

$$\frac{dNG}{dQ_r} = (1 - f(Q_r))\Delta PS_{Q_r} - f_{Q_r}\,(\Delta PS(Q_r) + C_P) = 0. \tag{2}$$

By rearranging Equation (2), we obtain

$$(1 - f(Q_r))\,(-\Delta PS_{Q_r}) = -f_{Q_r}\,(\Delta PS(Q_r) + C_P)\,. \tag{3}$$

Note that $(1 - f(Q_r))$ is the probability of staying in power, and $-\Delta PS_{Q_r}$ is marginal gain in surplus with lower Q_r. Equation (3) states that the marginal expected gain in producer surplus from reducing supply is equal to the expected economic loss associated with the marginal increase in the probability of losing power due to restricted supply. Specifically, this expected economic loss is the product of the marginal increase in the probability of losing power, f_{Q_r}, and the loss of both producer surplus and benefit from holding power for the regulator, $(\Delta PS(Q_r) + C_P)$.

This model suggests that the producer's gain from the regulation will increase, for example, when demand is more inelastic or when the vulnerability to losing power due to restricted supply is low. Obviously, when there is a large potential to get an increased producer surplus, then the restrictions on supply will be stronger. On the other hand, the more that the politician gains from their power (i.e., larger C_p) or the more vulnerable they are (i.e., higher $f(Q_r)$), the less they engage in introducing cartels and monopolies. This model suggests that manipulation of power to benefit the few is less likely in a democracy where consumers are aware of the political process and are able to mobilize their power against the artificial restriction of supply.

Now let us see how the rent generated from the regulation might be divided between the industry and the politician (i.e., "sharing of spoils"). Let $\alpha \in [0, 1]$ be the relative power of the politician to the industry when dividing the spoils. The probability of losing power may be a function of the politician's portion in the spoils (denoted by X). Specifically, the probability of the politician losing position is $(f(Q_r, X))$. Again, as before, the politician's loss in case of losing his position is denoted by C_P. Therefore, the net gain for the politician from the regulation is $X - f(Q_r, X) \cdot C_P$. The industry gains $\Delta PS(Q_r)$ as long as the politician stays in power, minus the kickback money X to the politician with certainty. So, the net gain of the industry $(1 - f(Q_r, X)) \cdot \Delta PS(Q_r) - X$. The optimal Q_r and X can be determined by solving the following optimization problem:

$$\text{Max}_{\{Q_r, X\}} \Big\{\alpha\, (X - f(Q_r, X) \cdot C_P) + (1 - \alpha)\Big(\big(1 - f(Q_r, X)\big)\Delta PS(Q_r) - X\Big)\Big\} \quad (4)$$

subject to $Q_m \le Q_r \le Q_{pc}$ and $0 \le X \le \Delta PS(Q_r)$.

Assuming an interior solution, the first-order conditions for Q_r and X are:

$$-af_{Q_r}C_p + (1-a)\big[(1-f(Q_r,X))\,\mathit{\Delta}PS_{Q_r} - f_{Q_r}\mathit{\Delta}PS(Q_r)\big] = 0, \tag{5}$$

$$a(1-f_XC_p) - (1-a)\,(1+f_X\mathit{\Delta}PS(Q_r)) = 0, \tag{6}$$

where $f_{Q_r} = \partial f(Q_r,X)/\partial Q_r$, $f_X = \partial f(Q_r,X)/\partial X$, and $\mathit{\Delta}PS_{Q_r} = \partial \mathit{\Delta}PS(Q_r)/\partial Q_r$.

Rearranging terms in Equation (5), we obtain

$$(1-\alpha)\,(1-f(Q_r,X))\,\Delta PS_{Q_r} = f_{Q_r}\big[\alpha C_p + (1-\alpha)\,\Delta PS(Q_r)\big]. \tag{7}$$

The left-hand side of Equation (7) is the weighted marginal gain to the industry–politician coalition from reduction in quantity (i.e., expected increase in producers' surplus). The right-hand side is the expected marginal cost from a marginal reduction in regulated output. A reduction in probability of winning will reduce the well-being of both the politician and the industry. Equation (7) states that at the optimal level of Q_r, the weighted marginal gain of Q_r is equal to the weighted marginal cost. The greater is the industry power $(1-\alpha)$, the stricter is the regulation (i.e., lower Q_r values). For example, when a politician depends strongly on domestic manufacturers, he may set regulations that limit import opportunities. This was a key element in the export substitution strategy in Latin America.

Similarly, by rearranging Equation (6) we obtain

$$\frac{\alpha}{1-\alpha}\,(1-f_XC_p) = 1 + f_X\mathit{\Delta}PS\,(Q_r)\,. \tag{8}$$

The left-hand side of Equation (8) is the marginal gain to the politician from increased portion of the spoils, weighted by its relative political power $a/(1-a)$. Note that the marginal gain from increased donation is income plus the expected extra political gain from higher spending (remember that f_X is negative; the more the politician spends on elections, the less likely he or she is to lose). The right-hand side of the equation is the marginal cost to the industry. It is the direct expenditure (1 unit of X) minus the gain due to reduction in expected political risk due to donation $f_X \Delta PS(Q_r)$. When α is higher, the politician has more political power, and, thus can negotiate a larger contribution from industry for a given level of extra surplus he or she provides the industry by regulation. Also, when the marginal effect of campaign contribution is larger, the bigger the donation (i.e., X) will be.

From this simple "spoil-sharing" model we can see that factors determining patterns of political payoffs may include the strength of politician (a), the effectiveness of campaign spending (f_X), gain to producers ($\Delta SP(Q_r)$), probability of getting caught ($f(Q_r, X)$), and price for getting caught (C_p). One can infer that complexity with lack of transparency leads to corruption, that lack of awareness by losers allow for more exploitation, and that political awareness matters. Numerous day-to-day examples, such as gifts to authority figures, licensing, and regulations, can be explained using this model. Rent-seeking behavior may be used to slow reforms or changes, such as introduction of policies that limit new technologies or new export practice.

1.3. *Modeling competing interests*

Different from earlier studies on political economy that focus on voters, politicians, or political parties, Becker (1983) proposes a theory postulating that political equilibrium is a result of competition among interest groups. He argues that each interest group will invest its resources (e.g., time, money, energy, and social connections) to build up political pressure and maximize their incomes. Interest groups vary in their resource endowment and in their capability to generate political pressure. Therefore, the outcomes for interest groups may differ in the political equilibrium. In this subsection, we briefly introduce this model.

Suppose there are two interest groups, s and t. One can view group s as the group that enjoys subsidy and view group t as the group that is taxed. The numbers of members in groups s and t are n_s and n_t, respectively. Within each group, the members are identical. Each group will invest its resources to generate political pressure to either increase its subsidy or reduce its tax. Assume that each member in group s invests a_s amount of resources and each member in group t invests a_t. The political pressure produced by the groups is, therefore, $p_j = p_j(m_j, n_j)$ where $m_j = a_j n_j$, and $j \in \{s, t\}$. The pressure from both groups will determine the payoffs for each group because of the competition between the two groups. Moreover, the aggregated payoffs of the two groups should be zero because the subsidy for group s will be from the tax from group t. Specifically, we have

$$n_s G(R_s) = I^s(p_s, p_t, x), \tag{9}$$

$$n_t F(R_t) = -I^t(p_s, p_t, x), \tag{10}$$

$$I^s(p_s, p_t, x) + I^t(p_s, p_t, x) \equiv 0, \tag{11}$$

where R_s and R_t are subsidy rate and tax rate per member in groups s and t, respectively; functions $G(\cdot)$ and $F(\cdot)$ capture the deadweight losses from subsidy and tax, reflecting distortion effect of subsidy and tax; and finally, $I^s(\cdot)$ and $I^t(\cdot)$ are "influence" functions that translate the political pressure and other variables (labeled as x) into subsidy amount or tax revenue.

For a member in group s or t, her overall payoff can be written as,

$$Z_s = Z_s^0 + R_s - a_s, \tag{12}$$

$$Z_t = Z_t^0 - R_t - a_t, \tag{13}$$

where Z_s^0 and Z_t^0 are initial payoffs prior to any political redistribution. Suppose both groups are politically active, i.e., $a_s > 0$ and $a_t > 0$. The payoff maximization conditions for the two groups are:

$$\frac{dR_s}{da_s} = 1, \text{ and } \frac{dR_t}{da_t} = -1. \tag{14}$$

Based on Equations (9)–(11), the conditions in (14) are equivalent to

$$\frac{dR_s}{da_s} = \frac{1}{n_s G'} \frac{\partial I^s}{\partial p_s} \frac{\partial p_s}{\partial m_s} \frac{\partial m_s}{\partial a_s} = \frac{I_s^s p_m^s}{G'} = 1, \tag{15}$$

$$\frac{dR_t}{da_t} = -\frac{1}{n_t F'} \frac{\partial I^t}{\partial p_t} \frac{\partial p_t}{\partial m_t} \frac{\partial m_t}{\partial a_t} = \frac{I_t^s p_m^t}{F'} = -1. \tag{16}$$

The second equation in expression (15) holds because $\partial m_s/\partial a_s = n_s$, $I_s^s \equiv \partial I^s/\partial p_s$, and $p_m^s \equiv \partial p_s/\partial m_s$. The second equation in expression (16) holds for similar reasons. Becker (1983) shows that the sufficient conditions for the optimization are $I_{ss}^s < 0$, $I_{tt}^s > 0$, $p_{mm}^s \leq 0$, $p_{mm}^t < 0$, $G'' > 0$, and $F'' < 0$. Assuming that each group, when it selects its political investment level a_j, takes the other group's investment level as given. Therefore, expression (15) can be viewed as a response function of group s's investment level, a_s, to group t's investment level, a_t. Similarly, expression (16) is group t's response function to group s's investment level, a_s. The equilibrium is reached under a pair of (a_s^*, a_t^*) that satisfies both (15) and (16).

Figure 2 presents the response functions and equilibria, with the initial equilibrium at point e_0. Suppose now group s becomes more efficient in generating political pressure, say, due to their leadership change. In other words, group s can respond with higher political pressure for any given pressure generated by group t. This change can be reflected as an upward shift of the response curve shifts from s_0 to s_1, causing the equilibrium to move from e_0 to e_1. We can see that when compared with the initial equilibrium e_0, the new

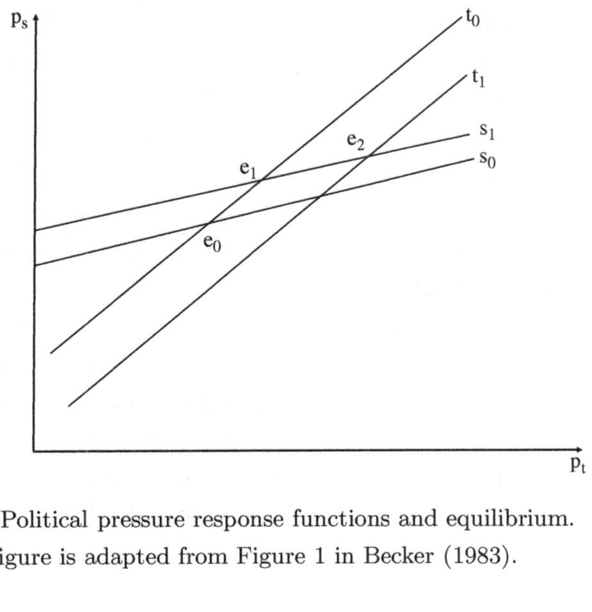

Figure 2. Political pressure response functions and equilibrium.
Note: This figure is adapted from Figure 1 in Becker (1983).

equilibrium e_1 implies higher political pressure from both groups because the slopes of the response curves are positive. However, based on Equation (15), the upward shift from s_0 to s_1 will cause both the subsidy to group s and the tax on group t to increase. Becker (1983) concludes that when a group is more efficient in exerting political pressure, this group can either increase its subsidy or decrease its tax.

If group t also enhances its efficiency to generate political pressure, then its response curve will move, say, to t_1. In this case, the equilibrium will be settled at e_2. As a result, the pressure generated by both groups would increase, but the equilibrium influence of each group will be undetermined because it depends on the relative changes in the influence of the two groups. Therefore, what matters most for the political outcome of a group is not its absolute efficiency in generating political pressure; it is the group's *relative* efficiency that will eventually determine the political outcome (Becker, 1983). Becker further argued that, due to the free-riding problem, smaller political groups (e.g., farmer groups) tend to have relatively higher efficiency in generating political influence.

1.4. *A game-theoretical framework*

Another useful framework to analyze the interaction between political groups is Nash–Harsanyi bargaining game, which models bargaining and negotiations among groups and predicts the results therein. The framework was developed under a series of seminal works by Nash (1950, 1951, 1953) and Harsanyi (1962a,b, 1963). Rausser *et al.* (2011, Chapters 2 and 3) provide a comprehensive review of this framework. In this subsection, we briefly introduce a bargaining game under which the reservation payoff (i.e., payoff when no agreement is reached by political groups) of each group is exogenously given. For the bargaining game with endogenously determined reservation payoffs, we refer readers to Chapter 3 of Rausser *et al.* (2011).

We start with a model pertaining to two players, and then expand this model to include n players. First, consider two groups, 1 and 2, that aim to maximize their individual payoffs through bargaining with the other group to reach an agreement (e.g., a policy intervention). Suppose their reservation payoffs are $\underline{u}_1$ and $\underline{u}_2$, respectively. In other words, if no agreement is made between the two groups, then group 1 will receive $\underline{u}_1$ and group 2 $\underline{u}_2$. Let P denote the payoff space of the two groups, which includes all vectors, $u \equiv (u_1, u_2)$, of potential payoffs to groups 1 and 2. We assume that P is compact and convex. Define H as a subset of P such that the element in H is not (strictly or weakly) dominated by any element in P. That is, for any element u^H in set H, there does not exist an element in P, u, such that $u_1 \geq u_1^H$ and $u_2 \geq u_2^H$ (i.e., H is the efficiency frontier of P). Define P^* as another subset of P such that $P^* \equiv \{u \in P : u_1 \geq \underline{u}_1,\ u_2 \geq \underline{u}_2\}$ and H^* as the efficiency frontier of P^*. Furthermore, let $\underline{u}$ denote the optimal solutions of the bargaining problem.

Based on the individual rationality axiom, it is readily checked that no payoff outside of set P^* will be reached as an agreement by the two groups. In other words, it must be true that $\underline{u} \in P^*$. Furthermore, the rationality assumption will imply that no Pareto improvement can be made to optimal solutions $\underline{u}$. That is, one cannot find a payoff vector, $u' \in P^*$, such that when compared with $\underline{u}$, one group is better off and the other group is not harmed, indicating that $\underline{u} \in H^*$. This axiom is termed Pareto optimality. Prior to Nash's game-theoretical framework of the bargaining problem, economic theories could only refine the optimal solutions to H^*, which is typically a set instead of a unique solution.

Based on the individual rationality axiom, the Pareto optimality axiom, and three additional axioms, Nash (1950) showed that the optimal solution to the bargaining problem is unique and can be obtained by solving a straightforward optimization problem. The three additional axioms are symmetry, linear invariance, and independence of irrelevant alternatives. The symmetry axiom states that P^* is symmetric: if a vector $(a, b) \in P^*$ then $(b, a) \in P^*$. The linear invariance axiom states that an order-preserving linear transformation of a player's utility function does not affect the optimal solution of the bargaining problem. Finally, the axiom of independence of irrelevant alternatives states that removing irrelevant alternative payoff vectors from set P does not affect the optimal solution of the bargaining problem. Here the irrelevant alternative payoff vectors include any vectors except the reservation payoff vector and the optimal solution of the bargaining problem based on the original payoff set P.

Based on the aforementioned five axioms, Nash (1950) showed that the optimal solution of the two-player bargaining game can be obtained by solving

$$\max_{(u_1,u_2)\in P^*} \left[(u_1 - \underline{u}_1)(u_2 - \underline{u}_2)\right]. \tag{17}$$

This two-player bargaining game can be easily expanded to an n-player game. Let $\underline{u} \equiv (\underline{u}_1, \ldots, \underline{u}_n)$ and $u \equiv (u_1, \ldots, u_2)$ be the reservation payoff and payoff of players $(1, \ldots, n)$, respectively. Also, we expand sets P and P^* from two dimensions to n dimension accordingly and label them as P_n and P_n^*. The optimal solution of the n-player bargaining game is the solution to the following optimization problem:

$$\max_{u\in P_n^*} \Pi_{i\in\{1,\ldots,n\}}(u_i - \underline{u}_i). \tag{18}$$

The n-player bargaining game can be further generalized to accommodate heterogeneous bargaining power across players (Britz *et al.*, 2010). Let α_i denote the bargaining power (i.e., the weight) of player i. Then, the bargaining game solution can be obtained by solving:

$$\max_{u\in P_n^*} \Pi_{i\in\{1,\ldots,n\}}(u_i - \underline{u}_i)^{\alpha_i}. \tag{19}$$

In the next section we will see how this model is applied in agricultural economics.

2. Applications in Agriculture

In this section, we will discuss the political economy of biotechnology, biofuels, and water. We chose these three areas because their development was controversial and often involved competition between various interest groups. Therefore, they serve as good examples of applications of political economy in agriculture.

2.1. *Economics of biotechnology regulations*

Biotechnology in agriculture, such as genetically modified organisms (GMOs), is perhaps the most controversial topic related to agriculture nowadays. Various interest groups may hold starkly different opinions toward biotechnology, generating political pressure from different directions in order to shape the regulation of biotechnology. Graff *et al.* (2009) provide a political-economy framework incorporating multiple competing interests to understand the formation of biotechnology regulations in the United States, the European Union, and developing countries. They model the agricultural biotechnology regulator's problem as follows:

$$\begin{aligned}
&\text{Max (regulator's welfare} + A_1 \times \text{consumer surplus} \\
&\quad + A_2 \times \text{food retailers' producer surplus} \\
&\quad + A_3 \times \text{farmers' producer surplus} \\
&\quad + A_4 \times \text{major biotechnology suppliers' producer surplus} \\
&\quad + A_5 \times \text{new biotech innovators' producer surplus} \\
&\quad + A_6 \times \text{competing input suppliers' producer surplus} \\
&\quad + A_7 \times \text{academic institutions and scientists' benefits} \\
&\quad + A_8 \times \text{activist organizations' benefits} \\
&\quad + A_9 \times \text{environmental welfare}),
\end{aligned} \tag{20}$$

where the parameters A_1 to A_9 reflect the weight that the regulator assigns to each interest group. Note that the weights are normalized against the regulator's welfare (i.e., the regulator's welfare has weight at 1 in Equation (20)). An interest group can influence its weight by generating pressure on the regulator, by, for example, making political contributions, lobbying, protesting, or voting. The regulator maximizes the weighted sum of all interest groups' welfare, including his or her own.

Consumer surplus in Equation (20) reflects the heterogeneous taste, preference, and willingness to pay toward biotechnology. Studies (e.g., Paarlberg, 2001; Wu, 2004) have shown that consumers in developed countries do not benefit very much from biotechnology like GMOs because the food expenditures of these consumers are already relatively low. Furthermore, these consumers might be concerned by the potential health risks imposed by GMOs. This is perhaps why the majority of food consumers in the U.S. largely ignore the welfare impact of GMOs and influence GMOs only through individual purchase and voting.

Producer groups listed in Equation (20) have a heterogeneous preference for GMOs.[2] Food retailers may benefit or lose from the production of GMOs depending on consumers' response to GMOs. Organic food stores may benefit from loose regulations of GMOs because they can easily differentiate their products and charge a price premium. Farmers may benefit from the increased yields of genetically modified crops, but farmers who do not adopt GMOs would be worse off when wide adoption increases crop production and thus decreases crop prices. Although new biotech innovators will almost surely benefit from a *laissez-faire* biotechnology regulation, existing biotechnology suppliers may gain or lose from such regulation. This is because, on the one hand, a *laissez-faire* biotechnology regulation will make entry into the biotechnology sector much easier, and therefore the incumbents will have more competition from new entrants. On the other hand, under *laissez-faire* regulation, it will be relatively easy for the incumbents to expand their own innovation and product line. By definition, the competing input suppliers will suffer from a *laissez-faire* biotechnology regulation.

Academic institutions and scientists play a unique role in the political economy of biotechnology. First, their research outputs are often consulted in the decision-making process regarding

[2]Even within one group, the preference need not be homogeneous. Therefore, one can modify Equation (20) to divide one group into multiple sub-groups and assign new weights to these sub-groups. For example, food retailers can be further divided into large food stores (e.g., Kroger), organic food stores, and farmers' markets.

biotechnology regulation. For instance, studies on the health impact of DDT (an insecticide) partially resulted in the ban of its use in the U.S. in 1972. Therefore, stringent regulation may increase demand, and hence financial support, for research from academic institutions and scientists. Second, academic institutions and scientists may gain or lose under biotechnology regulations in terms of research grants, royalty income, and public esteem in the agricultural sector. The relationship between biotechnology regulations and the gains or losses of academic institutions is an interesting area for both theoretical and empirical research.

Graff *et al.* (2009) noted that one should differentiate the welfare of activist organizations and environmental welfare, even though the latter is often the reason to continue the activities of activist organizations. The welfare of activist organizations is determined, at least partially, by their funding from grants and donations, organization size, and reputation. However, environmental welfare is something that accrues to the whole society, not just the activist organizations.

Based on the discussion about these interest groups related to biotechnology, Graff *et al.* (2009) conjecture that the following groups are most likely to support a *laissez-faire* biotechnology regulation: new biotech innovators, farmers who benefit from the increased yield or reduced costs caused by biotechnology, and consumers who benefit from reduced food prices but do not worry much about the potential risk of biotechnology. Groups that support strict biotechnology regulation may include consumers who are price-insensitive and concerned by the potential risk of biotechnologies, brand-conscious food retailers, competing input suppliers, activist organizations, and regulators.

Based on the aforementioned model and discussion, Graff *et al.* (2009) compared biotechnology regulations in the U.S. and those in Europe. They pointed out that, although European consumers could have reduced their expenditures on food had GMOs been allowed in European markets, the cost of organizing consumer groups to promote GMOs could be much higher than the reduced food expenditures. It could also be the case that European consumers were willing to pay a price premium to avoid the potential health and environmental risks of GMOs. Therefore, not much pressure existed from the consumers' side in Europe to promote the adoption of GMOs. On the supply side, European farmers effectively benefited from the ban on GMOs that served as a non-tariff trade barrier, allowing the farmers to charge a price premium over GMO products. Perhaps the most powerful opponents to GMOs in Europe are the producers of conventional pest-control products for the clear reasons that the adoption of GMOs will reduce the demand for their products. Finally, activist organizations in Europe are strong.

In many developing countries, GMOs face stringent regulations as well. Consumers and farmers perhaps would significantly benefit from GMO adoption that could increase food supply and reduce production costs. However, due to the large numbers of consumers and farmers in developing countries, these two groups cannot efficiently generate political pressure on regulators for loosening regulations on GMOs. Producers of traditional agricultural inputs (e.g., pesticides and herbicides) who would be harmed by GMO adoption can easily form a group and generate political influence on regulators.

Stringent regulations on GMOs have significantly hindered the development of "second-generation" biotechnology that is more focused on the nutrient and environmental traits of crops, causing large welfare losses to farmers and consumers. Recent breakthroughs in gene-editing technologies, such as the clustered regularly interspaced short palindromic repeats (CRISPR)/CRISPR-associated protein (Cas) technologies, have the potential to accelerate innovations in new crop varieties. However, the new technologies are facing similar regulations and low social acceptance to those of GMOs in Europe and many developing countries (Miao and Khanna, 2020). Further research from scientists and economists on the benefits and risks of these new technologies will assist societies in understanding the true values of these technologies with more certainty.

2.2. *Political economy of biofuels*

In Chapter 5, we employed social welfare models to analyze the welfare gains or losses of consumers and producers, as well as changes in government outlays due to biofuel production and policy. In this subsection, however, we shift to the political economy and examine some key factors that influenced biofuel policies in the U.S., Brazil, and some other countries following Zilberman *et al.* (2014).

Similar to Equation (20), we develop a political economy model of biofuel policies as follows:

$$\begin{aligned}
&\text{Max(policymakers' welfare}\\
&\quad + B_1 \times \text{food and fuel consumers' surplus}\\
&\quad + B_2 \times \text{farmers' producer surplus}\\
&\quad + B_3 \times \text{environmentalists' welfare}\\
&\quad + B_4 \times \text{oil companies' producer surplus}\\
&\quad + B_5 \times \text{first-generation biofuel producers' surplus}\\
&\quad + B_6 \times \text{second-generation biofuel producers' surplus}\\
&\quad + B_7 \times \text{other energy producers' surplus}\\
&\quad + B_8 \times \text{automobile companies' producer surplus}\\
&\quad + B_9 \times \text{welfare of some other groups}), \qquad (21)
\end{aligned}$$

where parameters B_1 to B_9 are the weight assigned to different interest groups by policymakers.

During the early 2000s, U.S. policymakers were concerned with energy independence, the trade deficit, and climate change. Developing biofuels can serve as means to mitigate these concerns. Obviously, corn ethanol produced domestically will replace gasoline and thus reduce crude oil imports, which will both enhance energy independence and decrease the trade deficit. Although not policymakers' top priority back then, mitigating climate change was also cited as a reason for supporting biofuels in the United States. In Brazil, a major driver of sugar cane ethanol in the 1970s was the concern of trade deficit, which did not allow the country to import much crude oil.

Changes in food and fuel consumers' surplus due to biofuels vary significantly among countries. In developed countries such as the U.S., the production of biofuels only had a mild impact (about 5%) on retail food prices (Harrison, 2009). Because only a small portion of household income is devoted to food in these countries, this mild food price increase did not translate into large welfare loss to consumers. In developing countries, however, since a large portion of household income was spent on food, food price increases caused large welfare losses to consumers (Wright, 2014). Fuel consumers gained from biofuel because fuel price was lowered due to biofuel production, but the gains mainly accrued to consumers in developed countries because many consumers in developing countries do not have cars (Zilberman *et al.*, 2014).

Obviously, corn producers in the U.S. and sugarcane producers in Brazil benefited from biofuel production. Thus, they supported biofuel development. Environmentalists' support for biofuel, however, is significantly affected by research results on biofuel's greenhouse gas (GHG) emission reduction benefits. After the publication of two *Science* articles in 2008 (i.e., Fargione *et al.*, 2008; Searchinger *et al.*, 2008) which showed that biofuel production might actually increase GHG emissions, environmentalists' support for the corn-starch-based biofuel largely shifted to disapprobation, becoming more inclined to second-generation biofuels. Most oil companies and producers viewed biofuel as a competitor and thus opposed it, although a few big oil companies (e.g., BP and Shell) invested in the development of biofuels.

Zilberman *et al.* (2014) noted that both first- and second-generation biofuel producers benefited from biofuel production. Particularly, for the first-generation biofuel producers who are also corn growers, the benefits arose from both the rising corn price and corn ethanol profits. Producers of other alternative energy, such as solar and wind energy, viewed biofuel as a competitor because they were competing for a limited amount of government support and natural resources, such as land. Likewise, companies that make electric vehicles may oppose biofuels while their flex fuel counterparts would support biofuels. Finally, some other interest groups such as airlines and the military welcomed the development of biofuels due to concerns about stricter climate regulation, energy independence, and the impossibility to power their aircraft using batteries in the near future.

2.3. *Political economy of water*

Mark Twain supposedly said, "Whiskey is for drinking, water is for fighting." Conflicts about water ownership and use have existed forever and are subject to political debate and regulation. In particular, the allocation of water rights, water transactions, and water quality has been subject to policy debate and regulation.

Zilberman *et al.* (2023) argue that several factors affected the evolution of water policy in the United States and other countries over time. First, the relative abundance of water. Second, the emphasis on supply expansion and development. Third, the capacity of the government to invest in water projects. Fourth, the concern for the environment. During early settlement in the U.S., the federal government was relatively poor but had the power to distribute rights to water and other resources. The government was interested in the expansion of agriculture, which led to the introduction of water rights, where individuals established rights to use water by diverting them from larger bodies. With the prior appropriation system prevalent in the West, priority in time set priority in use, and there were restrictions on water trading. In the early days, farmers established water districts to divert water for mining, urban consumption, and agricultural activities. Starting at the beginning of the 20th century, as the government's financial capacity improved, it invested in water projects for irrigation and hydroelectric power. Some of these water projects did not pass benefit-cost analysis, but the power of agriculture interest groups and real-estate development led to their establishment. However, both the emergence of the environmental movement and increased concern about government spending led, in the 1970 and 1980s, to the establishment of principles and guidelines for new water project developments that approximate benefit-cost analysis, and they resulted in the decline of new water projects. With constraints on supply expansion, irrigated agriculture becomes more intensive, relying more heavily on sprinkler irrigation, low-pressure center pivot irrigation, and drip irrigation.

As water scarcity increased, there was an increasing awareness of the need to move from water rights to water trading, especially in California and Australia, where water rights owners were not allowed to sell water. The survey by Schoengold and Zilberman (2007) reviewed studies that suggest the transition from water rights to water markets may lead to the adoption of new technologies, increased agricultural productivity, and overall social welfare. However, the owner of water rights may lose from the transition to water markets if they are not allowed to keep most of the revenue from the sale of water. Therefore, the introduction of transferable rights (so water rights owners keep most of the proceeds from the sale) is more politically accepted by water rights owners than if the state keeps significant parts of the proceeds. Some environmental groups may oppose moving to water trading as it may increase agricultural production and reduce wilderness. Furthermore, the transition to water markets from water rights requires monitoring and new equipment investment. Uncertainty about water rights is another reason for the delay of the transition to markets, especially when the state has a limited capacity to enforce reallocation in an emergency. Partial trading was introduced in California in response to drought situations, but trading remains limited and temporary due to the state's legal constraints and limited capacity to impose reform. On the other hand, Australia has moved to a water trading system in response to the Millennium drought (2001–2009) (Hanemann and Young, 2020).

In much of the world, groundwater is the main source of irrigation, and traditionally, landowners have been entitled to pump the water under their land. That led to inefficiency because of the "Tragedy of the Commons" and depletion of groundwater resources. Government actors may have recognized a need to control over-pumping, but farming communities may have used their political influence to oppose it. In contrast, other politicians might have opposed restrictions on groundwater pumping because of its short-term impact on food prices or supplies. The result is the tendency to over-pump, which may trigger a depletion of aquifers and a water and farming crisis. In some cases, a political establishment will invest in a water project to augment groundwater (if the government resources and farming lobbies are strong). In other cases, farming activities may decline, leading to poverty and migration.

Water quality is another source of political debate. Increased fertilizer use has led to a large accumulation of nitrates and other chemicals in the groundwater. Furthermore, runoff from agricultural land may lead to the transfer of chemicals to lakes and other bodies of water, resulting in eutrophication; harmful algal blooms that lead to fish kills and dead zones. An important example is the dead zone in the Gulf of Mexico, where the alleviation requires fertilizer use reduction in the Midwest and thus the cooperation of farmers. There is a growing need for creative technological and politically feasible solutions. Water quality contamination exists in many other parts of the world, endangering human health and reducing clean water availability. One solution is the development of affordable and sound environmental technologies to cleanse the water and allow its use for consumption, an expensive implementation but already in effect in countries such as Israel and Spain (Simpson, 2018; Zarzo, 2021). Further development of these technologies and policies that enhance their adoption requires a significant public investment and may take time (Zilberman *et al.*, 2023).

The increased scarcity of water resources and increased technological sophistication and demand for water are pushing increased reliance on water markets and trading that reduce inefficiency. However, the pace of the change is affected by political and economic situations that vary across locations (Saleth and Dinar, 2004). Thus, seeking solutions that enhance efficiency while overcoming said constraints offers a valuable line of research.

3. Conclusion

In this chapter, we have introduced a few popular political economy models including the median voter model, the spoil-sharing model, the competing interest model, and the Nash–Harsanyi bargaining game. Their applications in agriculture were discussed with a focus on biotechnology regulation, biofuel policies, as well as water rights and trading. Political economy is an expansive research field and offers a unique perspective to understanding policy evolution and resource allocation. It can be applied to many areas in agricultural economics and what we have discussed in this chapter are only a few, although important, applications. For instance, agricultural economists have examined crop insurance and agricultural innovations from the perspective of political economy (e.g., Robert, 2003; Alston and Pardey, 2021; Chapter 7 in this book). We leave them to our readers for further exploration.

References

Alston, J.M. and P.G. Pardey. 2021. The Economics of Agricultural Innovation. *Handbook of Agricultural Economics* (Vol. 5, Chapter 75). Elsevier, Amsterdam.

Anderson, K., G. Rausser, and J. Swinnen. 2013. Political Economy of Public Policies: Insights from Distortions to Agricultural and Food Markets. *Journal of Economic Literature* 51(2): 423–477.

Becker, G.S. 1983. A Theory of Competition among Pressure Groups for Political Influence. *The Quarterly Journal of Economics* 98(3): 371–400.

Besley, T. and S. Coate. 1997. An Economic Model of Representative Democracy. *The Quarterly Journal of Economics* 112(1): 85–114.

Black, D. 1948. On the Rationale of Group Decision-Making. *Journal of Political Economy* 56(1): 23–34.

Britz, V., P.J.-J. Herings, and A. Predtetchinski. 2010. Non-Cooperative Support for the Asymmetric Nash Bargaining Solution. *Journal of Economic Theory* 145(5): 1951–1967.

Downs, A. 1957. An Economic Theory of Political Action in a Democracy. *Journal of Political Economy* 65(2): 135–150.

Graff, G.D., Gal Hochman, David Zilberman. 2009. The political economy of agricultural biotechnology policies. *AgBioForum* 12(1): 34–46.

Grossman, G.M. and E. Helpman. 1994. Protection for Sale. *The American Economic Review* 84(4): 833.

Fargione, J., J. Hill, D. Tilman, S. Polasky, and P. Hawthorne. 2008. Land Clearing and the Biofuel Carbon Debt. *Science* 319(5867): 1235–1238.

Hanemann, M. and M. Young. 2020. Water Rights Reform and Water Marketing: Australia vs the US West. *Oxford Review of Economic Policy* 36(1): 108–131.

Harrison, R.W. 2009. The Food versus Fuel Debate: Implications for Consumers. *Journal of Agricultural and Applied Economics* 41(2): 493–500.

Harsanyi, J.C. 1962a. Measurement of Social Power, Opportunity Cost, and the Theory of Two-Person Bargaining Games. *Behavioral Science* 7: 67–80.

Harsanyi, J.C. 1962b. Measurement of Social Power in N-Person Reciprocal Power Situations. *Behavioral Science* 7: 81–91.

Harsanyi, J.C. 1963. A Simplified Bargaining Model for N-Person Cooperative Game. *International Economic Review* 4: 194–220.

Hotelling, H. 1929. Stability in Competition. *The Economic Journal* 39(153): 41–57.

Innes, R. 2003. Crop Insurance in a Political Economy: An Alternative Perspective on Agricultural Policy. *American Journal of Agricultural Economics* 85(2): 318–335.

Nash, J.F. 1950. The Bargaining Problem. *Econometrica* 18: 155–162.

Nash, J.F. 1951. Non-Cooperative Games. *Annals of Mathematics* 54: 286–295.

Nash, J.F. 1953. Two-Person Cooperative Games. *Econometrica* 21: 128–140.

Olson, M. 1965. *The Logic of Collective Action: Public Goods and the Theory of Groups*. Harvard University Press.

Paarlberg, R.L. (2001). *The Politics of Precaution: Genetically Modified Crops in Developing Countries*. Baltimore, MD: Johns Hopkins University Press.

Rausser, G.C. 1982. Political Economic Markets: PERTs and PESTs in Food and Agriculture. *American Journal of Agricultural Economics* (1982): 821–833.

Rausser, G.C. 1992. Predatory Versus Productive Government: The Case of US Agricultural Policies. *Journal of Economic Perspectives* 6(3): 133–157.

Rausser, G.C. and W.E. Foster. 1990. Political Preference Functions and Public Policy Reform. *American Journal of Agricultural Economics* 72(3): 641–652.

Rausser, G.C., J. Swinnen, and P. Zusman. 2011. Political Power and Economic Policy: Theory, Analysis, and Empirical Applications. Cambridge University Press, Cambridge.

Saleth, R.M. and A. Dinar. 2004. *The Institutional Economics of Water: A Cross-Country Analysis of Institutions and Performance*. World Bank Publications.

Schoengold, K. and D. Zilberman. 2007. The Economics of Water, Irrigation, and Development. *Handbook of Agricultural Economics* 3: 2933–2977.

Searchinger, T., R. Heimlich, R.A. Houghton, F. Dong, A. Elobeid, J. Fabiosa, S. Tokgoz, D. Hayes, and T.-H. Yu. 2008. Use of U.S. Croplands for Biofuels Increases Greenhouse Gases Through Emissions from Land-Use Change. *Science* 319(5867): 1238–1240.

Simpson, K. 2018. What the world can learn from Israel's water reuse programs. *Medill Reports*. Medill School of Journalism, Northwestern University. October 18. Available at: https://news.medill.northwestern.edu/chicago/what-the-world-can-learn-from-israels-water-reuse-programs/ (accessed January 1, 2024).

Swinnen, J. and F.A. van der Zee. 1993. The Political Economy of Agricultural Policies: A Survey. *European Review of Agricultural Economics* 20(3): 261–290.

Waterfield, G., S. Kaplan, and D. Zilberman. 2020. Willingness to Pay Versus Willingness to Vote: Consumer and Voter Avoidance of Genetically Modified Foods. *American Journal of Agricultural Economics* 102(2): 505–524.

Wright, B. 2014. Global Biofuels: Key to the Puzzle of Grain Market Behavior. *The Journal of Economic Perspectives* 28(1): 73–97.

Wu, F. (2004). Explaining public resistance to genetically modified corn: An analysis of the distribution of benefits and risks. *Risk Analysis* 24(3): 715–726.

Zarzo, D. 2021. Water Reuse in Spain. *IDA Global Connections*, Fall 2021 Issue. Available at: https://issuu.com/idadesal/docs/digital_aaff_ida_fall21/30 (accessed January 1, 2024).

Zilberman, D. 1984. Technological Change, Government Policies, and Exhaustible Resources in Agriculture. *American Journal of Agricultural Economics* 66(5): 634–640.

Zilberman, D., G. Hochman, S. Kaplan, and E. Kim. 2014. Political Economy of Biofuel. *Choices* 29(1): 1–5.

Zilberman, D., A. Huang, L. Goldberg, and T. Reardon. 2023. The Evolution of Symbiotic Innovation, Water, and Agricultural Supply Chains. *Applied Economic Perspectives and Policy* 45(3): 1592–1603.

Zilberman, D., S. Kaplan, E. Kim, and G. Waterfield. 2014. Lessons from the California GM Labelling Proposition on the State of Crop Biotechnology. In *Handbook on Agriculture, Biotechnology and Development*. Edward Elgar Publishing.

Chapter 7

Agricultural Innovation

Innovation gave birth to new technologies that had changed agriculture. From the self-scouring steel plow in the 1830s to automated combines nowadays, and from synthetic nitrogen fertilizer in the early 20th century to today's nitrogen-fixing function of genetically edited crops (Yan *et al.*, 2022), new technologies have offered agriculture numerous means to increase productivity and reduce production externalities. In this chapter, we provide an overview of the innovation literature in agricultural economics, discussing the definition and measurement of technological change, a few key models and their insights, as well as political economy and public policies about agricultural innovation or innovation in general. We then conclude with some interesting and possibly fruitful future research directions in the realm of agricultural innovation.

1. Nature of Technological Change and R&D

The first set of questions we need to ask are: What is technological change and how is it measured? In short, technological change reflects the ability to get more output from the same amount of inputs. It can be reflected by an increase in an index of quantity of output per unit of input, or by a change in production function parameters.

The first controversy we encounter in the economic literature on technological change concerns how one accounts for changes in input use when measuring technological change. Here we have two schools of thought.[1] First, Heady (1949) and Denison (1967) claim that technological change accounts for all the growth in output that is not accounted for by growth in *physical* input use. They measure an exogenous shift of isoquants where input measures are unchanged. They include changes in *quality* of input as part of technological change and measure use of input in each single period. The second school of thought, represented by Jorgenson and Griliches (1967), claims that technological change reflects changes in production functions that cannot be explained otherwise. Specifically, technological change reflects changes that cannot be explained in terms of increased quality or quantity of inputs. Technological changes are measured in input-output ratios when quality changes are considered. This thought enlightens two manifestations of technological change: increase in knowledge of the production process and improvement in input quality. Accordingly, Peterson and Hayami (1977) define technological change as "[t]he phenomena of input quality improvements or an increase in knowledge leading to increase in output per unit of input" (p. 500).

This definition tries to generate a compromise in the embodied-disembodied argument. For years, economists have asked: do technological changes embody themselves in new machinery (input changes) or are they slow processes of change in production techniques (management)? The disembodied hypothesis relied on evidence from the airplane industry when the time required to assemble a plane declined with the increase in the number of planes produced. People developed the notion of a "learning curve" where output/labor = f (time) or output/labor = f (output); function f is found to be logarithmic. This relationship became the basis for Arrow's (1962) "learning by doing" theory.

The book by Salter (1960) is a cornerstone of an alternative approach: the "Putty Clay" approach. Here, as we have seen in our

[1]Godin (2015) documented the evolvement of the "technological change" concept in the 20th century.

production chapter, it is assumed that there is a choice of input-output coefficients before a new technology is introduced and, once an investment takes place, an input/output ratio is fixed. In other words, before the new machinery is introduced, the production is in the putty stage; after the new machinery is adopted, the production has the "clay" and the input/output ratio is virtually constant. The new technology is considered embodied in the machinery that need to be bought. Technological change reflects itself in the putty stage that every year the machinery is better. Note, however, that these two theories — embodied versus disembodied — are more complementary than contradictory. It is true that new machinery, embodying new knowledge, is introduced constantly, but use efficiency improves with experience, as the user acquires new managerial ability.

A second important issue relates to the direction of technological change. With technological change, is the neoclassical production function (the *ex-ante* one, *a la* Salter, 1960) changing in a neutral or a biased manner? Technological change can be described as a shift of the unitary isoquant toward the origin (one unit of output can be produced with less inputs), but the shift can be "parallel" (that is, the quantity of all inputs declines proportionally to their use) or biased (some inputs reduce more than other).

Suppose the production function is $f(k,l)$, where k and l stand for capital and labor, respectively. There are three measures of technological bias. All three measure what occurs to the ratio of capital share to labor share (i.e., $f_k k/f_l l$, where f_k is the marginal product of capital k and f_l is the marginal product of labor l) along a certain line and can be interpreted as measures of what happens to the ratio of overtime along that particular line. Hicks' measure focuses on bias along the fixed capital/labor ratio; Harrod's measure pays attention to bias along fixed capital/output ratio; and, finally, Solow's measure emphasizes bias along fixed labor/output ratio. For instance, Hick's measure of technological bias can be written as,

$$\frac{\partial\left(\frac{f_k k}{f_l l}\right)}{\partial t}\Big|_{\text{given } \frac{k}{l}} \gtreqless 0 \Rightarrow \begin{cases} \text{labor saving} \\ \text{neutral} \\ \text{capital saving,} \end{cases} \tag{1}$$

where t stands for time.

Given these definitions, the question is: What is the nature of technological change in the real world? According to Salter (1960), technological changes are neutral. He states that manufacturers want to minimize cost and do not care if this is due to labor or capital savings. Therefore, they will encourage research possibilities that reduce both capital and labor requirements. He agrees that observed data indicate that capital/labor ratio is increasing over time, but he explains it as the consequence of the increase in the relative price of labor (the economy is moving along the iso-quants toward a more intensive use of capital, but the shape of the isoquants remains unchanged). Salter criticizes an alternative approach, the induced innovation approach, which maintains that research and innovation efforts that shift production functions are affected by relative prices (more to follow on the induced innovation approach).

Hayami and Ruttan (1970) apply the induced innovation approach to show that differences in endowment determine differences in relative prices which affect the direction of R&D in different countries. Binswanger (1974) extended their work and developed an empirical model for understanding technological bias. Atkinson and Stiglitz (1969) have a theory following Joan Robinson's ideas. Given an initial isoquant, an initial technology, the R&D activity is close to this technology and the *ex-ante* production function becomes less and less elastic and sensitive as prices change. Thus, even in the *ex-ante* production function, we may find regions of extreme rigidity. The result will be that a country might be very efficient along one k/l ratio, but less so along another.

2. Understanding Directions of Technical Changes: Predominant Models

One focus of the innovation literature concerns the directions of technical changes and the drivers of the directions. Are technologies becoming more labor-augmenting or land-augmenting? What are the underlying forces that determined the directions of technical changes? There are two major strands of literature in this realm. One proposed the induced innovation hypothesis and the other introduced the directed innovation hypothesis. In this section, we discuss them briefly by focusing on two representative papers.

2.1. *Induced innovation hypothesis: Binswanger (1974)*

Before we introduce this model, note that it is agreed that technological change includes many processes, but two are important: innovation and diffusion. Both processes involve investment — innovation is an investment in R&D and diffusion is an investment in the products of R&D. Here, we analyze the determination of the direction of an innovative effort. It is assumed that the innovator is the user of the new technology — an unlikely assumption in agriculture, where there is a separation between a developer of new technology and its users. However, it is reasonable in other industries, where a firm develops, in part or totally, its technologies. This model is also relevant for a competitive economy.

The model is based on the Evenson and Kislev (1976) model of applied research, where research is viewed as a search for new products, input processes, and so on. Research outcome is a random draw from a distribution. Basic research defines the distribution — probability of success — and applied research uses the probability rule and searching. To fix ideas, Evenson and Kislev (1976) model the optimal number of trials in a series of agricultural experiments, searching for new crop varieties with higher yields. Binswanger (1974) assumes that R&D activities can be modeled using a similar framework. The output of R&D activities are parameters of production function and, as the R&D effort increases, one may expect to see technologies with lower input-output ratios.

Let us assume that the firm's production function is $Y = f\left(\frac{K}{A}, \frac{L}{B}\right)$, where A and B are measures of capital and labor productivity and, as they decline, productivity increases. Now assume that we start with initial parameters, A_0 and B_0, and implement

R&D efforts to develop new technology. The measure of success is

$$A^* = \frac{A_0 - A_1}{A_0}, \quad \text{and} \quad B^* = \frac{B_0 - B_1}{B_0}. \tag{2}$$

Suppose there are two research lines, M and N. M is mainly capital saving and N is labor-saving. Let n be the number of research units (or simply, research input) under research line N, and m be the number of research units under research line M. Let α^N be the impact of one unit of successful research type N on capital saving, and α^M be the impact of one unit of successful research type M on capital saving. The impact of one unit of successful research on labor-saving, β^N and β^M, is defined analogously. Finally, let $\mu(m)$ denote the expected amount of successful research type M when input is m, where $\mu' > 0 > \mu''$. Similarly, let $\mu(n)$ denote the expected amount of successful research type N when input is n. The two research lines are complements if $\alpha^M > \beta^M > 0$ and $\beta^N > \alpha^N > 0$. The two research lines are substitutes if $\alpha^M > 0 > \beta^M$ and $\beta^N > 0 > \alpha^N$. The total expected effect of R&D are

$$\begin{aligned} A^* &= \mu(n)\,\alpha^N + \mu(m)\,\alpha^M = A^*(m,n), \\ \text{and } B^* &= \mu(m)\,\beta^M + \mu(n)\,\beta^N = B^*(m,n). \end{aligned} \tag{3}$$

Assume a Leontief production function, $Y = \min(\frac{K}{A}, \frac{L}{B})$ and a fixed output Y (imagine building a plant with fixed capacity). Suppose that if there is no R&D, then K_0 and L_0 are needed to produce Y. However, firms can conduct R&D to improve the efficiency of capital and labor and perhaps reduce the need for these two inputs. Risk-neutral firms will maximize the expected profits by choosing optimal R&D investment m and n:

$$\begin{aligned} \max_{m,n}[&PY - RK_0 - WL_0 + RK_0A^*(m,n) \\ &+ WL_0B^*(m,n) - mP^M - nP^N], \end{aligned} \tag{4}$$

where P, R, W, P^M, and P^N are prices of final product, capital, labor, research input for type M, and research input for type N, respectively. Solving this optimization problem yields the optimal R&D levels in the two research lines, m^* and n^*.

By defining technological bias as

$$\text{Technological Bias} = A^*(m^*, n^*) - B^*(m^*, n^*) \gtreqless 0 \Rightarrow \begin{cases} \text{capital saving} \\ \text{neutral} \\ \text{labor saving} \end{cases}, \tag{5}$$

Binswanger (1974) found that bias and research scale depend on the price and productivity of research line, cost of each factor, and the output level. For instance, if research line M is more likely to be successful (i.e., larger $\mu(m)$) or to have larger impact on efficiency (i.e., larger α^M), then technological change will be more likely to be capital-saving. Likewise, a decrease in input price of research line M will have the same impact on the direction of technological change. Moreover, larger production level, Y, will call for more research. Finally, factor price ratio, W/R, also plays a role in determining the direction of bias. If labor becomes relatively more expensive (i.e., increasing W/R) then technological change tends to be labor-saving, which is consistent with the induced innovation hypothesis.

The work by Binswanger (1974) is among a host of endeavors that seek to establish the microeconomic foundation for the induced innovation hypothesis. Nevertheless, the theoretical ground of the model is limited. For instance, the production function is in a restricted form, Leontief, and the model ignores risk and risk aversion. To include risk and risk aversion, one can re-write the optimization problem as,

$$\max_{m,n} EU\left[PF\left(\frac{K}{A}, \frac{L}{B}\right) - WL - RK - mP^M - nP^N\right],$$

$$\text{s.t.,} \quad A = A_0[1 - A^*(m,n)] \quad \text{and} \quad B = B_0[1 - B^*(m,n)]. \tag{6}$$

Another limitation of Binswanger's (1974) model is that it ignores market structure. In agriculture the farm input sector is independent from the farming sector. The input producers are monopolists or oligopolists and use their power to determine the quantity and quality of research. The input producer has to take into account the realities of the adoption process in their decision-making, and R&D decisions depend on adoption procedure parameters and are also determined simultaneously with promotion choices. Moreover, the R&D process in the Binswanger (1974) model is limited to biological and chemical technological changes. In mechanical changes, there is a specific dynamic aspect that is ignored. The research process can be then described by an optimal control model.

2.2. *Directed innovation hypothesis: Acemoglu (2002)*

In what follows we briefly introduce the model in Acemoglu (2002) that proposes the directed innovation hypothesis. Let $y = F(L, Z, A)$ denote the aggregate production function, where y is output, L is labor, Z can be viewed as capital or land, and A stands for a technology index. We further assume that $\partial F/\partial L > 0$, $\partial F/\partial Z > 0$, and $\partial F/\partial A > 0$. Thus, larger A indicates technological improvement. Acemoglu (2002) defines that, if the production function is in the form of $y = F(AL, Z)$ then a technological improvement is called *L-augmenting*; if the production function has the form of $y = F(L, AZ)$ then a technological improvement is called *Z-augmenting*. Moreover, a technological change is called *L-biased* if $\partial((\partial F/\partial L)/(\partial F/\partial Z))/\partial A > 0$ and *Z-biased* if $\partial((\partial F/\partial Z)/(\partial F/\partial L))/\partial A > 0$. Note that an *L-augmenting* technological improvement is not necessarily an *L-biased* improvement. Consider the following constant elasticity of substitution (CES) production function

$$y = \left[\gamma\cdot (A_L L)^{\frac{\sigma-1}{\sigma}} + (1-\gamma)\cdot (A_Z Z)^{\frac{\sigma-1}{\sigma}}\right]^{\frac{\sigma}{\sigma-1}}, \qquad (7)$$

where $\gamma \in (0, 1)$ is a share parameter reflecting the importance of a factor, A_L and A_Z are technology indices, and $\sigma > 0$ but $\sigma \neq 1$ is the elasticity of substitution parameter between factors L and Z. When σ approaches to 1 (respectively, 0 and $+\infty$), then the function is Cobb–Douglas (respectively, Leontieff and linear). When $\sigma > 1$, Acemoglu (2002) views the two factors as gross substitutes because in this case the demand for one factor increases as the price of the other factor increases. When $\sigma < 1$, the two factors are viewed as gross complements. Clearly, A_L is L-augmenting whereas A_Z is Z-augmenting.

If we define Ω as the ratio of marginal product of Z to marginal product of L, then it is readily checked that

$$\Omega \equiv \frac{\partial y/\partial Z}{\partial y/\partial L} = \frac{1-\gamma}{\gamma}\left(\frac{A_Z}{A_L}\right)^{\frac{\sigma-1}{\sigma}}\left(\frac{Z}{L}\right)^{-\frac{1}{\sigma}}. \tag{8}$$

From this equation we obtain

$$\frac{\partial \Omega}{\partial A_Z} = \frac{1-\gamma}{\gamma}\cdot\frac{\sigma-1}{\sigma}\cdot\frac{1}{A_L}\cdot\left(\frac{A_Z}{A_L}\cdot\frac{Z}{L}\right)^{-\frac{1}{\sigma}}. \tag{9}$$

Equation (9) shows that if $\sigma > 1$ (i.e., L and Z are gross substitutes) then $\partial\Omega/\partial A_Z > 0$ and thus A_Z is Z-biased, and that if $\sigma < 1$ (i.e., L and Z are gross complements) then A_Z is instead L-biased. Similarly, if $\sigma > 1$ then A_L is L-biased, and if $\sigma < 1$ then A_L is Z-biased. Note that an increase in A_Z will increase the marginal product of both Z and L. However, when $\sigma < 1$ (i.e., L and Z are gross complements), an increase in A_Z will increase the marginal product of L by a larger amount than that of Z. When $\sigma > 1$ the opposite is true.

The model focuses on two sectors: an intermediate good sector and an innovating sector.[2] The former produces a labor-intensive good, denoted by Y_L, and a capital-intensive good, denoted by Y_Z. When producing Y_L, L-augmenting innovations are used, and when producing Y_Z, Z-augmenting innovations are used. The innovating sector consists of technology monopolists who supply technologies that are used in the intermediate goods sector. Specifically, Y_L and Y_Z are specified by

$$Y_L = \frac{1}{1-\beta}\left(\int_0^{N_L} x_L(j)^{1-\beta}dj\right)L^{\beta} \quad \text{and}$$

$$Y_Z = \frac{1}{1-\beta}\left(\int_0^{N_Z} x_Z(j)^{1-\beta}dj\right)Z^{\beta}, \tag{10}$$

[2]To close the model, a consumer utility function with constant relative risk aversion and an aggregate production function with constant elasticity of substitution $\left(\text{i.e., } Y \equiv \left(\gamma Y_L^{\frac{\epsilon-1}{\epsilon}} + (1+\gamma)\,Y_Z^{\frac{\epsilon-1}{\epsilon}}\right)^{\frac{\epsilon}{\epsilon-1}}\right)$ are included in the model. In each period, the sum of consumption, investment, and R&D expenditure is no higher than the aggregate production level.

where $\beta \in (0,1)$ is a parameter; $x_L(j)$ is L-augmenting innovation of type j and N_L stands for the range of L-augmenting innovations; and $x_Z(j)$ and N_Z can be interpreted similarly for Z-augmenting innovations.

Assuming competitive markets for intermediate goods, the optimization problems of firms that produces Y_L or Y_Z are

$$\max_{L,\{x_L(j)\}} p_L Y_L - w_L L - \int_0^{N_L} \kappa_L(j)\, x_L(j) dj \quad \text{and}$$
$$\max_{Z,\{x_Z(j)\}} p_Z Y_Z - w_Z Z - \int_0^{N_Z} \kappa_Z(j)\, x_Z(j) dj, \tag{11}$$

where p_L and p_Z are prices of goods Y_L and Y_Z, respectively; w_L and w_Z are prices of factors L and Z; and $\kappa_L(j)$ and $\kappa_Z(j)$ are prices of innovations $x_L(j)$ and $x_Z(j)$, respectively. Taking these prices as well as N_L and N_Z as given, the first-order conditions of the optimization problems in (11) are:

$$x_L(j) = \left(\frac{p_L}{\kappa_L(j)}\right)^{1/\beta} L \quad \text{and}$$
$$x_Z(j) = \left(\frac{p_Z}{\kappa_Z(j)}\right)^{1/\beta} Z, \tag{12}$$

$$w_L = \frac{\beta}{1-\beta} p_L \left(\int_0^{N_L} x_L(j)^{1-\beta} dj\right) L^{\beta-1} \quad \text{and}$$
$$w_Z = \frac{\beta}{1-\beta} p_Z \left(\int_0^{N_Z} x_Z(j)^{1-\beta} dj\right) Z^{\beta-1}. \tag{13}$$

Equation (12) shows that the demand for innovations increases in the output prices of the intermediate goods and factors employed but decreases in innovation prices. Equation (13) simply shows the marginal cost of a factor (L or Z) is equal to its marginal benefit.

We now examine the innovating monopolists' optimization problem. For simplification, we assume that the marginal cost of all innovations is the same and denoted by ψ. Therefore, the profit maximization problem of supplying innovation $x_L(j)$ is

$$\max_{\kappa_L(j)}\{\pi_L(j) = (\kappa_L(j) - \psi)\, x_L(j)\}. \tag{14}$$

Based on $x_L(j)$ in Equation (12), the first-order condition in optimization problem (14) implies that the profit-maximizing price for the innovation is $k_L(j)^* = \psi/(1-\beta)$. For simplicity, Acemoglu (2002) normalizes ψ to be $1-\beta$. Therefore, the optimal price for L-augmenting innovations is 1. Similarly, the optimal price for Z-augmenting innovations is also 1. The innovation demand in Equation (12) and the optimal prices demonstrate that maximized instantaneous profits from supplying the L-augmenting and Z-augmenting technologies are

$$\pi_L = \beta p_L^{1/\beta} L \quad \text{and} \quad \pi_Z = \beta p_Z^{1/\beta} Z. \tag{15}$$

Consider a steady state and let the interest rate be r. Then the innovating monopolists' net present values from supplying the innovations over the lifetime can be written as

$$V_L = \frac{\beta p_L^{1/\beta} L}{r} \quad \text{and} \quad V_Z = \frac{\beta p_Z^{1/\beta} Z}{r}, \tag{16}$$

from which we obtain Acemoglu's (2002) key message:

$$\frac{V_Z}{V_L} = \left(\frac{p_Z}{p_L}\right)^{\frac{1}{\beta}} \cdot \frac{Z}{L} = \left(\frac{1-\gamma}{\gamma}\right)^{\frac{\epsilon}{\sigma}} \left(\frac{N_Z}{N_L}\right)^{-\frac{1}{\sigma}} \left(\frac{Z}{L}\right)^{\frac{\sigma-1}{\sigma}}, \tag{17}$$

where $\sigma \equiv \epsilon - (\epsilon - 1)(1-\beta)$ is the derived elasticity of substitution between factors L and Z.[3] Note that the relative profitability from

[3]The second equation in (17) holds because (a) $\frac{p_Z}{p_L} = \frac{\partial Y/\partial Y_Z}{\partial Y/\partial Y_L} = \frac{1-\gamma}{\gamma}\left(\frac{Y_Z}{Y_L}\right)^{-\frac{1}{\epsilon}}$ in competitive market equilibrium; and (b) $Y_L = \frac{1}{1-\hat{a}} p_L^{(1-\beta)/\beta} N_L L$ and $Y_Z = \frac{1}{1-\beta} p_Z^{(1-\beta)/\beta} N_Z Z$ obtained by substituting (12) into (10).

Z-augmenting innovations and L-augmenting innovations, V_Z/V_L, determines innovators' incentive to supply a certain type of innovation. The larger the V_Z/V_L value, the greater incentive to provide Z-augmenting innovation. The first equation in (17) shows that two forces influence the relative profitability and thus the direction of technical changes: the price effect, denoted by $(p_Z/p_L)^{1/\beta}$, and the market size effect, denoted by Z/L. Clearly, the price effect will increase the incentive to supply innovations that produce the more *expensive* intermediate goods, while the market size effect will increase innovations that augment the more *abundant* factor. Note that an exogenous increase in relative abundance of one factor has both price and market size effects on the direction of innovation. The price effect occurs because an increase in the abundance of a factor decreases its relative price, and, therefore, decreases the incentive to supply, whereas an increase in the abundance increases the market size for innovation augmenting this factor, and, therefore, increases the incentive to supply. If the price effect dominates the market size effect, then an increase in the relative abundance of a factor will decrease innovations augmenting this factor. However, if the market size effect dominates the price effect, then the opposite is true.

The second equation in (17) reveals conditions under which one effect dominates the other. The conditions are strikingly straightforward: If $\sigma < 1$, then the price effect dominates the market size effect; if $\sigma > 1$, then the opposite is true. The intuition is as follows. As noted earlier, when $\sigma < 1$ then the two factors are gross complements. In this case, an increase in the abundance of factor Z would increase the demand for factor L, and thus its price, significantly. Therefore, the relative price between Z and L will decrease so much that the overall incentive to supply Z-augmenting innovations will decrease. When $\sigma > 1$ then the two factors are gross substitutes, and thus an increase in the abundance of Z will decrease the prices of both Z and L. In this case, the relative prices of these two factors may not change very much and therefore the price effect is moderate and dominated by the market size effect.

Interestingly, by using Equation (13) we can re-write the first equation in (17) as

$$\frac{V_Z}{V_L} = \frac{w_Z}{w_L} \cdot \frac{Z}{L} \cdot \frac{N_Z}{N_L}, \tag{18}$$

which shows that the induced innovation hypothesis proposed by Hicks (1932) only partially captured the incentives to innovate by emphasizing on the relative factor price, w_Z/w_L, while overlooking the market size effect that is reflected by Z/L.

3. Politics, Policies, and Innovations

In addition to market forces, political forces or public policies can also have a significant influence on innovations. In this section, we discuss three important papers that examine the relationship between innovation and political forces or public policies.

3.1. *Political forces and innovation: de Gorter and Zilberman (1990)*

Although innovation was not directly mentioned, de Gorter and Zilberman (1990) analyze the role of political influence and market features on public expenditure, with various R&D projects as motivating examples. Focusing on a closed economy under perfect competition markets, they highlight the role of demand elasticity and political influence on R&D investment. In this subsection, we will briefly review their model.

Let $U(q, Z) = u(q) + Z$ be the utility function of a representative consumer, where q is a specific commodity (e.g., wheat) and Z is a numeraire good. On the production side, let $C(q, E)$ denote the cost function of a representative producer who produces the commodity, with E representing the public expenditure on R&D. The funding source of the public expenditure can be consumers (via tax), or a group of producers (via, e.g., producer associations), or both. Suppose that $\alpha \in [0, 1]$ is the portion of public expenditure sponsored by consumers via tax. Obviously, if the public expenditure is fully funded by consumers (respectively, producers) then $\alpha = 1$ (respectively, $\alpha = 0$). We assume that $C_q > 0$, $C_{qq} > 0$, $C_E < 0$, $C_{EE} > 0$, and $C_{qE} < 0$ to ensure that the cost function is convex in both q and E, and that an increase in E will reduce the marginal cost of q (i.e., shifting the supply curve rightward).

Let p be the price of the commodity and Y be the income of the representative consumer. The consumer maximizes her utility by choosing the consumption quantity:

$$\max_q \{u(q) + Y - pq - \alpha E\}. \tag{19}$$

For the representative producer, the profit-maximizing problem can be written as,

$$\max_q \{pq - C(q, E) - (1 - \alpha)E\}. \tag{20}$$

Due to perfect competition, both consumers and producers are price takers. We can thus derive the demand and supply relationships based on problems (19) and (20) as follows: $q^D = D(p) \equiv u_q^{-1}(p)$ and $q^S = S(p, E) \equiv C_q^{-1}(p, E)$, where subscript q denotes derivative with respect to q. Competitive market equilibrium will be reached when $q^D = q^S$ (or, equivalently, $u_q = C_q$, marginal utility equal to marginal cost), which determines the equilibrium price and quantity as functions of expenditure: $p^*(E)$ and $q^*(E)$.

By applying the implicit function theorem to the equilibrium condition, $u_q(q) = C_q(q, E) = p^*$, one can obtain the impact of public good expenditure on equilibrium quantity and price. Specifically,

$$q_E^* = \frac{C_{qE}}{u_{qq} - C_{qq}} = \frac{C_{qE}\eta^S\eta^D}{p(\eta^S - \eta^D)} \quad \text{and} \quad p_E^* = \frac{C_{qE}}{1 - \eta^D/\eta^S}, \tag{21}$$

where $\eta^S \equiv S_p \cdot p/q = p/(C_{qq} \cdot q)$ and $\eta^D \equiv D_p \cdot p/q = p/(u_{qq} \cdot q)$ are price elasticities of supply and demand, respectively. Because $C_{qE} < 0$, $\eta^S > 0$, and $\eta^D < 0$, one can readily check that $q_E^* > 0$ and $p_E^* < 0$. Equation (21) shows that the quantity and price effect of R&D expenditure depends on the marginal cost effect of the said expenditure, as well as the supply and demand elasticities. For instance, if the R&D expenditure has large impact on marginal cost in terms of absolute value or if the demand is inelastic, then an increase in R&D expenditure tends to have large price effect.

Plugging $q^*(E)$ and $p^*(E)$ into the utility function and the profit function, we obtain

$$\begin{cases} U^*(E) \equiv u(q^*(E)) + Y - p^*(E)\,q^*(E) - \alpha E \\ \pi^*(E) \equiv p^*(E)\,q^*(E) - C(q^*(E), E) - (1-\alpha)E. \end{cases} \tag{22}$$

Differentiating equations in (22) with respect to E and using the equilibrium condition $C_q|_{q^*} = u_q|_{q^*} = p^*$ yields

$$\begin{cases} U_E^* = -q^*(E)\,p_E^* - \alpha. \\ \pi_E^* = -C_E + q^*(E)p_E^* - (1-\alpha). \end{cases} \tag{23}$$

The equations in (23) show that a one-unit increase in R&D expenditure, E, will have three effects: (1) it will decrease the consumer's utility and the producer's profit by α and $1-\alpha$, respectively; (2) it will increase consumer's utility by $-q^*(E)\,p_E^*$ due to the price effect, but decrease the producer's profit by the same amount (i.e., consumers spend less on the same quantity of goods and accordingly, producers receive less); and (3) it will reduce the producer's production cost by C_E.

The total social welfare is $W^*(E) = U^*(E) + \pi^*(E)$. Taking derivative of $W^*(E)$ with respect to E yields $W_E^* = U_E^* + \pi_E^* = -C_E - 1$, which indicates that, assuming an interior optimal solution for E, at the socially optimal R&D expenditure level, the marginal cost of R&D expenditure (i.e., 1) should be equation to the marginal benefit of the expenditure (i.e., $-C_E$). However, the socially optimal R&D expenditure level (denoted by E^*) may not be the same as the expenditure level that is optimal to the producers (denoted by E_1^*) or that to the consumers (denoted by E_2^*). Note that E^* does not depend on the value of α, but E_1^* and E_2^* do (see equations in (23)). Depending on who funds the expenditure and who determines the quantity of fund, there are four scenarios to consider: (a) consumers solely fund the expenditure and determine its quantity; (b) producers solely fund the expenditure and determine its quantity; (c) consumer solely fund the expenditure but producers determine the expenditure quantity (government "captured" by producers); and (d) producers solely fund the expenditure but consumers determine the quantity (government "captured" by consumers). Assuming interior solutions, under scenarios a) to c), the R&D expenditure is determined by $-q^*(E)p_E^* - 1 = 0$, $-C_E + q^*p_E^* - 1 = 0$, and $-C_E + q^*p_E^* = 0$, respectively. Obviously, under scenario d) consumers would select infinite amount of R&D expenditure (i.e., $E_2^* = \infty$). We can see the optimal R&D expenditures will likely differ across the four different scenarios, indicating that the political influence will affect R&D expenditure.

Note that at the social optimum E^*, we have $-C_E = 1$ and thus $U_E^* = -q^*(E)p_E^* - \alpha = -\pi_E^*$. Therefore, evaluated at E^*, if $-q^*(E)p_E^* > \alpha$ then $U_E^* > 0$ and $\pi_E^* < 0$, indicating $E_1^* < E_2^*$. In other words, if α is small or if the demand is more inelastic (i.e., price effect of R&D is larger, see Equation (23)), then it is likely the case that $E_2^* > E^* > E_1^*$. In plain English, this means that if consumers only support a small portion of R &D or if the R&D will reduce price considerably, then consumers will prefer R&D expenditure that is larger than the social optimal expenditure and producers will prefer an expenditure that is smaller than social optimum. In contrast, when α is large or when the demand is more elastic, then the opposite is true. de Gorter and Zilberman (1990) use these results to explain why producers are more willing to fund R&D on specialty crops (high demand elasticity) but less willing to fund R&D on major row crops (low demand elasticity).

3.2. *Political connection and innovation: Akcigit et al. (2023)*

Akcigit *et al.* (2023) explore how political connection can prevent innovation. Assume that an incumbent firm's production function is $y = l$, where y is output and l labor input. The demand function facing the incumbent is $p = q^\beta y^{-\beta}$, where p is output price and q stands for product quality that is determined by innovation. Larger

q indicates higher quality. Suppose that labor cost is w per unit and that regulatory burdens increase the marginal cost of production by a portion of τ. We also assume a monopolistic market. Therefore, the profit maximization problem of an incumbent without any political connection to remove the regulatory burdens is

$$\pi^n = \max_l \{py - (1+\tau)\,wl\}, \quad \text{s.t.} \quad p = q^\beta y^{-\beta} \quad \text{and} \quad y = l. \quad (24)$$

Solving this optimization problem we obtain the optimal labor demand $l^* = q \cdot [(1-\beta)/((1+\tau)\,w)]^{1/\beta}$, the optimal revenue $R^* = q \cdot [(1-\beta)/((1+\tau)\,w)]^{(1-\beta)/\beta}$, the corresponding labor productivity $R^*/l^* = [(1+\tau)\,w]/(1-\beta)$, and the maximized profit $\pi^{n*} = \pi \cdot (1+\tau)^{-(1-\beta)/\beta} q$, where $\pi \equiv \beta((1-\beta)/w)^{(1-\beta)/\beta}$.

If the incumbent has political connections they can utilize them to remove the regulatory burdens at a fixed cost w^p, then the profit maximization problem would be

$$\pi^p = \max_l \{py - wl - w^p\}, \quad \text{s.t.} \quad p = q^\beta y^{-\beta} \quad \text{and} \quad y = l. \quad (25)$$

Solving problem (25) we obtain the optimal labor demand $\hat{l} = q \cdot [(1-\beta)/w]^{1/\beta}$, the optimal revenue $\hat{R} = q \cdot [(1-\beta)/w]^{(1-\beta)/\beta}$, the corresponding labor productivity $\hat{R}/\hat{l} = w/(1-\beta)$, and the maximized profit $\widehat{\pi^p} = \pi q - w^p$.

One can readily check that $\hat{l} > l^*$, $\hat{R} > R^*$, and $\hat{R}/\hat{l} < R^*/l^*$, indicating that an incumbent, if transitioned from being politically unconnected to connected, would hire more labor, generate higher revenue, but operate at lower productivity level. By comparing π^{n*} with $\widehat{\pi^p}$, we can see that, if $q > \hat{q}^s \equiv w^p/[\pi \cdot (1-(1+\tau)^{-(1-\beta)/\beta})]$, then the incumbent will prefer to be politically connected.

Due to the specific form of the production function (i.e., $y = l$), the productivity level here is equal to the monopolistic price. One may conclude that political connection is welfare-enhancing because now the price is lower and output is higher. This is only true in a static scenario, where innovations and new market entrances are ignored. However, in a dynamic framework where innovations increase product quality and market entrants with new innovations replace incumbent firms, political connections may prevent the entrance of new firms and thus dampen the dynamism of the market. To see this, let us introduce entrances and exits into the model.

Imagine that a potential entrant works on innovation aiming to improve the product quality, q, in the existing market. The success of the innovation occurs at Poisson arrival rate δ. The size of the success, λ, is a random variable with cumulative distribution function $F(\lambda)$. So, the product quality of the entrant with successful innovation is $q' = (1 + \lambda)q$, and the demand is determined by $p' = (q')^{\beta}(y')^{-\beta}$, where p' and y' is the price and quantity of the new product. If the entrant and the incumbent are in the same status regarding political connections (i.e., both have connections or none have connections), then the entrant will be able to replace the incumbent as long as $\lambda > 0$.[4] In this case, because the success of innovation occurs following a Poisson distribution with rate δ, the incumbent is replaced at rate δ.

When the incumbent is politically connected whereas the entrant is not, then not every successful innovation with $\lambda > 0$ will cause the incumbent to be replaced. Note that the lowest price that a politically connected incumbent can charge is w, the marginal production cost of the product without any regulatory burdens. However, the lowest price that a politically unconnected entrant can charge is $(1+\tau)w$. Therefore, in order to have the price-adjusted quality of the entrant's product (i.e., $(1 + \lambda)q/[(1 + \tau)\, w]$) greater than that of the incumbent's product (i.e., q/w), the entrant's innovation must be at least able to improve the existing quality by a portion of $\lambda^* = \tau$. Here we assume that the entrant and the incumbent will engage in a quality-adjusted price competition until one of them exits, then the market structure will return to be monopolistic.

To analyze the incumbent's decisions on whether to establish political connection, one more assumption is in order: with probability α the entrant has political connection and with probability $1 - \alpha$ it has no political connection. If the incumbent firm chooses not to be politically connected, then the net present value of its lifetime

---

[4]For simplicity we assume that products of the entrant and the incumbent are perfect substitutes after adjusting quality.

profit, denoted by $V_0(q)$, is

$$rV_0(q) = \pi \cdot (1+\tau)^{-1} \cdot q - \delta \cdot V_0(q), \tag{26}$$

where r is the interest rate and $\pi(1+\tau)^{-1}q$ is the instantaneous profit after setting $\beta = 1/2$. Equation (26) states that the instantaneous rent of the incumbent is equal to the instantaneous profit minus the expected loss caused by the incumbent being replaced by an entrant in the next moment. Based on Equation (26) we can solve $V_0(q)$ out as

$$V_0(q) = \frac{\pi \cdot (1+\tau)^{-1} \cdot q}{r+\delta}. \tag{27}$$

If the incumbent establishes political connection, the net present value of its lifetime profit, denoted by V_1, is

$$rV_1(q) = \pi q - w^p - \delta\left[\alpha + (1-\alpha)\,Pr\ (\lambda > \lambda^*)\ \right] V_1(q). \tag{28}$$

The interpretation of Equation (28) is similar to that of Equation (26). The instantaneous rent of the incumbent is equal to the instantaneous profit minus the expected loss from the incumbent being replaced by an entrant. Note that the chance that the incumbent is replaced by an entrant is δ (i.e., the chance that an innovation arrives) multiplied by the sum of α (i.e., the chance that the entrant is politically connected) and $(1-\alpha)\,Pr\ (\lambda > \lambda^*)$ (i.e., the chance that the entrant is not politically connected but the innovation is sufficiently large). Rearranging Equation (28), one can solve $V_1(q)$ as

$$V_1(q) = \frac{\pi q - w^p}{r + \delta[\alpha + (1-\alpha)\,Pr\ (\lambda > \lambda^*)\ ]}. \tag{29}$$

The incumbent will establish the political connection if $V_1(q) > V_0(q)$, which is equivalent to

$$q > \hat{q}^d \equiv \frac{w^p}{\pi(1 - \frac{r+\widetilde{\delta}}{r+\delta} \cdot \frac{1}{1+\tau})}, \tag{30}$$

where $\widetilde{\delta} \equiv \delta[\alpha + (1-\alpha)\,Pr\ (\lambda > \lambda^*)\ ]$. Recall that in the static framework the threshold quality above which the incumbent will establish political connection is $\hat{q}^s = w^p/[\pi \cdot (1-(1+\tau)^{-1})]$ after we set $\beta = 1/2$. One can check that $\hat{q}^d < \hat{q}^s$, indicating that in a dynamic framework the incumbent has more incentive to establish political connection. By doing so, the incumbent makes new firm entrance less likely to occur and thus it can survive longer. As a result, the innovations that can be eventually used in production occur at a lower rate. Specifically, as discussed earlier, when the incumbent does not have political connection, the implemented innovations occur at rate δ. When the incumbent has political connection, however, the implemented innovations occur at rate $\widetilde{\delta} \leq \delta$, where the equality holds when $\alpha = 1$ or $Pr\ (\lambda > \lambda^*)\ = 1$, or both. The results show that if the entrant has political connection with certainty, then the implemented innovations occur at the same rate as that when neither the incumbent nor the entrant is politically connected.

3.3. *Innovation incentive systems: Wright (1983)*

Public policies or institutional arrangements, such as patents, prizes, and contracts, have been used as tools to incentivize and support innovations. However, few studies have compared their efficiency to promote innovations.[5] Wright (1983) is perhaps the first study that examines and compares the efficiency of these tools considering asymmetric information. In this subsection, we briefly introduce the model developed in the study.

Wright (1983) assumes that the analysis framework is static with numerous homogeneous and risk-neutral inventors. The research target is a process invention that, if successful, can generate benefit B for society. For each inventor, the cost of generating μ units of research activity is $c(\mu)$. Assuming perfect competition, for each inventor the optimal research activity, denoted by μ^*, will be achieved at the minimum average cost. For simplicity, μ^* is normalized to be 1, setting the number of firms in the industry equal to the number of research activity unit in the market. Let $m \equiv \Sigma\mu$ be the total

[5]Clancy and Moschini (2013) offer a comprehensive review regarding the innovation incentives provided by patents, prizes, and research contracts.

research activity in the society. The total cost of all research activity is denoted by $C(m) \equiv \Sigma c(\mu)$, with $C'(m) > 0$ and $C''(m) \geq 0$. Let $P(m)$ denote the probability that at least one firm out of m firms will be successful.

Given the above assumptions, the socially optimal level of research activity, denoted by m_0, will be determined by $B \cdot P'(m_0) = C'(m_0)$. That is, the social optimum is reached when the marginal benefit of research (i.e., $B \cdot P'(m_0)$) is equal to the marginal cost (i.e., $C'(m_0)$). With complete information, the social optimal can be reached by a research administrator offering a payment $B \cdot P'(m_0)$ for each unit of research activity provided by the inventing firms. Or, the same social optimum can be achieved by directly contracting with inventing firms for m_0 units of research activity under price $B \cdot P'(m_0)$. However, Wright (1983) shows that a patent or prize policy that rewards the successful firms with full benefit of the invention may not induce the socially optimal level of research activity. The reason is explained as follows.

Due to the homogeneity assumption of firms, each firm has an equal chance to be successful. If there are multiple successful firms, then the award is shared equally among these firms. Therefore, under the "full-benefit" patent or prize, the expected award for a firm is $B \cdot P(m)/m$ per unit of research activity,[6] which is the marginal benefit of research activity for an individual firm. Because $P''(m) < 0$, we have $B \cdot P(m)/m > B \cdot P'(m)$. As a result, in the equilibrium under the "full-benefit" patent or prize, the marginal benefit and marginal cost of research activity, thus the quantity of research activities, are higher than the corresponding socially optimal levels. This result is known as the "common pool problem" in the innovation literature following Dasgupta and Stiglitz (1980), analogous to the inferior outcome from competitive fishing in a common fishery described by Gordon (1954). One strategy to fix this "common pool problem" under complete information is to just offer a portion (say, γ) of the full benefit to the successful firms, such

[6]This intuitive conclusion can also be readily shown by using the properties of Binomial distribution.

that $\gamma \cdot B \cdot P(m)/m = B \cdot P'(m)$. This can explain why patents have limited, instead of infinite, life.

However, in reality, it is rare to have complete information. For activities as complex as research, it is impossible for policymakers to know the specific research costs or the benefits of a successful research outcome, while the inventing firms may have much better information on their costs and potential benefits. Wright (1983) goes one step further from complete information, studying two scenarios under which cost and, separately, benefit of invention are known to the firms but unknown to policymakers. Here we discuss them briefly.

The first scenario involves random research costs with non-random benefits. A heuristic approach is employed to approximate welfare losses or gains from patents or prizes when compared to a direct contract of research activities. Figure 1 depicts equilibrium research activities when a prize is promised by policymakers under

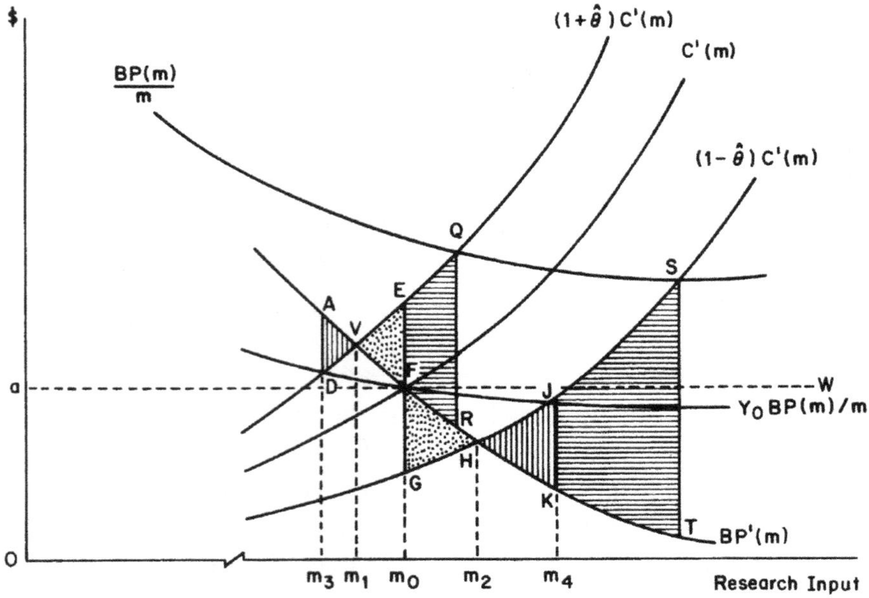

Figure 1. Social welfare of prizes when cost information is asymmetric.
Note: The figure is a reprint of Figure 1 in Wright (1983). Copyright American Economic Association; reproduced with permission of the author and of the *American Economic Review*.

this scenario. Note that Wright's analysis is *ex-ante*, and the solutions are optimal only in the sense of expectation. Assume that, from the policymaker's point of view, the marginal cost is $(1+\widehat{\theta})C'(m)$ and $(1-\widehat{\theta})C'(m)$ with equal chance. As we discussed before, if full benefit were to be awarded to successful inventing firms, the expected return per unit of research activity would be $B \cdot P(m)/m$, which is larger than the marginal benefit of research activity, $B \cdot P'(m)$, resulting in over-investment in research and welfare losses. As depicted in Figure 1, the line $B \cdot P(m)/m$ crosses lines $(1+\widehat{\theta})C'(m)$ and $(1-\widehat{\theta})C'(m)$ at points Q and S, respectively, resulting in much larger research activity than m_0, the *ex-ante* socially optimal research level. To reach this level by using prize or patent, the policymaker should only award a portion (i.e., Y_0) of the full benefit to successful inventing firms, depicted by line $Y_0 \cdot B \cdot P(m)/m$ in Figure 1. With this prize or patent, the social welfare gains (or losses) of using prize or patent when compared with contracting form m_0 units of research can be measured by $\Delta w = 0.5 \times [(\alpha_{VEF} - \alpha_{AVD}) + (\alpha_{FHG} - \alpha_{HJK})]$, where α stands for "area." Wright (1983) shows that under certain assumptions, Δw can be approximated by a function of elasticity of supply of research activity, elasticity of the average probability of research success, and the elasticity of marginal probability of research success.

Under the second scenario, the invention benefit, B, is assumed to be random whereas the invention cost is assumed to be deterministic. Here, the social optimal research activity under complete information, m_0, can be reached by either direct contracting or a discounted prize. The welfare gains and losses of awarding a patent when compared with awarding a contract or prize to fix the research activity at m_0 can also be approximated by another function of elasticities of research activity, average probability of research success, and marginal probability of success. Wright (1983) numerically shows that when success probability of research is high, then contracts are preferred to prizes and patents. When success probability is low but the elasticity of research supply is high, patents would be preferred to prizes and contracts. Prizes will likely outperform patents and contracts when success probability is moderate and the elasticity of research supply is small.

4. Agricultural Innovation and Climate Change

Agricultural innovation is expected to be a major tool for agriculture to respond to climate change. A few studies have explored the impact of climate change on agricultural innovation. Based on country-level patent data over the world, Miao and Popp (2014) show that drought promotes innovations of drought-tolerant seeds. Miao (2020) finds similar results using patent data for drought-tolerant traits of 10 major crops in the United States, showing that drought-tolerant innovations of these crops are quite sensitive to drought severity measured by Palmer Drought Severity Index (PDSI): a one-unit increase in PDSI will increase drought-tolerant trait patents by about 40%–60%.

A recent paper by Moscona and Sastry (2023) also investigates the impact of climate change on agricultural innovation. However, this paper pushes the research frontier one step further: after quantifying the responsiveness of agricultural innovation to climate change, they analyze how much the agricultural innovation mitigates climate change's impact on agriculture. Here we briefly describe this study.

First, Moscona and Sastry (2023) develop a theoretical framework to predict the direction of technological change under climate change. Finding the prediction ambiguous, they proceed the analysis with a novel empirical approach to examine the interaction between climate change effect and agricultural innovation. Their theoretical framework starts with a few assumptions. First, the production function for farm $i \in [0, 1]$ is

$$Y_i = \alpha^{-\alpha}(1-\alpha)^{-1}G(A_i, \theta)^{\alpha}T_i^{1-\alpha}, \tag{31}$$

where Y_i is crop yield, $\alpha \in [0, 1]$ is a parameter reflecting the relative importance of inputs, A_i can be viewed as local climate partially governing farm i's productivity, θ measures the overall technological advancement (or, technology quality), and finally, T_i is the quantity of technology adopted on farm i. Note that $\alpha^{-\alpha}(1-\alpha)^{-1}$ is included for modeling convenience. It is further assumed that $G(A_i,\ \theta) > 0$, $\partial G/\partial A_i > 0$, $\partial G/\partial\theta > 0$, and $\partial^2 G/\partial\theta^2 < 0$.[7] With crop price, p, and technology price, q, the optimal technology demand from farm i is $T_i^* = \alpha^{-1} p^{\frac{1}{\alpha}} q^{-\frac{1}{\alpha}} G(A_i, \theta)$.

Moscona and Sastry (2023) assume that the innovator is a monopolist who determines technology price, q, and overall technology quality, θ. With marginal cost of producing the technology input at $1-\alpha$ and the development cost at $C(\theta)$, where $C'(\theta) > 0$ and $C''(\theta) > 0$, the innovator's optimization problem can be written as,

$$\max_{q,\theta}\left[(q-(1-\alpha))\,\alpha^{-1} p^{\frac{1}{\alpha}} q^{-\frac{1}{\alpha}} \int G(A_i,\theta)\, dF(A_i) - C(\theta)\right], \quad (32)$$

where $F(A_i)$ is the cumulative distribution function of productivity A_i. By solving the optimization problem in Equation (32), we can obtain that $q^* = 1$ and $\theta^* = \text{argmax}\{p^{1/\alpha} \int G(A_i,\ \theta)\, dF(A_i) - C(\theta)\}$. See Online Appendix B of Moscona and Sastry (2023) for detailed derivations.

Moscona and Sastry (2023) define climate substitutability of technology as following: If $G_{12} \leq 0$, then technological advances are climate substitutes; if $G_{12} \geq 0$, then climate complements. Intuitively, if technology advances can decrease the marginal product of climate, G_1, then the technology is substituting for climate. On the other hand, if technological advances increase the marginal product of climate, then the technology is complementing climate. Moscona and Sastry (2023) show that if crop price is fixed (e.g., in a small open economy), then damaging climate change will increase climate-substituting technology but decrease climate-complementing technology. In a larger economy where crop price is

[7]Note that $\partial G/\partial A_i > 0$ could be a strong assumption. Many studies (e.g., Schlenker and Roberts, 2009) have shown that the impact of weather on crop yield is non-linear: above a threshold value, an increase in temperature or precipitation will harm crop yield. Therefore, a more realistic assumption could be $\partial G/\partial A_i > 0$ when A_i is small whereas $\partial G/\partial A_i < 0$ when A_i is large. Exploring how the theoretical results in Moscona and Sastry (2023) would change under this more realistic assumption could be an interesting exercise.

endogenously determined, however, a damaging climate change will still encourage climate-substituting technology, but its impact on climate-complementing technology is ambiguous. The idea is that damaging climate change reduces crop production and, thereby, increases crop price. An increased crop price indicates increased marginal product value of technology. This positive price effect on technology innovation will further strengthen the increased demand for climate-substituting technology, but will weaken or even reverse the decreased demand for climate-complementing technology. Therefore, the direction of changes in climate-complementing technology is ambiguous.

To empirically determine the impact of climate change on agricultural innovation, Moscona and Sastry (2023) harmonize the U.S. Department of Agriculture Variety Name List, Plant Variety Protection certificates, and U.S. patents on non-livestock agriculture to construct various measures of agricultural innovation and conduct econometric analysis. Climate stress is measured by the difference between observed temperature and a crop's upper threshold for optimal growing temperature. Their econometric analyses, together with numerous robustness checks, show that historical climate change had incentivized agricultural innovation: Based on data for 69 crops, climate change over 1950–2016 caused, on average, about 20% increase in agricultural innovation.

After quantifying the impact of climate change on agricultural innovation, Moscona and Sastry (2023) creatively move one step further to quantify to what extent the climate-induced innovation has mitigated the negative impact of climate change on agriculture. Using land value as the dependent variable, the authors explore how the exposure to agricultural innovation of one county may mitigate the negative impact of climate change on land value, where the exposure to innovation is measured by a county's exposure to extreme temperature, justified by the relationship between extreme temperature and innovation discussed in the previous paragraph. Moscona and Sastry (2023) find that in the past six decades, agricultural innovation had mitigated the negative impact of climate change by about 20%. Future agricultural innovation is estimated to reduce climate change impact on agriculture by about 13%, indicating that agricultural innovation itself is far from enough to eliminate the negative impact of climate change on U.S. agriculture.

Moscona and Sastry (2023) is the first study that attempts to examine the extent to which agricultural innovation may mitigate climate change's impact on agriculture. It opens a new field of research in agricultural economics and in the literature of climate change adaptation. Numerous subsequent research inquiries can be explored following Moscona and Sastry (2023). For instance, it might be of interest to further explore the role of public research (e.g., research in agricultural experiment stations) in mitigating climate change impact, where Moscona and Sastry (2023) do not find conclusive results, likely due to their rough measurement of agricultural innovation. Second, understanding crop heterogeneity in innovation's impact on mitigating the climate effect can be of policy relevance because it would be a prerequisite for optimal allocation of research fund across crops. Furthermore, it is not well understood how agricultural innovation affects the response to climate change on a spatial level. As Evenson (1989) and Moscona and Sastry (2022) point out, technologies developed based on local environment and climate may hinder technological spillover, which may in turn inhibit farmers from better adapting to climate change.

5. Conclusions

The literature on innovation is vast, and this chapter only covers a few topics about agricultural innovation that the authors are most interested in, leaving many important topics undiscussed, such as returns to agricultural R&D, efficiency of various schemes managing R&D funds, innovation and market power, as well as the relationship between agricultural innovation and agricultural productivity. Readers can find discussions of these topics in Huffman and Just (1994), Fuglie *et al.* (1996), Moschini and Lapan (1997), Alston and Pardey (2021), and Pardey and Alston (2021).

Innovation, from an idea to the final products or processes that can be adopted by end users, involves complex activities, such as research, manufacture, and marketing. Its emergence and success can be affected by numerous factors, such as existing knowledge stock, breakthroughs in basic research, supply of researchers, political forces, market structure, infrastructure of supply chains, and consumers' ever-changing tastes, to name a few. Sunding and Zilberman (2001) divide the innovation process into five stages: discovery, registration, development, production, and marketing. A recent article by Zilberman *et al.* (2022) provides a comprehensive discussion about innovation supply chain originating from innovative ideas and culminating with final marketed products, where adoption starts. We discuss adoption in the next chapter.

References

Acemoglu, D. 2002. Directed Technical Change. *The Review of Economic Studies* 69(4): 781–809.

Akcigit, U., S. Baslandze, and F. Lotti. 2023. Connecting to Power: Political Connections, Innovation, and Firm Dynamics. *Econometrica* 91(2): 529–564.

Alston, J.M. and P.G. Pardey. 2021. The Economics of Agricultural Innovation. Barrett, C.B. and D.R. Just (Eds.), *Handbook of Agricultural Economics*, Vol. 5, Chapter 75, pp. 3895–3980.

Atkinson, A.B. and J.E. Stiglitz. 1969. A New View of Technological Change. *The Economic Journal* 79(315): 573–578.

Arrow, K.J. 1962. The Economic Implications of Learning by Doing. *The Review of Economic Studies* 29(3): 155–173.

Binswanger, H.P. 1974. A Microeconomic Approach to Induced Innovation. *Economic Journal* 84(336): 940–958.

Clancy, M.S. and G.C. Moschini. 2013. Incentives for Innovation: Patents, Prizes, and Research Contracts. *Applied Economic Perspectives and Policy* 35(2): 206–241.

Dasgupta, P. and J. Stiglitz. 1980. Uncertainty, Industrial Structure, and the Speed of R&D. *The Bell Journal of Economics* 11(1): 1–28.

de Gorter, H. and D. Zilberman. 1990. On the Political Economy of Public Goods Inputs in Agriculture. *American Journal of Agricultural Economics* 72: 131–137.

Denison, E.F. 1967. *Why Growth Rates Differ: Postwar Experience in Nine Western Countries.* Brookings Institution, Washington, DC.

Evenson, R.E. 1989. Spillover Benefits of Agricultural Research: Evidence from U.S. Experience. *American Journal of Agricultural Economics* 71(2): 447–452.

Evenson, R.E. and Y. Kislev. 1976. A Stochastic Model of Applied Research. *Journal of Political Economy* 84(2): 265–282.

Fuglie, K., N. Ballenger, K. Day, C. Klotz, M. Ollinger, J. Reilly, U. Vasavada, and J. Yee. 1996. *Agricultural Research and Development: Public and Private Investments under Alternative Markets and Institutions.* Washington, DC: U.S. Department of Agriculture, Economic Research Service, Agricultural Economic Report No. 735.

Godin, B. 2015. Technological Change: What do Technology and Change Stand For? Working Paper. Project on the Intellectual History of Innovation, Montréal.

Gordon, H.S. 1954. The Economic Theory of a Common-Property Resource: The Fishery. *Journal of Political Economy* 62(2): 124–142.

Hayami, Y. and V.W. Ruttan. 1970. Factor Prices and Technical Change in Agricultural Development: The United States and Japan, 1880–1960. *Journal of Political Economy* 78(5): 1115–1141.

Heady, E.O. 1949. Basic Economic and Welfare Aspects of Farm Technological Advance. *Journal of Farm Economics* 31(2): 293–316.

Hicks, J.R. 1932. *The Theory of Wages.* Macmillan, London, UK.

Huffman, W.E. and R.E. Just. 1994. Funding, Structure, and Management of Public Agricultural Research in the United States. *American Journal of Agricultural Economics* 76(4): 744–759.

Jorgenson, D.W. and Z. Griliches. 1967. The Explanation of Productivity Change. *Review of Economic Studies* 34(3): 249–283.

Miao, Q. and D. Popp. 2014. Necessity as the Mother of Invention: Innovative Responses to Natural Disasters. *Journal of Environmental Economics and Management* 68(2): 280–295.

Miao, R. 2020. Climate, Insurance and Innovation: The Case of Drought and Innovations in Drought-Tolerant Traits in US Agriculture. *European Review of Agricultural Economics* 47(5): 1826–1860.

Moschini, G. and H. Lapan. 1997. Intellectual Property Rights and the Welfare Effects of Agricultural R&D. *American Journal of Agricultural Economics* 79: 1229–1242.

Moscona, J. and K.A. Sastry. 2022. Inappropriate Technology: Evidence from Global Agriculture. Working Paper, Harvard University.

Moscona, J. and K.A. Sastry. 2023. Does Directed Innovation Mitigate Climate Damage? Evidence From U.S. Agriculture. *The Quarterly Journal of Economics* 138(2): 637–701.

Pardey, P. and J. Alston. 2021. Unpacking the Agricultural Black Box: The Rise and Fall of American Farm Productivity Growth. *The Journal of Economic History* 81(1): 114–155.

Peterson, W. and Y. Hayami. 1977. Technical Change in Agriculture. Lee Martin (Ed.), *A Survey of Agricultural Economics Literature*, pp. 497–540. University of Minnesota Press, Minneapolis, MN.

Salter, W.E.G. 1960. *Productivity and Technical Change.* Cambridge University Press, Cambridge, UK.

Schlenker, W. and M.J. Roberts. 2009. Nonlinear Temperature Effects Indicate Severe Damages to US Crop Yields under Climate Change. *Proceedings of the National Academy of Sciences* 106(37): 15594–15598.

Sunding, D. and D. Zilberman. 2001. The Agricultural Innovation Process: Research and Technology Adoption in a Changing Agricultural Sector, B.L. Gardner and G.C. Rausser (Eds.), *Handbook of Agricultural Economics*, Volume 1, Part A, Chapter 4, pp. 207–261.

Yan, D., H. Tajima, L.C. Cline, R.Y. Fong, J.I. Ottaviani, H.-Y. Shapiro, E. Blumwald. 2022. Genetic Modification of Flavone Biosynthesis in Rice Enhances Biofilm Formation of Soil Diazotrophic Bacteria and Biological Nitrogen Fixation. *Plant Biotechnology Journal* 20(11): 2135–2148.

Wright, B.D. 1983. The Economics of Invention Incentives: Patents, Prizes, and Research Contracts. *American Economic Review* 73(4): 691–707.

Zilberman, D., T. Reardon, J. Silver, L. Lu, and A. Heiman. 2022. From the Laboratory to the Consumer: Innovation, Supply Chain, and Adoption With Applications to Natural Resources. *Proceedings of the National Academy of Sciences* 119(23): e2115880119.

Chapter 8

Technology Adoption

Technological change is a multistage process, which includes both technological innovation and adoption. Both processes require some investment and sacrifice: in some industries, the firms apply their own innovations, while in others, firms apply innovations from other firms. At a society-wide level, a certain level of technological adoption is necessary to make a dividend on innovation. Technological innovations will not generate much real-world impact unless they are adopted by society. Also, investments in innovations will not be recouped without a certain level of adoption of the innovations. Thus, social scientists, including economists, have long been concerned with technological adoption, and a large literature has been devoted to understanding the rationale for the uptake of a technology. This literature distinguishes between two concepts: adoption, the decision to use technology (measured on the individual level), and diffusion, the aggregate of adoption measured as the proportion of users in relation to potential users. The literature aims to understand who adopts a new technology, why they adopt it, and how they adopt it.

This chapter provides an overview of various theories and models on technology adoption, ranging from early models developed by sociologists to recent models by economists. Earlier models developed by sociologists in the 1960s–1970s mainly aimed to explain the S-shaped diffusion curve. However, these models were criticized for ignoring the economic drivers of adopters. Economists incorporated economic behavior such as profit maximization, risk consideration, and even dynamics into decision models of technology adoption. In recent years, advances in behavior economics enriched the literature on technology adoption. We, therefore, include a brief review of the roles of behavioral factors in affecting adoption.

1. Early Models

Early studies about technology diffusion can be at least traced back to 1890, when Gabriel Tarde, a French sociologist, published *The Laws of Imitation.* Emphasizing diffusion (since data on the aggregate was readily available), these studies viewed societal-wide uptake as time-consuming: it took about 40 years for a complete adoption of the mechanical tractor and about three to five years to complete the adoption of the tomato harvester. Other types of technological adoption (e.g., modern fertilizers and new crop varieties) also took time.

Ryan and Gross (1943) and Griliches (1957) found that the diffusion of hybrid corn in the United States followed S-shaped diffusion curves, depicted in Figure 1. At the "early adoption" stage, diffusion is slow, but at the "takeoff" stage, the diffusion rate becomes very high, although there is still a critical mass of non-adopters. As diffusion reaches the "saturation" stage, the rate of diffusion becomes quite low. This procedure was often modeled as a logistic function. Let P_t be diffusion (i.e., adoption ratio) at time t. Then we have

$$P_t = \frac{k}{1 + e^{-(a+bt)}}, \tag{1}$$

where k is the equilibrium ratio of diffusion, a is a measure of the initial level of diffusion, and b is the measure of the rate of diffusion.[1] Equation (1) implies that at each moment the log-ratio of adopters

[1]Note that the maximum level of diffusion ratio, k, can be less than 1. Therefore, $k \leq 1$.

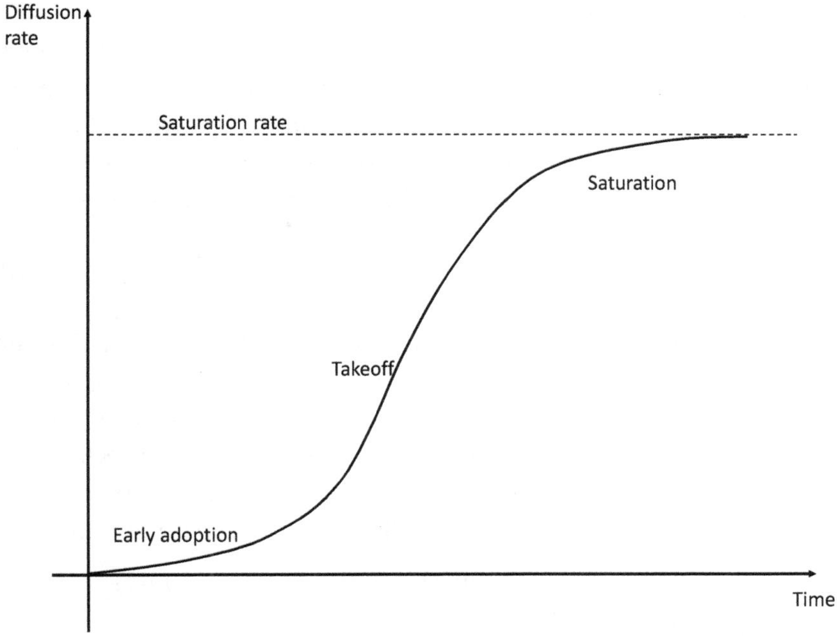

Figure 1. Diffusion rate and time.

to non-adopters is a linear function of time:

$$\log \frac{P_t}{k - P_t} = a + bt, \tag{2}$$

which can be estimated by using simple regressions in applied analyses. Griliches (1957) estimated the three coefficients (k, a, and b) to observe the effect of profitability on hybrid corn adoption in Iowa. Comparing diffusion rates in different areas, he demonstrated that diffusion was faster and more complete when the technology was more profitable.

1.1. *The imitation model*

Rogers (1962), a sociologist, argued that imitation is a key driver of technology diffusion: an individual who sees someone else using a technology may wish to imitate this person. The basic mathematics of imitation is similar to the mathematics of infectious diseases — the imitator catches the new technology from the early adopter.

Mansfield (1961) offered a formalization of imitation driving diffusion: he considered an industry with n identical firms, with $m(t)$ as the number of firms that have adopted a certain technology by time t and $n - m(t)$ for those that had not. The rate of adoption at time t among the non-adopters is defined by $\Delta m(t)/(n - m(t))$, where $\Delta m(t) \equiv m(t+1) - m(t)$. Mansfield (1961) assumed that

$$\frac{\Delta m(t)}{n - m(t)} = f\left(\frac{m(t)}{n}, \pi, c\right), \tag{3}$$

where π and c stand for profitability and adoption cost of the new technology, respectively. In other words, the adoption rate among non-adopters is a function of the portion of firms that have already adopted as well as the profitability and costs of the new technology. By using Taylor expansion, and discarding all elements of order greater than the second, Equation (3) can be approximated as

$$\begin{aligned}\frac{\Delta m(t)}{n - m(t)} &\approx \beta_1 + \beta_2\frac{m(t)}{n} + \beta_3\pi + \beta_4 c + \beta_5\pi\frac{m(t)}{n} \\ &\quad + \beta_6 c\frac{m(t)}{n} + \beta_7\pi c + \beta_8\pi^2 + \beta_9 c^2,\end{aligned} \tag{4}$$

where β's are coefficients from the Taylor expansion.[2]

To solve for $m(t)$, Mansfield moved to infinitesimal and got a differential equation based on Equation (4),

$$\frac{dm(t)}{dt} = [n - m(t)]\left[A + b\frac{m(t)}{n}\right], \tag{5}$$

where $A \equiv \beta_1 + \beta_3\pi + \beta_4 c + \beta_7\pi c + \beta_8\pi^2 + \beta_9 c^2$ and $b \equiv \beta_2 + \beta_5\pi + \beta_6 c$. Solving this differential equation, we obtain

$$\frac{m(t)}{n} = \frac{e^{\gamma+(A+b)t} - \frac{A}{b}}{1 + e^{\gamma+(A+b)t}}, \tag{6}$$

where γ is the integration constant. It is reasonable to assume that when time goes back infinitely (i.e., $t \to -\infty$), the adoption will be

[2] Mansfield (1961) assumed that the coefficient of $\left(\frac{m(t)}{n}\right)^2$ is zero, claiming that data support the assumption.

zero ($A = 0$). Therefore, we obtain

$$\frac{m(t)}{n} = \frac{1}{1 + e^{-(\gamma + bt)}}, \tag{7}$$

which is the same as Equation (1) when k in Equation (1) is set to 1.

Mansfield predicts that the proportion of adopting firms will be a symmetrical S-shaped curve over time. As the new technology becomes more profitable, the rate of diffusion quickens and the cost of the adoption process declines.

While Mansfield's model is elegant, there are a few reasons why it is unsatisfactory. First, it assumes identical firms and ignores differences between firms due to size, wealth, and education (another paper by Mansfield (1963) showed that these differences matter). Second, it does not consider the dynamic, or the learning-by-doing, aspect of adoption that reduces the cost of innovation. Third, the model lacks basic economic mechanisms of decision-making. In particular, it evades questions of utility, focusing solely on imitation as the driver of uptake.

1.2. *The threshold model*

The threshold model, introduced by David (1975) and presented in Sunding and Zilberman (2001), distinguishes between micro-level behavior, heterogeneity among decision-makers, and dynamic processes. The micro-level decision maker decides whether to adopt (in the case of indivisible technologies) and the level of (in the case of divisible technologies) by maximizing profit, expected utility, or some other objectives. But individuals are different: at a given period, some people adopt and others do not, divided by a threshold, which determines the rate of diffusion. Over time, dynamic processes of learning and technological improvement that reduce the cost of technology change the rate of diffusion.[3]

[3]Of course, sometimes alternative technologies appear and technologies are dis-adopted, while in other cases technologies are abandoned because people have bad experience with them. The term "threshold" comes from the fact that in some models, for example purchasing luxury cars, the consumers are divided according

In real life, there are many sources of heterogeneity, and identifying the key parameters that determine the set of adopters is a major statistical challenge. With the availability of data on individual behavior as well as the statistical tools of *logit* and *probit*, researchers can apply the threshold model to estimate the parameters that will affect the likelihood of adoption by different individuals at every moment. For simplicity, in this chapter, we consider a farming industry in which farm sizes differ. Let l denote farm size and assume its density function is $g(l)$. Therefore, the total number of farms and total land acreage in the farming industry are $N \equiv \int_0^\infty g(l)dl$ and $L \equiv \int_0^\infty lg(l)dl$, respectively. Suppose that farmers are facing a new technology which, at time t, costs F_t to be established on a farm and generates $\Delta\pi_t$ more profits per acre than does the conventional technology. If farmers are attempting to maximize their profits, then farmers with farm size such that $l \cdot \Delta\pi_t \geq F_t$ will adopt the new technology. Define $l_t^* \equiv F_t/\Delta\pi_t$ as the threshold farm size above which farmers will adopt the new technology. The share of farms that have adopted the new technology by time t is

$$Y_t = \frac{\int_{l_t^*}^\infty g(l)dl}{N}. \tag{8}$$

By using Leibniz's formula, from Equation (8) we obtain

$$\frac{\partial Y_t}{\partial t} = -\frac{g\left(l_t^*\right)}{N}\frac{\partial l_t^*}{\partial t}. \tag{9}$$

It is reasonable to assume that $\frac{\partial l_t^*}{\partial t} < 0$ because the fixed establishment cost of the new technology is expected to be decreasing over time and the profitability advantage of the new technology is likely to increase due to the increased efficiency of using the new technology over time (i.e., "learning by using"). Moreover, because $g\left(l_t^*\right)$ is always positive, we can conclude that $\partial Y_t/\partial t > 0$. Differentiate

to income and at each moment there is a threshold level of income above which people are assumed to adopt the technology. But this threshold level declines over time.

Equation (9) with respect to t, we have

$$\frac{\partial^2 Y_t}{\partial t^2} = -\frac{1}{N}\left[\frac{\partial g\left(l_t^*\right)}{\partial l_t^*}\left(\frac{\partial l_t^*}{\partial t}\right)^2 + g\left(l_t^*\right)\frac{\partial^2 l_t^*}{\partial t^2}\right]. \tag{10}$$

In Equation (10), the curvature of the diffusion curve depends on (1) the slope of the density function at the threshold acreage (i.e., $\partial g(l_t^*)/(\partial l_t^*)$), (2) the relationship between the threshold acreage and time (i.e., $\partial l_t^*/\partial t$), (3) the value of density function at the threshold acreage (i.e., $g(l_t^*)$), and (4) the curvature of l_t^* as a function of t. As long as $\partial^2 Y_t/\partial t^2$ is positive when t is small and negative when t becomes larger, the diffusion curve will assume an S-shaped curve. For instance, if the adoption threshold farm size, l_t^*, decreases over time at a constant rate (i.e., $\partial^2 l_t^*/\partial t^2 = 0$); if the farm size distribution is unimodal, as in Figure 2, then $(\partial^2 Y_t)/(\partial t^2)$ will be small and positive when t is small. As t increases, $(\partial^2 Y_t)/(\partial t^2)$ first

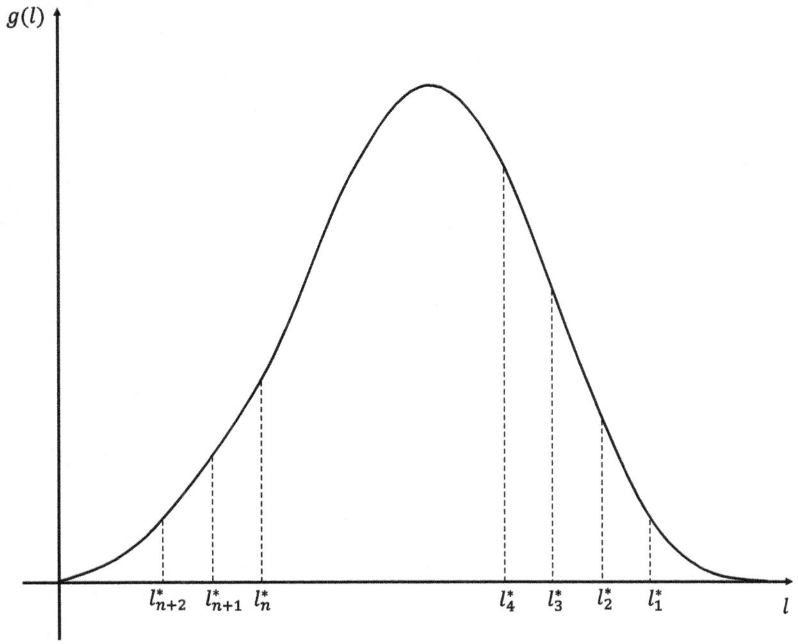

Figure 2. Unimodal farm size distribution.

increases and then decreases to 0 and then negative. In this case, the diffusion curve is S-shaped.

The diffusion in cases of divisible technologies can be computed in similar ways. For instance, with a new seed variety, farmers may experiment with it on a small portion of their plot. With learning-by-doing, the uncertainty of the technology may decline. Thus, the land share of the technology, as well as the number of adopters, will increase, resulting in S-shaped behavior of diffusion as well.

2. Static Expected Utility Models

The imitation model and threshold model discussed above do not consider any risks associated with new technologies. However, risks are prevalent, particularly for new technologies, because potential adopters have little experience with them. In this section, we discuss the static expected utility model concerning technology adoption developed by Just and Zilberman (1983). Note that we discussed this model in Chapter 4 but mainly to focus on diversification. In this section, however, we will focus on the insight into technology adoption derived from the Just and Zilberman (1983) model.

Consider a farmer who is considering (1) whether or not to adopt a new crop variety on their farm, and (2) if they adopt, then how much of their land will be devoted to the new crop variety.[4] Suppose the profit per acre of the conventional crop is $\pi_0 = m_0 + \epsilon_0$, where m_0 is a constant but ϵ_0 is a random variable with $E(\epsilon_0) = 0$ and $Var(\epsilon_0) = \sigma_0^2$. The profit per acre of the new crop variety is $\pi_1 = m_1(f) + v_1(f)\epsilon_1$, where f is the cost per acre incurred for planting the new crop variety, $m_1(f)$ and $v_1(f)$ are deterministic functions of f, and ϵ_1 is a random variable with $E(\epsilon_1) = 0$ and $Var(\epsilon_1) = \sigma_1^2$. Moreover, if the farmer adopts the new crop variety, then a fixed cost,

[4]This is a quite general decision problem regarding technology adoption, particularly in agriculture, and the framework illustrated below developed by Just and Zilberman (1983) has been used in many other studies such as Miao and Khanna (2017a,b) and Majeed *et al.* (2023). As of February 2025, the paper has been cited more than 600 times according to Google Scholar, and the citation per year of this paper is still trending up after 42 years since its publication.

k, would be incurred regardless of the portion of land devoted to the new variety. Suppose the farm size is $\overline{L}$ and the farmer fully utilizes their land. The land devoted to the conventional crop variety and the new variety is denoted by L_0 and L_1, respectively. The technology adoption decision problem can be written as

$$\max_{\substack{I\in\{0,1\}\\ L_0,L_1,f}} E\{U(p_L\overline{L} + \pi_0 L_0 + I \cdot (\pi_1(f)L_1 - k))\} \tag{11}$$

$$\text{s.t. } L_0 + I \cdot L_1 = \overline{L}, \text{ and } L_0, L_1, f \geq 0,$$

where E is the expectation operator; I is an adoption index, with $I = 0$ indicating non-adoption and $I = 1$ adoption; and p_L is end-of-season land price.

To solve the maximization problem in Equation (11), one can compare the expected utility under two scenarios. The first one is the non-adoption scenario where $I = 0$. Under this scenario, the farmer's expected utility is

$$V_0 = E\{U(p_L\overline{L} + \pi_0\overline{L})\}. \tag{12}$$

The second is the adoption scenario under which the farmer chooses the size of L_1 (i.e., acreage devoted to the new crop variety) to maximize their expected utility:

$$V_1 = \max_{L_1\in(0,\overline{L}],f>0} E\{U(p_L\overline{L} + \pi_0\left(\overline{L} - L_1\right) + \pi_1(f)L_1 - k)\}. \tag{13}$$

In Section 2.3.3 of Chapter 4, we discussed the solutions to problem (13) and the comparative static analyses in detail. Here, we expand upon the discussion in that section to suggest that the input accompanying the new crop variety increases the variance of new variety profits (i.e., $\partial v_1/\partial f > 0$). If the relative risk aversion is increasing, then larger farmers tend to use less of such input than do small farmers. However, if the input decreases the variance and if the relative risk aversion is increasing, then larger farmers tend to use more of such input.

The farmer will make the optimal choices by comparing V_0 and V_1. If $V_0 > V_1$ then the farmer will not adopt the new crop variety. If $V_0 \leq V_1$, then the farmer will adopt and plant the new variety on

L_1^* acres of their land, where L_1^* is the optimal solution to problem (13). That is,

$$I^* = \begin{cases} 0 & \text{if } V_0 > V_1 \\ 1 & \text{if } V_0 \leq V_1. \end{cases} \tag{14}$$

As Just and Zilberman (1983) point out, it is difficult to compare V_0 and V_1 without knowing the farmer's risk preference and the impact of input f on the risk of the new crop variety. However, because farm size has direct risk implication (i.e., the variance of total profit increases as farm size increases), under conditions of a positive fixed establishment cost for a new crop adoption (i.e., $k > 0$) and increasing relative risk aversion matched with non-increasing absolute risk aversion, Just and Zimmerman outline three possibilities. The first one is that no farms will adopt the new crop variety due to its high establishment cost. The second one is that farms smaller than a threshold will not adopt due to the high establishment cost, but farms larger than the threshold will adopt. The last one pertains to two farm size thresholds that divide farms into three groups. Farmers with a farm size smaller than the lower threshold will not adopt because the fixed establishment cost cannot be justified by the profits of the new crop; farmers with a farm size larger than the lower threshold but smaller than the higher threshold will adopt because they can justify the fixed cost and the disutility from the increased risk is not yet too large. Finally, farmers with farm size larger than the higher threshold will not adopt because the disutility from the increased risk is too large.[5]

3. Dynamic Models

Although the earlier adoption models and the static expected utility models capture some important aspects of technology adoption, such as the S-shaped diffusion curve and risky returns of new technology,

[5]Note that the last case only occurs when the covariance between the conventional crop profits and new crop profits is larger than the variance of conventional crop profits.

they miss some other important features of technology adoption. First, both the costs and benefits of technology adoption are dynamic. The new technology itself is likely to become less expensive as its producers get more efficient in producing the new technology through, say, "learning-by-doing." Compared to the $10,000 word processor which Jimmy Carter bought in 1981 to write his memoir (Bird, 2021), a word processor available today is far less expensive and more powerful. Moreover, through "learning-by-using," adopters can enlarge the benefits derived from the new technology over time. Second, technology improvement is unpredictable. A potential user looking to purchase a technological innovation may consider whether the future price of the good or even whether another improvement is in the pipeline. Sometimes delaying adoption may be a better decision than adopting today. In this section, we will introduce several models that explicitly consider the aforementioned factors in technology adoption.

3.1. *Learning and adoption of new technologies*

In this subsection, we will explicitly consider the "learning by doing" and "learning by using" effects on technology adoption. Consider a farmer facing a new technology that can increase their instantaneous profit by $\Delta\pi(\tau - t)$ at any time $\tau \geq t$ if the technology is adopted at time t. Note that "learning-by-using" implies $\frac{\partial \Delta\pi(\tau-t)}{\partial \tau} > 0$ and $\frac{\partial \Delta\pi(\tau-t)}{\partial t} < 0$. In other words, the longer the adopter has used the technology, the larger the benefit she can obtain from it.

It is also reasonable to assume that the rate of "learning-by-using" is decreasing over time (i.e., $\frac{\partial^2 \Delta\pi(\tau-t)}{\partial \tau^2} < 0$ and $\frac{\partial^2 \Delta\pi(\tau-t)}{\partial t^2} > 0$). Let $K(t)$ be the one-time adoption cost of the new technology at time t. We assume that the adoption cost decreases over time in a decreasing rate, i.e., $K'(t) < 0 < K''(t)$. Set the current time to be 0. The farmer's decision problem is to decide the optimal time $t \geq 0$ to adopt the new technology, considering the effects of "learning-by-using" and "learning-by-doing" on the benefits and costs of adoption. Let the discount rate be r, the farmer's optimization problem can be written as

$$\max_t e^{-rt}\left(\int_t^\infty \Delta\pi(\tau - t)e^{-r(\tau-t)}d\tau - K(t)\right). \qquad (15)$$

Assuming an interior solution, then the first-order condition of the maximization problem in (15) is

$$-\Delta\pi\,(0) + \int_t^\infty \frac{\partial\Delta\pi(\tau - t)}{\partial t}e^{-r(\tau-t)}d\tau + rK(t) - \frac{\partial K(t)}{\partial t} = 0. \quad (16)$$

Equation (16) illustrates the gains and losses from delaying the adoption per one marginal moment from the optimal adoption time, t^*. Specifically, the first term, $-\Delta\pi\,(0)$, indicates the direct profit loss from delaying the adoption at t^*. The second term, $\int_t^\infty \frac{\partial\Delta\pi(\tau-t)}{\partial t}e^{-r(\tau-t)}d\tau$, is the loss of total profits over the technological lifetime caused by the reduced "learning-by-using" due to the delay (note that here we assume the lifespan of the technology is infinite). The third term, $rK(t)$, is the saved interest for the one-time adoption cost due to the delay. Finally, the fourth term, $-\partial K(t)/\partial t$, is the saved adoption cost due to the delay. In the optimal solution, the sum of these four terms is 0.

It is readily checked that an increase in interest rate, r, will reduce the loss from decreased "learning-by-using" (i.e., the second term in Equation (16)), and increase the saved interest for the adoption cost (i.e., the third term in Equation (16)). Therefore, higher interest rates tend to delay new technology adoption. Moreover, if production technology is constant returns to scale, then both the profit increase from the new technology and the "learning-by-using" effect will be proportional to farm size, so large farms would adopt the new technology earlier than small farms.

3.2. *A deterministic dynamic model*

In addition to "learning-by-doing" and "learning-by-using," drivers of the changes in benefits and costs of technology adoption include variations in the environment and resource availability. For instance, climate change has increased the frequency of droughts and, therefore, spurred the adoption of drought-tolerant seeds. The depletion of an aquifer may increase the adoption of more efficient irrigation technology, such as drip irrigation. Shah *et al.* (1995) developed a deterministic dynamic model to illustrate the adoption of advanced irrigation technology considering the decreasing availability of irrigation water. Although focused on irrigation, the model in Shah *et al.* (1995) can be readily transferred to understanding technology adoption under several changing resource or environmental constraints. In this subsection we briefly discuss this model.

Suppose farmers are facing two irrigation technologies: a conventional technology (e.g., furrow irrigation) and a modern technology (e.g., drip irrigation). The modern technology can increase water use efficiency, but at a higher establishment cost. Assuming constant returns to scale production function, we denote the output per acre as $y = f(e)$, where e is effective water use per acre and is determined by $e = h_i(\alpha)a$, as we discussed in the production chapter. Here α is land quality, a is actual water use, and $h_i(\alpha)$ reflects how efficient the land with quality α, together with the irrigation technology ($i = 1$ indicating the conventional technology, and $i = 2$ the modern technology), will use the actual water applied to it. We assume that $h_1(\alpha) = \alpha < h_2(\alpha) \leq 1$ and $h_2'(\alpha) > 0 > h_2''(\alpha)$, which implies that modern technology improves the water use efficiency of any land when compared with the conventional technology and that the improvement is decreasing as land quality increases.

Let the range of α be $[\alpha_L, 1]$, where α_L is the lower bound of land quality. Furthermore, let $g(\alpha)$ be the density function of land quality α. By normalizing total land area to be 1, we have $\int_{\alpha_L}^{1} g(\alpha)\, d\alpha = 1$. Further, let $\delta_{it}(\alpha)$ denote the share of land with quality α that adopts technology $i \in \{1, 2\}$ at time t. Then we have $0 \leq \sum_{\mathrm{i}} \delta_{it}(\alpha) \leq 1$ for any t and α. Therefore, we have

$$0 \leq \int_{a_L}^{1} \left(\sum_{\mathrm{i}} \delta_{it}(\alpha) g(\alpha) \right) d\alpha \leq 1. \tag{17}$$

Finally, let k_i denote the per-acre cost of using technology i at time t. Then, we write out the expressions for the total output

(Y_t), total water used (A_t), and total technology cost (K_t) at time t. They are:

$$Y_t = \int_{a_L}^{1} \left[\sum_{\text{i}} \delta_{it}(\alpha) f\left(h_i(\alpha) a_{it}\right) \right] g(\alpha) d\alpha, \tag{18}$$

$$A_t = \int_{a_L}^{1} \left[\sum_{\text{i}} \delta_{it}(\alpha) a_{it} \right] g(\alpha) d\alpha, \tag{19}$$

$$K_t = \int_{a_L}^{1} \left[\sum_{\text{i}} \delta_{it}(\alpha) k_{it} \right] g(\alpha) d\alpha. \tag{20}$$

Denote the stock of available groundwater at time t by S_t. Excluding any recharge of the groundwater, we have

$$\dot{S}_t = -A_t. \tag{21}$$

Let $U(Y_t)$ be the instantaneous benefit from consuming total output Y_t, and $c(S_t)$ be the cost of extracting one additional unit of groundwater when the water stock is S_t at time t. Therefore, the total social welfare at time t is $U(Y_t) - c(S_t)A_t - K_t$. The social planner's goal is to maximize net social welfare over time 0 to T by optimally choosing land share allocated to each technology (i.e., δ_{it}) and water use under each technology (i.e., a_{it}). Denoting discount rate by r, the social planner's optimization problem can be written as

$$\max_{\delta_{it}, a_{it}} \int_0^T e^{-rt} [U(Y_t) - c(S_t)A_t - K_t] dt, \tag{22}$$

s.t. (17) to (21), $S_T \geq 0$, and given S_0.
The current Hamiltonian value is

$$\begin{aligned} H = \Bigg[& U(Y_t) - c(S_t)A_t - K_t - \lambda_t A_t - p_t Y_t + w_t A_t + \gamma_t K_t \\ & + \int_{\alpha_L}^{1} \left\{ \sum_i \delta_{it} \left[p_t f(h_i(\alpha) a_{it}) - w_t a_{it} - \gamma_t k_t \right] \right. \\ & \left. + \mu_t(\alpha) \left[1 - \sum_i \delta_{it}(\alpha) \right] \right\} g(\alpha) d\alpha \Bigg], \end{aligned} \tag{23}$$

where λ_t is the shadow cost of groundwater stock at time t, and p_t, w_t, γ_t, and $\mu_t(\alpha)$ are the shadow prices of the output, water applied, aggregate technology cost, and land capacity constraints. The maximization of the current value Hamiltonian requires

$$\dot{\lambda}_t = r\lambda_t - \frac{\partial H}{\partial S_t} = r\lambda_t + A_t c'(S_t), \tag{24}$$

$$\frac{\partial H}{\partial Y_t} = U'(Y_t) - p_t = 0, \tag{25}$$

$$\frac{\partial H}{\partial A_t} = -c(S_t) - \lambda_t + w_t = 0, \tag{26}$$

$$\frac{\partial H}{\partial K_t} = \gamma_t - 1 = 0, \quad \text{and} \tag{27}$$

$$\max_{\delta_{it}, a_{it}} \sum_i \delta_{it}[p_t f(h_i(\alpha)a_{it}) - w_t a_{it} - \gamma_t k_t] + \mu_t(\alpha)\left[1 - \sum_i \delta_{it}(\alpha)\right]. \tag{28}$$

Equation (24) indicates that the change in the shadow price of the stock at time t, $\dot{\lambda}_t$, is the interest of the shadow price, $r\lambda_t$, minus the extraction cost increase caused by the marginal depletion of the groundwater stock (note that $c'(S_t) < 0$). Equation (25) states that the shadow price of total output is equal to the marginal benefit of the output. Equation (26) states that the shadow price of applied water is equal to the extraction cost of one additional unit of water plus the shadow price of groundwater stock. Equation (27) implies that the shadow price of technology cost is one. Finally, Equation (28) requires that optimal δ_{it} and a_{it} should be chosen for all kinds of land at the micro-level.

Obtaining the optimal solutions from expressions (24)–(28) is quite technical and we refer readers to Shah *et al.* (1995) and Caswell and Zilberman (1986) for details. Here we focus on the insights of technology adoption derived from the model. Shah *et al.* (1995) show that under the conditions that $h_1(\alpha) = \alpha \leq h_2(\alpha) \leq 1$, $h(1) = 1$, and $h_2'(\alpha) > 0 > h_2''(\alpha)$, there is a land quality threshold value, denoted by α_t^s, above which the modern technology will not be adopted. This is because the gains from modern technology are smaller for high-quality land than for low-quality land, and the smaller gains cannot justify the adoption cost. They also show that there is another land quality threshold, denoted by α_t^m, below which the land will be left idle (i.e., neither the conventional technology nor the modern technology will be adopted on the land). Therefore, at time t, the modern technology is adopted on land with quality over $[\alpha_t^m, \alpha_t^s]$, and the conventional technology is adopted on land with quality higher than α_t^s. The dynamics of α_t^m and α_t^s determine the diffusion of modern technology over time.

Shah *et al.* (1995) show that if $\epsilon_i \equiv -f''(e)e/f'(e) > 1$ and $\eta_i \equiv h_i'(\alpha)\alpha/h_i(\alpha) \in [0,1]$, then $\partial\alpha_t^s/\partial p_t > 0$ and $\partial\alpha_t^m/\partial p_t < 0$, which indicates that an increase in output price will increase the adoption of modern technology. From equation (26), we obtain $\dot{w}_t = c'(S_t)\dot{S}_t + \dot{\lambda}_t$. Based on equations (21) and (24), we have $\dot{w}_t = r\lambda_t \geq 0$, indicating that water price is always non-decreasing. Shah *et al.* (1995) show that if $\epsilon_i > 1$ and $\eta_i \in [0,1]$, then the increase in water price will increase both α_t^m and α_t^s, leaving the diffusion of modern technology determined by the distribution of land quality. If the land quality distribution is unimodal, then the modern technology diffusion may be S-shaped. Figure 3 provides an example of the

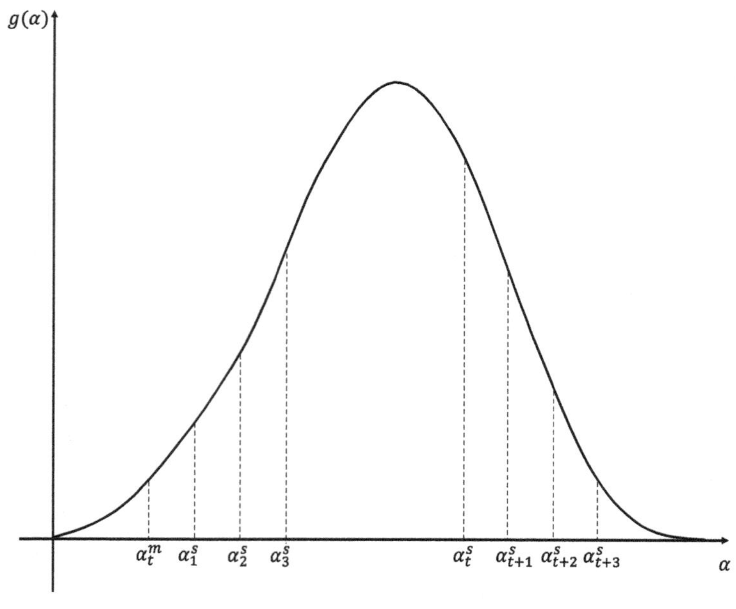

Figure 3. Unimodal land quality distribution.

relationship between modern technology diffusion and land quality distribution. In this example, we assume that α_t^m is affected little by the increasing water price over time, whereas α_t^s increases by the same amount each period. In this case, the rate of adoption of modern technology will increase initially but then decrease, creating an S-shaped diffusion curve.

3.3. *Real option models*

Technology adoption, like many other investments, involves various degrees of irreversibility. For instance, time spent on studying, purchasing, and learning how to use the new technology cannot be recovered. Newly purchased equipment, if to be re-sold, often endures significant discounts. Moreover, benefit and cost uncertainties are prevalent among new technologies. The benefits of drought-tolerant varieties depend on the weather of the growing season because these varieties may perform better than traditional varieties during dry years but worse during wet years. The cost of new machinery may fluctuate considerably over time due to trade frictions, wars, or disease outbreaks (think about human history over 2018–2023). Real option models consider both irreversibility and uncertainty associated with technology adoption, shedding new insights that are missing in the aforementioned models in this chapter. Real option models view technology adoption as an option (right, but not an obligation to adopt), which can be exercised at any time chosen by the adopter. As new information in future periods may mitigate the uncertainty related to the benefits and costs of the new technology, under certain conditions delaying adoption may be the optimal choice. We here use a simple two-period model to illustrate this point.

Suppose that a farmer is considering adopting a new technology (e.g., an irrigation system). Let R_i denote the revenue generated by the new technology in period $i \in \{1, 2\}$. Suppose R_1 is deterministic and R_2 is random. With equal chance, R_2 can take values of 100 and 200. The farmer will be certain about the value of R_2 at the beginning of period 2. For simplicity, we assume that the adoption cost, K, is constant over the two periods, with a fixed value at $K = 150$. We also ignore the discount rates. Now, the question is, should the farmer adopt the new technology in period 1 or delay the decision to period 2?

If the farmer adopts in period 1, then the expected net present value (NPV) of adoption is

$$NPV_0 = R_1 - K + E(R_2) = R_1 - 150 + 0.5 \times (100 + 200) = R_1. \quad (29)$$

The standard NPV approach would recommend adoption in period one as long as $R_1 > 0$. However, what if the farmer waits till period 2 and based on their decision on new information in that period? Doing so, she would forgo the revenue in period 1 (i.e., R_1) but she avoids the possibility of losing money in period 2. This is because, if she adopts in period 1, then, in period 2, she has a 50% chance of receiving a low return, 100. If R_1 is smaller than 50, then receiving 100 in period 2 indicates that the total revenue in the two periods cannot cover the adoption cost. Overall, if she delays the adoption decision to period 2 after the new information about period 2 revenue is revealed, she will adopt when the revenue is 200 and not adopt when the revenue is 100. In sum, the expected NPV of delaying the decision to period 2 is

$$NPV_1 = E\left[\max\left(R_2 - K, 0\right)\right] = 0.5 \times 0 + 0.5 \times (200 - 150) = 25. \quad (30)$$

By comparing NPV_0 and NPV_1, we can conclude that, if $R_1 \leq 25$, then the farmer should delay the adoption decision to period 2. If $R_1 > 25$, then the farmer should adopt in period 1. We can see that the real option approach recommends a higher period 1 revenue (25 instead of 0) to trigger the adoption than does the standard NPV approach. This is because the standard NPV approach ignores the value of the "option" that the farmer owns to adopt in period 2, which should be viewed as part of the opportunity cost of adopting the technology in period 1. Therefore, we can define the option value (the value of flexibility) as $\max[NPV_1 - NPV_0, 0]$. In this case, the option value is $\max[25 - R_1, 0]$.

The two-period example above illustrates a powerful framework to model adoption decisions or other decisions under irreversibility and uncertainty. Two-period real option models have the essence of real option models (i.e., new information revealed in a future period and the decision-maker has the option to delay an action to benefit from the new information) and are very much tractable. As a result, they are widely used in the literature. For instance, Arrow and Fisher (1974) used a two-period model to study whether an area should be developed or preserved. Moledina *et al.* (2003) examined firms' strategic abatement behaviors under emission tax and permit using a two-period real option framework. Miao *et al.* (2012) studied investment in cellulosic biofuel technologies under a waivable mandate by using a two-period real option model. Finally, Miao *et al.* (2022) employed a two-period real option model to study whether or not to convert a parcel of land into a new use considering uncertainties of returns from alternatives.

An extension of the above two-period example into a multi-period framework is straightforward. Let r denote the discount rate and $\Delta\pi(s_t)$ the profit difference between the new technology and traditional technology, where s_t is a random variable. The farmer's decision problem is to optimally choose the adoption time, T, to maximize the expected benefits from adoption. The problem can be written as

$$\max_{T\in\{0,1,\ldots,\infty\}} \sum_{t=T}^{\infty} E_{s_t}\left[\frac{\Delta\pi(s_t)}{(1+r)^t}\right] + \frac{K}{(1+r)^T}, \tag{31}$$

where E_{s_t} is the expectation operator with respect to s_t. The solution to problem (31) involves identifying an adoption policy under which whenever the realization of a random variable s_t reaches a threshold value, then adoption will occur. The properties of the stochastic process $\{s_t\}$ determine the optimal adoption time. A general insight from the solutions to problem (31) is that, when the variance of s_t increases the expected optimal adoption time will be larger. Intuitively, when future returns are becoming more uncertain and adoption involves irreversible costs, then delaying the action may be a rational choice. Dixit and Pindyck (1994) provide a comprehensive set of treatments on real option models like the one in (31) and its many other variations. Recent applications of the real option models include Ye *et al.*'s (2022) study on the impact of renewable energy policies on renewable energy technology development and adoption, focusing on the increased risk of technology obsolescence caused by the policies.

4. Beyond Profit and Utility Maximization

The preceding models (except the imitation models) in this chapter are based on neoclassical economic theory, where decision rules are derived from maximizing expected profits or utility. In the past four decades, however, developments in behavioral economics, experimental economics, and many other fields in economics have significantly enriched our understanding of people's decision-making associated with technology adoption. A large literature has focused on understanding people's loss, ambiguity, time, and social preferences and their implications on technology adoption. In this section, we provide a brief review along these lines of research.

An emerging body of research employs prospect theory to understand farmers' technology adoption behavior.[6] Liu (2013) conducted field experiments to examine Chinese cotton farmers' adoption decisions regarding Bt cotton, finding that higher loss aversion delays the adoption of Bt cotton, but overweighting small probabilities accelerates the adoption. Bocquého *et al.* (2015), in contrast, find that both loss aversion and overweighting small probabilities decrease bioenergy crop adoption of farmers based on a survey and experiments conducted in France. Also focusing on bioenergy crop adoption but using a numerical simulation approach, Anand *et al.* (2019) find that an increase in loss aversion will decrease miscanthus adoption but will increase switchgrass adoption.

Studies on technology adoption based on expected utility theory or prospect theory assume that farmers know the probability distribution of the returns of a new technology, which is a strong assumption because the returns are determined by numerous factors including the uncertain technical characteristics of the new

[6]See Chapter 4 for an introduction of prospect theory.

technology, market environment of output, and individual adopter's capability of managing the technology (Chavas and Nauges, 2020). A few recent studies in agricultural technology adoption have considered the impact of ambiguity aversion on adoption. Barham *et al.* (2014) conducted field experiments with U.S. Midwestern farmers and found that farmers with higher ambiguity aversion tend to adopt genetically modified (GM) maize earlier, due to GM maize reducing the ambiguity of pest-damage levels. In contrast, Ward and Singh (2015) do not find that ambiguity aversion has an obvious impact on the adoption of drought-tolerant rice in rural India. Based on a MaxMin expected utility model, Bryan (2019) shows that the ambiguity created by rainfall index insurance decreases the demand for such insurance and the incentivizing impact of the insurance on technology adoption among ambiguity-averse farmers. Chapter 4 describes an example employing the α-MaxMin model to understand people's adoption decisions under ambiguity.

Because the benefits of technology adoption can be recouped over years of the lifespan of the technology, how farmers discount returns in the future is critical for estimating the overall benefit of adoption. Studies (e.g., Duquette *et al.*, 2012) have shown that farmers' discount rate can be as high as 40% (i.e., \$1,000 one year from now is only as good as about \$700 right now). Standard intertemporal decision-making models have been assuming a constant discount rate since the seminal work by Samuelson (1937) that predicted time-consistent behaviors. Although convenient, these models encounter difficulties in explaining some "anomalies" in people's intertemporal decisions, such as preference reversals (Thaler, 2015; Ch. 11). Existing studies (see Frederick *et al.* (2002) for a comprehensive review) in experimental economics literature have shown that hyperbolic discounting (the discount rate becomes smaller as time departs further away from present) can better fit people's observed discount rates over time and better explain intertemporal behaviors. Although Tanaka *et al.* (2010) and Liebenehm and Waibel (2014) estimate farmers' time preference parameters based on hyperbolic discounting models, few studies have examined the role of hyperbolic discounting in agricultural technology adoption. Some early works in this realm include Duflo *et al.* (2011) and Clot *et al.* (2017). The former study found that a small and time-limited price discount of fertilizer after harvest, when farmers have relatively abundant cash, increases fertilizer use among farmers with hyperbolic discounting by inducing a commitment to using fertilizer. Clot *et al.* (2017) find that farmers with higher risk aversion are more impatient, and less likely to enroll in long-term conservation programs in which program failure is possible.

Because technology adoption is a complicated process that involves farmers' judgment on various potential effects of a new technology on farm operation, studies have shown that farmers' human capital (education and on-the-job learning) affects technology adoption via different channels (Huffman, 2020; Foster and Rosenzweig, 2010). Huffman (1977) shows empirical evidence that farmers with higher human capital can respond to technical and economic changes more efficiently. A natural inference from this conclusion is that farmers with higher human capital will be more likely to succeed in harvesting the benefits of new technology and to adopt (Huffman, 2001; Abdulai and Huffman, 2014; Pannell and Zilberman, 2020). Farmers with higher education levels are often more patient and therefore are more willing to make investments to increase future returns (Liebenehm and Waibel, 2014). Moreover, human capital is likely to be positively correlated with cognitive ability, which accelerates adoption (Barham *et al.*, 2018; Dessart *et al.*, 2019).

A factor that is closely related to human capital in the realm of technology adoption is learning, which has been a focus of many studies in the adoption literature (see Foster and Rosenzweig (2010) for a comprehensive review). Learning mitigates the uncertainty of the new technology and increases the adopters' ability to better use the technology (Foster and Rosenzweig, 1996). Therefore, educating farmers on the new technology, either through public extension services or peer farmers, may accelerate adoption (Genius *et al.*, 2014). Due to the positive externality of the learning conducted by early adopters, Foster and Rosenzweig (1995) suggest that subsidies for early adoption could be used to enhance adoption.

In addition to loss, ambiguity, and time preferences, the behavioral economics literature also considers the roles of social preferences, such as peer effects, social status, and social networks on technology adoption. Dessart *et al.* (2019) and Streletskaya *et al.* (2020) provide excellent reviews on behavioral economics and technology adoption. An interesting discussion about behavioral economics associated with agricultural production can be found in Wuepper *et al.* (2023). Based upon randomized controlled trials, many experimental economics studies have examined factors that constrain agricultural technology adoption. Bridle *et al.* (2020) provide a comprehensive review of recent experimental findings of these studies, with a focus on farmers in Sub-Saharan Africa and South Asia, outlining four obstacles to technology adoption: credit constraint, risk exposure, information scarcity, and limited access to input and output markets. The authors suggest that risk mitigation and enhanced access to information are critical for encouraging adoption.

5. Technology Adoption and Marketing

Based on the work of Kalish (1985), Rogers (2003), and Zilberman *et al.* (2012), we posit that individual decision-makers go through four stages in their adoption choice. First, the awareness of the new product may be influenced by observing other people and is consistent with the imitation model. Second, assessment that involves experimentation via producer-offered demonstrations or experimentation with products by friends and family. Third, the adoption decision that may be based on constrained optimization, but the information used for this decision is affected by the judgment of others and social norms. Behavioral economics provides some new insights into the way people make choices (Thaler, 2015). One important notion is loss aversion suggesting that people emphasize avoiding losses over achieving wins (see Chapter 4 for details). Therefore, they need various mechanisms of reassurance about the performance and the value of a new technology in evaluating it. Mechanisms like demonstration that allow for testing the technology before purchase, money-back guarantees, warranties, or insurance of performance that protect against failure are important in deciding to adopt a new technology.

Frequently, people may decide to rent a technology (e.g., a car) in order to experiment with it to reduce the perceptions of risk and increase the likelihood of adoption (Zilberman *et al.*, 2012). Credit support can also reduce the fixed cost of adoption. Furthermore, Kahneman (2011) distinguished between important, large-scale technologies that require deliberation and less important decisions that can be made *ad hoc*. While buying a new car requires some deliberation and rational decision-making, the decisions about complementary components are often made *ad hoc*. The fourth and final stage is re-evaluation to determine whether to purchase the product in the future.

Potential buyers are heterogeneous in terms of human capital, income, education, and preferences, and different buyers will adopt at different times. Another source of heterogeneity is self-efficacy, which is a person's perception of their own ability to influence the outcome of events (Bandura, 1994), separating innovators and imitators (Bass, 1969). Innovators are individuals who "decide to adopt an innovation independently of the decisions of other individuals in a social system" while imitators are adopters who "are influenced in the timing of adoption by the pressures of the social system" (Bass, 1969).

Over time, dynamic processes will change the key parameters and expand the range of adopters. These include learning about the technology (with experience, people better understand the parameters of the technology and their risk concern declines), learning by doing (i.e., a manufacturer improves the productivity of product production and it becomes cheaper), learning by using (the user benefits from experience with technology), and network externality (when the benefit of the technology depends on the number of users, for example, the telephone or internet). Therefore, more people find the technology attractive over time.

New products may be introduced in different forms. Lu *et al.* (2016) suggest that when it comes to an individual product with high fixed costs, early periods are characterized by few purchases for their own use, and some people are likelier to purchase the product to rent to individuals that are less able to buy or utilize the product. For example, large farmers will buy a combine and other farmers will contract services. Over time, as the price of the product declines, rental rates may decline, and ownership may spread. The first company that sold sprinklers in California was called "Rain for Rent." Over time, farmers purchased their own irrigation equipment. Rental agreements are important both to share the fixed costs and to allow farmers to test the technology. IBM leased mainframe computers to buyers and only a few very big organizations owned computers. Now, as the price of computers has gone down, most Americans own their own computers. Furthermore, as the product is established, variations of a product allow for different segments of users to own it. Ownership has two advantages: (i) reduced transaction costs (you have it when you need it) and (ii) pride of ownership. Potential buyers compare these gains with the extra costs of ownership, such as maintenance.

In addition to improvements in the technology that reduce cost, technological improvement results in increased functionality and efficiency. Once companies develop supply chains to market a technology, they need new models and features to resell it. The shorter the life of a technology, the more important is continuous innovation by companies to survive. These improvements in technology further advance the diffusion processes. One mechanism to enhance a technology is to provide a virtual ecosystem where others may contribute complementary products, like apps. For example, the diffusion of computers has been enhanced with the introduction of editing and business software, games, and online videos (Putler and Zilberman, 1988). Furthermore, suppliers of the technology aim to improve upon it to produce new versions, gaining from variations as consumers are more willing to pay for specific features. When an existing version of a product becomes obsolete, they are sold to new groups of buyers (e.g., low-income buyers) and the high-income premier segments purchase the newer versions. Furthermore, some producers will develop new brands and supply chains to emphasize their unique value proposition, as Apple did with moving from cell phones to smartphones.

In many cases with new products, however, producers may be uncertain that people will purchase their products. Having an intermediary that develops a supply chain to transmit a product between the producer and buyer thus carrying much of the risk on both ends, may facilitate the introduction and development of the new product. This is quite frequent, such as Costco develops a new supply chain to buy quinoa from producers in the Andes.

Phillips (2011) introduced the notion of *relentless innovation*, connecting to the experience of companies like Nokia and Blackberry that they must innovate or die. Another example is the shift away from driving as people, particularly younger generations, choose alternatives, such as ride-sharing or Uber/Lyft (additionally facilitated by being more adept with other technologies, like smartphones). Thus, car companies have more incentive to develop autonomous vehicles (AVs).

In the case of AV, new innovations will include improvements to the performance of the car as well as tailoring the car to reach different market niches. Thus, the automobile industry is likely to have several major producers and an ecosystem of small firms that produce the "apps" that complement the AV. Nobel Laureate Gary Becker (1965) and the seminal work of Rosen (1974) introduced the notion of household production functions and hedonic pricing, respectively. In this case, consumers would pay for features and components of technologies. The price of a product embodies the price of the value of its components. But, when an AV is introduced, people will have the convenience of riding their own car while also performing other activities, including entertainment, resting, or working. Because the AV will provide more amenities than traditional cars—transport in addition to the environment for business, living, and entertainment—one may expect more diverse sets of products in AV than in current vehicles. So, while we look at the AV as a mechanism to reduce dependence on the personal car, the literature suggests that it will actually enhance the range of functions performed by a vehicle, and especially personal vehicles. In the long-run, as prices decrease, it may even result in increased car ownership rates.

6. Conclusion

Technology adoption is a key step for farmers to enhance their productivity, competitiveness, and profitability. In this chapter, we have summarized major economic models explaining technology adoption, as well as technology adoption drivers beyond profit and utility maximization. We believe that technology adoption will continue to be an active research area in agricultural economics due to the continuous emergence of new technologies and the urgent need for new technologies to address challenges such as climate change and food security.

Two major related issues that affect adoption are regulation and acceptance. For example, governments regulate new medicines as well as the use of chemicals in agriculture. One of the major reasons for product regulation is safety. The literature on risk perception shows that people are more concerned with the unknown than the known, and are more concerned about the risk they cannot control (moving by an autonomous vehicle) than the risk they control (driving a car). As a result, certification from a trusted government may lead to consumers or retailers to start adopting a technology. The introduction of new technologies (e.g., AVs) will be gradual and will involve extra cautionary regulations, until concerns about risks are sufficiently reduced. We must keep in mind that the earliest cars had people running before them to warn against accidents. However, the regulatory procedures have an inherent benefit-risk tradeoff, often reflecting political and economic considerations. The often urgent need for new medicines, such HIV/AIDS treatments, leads to expedient processes, and one could expect a similar outcome with biotechnology in medicine compared to that in agriculture.

In the case of acceptance, consumers may oppose a new product for environmental or other reasons, and may fight politically to prevent its introduction, even when it is deemed sound to use it.

The introduction of a new technology that has multiple social ramifications and is regulated entails a political economic battle involving multiple constituents (Herring and Paarlberg, 2016). They include groups that are affected negatively by the technology or have an alternative solution to the problem that the technology addresses. Returning to biotechnology in agriculture, actors include chemical companies or groups supporting ecological agriculture and organic associations. At the same time, however, biotechnology in medicine was more readily accepted as it was perceived to address immediate needs and "life or death" situations. In the case of AVs, taxi drivers, and even Uber or Lyft drivers may try to impede their introduction while senior living facilities, safety agencies, and others will be more supportive. Overall, people and organizations that oppose the use of new technologies may use the political system to block its use, fully or partially. If they are powerful enough, they may be successful, as in the case of GMOs in Europe. Or they may be successful in delaying introduction, as in the case of some GMO traits in the U.S.

References

Abdulai, A. and W.E. Huffman. 2014. The Adoption and Impact of Soil and Water Conservation Technology: An Endogenous Switching Regression Application. *Land Economics* 90(1): 26–43.

Anand, M., R. Miao, and M. Khanna. 2019. Adopting Bioenergy Crops: Does Farmers' Attitude toward Loss Matter? *Agricultural Economics* 50(4): 435–450.

Arrow, K.J. and A.C. Fisher. 1974. Environmental preservation, uncertainty, and irreversibility. *Quarterly Journal of Economics* 88, 312–319.

Bandura, A. 1994. *Self-Efficacy.* John Wiley & Sons, Inc. New York, NY.

Barham, B.L., J.P. Chavas, D. Fitz, V. Ríos Salas, and L. Schechter. 2014. The Roles of Risk and Ambiguity in Technology Adoption. *Journal of Economic Behavior and Organization* 97: 204–218.

Barham, B.L., J.P. Chavas, D. Fitz, and L. Schechter. 2018. Receptiveness to Advice, Cognitive Ability and Technology Adoption. *Journal of Economic Behavior and Organization* 149: 239–268.

Bass, F.M. 1969. A New Product Growth for Model Consumer Durables. *Management Science* 15(5): 215–227.

Becker, G.S. 1965. A Theory of the Allocation of Time. *The Economic Journal* 493–517.

Bird, K. 2021. *The Outlier: The Unfinished Presidency of Jimmy Carter.* Penguin Random House LLC, New York, NY.

Bocquého, G., F. Jacquet, and A. Reynaud. 2015. Adoption of Perennial Crops and Behavioral Risk Preferences. An Empirical Investigation among French Farmers. Paper presented in the "Risk and Environment" Session at Journées de Recherche en Sciences Sociales, SFER, Nancy, France, December 11–12.

Bridle, L., J. Magruder, C. McIntosh, and T. Suri. 2020. Experimental insights on the constraints to agricultural technology adoption. Working Paper.

Bryan, G. 2019. Ambiguity Aversion Decreases the Impact of Partial Insurance: Evidence from African Farmers. *Journal of the European Economic Association* 17(5): 1428–1469.

Caswell, M.F. and D. Zilberman. 1986. The Effects of Well Depth and Land Quality on the Choice of Irrigation Technology. *American Journal of Agricultural Economics* 68(4): 798–811.

Chavas, J.P. and C. Nauges. 2020. Uncertainty, Learning, and Technology Adoption in Agriculture. *Applied Economic Perspectives and Policy* 42(1): 42–53.

Clot, S., C.Y. Stanton, and M. Willinger. 2017. Are Impatient Farmers More Risk-Averse? Evidence from a Lab-in-the-Field Experiment in Rural Uganda. *Applied Economics* 49(2): 156–169.

David, P.A. 1975. *Technical Choice Innovation and Economic Growth: Essays on American and British Experience in the Nineteenth Century.* Cambridge University Press, Cambridge, NY.

Dessart, F.J., J. Barreiro-Hurlé, R., and Van Bavel. 2019. Behavioural Factors Affecting the Adoption of Sustainable Farming Practices: A Policy-Oriented Review. *European Review of Agricultural Economics* 46, 417–471.

Dixit, A. and R. Pindyck. 1994. *Investment under Uncertainty.* Princeton University Press, Princeton, NJ.

Duflo, E., M. Kremer, and J. Robinson. 2011. Nudging Farmers to Use Fertilizer: Theory and Experimental Evidence from Kenya. *American Economic Review* 101(6): 2350–2390.

Duquette, E., N. Higgins, and J. Horowitz. 2012. Farmer Discount Rates: Experimental Evidence. *American Journal of Agricultural Economics* 94(2): 451–456.

Foster A.D. and M.R. Rosenzweig. 1995. Learning by Doing and Learning from Others: Human Capital and Technical Change in Agriculture. *Journal of Political Economy* 103(6): 1176–1209.

Foster A.D. and M.R. Rosenzweig. 1996. Technical Change and Human Capital Returns and Investments: Evidence from the Green Revolution. *American Economic Review* 86: 931–953.

Foster A.D. and M.R. Rosenzweig. 2010. *Microeconomics of Technology Adoption. Annual Review of Economics* 2: 395–424.

Frederick, S., G. Loewenstein, and T. O'Donoghue. 2002. Time Discounting and Time Preference: A Critical Review. *Journal of Economic Literature* 40(2): 351–401.

Genius, M., P. Koundouri, C. Nauges, and V. Tzouvelekas. 2014. Information Transmission in Irrigation Technology Adoption and Diffusion: Social Learning, Extension Services, and Spatial Effects. *American Journal of Agricultural Economics* 96(1): 328–344.

Griliches, Zvi. 1957. Hybrid Corn: An Exploration in the Economics of Technological Change. *Econometrica* 25(4): 501–522.

Herring, R. and R. Paarlberg. 2016. The Political Economy of Biotechnology. *Annual Review of Resource Economics* 8: 397–416.

Huffman, W.E. 1977. Allocative Efficiency: The Role of Human Capital. *Quarterly Journal of Economics* 91: 59–79.

Huffman, W.E. 2001. Human Capital: Education and Agriculture. B.L. Gardner and G.C. Rausser (Eds.), *Handbook of Agricultural Economics*, Vol. IA, pp. 333–381. Amsterdam, Netherlands: Elsevier Science/North-Holland.

Huffman, W.E. 2020. Human Capital and Adoption of Innovations: Policy Implications. *Applied Economic Perspectives and Policy* 42(1): 92–99.

Just, R.E. and D. Zilberman. 1983. Stochastic Structure, Farm Size and Technology Adoption in Developing Agriculture. *Oxford Economic Papers* 35(2): 307–328.

Kahneman, D. 2011. *Thinking, Fast and Slow.* Farrar, Straus and Giroux, New York, NY.

Kalish, S. 1985. A New Product Adoption Model with Price, Advertising, and Uncertainty. *Management Science* 31(12): 1569–1585.

Liebenehm, S. and H. Waibel. 2014. Simultaneous Estimation of Risk and Time Preferences among Small-Scale Cattle Farmers in West Africa. *American Journal of Agricultural Economics* 96(5): 1420–1438.

Liu E. 2013. Time to Change What to Sow: Risk Preferences and Technology Adoption Decisions of Cotton Farmers in China. *The Review of Economics and Statistics* 95(4): 1386–1403.

Lu, L., T. Reardon, and D. Zilberman. 2016. Supply Chain Design and Adoption of Indivisible Technology. *American Journal of Agricultural Economics* 98(5): 1419–1431.

Majeed, F., M. Khanna, R. Miao, E. Blanc-Betes, T. Hudiburg, and E.H. DeLucia. 2023. Carbon Credit Markets Can Reduce the Riskiness of Bioenergy Crop Production. *Journal of the Agricultural and Applied Economics Association* 2(2): 181–197.

Mansfield, E. 1961. Technical Change and the Rate of Imitation. *Econometrica* 29(4): 741–766.

Mansfield, E. 1963. The Speed of Response of Firms to New Techniques. *The Quarterly Journal of Economics* 77(2): 290–311.

Miao, R., D.A. Hennessy, and B.A. Babcock. 2012. Investment in Cellulosic Biofuel Refineries: Do Waivable Biofuel Mandates Matter? *American Journal of Agricultural Economics* 94(3): 750–762.

Miao, R. and M. Khanna. 2017a. Effectiveness of the Biomass Crop Assistance Program: Roles of Behavioral Factors, Credit Constraint, and Program Design. *Applied Economic Perspectives and Policy* 39(4): 584–608.

Miao, R. and M. Khanna. 2017b. Costs of Meeting a Cellulosic Biofuel Mandate with Perennial Energy Crops: Implications for Policy. *Energy Economics* 64: 321–334.

Miao, R., D.A. Hennessy, and H. Feng. 2022. Grassland Easement Evaluation and Acquisition with Uncertain Conversion and Conservation Returns. *Canadian Journal of Agricultural Economics* 70(1): 41–61.

Moledina, A.A., J.S. Coggins, S. Polasky, and C. Costello. 2003. Dynamic Environmental Policy with Strategic Firms: Prices Versus Quantities. *Journal of Environmental Economics and Management* 45(2): 356–376.

Pannell, D. and D. Zilberman. 2020. Understanding Adoption of Innovations and Behavior Change to Improve Agricultural Policy. *Applied Economic Perspectives and Policy* 42(1): 3–7.

Phillips, J. 2011. *Relentless Innovation: What Works, What Doesn't and What That Means For Your Business.* McGraw Hill Professional.

Putler, D.S. and D. Zilberman. 1988. Computer Use in Agriculture: Evidence from Tulare County, California. *American Journal of Agricultural Economics* 70(4): 790–802.

Rogers, E.M. 1962. *Diffusion of Innovations.* The Free Press, New York, NY.

Rogers, E.M. 2003. *Diffusion of Innovations* (5th ed.). The Free Press, New York, NY.

Rosen, S. 1974. Hedonic Prices and Implicit Markets: Product Differentiation in Pure Competition. *Journal of Political Economy* 82(1): 34–55.

Ryan, B. and N.C. Gross. 1943. The Diffusion of Hybrid Seed Corn in Two Iowa Communities. *Rural Sociology* 8(1): 15–24.

Samuelson, P.A. 1937. A Note on Measurement of Utility. *The Review of Economic Studies* 4(2): 155–161.

Shah, F.A., D. Zilberman, and U. Chakravorty. 1995. Technology Adoption in the Presence of an Exhaustible Resource: The Case of Groundwater Extraction. *American Journal of Agricultural Economics* 77(2): 291–299.

Streletskaya, N.A., S.D. Bell, M. Kecinski, T. Li, S. Banerjee, L.H. Palm-Forster, and D. Pannell. 2020. Agricultural Adoption and Behavioral Economics: Bridging the Gap. *Applied Economic Perspectives and Policy* 42(1): 54–66.

Sunding, D. and D. Zilberman. 2001. The Agricultural Innovation Process: Research and Technology Adoption in a Changing Agricultural Sector, B.L. Gardner and G.C. Rausser (Eds.), Handbook of Agricultural Economics, Volume 1, Part A, Chapter 4, pp. 207–261.

Tanaka, T., C.F. Camerer, and Q. Nguyen. 2010. Risk and Time Preferences: Linking Experimental and Household Survey Data from Vietnam. *American Economic Review* 100(1): 557–571.

Tarde, G. 1890. *Les Lois de l'imitation.* Paris: Alcan. English edition: The Laws of Imitation, translated by Parsons, E.C., The Mershon Company Press, Rahway, NJ.

Thaler, R.H. 2015. *Misbehaving: The Making of Behavioral Economics.* WW Norton & Company.

Ward, P.S. and V. Singh. 2015. Using Field Experiments to Elicit Risk and Ambiguity Preferences: Behavioural Factors and the Adoption of New Agricultural Technologies in Rural India. *The Journal of Development Studies* 51(6): 707–724.

Wuepper, D., S. Bukchin-Peles, D. Just, and D. Zilberman. 2023. Behavioral Agricultural Economics. *Applied Economic Perspectives and Policy* 45(4): 2094–2105.

Ye, F., N. Paulson, and M. Khanna. 2022. Are Renewable Energy Policies Effective to Promote Technological Change? The Role of Induced Technological Risk. *Journal of Environmental Economics and Management* 114: 102665.

Zilberman, D., J. Zhao, and A. Heiman. 2012. Adoption versus Adaptation, with Emphasis on Climate Change. *Annual Review of Resource Economics* 4(1): 27–53.

Chapter 9

Agricultural Supply Chain

Microeconomics seeks to understand the market for goods (e.g., bread, meat, oil), which tend to be studied in isolation with rather simple, and few, linkages. However, consumers frequently do not consume a raw good (e.g., wheat grain or a cow), but rather a processed good (e.g., a sandwich or hamburger), the outcomes of complex supply chains that innovators and producers have to take into account when developing their products. Economists have not paid much attention to supply chains (at least before the COVID-19 pandemic), and when they do, they often take supply chains as "given." But the reality is that every time an innovation is introduced, whoever controls the innovation, thinks about the design of a supply chain to implement it. This chapter emphasizes the role of supply chains as mechanisms to implement innovations in the context of agriculture, studying the design and performance of supply chains. We will do so by using many examples such as Tyson Foods, beer, and biofuels. We can apply the concept of the supply chain to just about any product or service (even education) to understand its elements, linkages, purposes, and external influences.

1. Product Characteristics and Hedonics

1.1. *Demand theory and supply chain*

Demand theory is a major element of economics. Its pursuit of generality resulted in a minimal set of assumptions and results. In particular,

(1) It assumes utility maximization subject to income constraint and the main result is that (compensated) demand is negatively sloped.
(2) All goods are treated equal without much attention to the intrinsic properties of goods (the only valuable distinction is between goods that are substitutes versus complements and between inferior, normal, and luxury goods).
(3) Preferences are considered as given.
(4) The number of goods is constant without new innovations.
(5) Consumption decisions are made within markets without attention to household-level choices.
(6) The household labor associated with consumption is not considered.

The traditional demand theory has been criticized by Nobel Laureates Gary Becker and Kelvin Lancaster to be elegant, general, and vacuous, but not very useful in addressing some of the most interesting and pressing issues (see Chapter 3 in this book). For example, it is not useful for assessing the demand for new products because it has limited capacity to identify sources of product improvement and product differentiation. But much of the modern economy is based on improving existing products. Lancaster (1966) emphasized more on the processing of raw goods rather than consumable goods, while Becker (1965) introduced the notion of *household production function* where family labor is used in conjunction with purchased goods to produce the final consumables with the desired characteristics for the household. We will develop a framework based on their work and relate it to our work on supply chains.

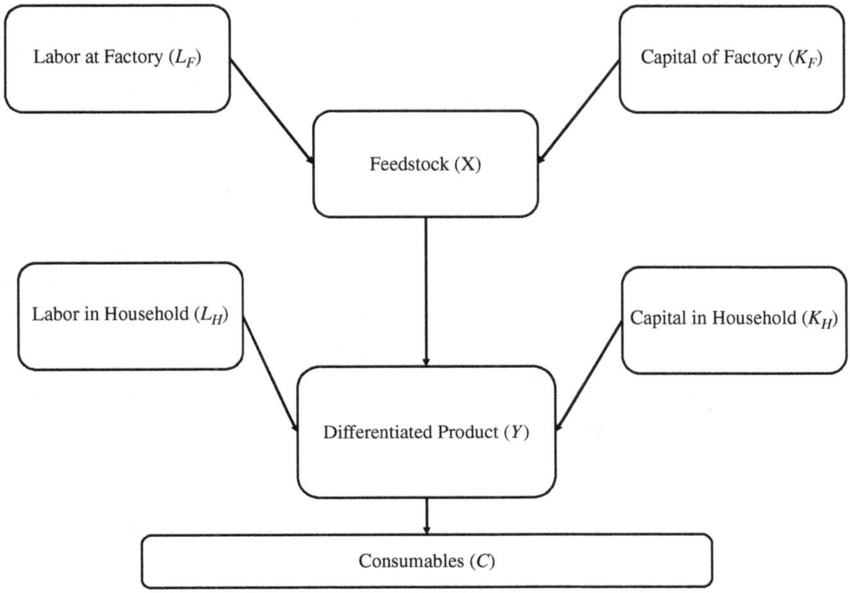

Figure 1. A supply chain from feedstock to consumables.

Like Becker and Lancaster, we will assume that there is a sequence in the production system, and this sequence is a supply chain. The starting point is a commodity, like cattle, that we call feedstock and is denoted by X. Feedstock is processed in a factory, with inputs like labor (L_F) and capital (K_F), to produce a differentiated product (Y), say, meat. Within the household, the product is further processed with family inputs including labor (L_H) and capital (K_H) to produce a consumable (C), like a steak. This basic model is presented in Figure 1. We can formalize it by denoting the production function of the differentiated product at the factory as $Y = f(K_F, L_F, X)$ and the production function of the consumable as $C = g(K_H, L_H, Y)$. Of course, this simple, one-dimensional model can be expanded to have vectors of each variable. For example, households may buy many types of differentiated products, using the labor of different family members and different types of equipment (i.e., capital), to produce different types of consumables.

Now let us assume that the household has initial income denoted by I and time T that can be used for household work L_H or work outside the home that earns wage W (in dollars). Let us also assume that the household operates in a market economy and the price of Y is P and the cost of using one unit of household capital is r.[1]

Thus, the net income after expenditures on Y and K_H is: $I_N = I - PY - rK_H + W \cdot (T - L_H)$. The household derives utility from the consumption of C and net income. The household utility is denoted by $U(C, I_N)$. To simplify, plug $C = g(K_H, L_H, Y)$ and $I_N = I - PY - rK_H + W \cdot (T - L_H)$ in the utility function. The household determines their purchase of Y, their amount of K_H and L_H. The optimization problem is,

$$\underset{\{Y, L_H, K_H\}}{\text{Max}} \; U\Big(g\left(K_{H,} L_H, Y\right), I - PY - rK_H + W \cdot (T - L_H)\Big). \quad (1)$$

The first-order conditions are derived using the chain rule:

$$\frac{dU(C, I_N))}{dC} \cdot \frac{dg(K_H, L_H, Y)}{dY} = P \cdot \frac{dU(C, I_N)}{dI_N}. \quad (2)$$

Let $\lambda = \frac{\frac{dU(C,I_N))}{dC}}{\frac{dU(C,I_N)}{dI_N}}$ denote the monetary value of consuming one unit of C at the optimal solution. Condition (2) implies that the optimal Y is determined when the value of its marginal product $\lambda \cdot \frac{dg(K_H, L_H, Y)}{dY}$ is equal to the price P. Similarly, one can derive the first-order conditions that denote the amount of household labor and capital allocated to producing C.

$$\frac{dU(C, I_N))}{dC} \cdot \frac{dg(K_H, L_H, Y)}{dL_H} = \frac{dU(C, I_N)}{dI_N} \cdot W. \quad (3)$$

$$\frac{dU(C, I_N))}{dC} \cdot \frac{dg(K_H, L_H, Y)}{dK_H} = \frac{dU(C, I_N)}{dI_N} \cdot r. \quad (4)$$

[1]For simplicity we avoid using a dynamic model on decisions about investments in durables that require multi-period analysis. Instead, we assume that the household pays a fee for each unit of equipment they use.

Conditions (3) and (4) suggest that the optimal level of household labor and capital allocated to producing C is where the value of their marginal products are equal to W and r, respectively. Condition (2) provides the foundation for the consumer demand for the differentiated commodity, Y, which will depend on the initial income, I, the cost of capital, r, and the cost of labor, W. Similarly, conditions (3) and (4) provide the basis to estimate how much household time and capital will be supplied to produce C, given the prices P, W, and r.

Our analysis is highly simplified. Certainly, there is heterogeneity among households where each household has its own demand function, and these demand functions are combined to produce aggregate demand. But the basic principle is that choices at the household level determine how much consumables that each household will derive and the demand for differentiated products. The analysis can also be expanded at the factory level to determine the optimal supply of Y given the prices of feedstock, capital, and labor at the factory. The interaction of the demand and the supply for Y will determine its price.

1.2. *Product characteristics and hedonics*

Now let us add another level of complexity based on a classic paper by Rosen (1974). Assume that Y, the differentiated product, can have different levels of quality, q. In this case, we assume that utility is now also a function of q and it becomes $U(C, I_N, q)$.[2] Every family must then determine both the quantity and the quality that they consume. In a competitive economy, the family faces a *hedonic pricing* formula, where price as a function of quality: $P(q)$. Hedonic pricing is a method of analysis used to assess the marginal value of a characteristic.

Generally, we expect that the price of the commodity will improve with its quality. In this case, the optimization problem of the

[2]For simplicity, we do not consider the more general case where production function of C is affected by q, such that $C = g(K_H, L_H, Y, q)$.

household becomes,

$$\underset{\{Y,L_H,K_H,q\}}{\text{Max}} \quad U(g\left(K_H, L_H, Y\right), I - P(q)Y - rK_H + W \cdot (T - L_H), q). \tag{5}$$

In this case condition (2) becomes,

$$\frac{dU(C, I_N, q))}{dC} \cdot \frac{dg(K_H,\, L_H, Y)}{dY} = \frac{dU(C, I_N, q)}{dI_N} \cdot P(q). \tag{6}$$

And conditions (3) and (4) will change accordingly. But more importantly, we have another first-order condition:

$$\frac{dU(C, I_N, q))}{dq} = \frac{dU(C, I_N, q)}{dI_N} \cdot \frac{dP}{dq}. \tag{7}$$

Now let $\mu(q) = \frac{\frac{dU(C,I_N,q))}{dq}}{\frac{dU(C,I_N,q)}{dI_N}}$ be the marginal monetary value of a unit of quality to the household. The optimal quality of Y purchased by a given household will be at the point where the quality's marginal monetary value is equal to the marginal increase in price caused by the increase in quality, namely, $\mu(q) = \frac{dP}{dq}$. The marginal monetary value of a unit of quality is an element in hedonic pricing. From this analysis, one can derive demand for both the quantity and quality of the product, which will be dependent on the hedonic pricing formula $P(q)$ as well as r, I, T, and W.

Rosen's analysis suggests that higher-income people purchase higher-quality products and that the marginal price of quality is increasing. Rosen's analysis also considered firms' behavior. When producers are heterogeneous, different producers will elect to produce products of different quality. Market forces will lead to an equilibrium that determines $P(q)$, and for each level of quality, the quantity of demand equals the quantity of supply.

Many products have different product characteristics, which capture different elements of quality. For example, foods have calories, vitamins, and protein, as well as taste and appearance indicators. Some elements of quality are continuous variables (e.g., calories or protein content in a food item) and others are discrete variables (e.g., a food product can be either organic or not). In addition, some

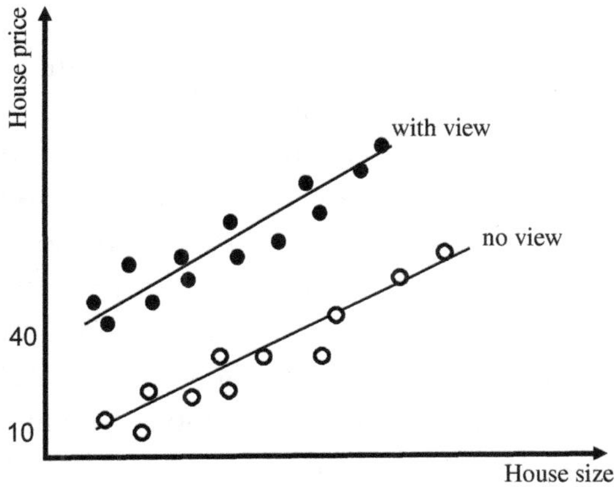

Figure 2. Relationship between house size and house price considering ocean view.

elements of quality are objective (e.g., vitamin content) while others are subjective (e.g., taste or beliefs). Each product characteristic has a hedonic price. Economists have developed mathematical formulas to estimate the price of a good as a function of its product characteristics. The most common use of hedonic pricing is in the valuation of houses. A simple model may assume that the price of a house in a given region of San Francisco (P_h) depends on its size S and whether or not it has an ocean view ($V = 1$ if it has an ocean view and 0 otherwise). A simple linear formula is:

$$P_h = \alpha S + \beta V,$$

where α is the hedonic price of the square foot and β is the shadow price of an ocean view. Figure 2 shows that if one has data on house prices, the two coefficients can be estimated. Of course, actual studies estimate more complex formulas with different hedonic prices for different room types, the safety of neighborhood, quality of yard, and so on.

1.3. *Hedonics, innovation, and supply chain*

Nowadays, because food demand is inelastic and increased supply reduces prices, a big challenge for agricultural firms and regions is not necessarily to produce more food, but rather to increase the value added.[3] Increasing value-added and quality of products is key to many industries. Innovation that improves product quality tends to change the hedonic price equation, and therefore the elements of the equation are changing over time. For example, drip irrigation allowed farmers to grow fruits and vegetables on lower-quality land (e.g., steep hills or sandy soil) where they were not grown before. After the introduction of drip irrigation, the price of lower-quality land increased, and because of the increased food supply, output prices declined, and the value of higher-quality land declined (Caswell and Zilberman, 1986). Moreover, the food system over the last 100 years has gone through a value-added revolution, where more processed food requires fewer labor requirements at the household level (Levenstein, 2003). Changes in food availability and in demand are shifting the hedonic prices of different food characteristics, including nutrients, taste, and convenience.

The way that changes in quality are introduced depends on the capacity of the innovating organization to implement their innovation through the design of supply chain and marketing activities. One example is the transition from early cell phones to smartphones, which resulted in new features of phones and a new valuation of their attributes. This transition was also associated with the emergence of Apple and Samsung and the decline of Nokia. To better understand these transitions, we need to understand product-changing innovation processes and associated supply chains.

2. Innovation and Supply Chains

Innovations are the foundation of changes in technologies and institutions. There is a large literature on the economics of innovation (Sunding and Zilberman, 2001) that provides classifications of innovations and explains their generation, implementation, and impacts.

[3]The main agricultural problem in the U.S. and developed world has been oversupply that led to subsidies to reduce acreage. At the same time, the global population is growing, and we need to increase food production. So, agribusinesses and governments work both to increase food security as well as the quality and value-added of food.

While most of the literature takes markets and supply chains as given when considering innovation implementation, we stipulate that implementation of innovations often involves creating or redesigning supply chains. Moreover, supply chains are not rigid entities, but rather flexible structures that both respond to and affect technologies and policies. In this section, we will first discuss innovation and innovation processes, and then link them to supply chains. Obviously, this is only an introduction. Both topics, together with the linkages between them, will get more coverage as we move forward in this chapter.

Innovations are new ways of doing things. Schumpeter (1934), the great Austrian economist who taught at Harvard, recognized the importance of innovation and technological change. He emphasized that economic systems were constantly evolving and that innovations were the key driving forces that led to the creation of new firms and markets and the destruction of old ones (which he called "creative destruction"). Innovating firms may acquire market power, but they often dissipate as new innovations and competitors emerge. These processes lead to increased availability of products and decreased costs. Schumpeter's ideas, in many ways, contrast with the traditional emphasis in microeconomics on equilibrium and competition. Many of the modeling tools of microeconomics can be used to illustrate and expand Schumpeterian ideas. Our analysis here is based on some of his concepts linking explicitly innovation processes with supply chains and markets that innovations induce or affect.

There are many ways to categorize innovations. One major distinction is between *embodied* and *disembodied* innovations (see Chapter 7 in this book). Embodied innovations are reflected by new products or services that can be sold, whereas disembodied innovations are mostly ideas and concepts. The owner of an embodied innovation can capture much of the benefit by selling it in the market, but it is much more difficult to capture the financial benefit from disembodied innovations. Therefore, the government may need to support the creation and adoption of disembodied innovations. A more detailed classification distinguishes between product innovation (e.g., tractor, automobile), process innovation (e.g., internal combustion engine), institutional innovation (e.g., banks), managerial innovation (e.g., double ledger accounting), and resource use innovation (e.g., growing flowers in Kenya). Classification can go even further. For example, innovations that address pest control problems can be classified as mechanical (e.g., using a hoe), chemical (e.g., pesticides), biological (e.g., exploiting predator-prey dynamics), genetic (e.g., new seed varieties), managerial (e.g., crop rotation), and informational (e.g., monitoring pests and weather). Different classification systems serve different purposes and there is no clear hierarchy.

Most innovations start from a concept, and the innovation process translates the concept into something that can be implemented, which can be a product, practice, or institution. Once this outcome is established, then we have supply chains that commercialize it. An example of a product innovation is the personal computer. Steve Jobs and Steve Wozniak thought about a user-friendly personal computer.[4] It resulted in the Apple I and II products. The supply chain of these products evolved from selling through a few stores (Apple I) to developing a national distribution system (Apple II). An example of a process innovation is pre-packaged fresh salads. It was originated by James R. Lugg, an agricultural scientist. He led a research team that, by mixing some gases appropriately, created a method to preserve salad greens for up to two weeks. They obtained a patent and commercialized it through a company called Fresh Express. In both cases, the innovations were embodied in products, and therefore were carried by the private sector. On the other hand, the notion of integrated pest management (IPM) was introduced by UC Berkeley entomologist A.E. Michelbacher in 1939 and was further refined by researchers at the university in the late 1950s. It emphasized the selection of appropriate pest treatment based on monitoring of pest population. It was a disembodied management practice and, at least in the beginning, it was promoted, taught, and implemented by the public sector through university and

[4]See http://www.computerhistory.org/atchm/steve-jobs/.

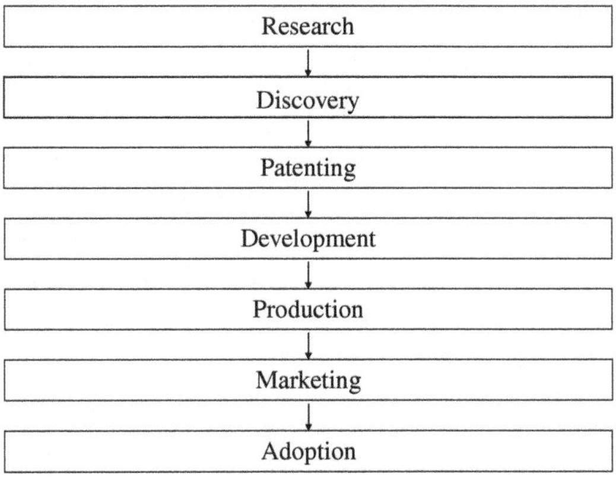

Figure 3. The innovation process.

government extension services. Since it has been proven profitable and its implementation requires specific skills, a new private sector of professionals and firms has emerged providing IPM services.

The transition of innovation from a concept to an implementable outcome (product or service) may follow multiple paths. Most innovations in the past were introduced by practitioners who refined them through trial and error. The wheel and the use of fire for cooking are two examples of this path. Even now many important innovations arise from practitioners. But in the past century, academic research has been the source of many important innovations, especially in chemistry, biology, medicine, engineering, and computer science. The transition from an idea to a product is frequently called the "Innovation Process", and it is depicted in Figure 3. In the case of, say, a medical innovation, researchers at the university come up with a discovery based on their research. The discovery leads to a new concept, an idea to solve a problem. The concept is then experimented with in the lab. After the concept is established, the scientist may seek a patent and publish the results. But to be ready for commercialization, the innovation must go through the development process, which includes upscaling and testing (both to make sure the product performs well and meets regulatory requirements). Once the product is ready, then commercialization starts with production and marketing that, hopefully, leads to consumer adoption.

This schematic analysis is far from perfect. There are a lot of feedback mechanisms within the system. The development process may discover bugs and flaws that prompt new research. The production process is gradual and responds both to consumer feedback and may require new developments. But this overall framework is useful for analysis of the institutional elements associated with innovation, which we will emphasize later. For example, while research may occur at the university, development may occur at start-ups and production at major companies. The transfer of technology from universities to the private sector is a major policy challenge. New institutions, like offices of technology transfer at universities, have emerged to facilitate this transfer. As we will discuss later, university researchers are also part of start-ups and the interaction of universities with industries to form the education–industry complex is a major factor that explains the strengths of California versus other regions.

Although useful, this schema ignores the basic issue that we emphasize, which is the creation and modification of supply chains. Supply chains are the organizational arrangements responsible for the creation and movement of a product from its raw materials to final customers. Once an innovation is working and generates new products or services, then its introduction to the market requires establishing or modifying supply chains. For example, when Apple introduced iPhone, it needed to develop new markets for its final product and for its components. It also needed to decide on how to distribute and market iPhones. For instance, Apple needed to decide what and how much to produce in-house and where to source inputs. Its decisions were constrained by the preferences of consumers and by the availability and capability of suppliers. The design of supply chains to implement this innovation is an economic problem that we will investigate in this chapter.

3. Modeling Supply Chains

In traditional agricultural systems, most of the production was done on a farm. A farmer would have grown food to feed her family and their livestock, harvested and processed the grain, fruit, vegetables, and meat, and then sold them. With innovations came specialization and the increase in activities occurring beyond the farm gate. Today a farm unit that specializes in growing crops is likely to obtain inputs such as seeds, fertilizers, pesticides, and irrigation water from input suppliers and then sell its crops to a packing house, which processes and sells the product to retailers for purchase by end consumers. Supply chain covers the various stages that the final product goes through.

Every product we consume — our car, phone, movies, the water we drink, and medicine — has a supply chain. Every supply chain has several segments, and each segment often has subsegments. Understanding supply chains and how they work is challenging, but crucial to a good analysis of the economy and its operation. As we mentioned earlier, supply chains change with new innovations and policies. New modes of transportation (e.g., train), discoveries (e.g., relativity, DNA), and political events lead to changes in what is produced and where, and the various linkages between producers and consumers. To understand the complexity of supply chains we must simplify how we represent them for analytical purposes.

3.1. *Two models of supply chains*

We will start with a simple two-segment supply chain for producing a processed agricultural product. The first segment of this supply chain is producing an agricultural product, called feedstock, and the second segment is processing the final product. You may think of fields that produce sugar cane and a refinery that processes them to produce sugar or ethanol; orchards that grow fruits and a packinghouse where the fruits are sorted, stored, and prepared for shipment; and cows that produce milk and dairy and farms that process and ship them as various products. Figure 4 presents a schema of such a supply chain. Note that the supply chain does not include the final consumers, who represent the demand for the final product. The company that owns the processing facility may be vertically integrated and produce the feedstock as well, it may purchase the feedstock from independent farmers, for example, through contract or via a market,

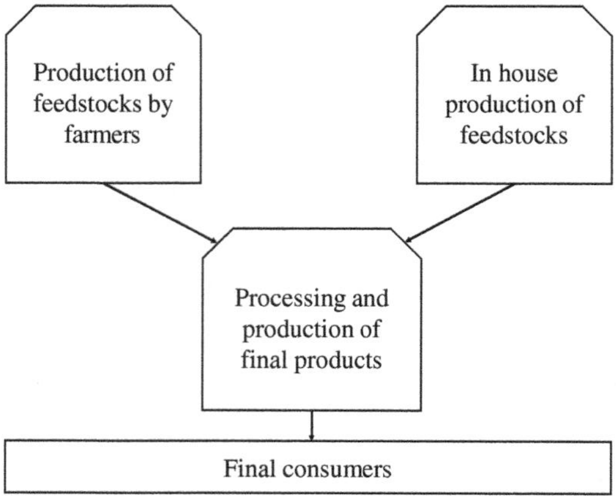

Figure 4. Two-segment supply chain.

or it may combine some in-house production of the feedstock with some purchase from suppliers outside the farm.

The two-segment supply chain is useful to analyze the supply chain choices associated with the implementation of new innovations. When an entrepreneur comes up with an innovation, say to produce flowers in Kenya for the European market, they need to have a source for the flowers and a processing facility that will collect, sort, and ship them. They also have to decide the parameters for processing and how to split production in-house versus purchasing from others. If the entrepreneur aims to maximize profits and has limited credit and other resources, the choice of the capacity and distribution of effort between internal and external sources is a constrained optimization problem. Establishing a flower exporting facility is a long-term investment requiring multiple years to pay off with uncertainty about future conditions. The entrepreneur attempts to maximize the expected discounted net present value of profits given credit or other resource constraints, as well as technologies they face.

We will solve these types of problems in the following sections, but note that the expected profits in each period include the revenue from sales of the final product (depending on the quantity produced and the demand for the product) minus the expenses (cost of processing, in-house production, and feedstock purchases).

We need to distinguish between the fixed costs of investing in facilities and permanent equipment versus the variable costs of production. The limited capacity to borrow and supervise may force the entrepreneur to rely on either feedstock produced by others, or a smaller processing facility with a significant in-house production facility. When we look at the decision problem of the entrepreneur as one occurring over time, we need to recognize that because of technological change and learning, the planned activities often change. Furthermore, the entrepreneur may have market power in the final product or feedstock market that could affect the prices they receive for output or the amount paid for feedstock. These considerations will affect the choices made for final output and the allocation between the feedstock purchased from outside suppliers and that produced in-house.

The decision of the entrepreneur also depends on government policies. For example, the initial investment may increase in the presence of programs that provide cheap credit to infrastructure investment in developing countries. In other situations, a foreign entrepreneur may have limited capacity to control land for feedstock production, which may limit the capacity to produce in-house and thus increase reliance on external providers.

While the two-segment supply chain is easy to demonstrate, a three-segment system (Figure 5) might be more appropriate for agriculture. The three-segment supply chain has been used generically in economic analysis (Reardon and Timmer, 2012) where there is a distinction between the upstream (farms), midstream (processing), and downstream (wholesalers and retailers). For example, Tyson Foods, a large livestock processor, relies mostly on contractors to produce its feedstock (poultry, chicken) but frequently supplies them with inputs like grains and genetic materials and provides guidance for production. In other cases, farm cooperatives may collectively purchase the input and sell the output of the farmers. The three-segment supply chain has also been applied to natural resource management. For example, Chakravorty *et al.* (2009) depicted the supply chain of water in agriculture with the water source (upstream), aqueduct (midstream), and distribution (downstream).

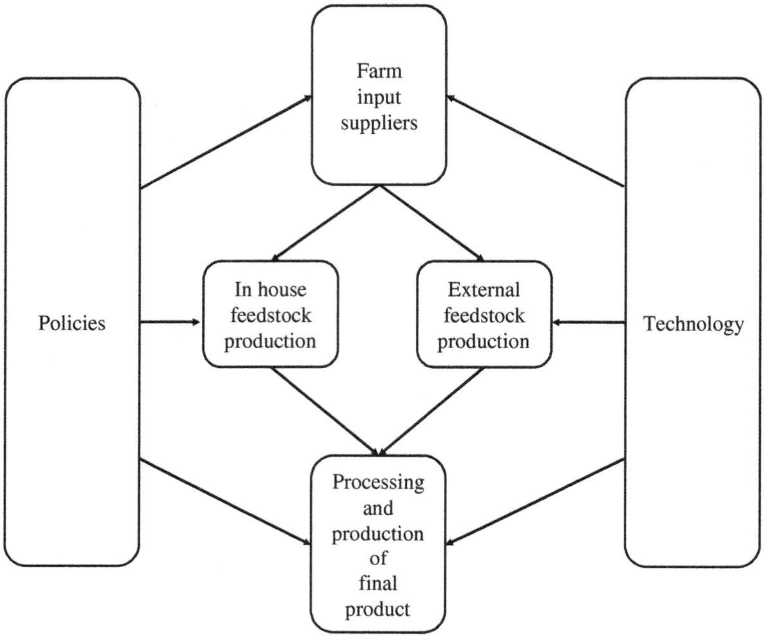

Figure 5. Three-segment supply chain.

Let us return to the example of Tyson Foods because it can be used to illustrate how innovations lead to the redesign of supply chains. According to Schaefer (2014), the company started in the 1930s when the founders realized that there was a large demand for poultry in New York that could be supplied by farmers in Arkansas. They thus started as a trucking company, buying poultry from farms in Arkansas and selling it in New York (a two-segment supply chain). Then they had another innovative idea to take advantage of their trucks and economies of scale (regarding purchasing) by providing their producers with feed, thus converting to a three-segment supply chain. Later, they realized that the new genetics improved the quality of chickens, so they decided to invest in R&D and start providing poultry producers with genetic materials. This meant that they added another element to the first segment of the three-segment supply chain, which is producing genetic material.

Further, it may be more useful, in many cases, to consider a four-segment supply chain, which includes farm inputs, farms, processing, and distribution. Each segment of the system can be broken down into subsegments, which means the detailed supply chain is much more complex and has many segments. For example, the input supply segment may include many elements — fertilizer, irrigation, and machinery. The supply chain of fertilizer may include feedstock (manure), processing to refined product (fertilizer), and distribution (shipping). This suggests that supply chains are nested systems, and the degree of detail that we consider depends on the problem at hand.

Our analysis has thus far deemphasized one aspect of the supply chain: marketing. Marketing is part of the distribution, but in many cases, there is a marketing chain nested inside the supply chain. A finished product may be purchased by wholesalers who then sell it to retailers, who in turn sell it to the general public. Companies may have their own salespeople and may use different strategies to promote sales at different stages of the supply chain. In some cases, they may go to trade shows and then establish contacts with potential buyers. There are many marketing tools like advertisements, demonstrations, samplings, and warranties. The introduction of the internet also affects the way sales are promoted. Some of these aspects will be discussed further in this chapter.

3.2. *Innovation-induced supply chains*

One of the major concepts that we emphasize in this chapter is innovation-induced supply chains. New innovations are likely to spur the creation of supply chains to implement these innovations. But these supply chains are often partial elements of larger supply chains. For example, the introduction of GMOs required a two-segment supply chain, involving the generation and insertion of traits into seeds, which then entered an existing supply chain. Monsanto had facilities to conduct research to identify, refine, and test traits. They decided to buy some seed companies to sell GMO seeds directly to farmers. Then, they sold other seed companies, like Pioneer, the right to insert the patented traits in their own seeds. Corn ethanol is another example of an innovation that required a three-segment supply chain. The first segment is the production of feedstock (corn) on farms; the second is processing that produces multiple outputs, ethanol and other byproducts (such as dried distillers' grain (DDG) used as animal feed); and the third segment is the distribution of some of the outputs, such as ethanol and DDG.

First, let us consider an innovation that leads to further differentiation of a product. For example, a new product trait that affects quality. Returning to Tyson Foods, around 1990 they decided to, instead of just selling whole chickens, extend their processing to provide a wide variety of products (whole chickens, chicken parts, and even pre-cooked and processed chicken products). In this case, the production system has to be expanded and become more complex. A distribution section with its own segments can be added and divided to accommodate the range of subproducts. Similarly, after introducing pre-packaged salads, Fresh Express, driven by "relentless innovation," introduced packages with salad dressing of different flavors. This again adds complexity to supply chains and the design of the supply chain must determine how to allocate production to different product features based on demand, relying on hedonic pricing.

In the case of process innovation that can be adopted by different products, the supply chain design must recognize the sequence of products and regions in which technology will be introduced. A process innovation, in many cases, does not fit immediately into an existing production system, and thus the production system needs to be modified to accommodate the new process innovation. The supply chain design must consider that the suppliers, in many cases, assist the end consumer in adapting the process to their needs. When IBM introduced mainframe computers, a product allowing users to manage various computations, they also provided sales engineers who helped to customize the design of the system to the buyers' needs and provided training to their staff. In the case of drip irrigation, especially when it was introduced, drip manufacturers were providing drip system designs to adapt to the specific conditions of the buyers. Furthermore, the introduction of drip irrigation to some crops required changing agronomical practices. In California, extension specialists modified the production of tomatoes for processing to allow for the use of drip irrigation (Taylor *et al.*, 2014). In these cases, the supply chain may also have an adaptation segment with contributions from agencies like Cooperative Extension.

The design of the supply chain is also affected by changes in processing or shipping technologies. The introduction of the railroad allowed for the expansion of the grain supply chain so that grains could be grown in the Midwest and shipped to the coast. The introduction of cold storage in transport allowed for the expansion of processed foods across regions and borders. For example, most seafood consumed in the U.S. comes from Asia (Belton *et al.*, 2015). The flower industry grew and became less localized with the introduction of cold storage in air freight. It allowed regions that have advantages in the production of flowers, like California, Florida, Israel, and Kenya, to become major producers of flowers internationally.

Similarly, policy affects supply chains. Introduction of policies that allowed breweries to sell beer on-site led to the proliferation of microbreweries in the US (Swinnen, 2011). Improved credit conditions, such as reduced interest rates through monetary policy, may lead to the introduction of new supply chains to implement innovations that become profitable, or increase the output volume of supply chains by reducing the cost of operation. The successful adoption of drip irrigation in California relative to other regions in developing countries can be explained by government investment in research and extension services that collaborate with manufacturers to adapt technologies to local conditions (Taylor *et al.*, 2014).

3.3. *Symbiotic supply chains*

Zilberman *et al.* (2022) emphasize the symbiotic relationship between the innovation supply chain and product supply chain. The former focuses on institutions undertaking innovation as a research and

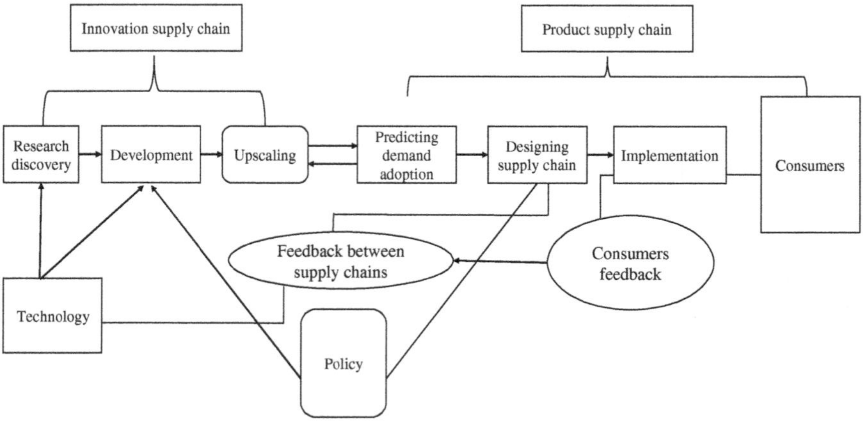

Figure 6. Symbiotic supply chains.

development process that leads to new products; and the latter centers on companies starting with innovative products and marketing them. Zilberman *et al.* (2022) combine the two supply chains, analyzing a sequence of actions from labs to consumers. They argue that the two supply chains affect each other and that, concurrently, they are influenced by economic and policy considerations.

Figure 6 presents the symbiotic relationship between the two supply chains, through which the transition from innovative ideas to final marketed products occurs. First, in the innovation supply chain, basic concepts are refined for commercial uses via developing, testing, and upscaling. Second, the product supply chain produces and markets the product. On the one hand, the output of the innovation supply chain, determining the characteristics of the product, will affect the formation of the product supply chain. On the other hand, feedback from each segment of the product supply chain can be incorporated in the innovation supply chain to further improve the product or to invent new products. Moreover, the two supply chains are influenced by public policies on R&D, education, trade, and intellectual property rights protection, among many others.

So far, we have illustrated how supply chains can be presented as a collection of activities that follow a logical sequence to produce final outputs from raw materials through intermediary outputs.

The design of a supply chain can be presented as an optimization of expected discounted profits subject to constraints. New innovations may lead to the establishment of new or redesigned supply chains, and similarly, government policies can affect the design of new and existing supply chains. The next two sections will introduce tools that allow the planner to design supply chains.

4. Designing Supply Chains — Static Analysis

As we argued, the introduction of new innovations is leading to the creation and modification of supply chains. In this section, we will present and solve the supply chain design issues mathematically. Like many economic problems, supply chain design is a constrained optimization problem. The design problem varies according to the nature of the innovation and the constraints facing the entrepreneurs who aim to implement the technology. For every design problem, we need to identify the objective function, decision variables, and constraints. In reality, every problem is unique, but we will attempt to investigate the impact of one category of innovation presented within a simple supply chain and analyze its implications. We will aim to develop some general lessons, but there is room for future research to analyze the impact of different types of innovation on different supply chain structures.

Here we consider a supply chain for a product processing agricultural feedstock. We design a two-segment supply chain that corresponds to Figure 4 in the previous section. The innovation may be a new product altogether, or a new location to produce a product. The optimization problem that we will solve is similar to the one presented by Du *et al.* (2016). We will start with a basic model, and then expand it. The main choices that a firm or entrepreneur who applies the innovation (referred to as the enterprise) are the total quantity of production and the amount of feedstock that will be produced in-house versus purchased through markets or contracts with third parties. Obviously, this model is abstract and ignores key variable inputs and equipment, but the role of a model is to emphasize key issues.

Let X_h denote the quantity of feedstock produced in-house and X_m as that purchased from a third party. The total feedstock is denoted by

$$X = X_h + X_m, \tag{8}$$

where $X_h \geq 0$ and $X_m \geq 0$. Let the final output be denoted by Q, and the production function is

$$Q = f(X) = f(X_h + X_m). \tag{9}$$

We assume that marginal productivity of feedstock, denoted by $MP(X) = \partial f(x)/\partial X$, is positive and non-increasing in X. The cost of production includes cost of processing the feedstock, $C_p(X)$, the cost of producing the feedstock in-house, $C_h(X_h)$, and the expenditure of purchasing feedstock from third parties, $E_m(X_m)$. The cost of producing the purchased feedstock from the third party is $C_m(X_m)$, but we assume that these suppliers are competitive and will charge the marginal cost of X_m per unit supplied. This marginal cost is denoted by $MC_m(X_m) = dC_m(X_m)/dX_m$. So, the outlay of expenditure on purchased feedstock is $E_m(X_m) = X_m MC(X_m)$. The total cost of the firm that considers introducing the innovation is therefore

$$TC = C_p(X) + C_h(X_h) + X_m MC_m(X_m). \tag{10}$$

Now assume that the price of Q is P and the enterprise is facing an inverse demand $P = D^{-1}(Q)$. The enterprise's revenue is thus $f(X_h + X_m)D^{-1}(Q)$. To simplify our analysis we will determine the profit-maximizing X_h and X_m and will use (9) to determine the optimal output. With the aforementioned notation, we write the supply chain design optimization problem as

$$\begin{aligned} L = \underset{\{X_h, X_m\}}{\text{Max}} \big[& f(X_h+X_m) D^{-1}(f(X_h+X_m)) - C_p(X_h+X_m) \\ & - C_h(X_h) - X_m MC_m(X_m) \big] \end{aligned} \tag{11}$$

$$\text{s.t. } X_m \geq 0 \text{ and } X_h \geq 0.$$

For convenience, define enterprise revenue R as $f(X_h+X_m)$ $D^{-1}(f(X_h+X_m))$ and enterprise cost C as $[C_p(X_h+X_m) + C_h(X_h) + X_m MC_m(X_m)]$. Thus Equation (11) is equal to the maximization of profits subject to the non-negativity constraint. First, assume that we have an interior solution. Using the chain rule, the differentiation of the first-order condition with respect to X_h yields

$$\frac{dL}{dX_h} = \frac{\partial f(X)}{\partial X}\left[D^{-1}(Q) + Q\frac{\partial D^{-1}(Q)}{\partial Q}\right] - \frac{\partial C_p(X)}{\partial X} - \frac{\partial C_h(X_h)}{\partial X_h} = 0. \tag{12}$$

We note the following:

Marginal productivity of input: $MP(X) = \dfrac{\partial f(X)}{\partial X}$;

Marginal revenue of output: $MR(Q) = D^{-1}(Q) + Q\dfrac{\partial D^{-1}(Q)}{\partial Q}$;

Marginal cost of processing $MC_P(X) = \dfrac{\partial C_p(X)}{\partial X}$; and,

Marginal cost of producing in-house $MC_h(X_h) = \dfrac{\partial C_h(X_h)}{\partial X_h}$.

Using these definitions, the first-order condition can be rewritten as

$$MR(Q)MP(X) = MC_P(X) + MC_h(X_h). \tag{13}$$

Condition (13) states that at the optimal level of X_h, the marginal contribution of a unit of X_h to the enterprise revenue, which is its marginal productivity (i.e., $MP(X)$) times the marginal revenue produced by each unit of output (i.e., $MR(Q)$) is equal to the sum of marginal cost of processing and producing one unit of feedstock in house.

The first order condition of X_m is:

$$\frac{dL}{dX_m} = \frac{\partial f(X)}{\partial X}\left[D^{-1}(Q) + Q\frac{\partial D^{-1}(Q)}{\partial Q}\right] - \frac{\partial C_p(X)}{\partial X} - MC_m(X_m) - \frac{\partial MC_m(X_m)}{\partial X_m}X_m = 0. \tag{14}$$

Now recall that expenditure on purchased inputs is $E_m(X_m)$. Let the marginal expenditure on purchased inputs $ME\,(X_m) = MC_m\,(X_m) + \frac{\partial MC_m(X_m)}{\partial X_m} X_m$. With this interpretation, the first-order condition (14) can be rearranged to yield

$$MR(Q)MP(X) = MC_P(X) + ME(X_m). \quad (15)$$

Condition (15) states that at the optimal level of X_m, the marginal contribution of a unit of X_m to the firm revenue is equal to the sum of marginal cost of processing and the marginal expenditure on purchased inputs. By comparing conditions (13) and (15) we note that

$$MC_h\,(X_h) = ME(X_m) \geq MC_m\,(X_m). \quad (16)$$

The inequality in expression (16) holds because $ME(X_m) - MC_m(X_m) = \frac{\partial MC_m(X_m)}{\partial X_m} X_m \geq 0$. Expression (16) shows at the optimal solution, the marginal cost of in-house production is equal to the marginal expenditure of purchasing from others and may be greater than the marginal cost of the third-party production. This reflects the monopsonistic power of the enterprise, meaning that at the optimal solution the enterprise may produce more in-house and purchase less from external sources to reduce the price of purchased inputs.

Furthermore, the enterprise is a monopoly in the output market and a monopsony in the purchased input market. This means that it will produce less output overall than would occur under competition, and it will use fewer inputs overall. Much of the burden of the reduction of inputs will be borne by the input suppliers, reflecting market power in both markets. The reduction in output produced and input purchased by the enterprise compared to a competitive environment will result in extra profit because of higher prices and lower purchased input cost. This extra profit is the compensation for the entrepreneurial effort. From a traditional welfare economics perspective, this outcome is inefficient, but entrepreneurs or firms may not engage in implementing an innovation in the absence of this extra profit.

Thus far we assume an interior solution. But there may be cases of corner solutions as well. For example, the internal cost of producing inputs may be very high due to a lack of internal expertise in the production of the input, or because the government may restrict activities or access to resources (e.g., land and water) needed to produce the feedstock. In this case, all the production will be carried out externally (i.e., $X_h = 0$) and the optimal outcome will occur at the X_m where

$$MR(Q)MP(X_m) = MC_P(X_m) + ME(X_m). \tag{17}$$

In this case, the marginal revenue associated with increased purchased input is equal to the marginal cost of processing it and the marginal expenditure of purchasing it. The enterprise will be a monopoly in the output market and a monopsony in the input market. If production in-house was prevented due to regulations, the production would be lower than if in-house production were allowed and thus regulations would reduce overall welfare. Further, purchases from other sources are higher when in-house production is banned, thus outside suppliers may support such a ban even though it reduces overall welfare.

The enterprise behaves in this case as a middleman, which is a monopoly in its output market and a monopsony in its input market. This is a very desirable position to be from a profitability perspective, as the middleman maximizes profits from its activities in both markets. But the middleman's presence also results in the largest reduction in overall welfare compared to other arrangements — all result in higher output and purchased input use levels, lower output price, and higher purchased input price. Apple's situation in the cellphone market largely resembles a middleman solution, and indeed it is the richest company in the world at the time of writing the book.

In some cases, purchasing from others may not be feasible (i.e., $X_m = 0$). This may occur when the innovation introduces both a new feedstock and process in a new region where there are no local farmers conducting such activities. For example, the introduction of sugarcane for ethanol in regions of mostly abandoned land or extensively used rangeland (e.g., in Brazil). It may also occur with the introduction of the production and processing of winter vegetables in a desert region where part of the innovation is to support production with a new source of water. In these cases, the optimal outcome will occur at the X_h where

$$MR(Q)MP(X_h) = MC_P(X_h) + MC_h(X_h). \tag{18}$$

In this case, the enterprise has a monopoly only in the output market. The overall production will be larger than if some feedstock productions were feasible under similar cost structures by local producers because the enterprise will use their monopsony power to reduce the purchases of inputs from these suppliers.

It is useful to assess how sensitive the outcomes of the enterprise behavior to changes in key parameters are. The extra gains from the markets' power associated with the innovation are greater when the price elasticities of final output demand and purchased input supply are smaller. Over time, these monopoly gains may not last, as other firms may enter the markets associated with the innovation, which is consistent with the Schumpeterian view that monopoly power tends to vanish as new entrants are aiming to capture extra rents associated with market power.

Frequently, the processing process is utilizing only part of the feedstock, and the rest is gone to waste. In this case, the final output is a function of "effective feedstock." When the innovation has higher feedstock use efficiency (higher percentage of feedstock utilized in production) it will result in a greater quantity of the final output and lower output price. It may reduce feedstock use (especially when the gain in overall output is modest), but in some cases the increase in input use efficiency will result in a large increase in output and increase in feedstock use, increasing the price of purchased feedstock. This is consistent with the analysis of Khanna and Zilberman (1997) on the impact of the adoption of resource-conserving technologies.

When not all feedstock is utilized, uses for the residue are introduced over time. These innovations expand the supply chain because the processing of the feedstock is expanded, and the new

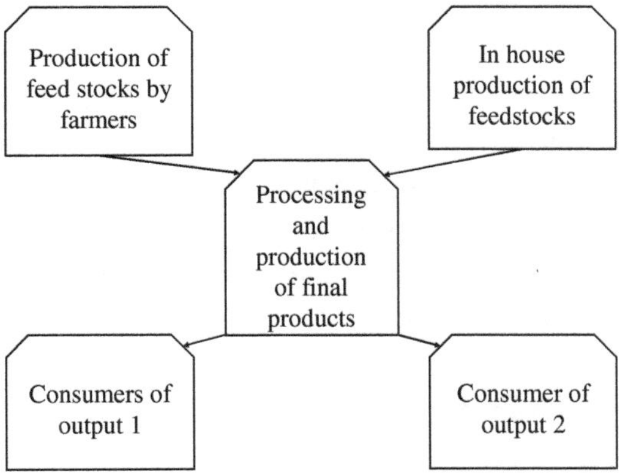

Figure 7. Expanded supply chain.

activity generates new outputs. In this case, the supply chain is producing two products with two different sets of consumers (see Figure 7). A more detailed analysis should consider a third segment of the supply chain (namely distribution of the two outputs). But in this case, the enterprise must decide whether it is profitable to add the additional processing of the feedstock to produce a second output. If the new processing is added, then the revenue stream from the feedstock is increasing, as well as the cost of processing. Under plausible conditions, this extra demand will lead to a larger volume of feedstock production. Two examples of such a situation are the use of bagasse (the residue of sugarcane) to produce ethanol and the use of dried distillers' grain (the residue from corn ethanol production) as animal feed. With these added options, optimal feedstock production is likely to increase.

Two other considerations that are important to address are credit and risk. The implementation of innovations requires investment — the enterprise may finance it by relying on some combination of its internal resources, issuing stock, receiving government support, or seeking financial loans. The outcome of an investment is uncertain and financial plans are, at best, a good estimate due to significant future uncertainty. Furthermore, credit availability by banks may be limited.

4.1. *Credit*

Both the processing activities and the in-house production requires an investment and are especially vulnerable to credit constraints. Rigorous analysis of the credit constraints requires a more detailed analysis, but we can adjust our model by modifying the conditions of the model (11) by adding a constraint to yield a modified optimization problem as follows:

$$L = \underset{\{X_h, X_m\}}{\text{Max}} \Big[f\left(X_h + X_m\right) D^{-1}\left(f\left(X_h + X_m\right)\right) \\ - C_p\left(X_h + X_m\right) - C_h\left(X_h\right) - X_m MC_m\left(X_m\right) \Big], \quad (19)$$

s.t. $\beta_p C_p\left(X_h + X_m\right) + \beta_h C_h\left(X_h\right) \leq g(W_0 \alpha\left(R - C\right))$ and X_m, $X_h \geq 0$,

where β_p is the proportion of in-house costs associated with the upfront investment in processing, β_h is the proportion of in-house costs associated with the upfront investment in input production, W_0 is the net worth of the enterprise, and α is the credit coefficient which translates this profitability potential to creditworthiness. Credit is given based on the value of asset generated by the enterprise, depending on its estimated profitability.

We assume that the credit constraint limits the upfront investment made by the enterprise and our formulation translates it to a constraint based on cost.[5] We will not solve this optimization here, but adding these constraints may change the outcomes because the extra cost of credit impacts the level of investment in processing facilities and in-house production. One expects that companies that are constrained by credit are likely to reduce their in-house production and may utilize much of their credit to finance processing facilities while relying on purchases from others for feedstock. One reason why a major wine company like Gallo invested mostly in their processing capacity was that they were not able to finance much of the land needed to produce grapes (i.e., their feedstock).

[5]We assume that external suppliers can obtain their own credit and therefore the enterprise is not burdened by financing them.

There are situations where external suppliers may not be able to obtain their own credit, most often occurring in developing countries where credit institutions and insurance schemes are limited. In these situations, the enterprise may need to finance, at least partially, external feedstock producers, which is likely to limit the size of the feedstock processing but may ultimately increase in-house production.

4.2. *Risk*

The analysis thus far assumed full certainty. In reality, implementation of innovation is subject to significant risk (Du *et al.*, 2016). The enterprise faces several types of risk. The four prominent forms are processing cost risk, output price risk, external supply risk, and in-house production risk. When refining technology is relatively new, the cost of the refining facility is subject to random shocks. Each form of risk presents its own set of considerations.

If the enterprise is risk-averse, and the marginal utility from the profit is declining, higher processing cost risk may result in a lower activity level. This suggests that as facilities become more reliable, the production and processing of feedstock may increase. An increase in output price risk will also tend to reduce the size of all activities. The introduction of future markets or price insurance may increase the likelihood of implementing innovation and increase the size of the production or processing activities. An increase in the riskiness of external suppliers may reduce overall activities and increase reliance on in-house production. Similarly, an increase in the riskiness of in-house production will reduce overall activities and increase the reliance on external suppliers. In cases of storable feedstock (e.g., corn for ethanol), one way to deal with supply risk is through storage. But this option is not available to people who rely on refining sugarcane for ethanol because the storability of sugarcane is low.

5. Designing Supply Chains — Dynamic Analysis

Implementing innovation is a lengthy process and the analysis of the supply chain designed to implement this innovation is better to be done within a dynamic framework. Such a framework needs to recognize the changes in the forces that shape the economics of the demand for and cost of the outputs resulting from the innovation and accommodate these changes in the design of the supply chain. In this section, we will first discuss some dynamic forces affecting the implementation of the technology and how to model them within a decision-making framework. Then we will analyze the implications of the dynamic consideration in the supply chain design.

5.1. *Economic factor in dynamic analysis of supply chain design*

Consider the same enterprise we discussed in the last section (developing a new product based on refining agricultural feedstock), concentrating on the case where they purchase all feedstock from others. In doing so, we will emphasize the impact of dynamics on the processing facility. There are several key features that affect the dynamic analysis in this context.

First is the stock of capital used in the processing facility. This capital stock includes buildings and equipment, and its definition may expand to include knowledge (human capital). This capital stock is increased by investments and may decline by depreciation. In mathematical representation, we will assume a planning horizon of $T + 1$ years and the time indicator, t, ranges from $t = 0$ to $t = T$. We assume that the enterprise makes an initial investment denoted by I_0 and the investment in year t is denoted by I_t. The investments contribute to the accumulation of capital, and let K_t be the capital stock at the beginning of period t. Capital may evolve over time according to the equation of motion

$$K_t = K_{t-1}(1 - \delta) + I_{t-1}, \tag{20}$$

where δ is the depreciation rate. For instance, if $\delta = 0.05$, then capital declines in value by 5% each year and to maintain capital stock, the enterprise must make an investment in capital each period of $I_t = \delta K_t$. The equation of motion implies that investment made in period $t - 1$ will bear fruit starting at period t.

Second, the output of the processing process depends on the feedstock input at time t, X_t, and the capital stock of the firm, K_t.

Another argument of the production function is time, as producers tend to improve productivity over time due to learning-by-doing. At each period, starting from period 1, the processing facility is refining X_t units of feedstock. The production function is

$$Q_t = f(X_t,\ K_t, t). \tag{21}$$

We assume that the marginal productivity of both capital and feedstock in producing the final output in period t is nonnegative and decreasing. Namely, $\frac{\partial f}{\partial X} \geq 0$, $\frac{\partial f}{\partial K} \geq 0$, $\frac{\partial^2 f}{\partial X^2} < 0$, and $\frac{\partial^2 f}{\partial K^2} < 0$. An increase in capital leads to an increase in the marginal productivity of the feedstock (i.e., $\frac{\partial^2 f}{\partial X \partial K} > 0$). Given other inputs, the productivity of the processing is increasing at a decreasing rate over time (i.e., $\frac{\partial f}{\partial t} \geq 0$, $\frac{\partial^2 f}{\partial t^2} \leq 0$).

Third, we assume that the processing cost at period t, $C_p\left(X_t, K_t\right)$ depends on feedstock and capital. The costs of processing decline with the use of capital but tend to increase with the volume of feedstock processed. We assume positive and increasing marginal processing costs of feedstock (i.e., $\frac{\partial C_p}{\partial X} > 0$; $\frac{\partial^2 C_p}{\partial X^2} \geq 0$). More capital reduces processing cost at a declining rate (i.e., $\frac{\partial C_p}{\partial K} \leq 0$ and $\frac{\partial^2 C_p}{\partial K^2} \geq 0$). Increased capital reduces the marginal costs of processing feedstock (i.e., $\frac{\partial^2 C_p}{\partial K \partial X} \leq 0$).

Fourth, we assume that marginal costs of the feedstock depend on feedstock input and time, $MC_m\left(X_t, t\right)$. The marginal cost of processing is increasing with the volume of feedstock (i.e., $\frac{\partial MC_p}{\partial \mathrm{X}} \geq 0$) and the marginal cost declines over time due to technological change (i.e., $\frac{\partial MC_m}{\partial t} \leq 0$), indicating that over time the expenditure on purchased input may decline for a given level of feedstock.

Fifth, the willingness to pay for the final output is likely to grow over time due to population growth, increase in income (if it is not an inferior good), and learning-by-using on behalf of users that increases the value of the technology to these users. Some factors, such as the emergence of competing products and increased efficiency in the use of the product, may reduce the demand over time. We assume that inverse demand $P_t = D^{-1}\left(Q_t, t\right)$ is increasing with time and declining with quantity.

With these assumptions, we can write the dynamic optimization problem of the enterprise. It must determine, at each period, the quantity to produce, feedstock to purchase, and the amount of investment to make. These decisions are subject to the equation of motion of capital in (20), the production function in (21), and the non-negativity of X_t, I_t, and K_t. We assume that the discount rate is r and that the entrepreneur maximizes the total net present value obtained from the enterprise. The optimization problem can be written as

$$L = \underset{\{I_t, X_t\}}{\text{Max}} \sum_{t=1}^{T} \frac{1}{(1+r)^t} \left[f(X_t, K_t, t) D^{-1} (f(X_t, K_t, t)) \right.$$
$$\left. - C_p(X_t, K_t) - X_t MC_m(X_t, t) - I_t \right] - I_0, \tag{22}$$

s.t.

$K_t = K_{(t-1)}(1 - \delta) + I_{t-1}$ for $t = 0 \ldots T-1$ (the equation of motion of capital),

$X_t, I_t, K_t \geq 0$ (non-negativity constraints),

$K_0 = 0$ (no initial capital).

In our formulation of the optimization problem the temporal profit of the enterprise at each period from *1* to T is equal to the revenue minus processing costs, purchased input costs, and investment costs. These profits are discounted to compute the net present value, and then the initial investment is subtracted. As problem in (22) is a quite standard dynamic optimization problem, we forego solving it here but will present some features of the solution.

First, the formula to determine the amount of feedstock used at each period (X_t) is identical to the level determined from the static model. Namely, at the optimal level of X_t, the marginal contribution of feedstock to firm revenue, $MR(Q_t)MP_x(X_t)$, is equal to the sum of marginal contribution of feedstock to the processing cost, $MC_{Px}(X_t)$, and the marginal outlay on purchased inputs $ME(X_t)$. Note that because now the production and cost functions have more arguments than do their counterparts under the static scenario, we modified the notation so that $MP_x(X_t)$ is the marginal productivity of feedstock.

Similarly, $MC_{Px}(X_t)$ is the marginal processing cost with respect to feedstock. We note that both productivity and marginal costs depend on other variables (capital and time), but for simplicity they are not included in the arguments.

$$MR(Q_t)MP_x(X_t) = MC_{Px}(X_t) + ME(X_t). \tag{23}$$

Second, the temporal marginal benefits of capital at each period, denoted by $MB_K(K_t)$ is equal to its marginal contribution to the firm's revenue, $MR(Q_t)MP_K(K_t)$, plus the marginal reduction in processing costs due to increased capital, $-\ MC_{PK}\,(K_t)$.

$$MB_K\,(K_t) = MR(Q_t)MP_K\,(K_t) -\ MC_{PK}\,(K_t). \tag{24}$$

Third, the temporal marginal benefit of investment at any moment, $MB_I\,(I_t)$, is the net present value of marginal contribution of the capital goods generated from this investment throughout the life of the project, considering discounting and depreciation. In particular,

$$MB_I\,(I_t) = \sum_{j=t+1}^{T} MB_K\,(K_j)\frac{(1-\delta)^{j-t-1}}{(1+r)^{j-t}}. \tag{25}$$

Thus, the temporal marginal benefit of investment in period 0 will start at period 1 and will continue till time T, but this benefit will decline because of discounting and depreciation. The greater the r and δ the smaller the future benefits of an investment. This analysis suggests that the volume of investment in period t is such that the temporal marginal benefit of the investment is equal to 1 monetary unit, which is the temporal marginal cost of investment.

$$MB_I\,(I_t) = \sum_{j=t+1}^{T} MB_K\,(K_j)\frac{(1-\delta)^{j-t-1}}{(1+r)^{j-t}} = 1. \tag{26}$$

5.2. *Implications of the dynamic considerations*

Our analysis suggests that in every period the enterprise operates as a middleman in the output and feedstock market. The extent that it gains monopoly or monopsony rents depends on its market power at each period. If over time more competitors enter — so that the innovation is losing its uniqueness — the above-normal profits of the enterprise decline.

The volume of operation of the enterprise increases over time when learning-by-doing increases the productivity of processing the feedstock or the supply of feedstock is increasing and becomes cheaper, or the demand for the final product is increasing. For example, the scale of new forms of biofuel depends on (i) the extent of increased productivity of conversion of feedstock to fuel, (ii) the increase of the productivity of the feedstock sector, and (iii) the increased demand either because of the increased price of fossil fuel or increased compensation for greenhouse gas emission sequestration (Khanna and Crago, 2012).

Since the enterprise starts with no capital, it must invest in the early period to build capital stock. Smaller interest or depreciation rates will increase the size of the initial investment. The investment is likely to grow if the demand for the final product increases. Capital goods that increase feedstock use efficiency are more valuable when the demand for the final product is high or when feedstock costs are high. If the interest rate and the depreciation are high and the demand is expected to grow over time, the investment may be spread over more years.

The dynamic analysis suggests that under plausible conditions, the introduction of a supply chain to implement an innovation of a new product or production in a new place may require a significant initial investment to overcome the initial condition ($K_0 = 0$). This is consistent with the evidence in the literature on the need to overcome threshold investments when establishing supply chains of foods, for example, new supermarket facilities and distribution chains (Reardon and Timmer, 2012). The optimal initial investment for implementing innovation is larger, and the net present value is larger as well when the investor faces a lower interest rate. So, foreign investors that obtain their capital in developed countries with lower interest rates may have an advantage in introducing new production systems in developing countries. This is in addition to the added knowledge they may have. That may be one of the reasons that foreign direct investment played a crucial role in the development of the food sector in developing countries (Reardon *et al.*, 2009). As the interest rate in China and other developing countries has declined, their dependence on finance from foreign and hedge funds has decreased.

Learning is another important feature of our analysis. In cases with large potential gain from learning-by-doing, the enterprise may not invest much in the early years, but instead, wait so that learning reduces the cost of processing and feedstock. An enterprise may implement innovation at a slower pace if the early demand for the final product is low, but they expect the demand to grow substantially over time. Of course, they can affect this growth through marketing. If the learning increases, it may reduce the volume of investment at late periods as the marginal gain from capital declines. This is especially the case when demand for the final product is not growing much.

The dynamic analysis thus far ignores credit and risk. The ability to obtain credit increases as the performance and profitability of the enterprise is more apparent. Thus, in the early years, credit constraints may restrict the volume of the enterprise and limit its ability to take advantage of its potential. Promising but resource-limited enterprises that control an innovation may be taken over by established companies or hedge funds with sufficient resources to invest. This is demonstrated by the several innovative but small agricultural biotechnology or seed firms that have been taken over by major companies such as Monsanto and Pioneer.

Our dynamic analysis allows for learning by the enterprise. There may be a significant degree of uncertainty about the processing technology and the enterprise may make limited investment in capacity aiming to master the technology better instead. Learning reduces the production risk the enterprise faces. Especially when the enterprise is risk averse, learning may lead to increased operation volume over time. Note that learning may reveal flaws that can either be corrected or may lead to a decline or closure of operation. Waiting for the results of learning may lead to outcomes where only after the kinks are gone may the large-scale investment in the technology start. For example, franchising of food technology may occur only after satisfactory operational procedures have been established. Ray

Kroc, the founder of McDonald's, spent a few years perfecting the operation of the company in its two first stores before large-scale franchising (Boas and Chain, 1976).

Our dynamic analysis did not consider the possibilities of in-house production. However, there may be situations when external suppliers are either unavailable or inefficient, and the enterprise must then establish feedstock activities, either by owning them outright or by financing and guiding contractors. In other cases, if feedstock suppliers are not able to keep pace with the growth of demand, the processor may either initiate its own production operation or investment in expanding existing suppliers or seeking out new suppliers.

Thus far we discussed the optimization problem and analyzed the properties of the solution assuming that the investment is being made. But a key condition for making the investment is that the maximum total net present value of the optimization problem in (22) is positive, and most often exceeds an established threshold. This suggests that enterprises that face lower interest rates are more likely to implement new innovations and establish the associated supply chains. Innovations that result in outcomes that are facing higher demand and technologies that have low rates of depreciation are more likely to be implemented. Implementation is most likely to occur when affordable and reliable sources of feedstock are available.

The internal rate of return (IRR) is used to compare a set of investments. It is the value of r at which the solution to the net present value optimization problem in (22) is equal to 0. There may be several solutions to this problem. Therefore, to find a realistic IRR, it is worthwhile to repeat the optimization problem for different levels of r, starting from 0%, until an r that yields NPV = 0 is found.

6. Marketing

One of the major challenges of business is to market its products. Marketing is the interaction between a business and its client to aim to enhance goodwill and induce sales or income. Firms use marketing tools (e.g., advertising, salespersons, money-back guarantees), and one can think about something parallel to a production function (maybe a revenue or income function) that will be a function of marketing tools. So, in essence, a firm may determine an optimal combination of marketing tools in a profit-maximizing way, similar to how a farmer uses inputs to maximize profits. A key to designing a marketing strategy is to understand consumer behavior — one element is adoption behavior, which is the pattern of decisions associated with using a new product or service. Another important aspect is that consumer choices are influenced by risks, including the risk of reliability of the product as well as the fit of the product to consumer needs, and, therefore, some marketing tools aim to reduce these risks.

The literature on adoption can provide a lot of insights into the design of marketing tools that enhance adoption. So, understanding individual behaviors, heterogeneity, and dynamics of diffusion processes is important in designing marketing tools. One cannot underestimate the importance of understanding demographics and recognizing the notion of "different strokes for different folks." People vary in their tastes, income, ability, and interest. Therefore, they vary in their assessment of the usefulness and value of a product. Marketing strategies determine the way in which a product or media text is sold to a target audience, the techniques used to attract and persuade consumers, and the process of planning and executing the conception, pricing, promotion, and distribution of ideas, goods, and services to satisfy customers.

The challenge of marketers is to target the right population in their choice of location of an enterprise (or social network and media for online activities), and the pricing and advertising strategies used. While in Chapter 8 we spoke about the shift of the threshold of adoption among different income levels, marketers think about the shift of the frontier of adoption among different segments of the population.

A key element associated with marketing is risk and uncertainty. If consumers had perfect and complete information, they would make the right choices by themselves. Marketing is used to address issues of asymmetric information and other transaction costs. Buying a new product or service can be difficult. One must deal with risks, credit, transportation, logistics, and product specifications. Marketers can help in this regard. While basic economic models of behavior under uncertainty deal mostly with price and quantity risks, marketing deals with these risks and more. When a new product is introduced, a potential buyer does not know what it does (performance), how well it works (reliability), and if it will work for that buyer (fit). Marketing thus emphasizes issues of performance risk, reliability risk, and fit risk. Marketing also reduces transaction and transition costs.

The purchase of a product may require adjustments by the buyer and the user. A new machine requires training and reassignment of labor. Learning how to use a product takes time and is often costly, at least initially. Additionally, finance for a new product may not be easily available, and if the buyer needs to obtain credit by themselves it takes time and effort (and sometimes can lead to buyer remorse). Therefore, marketers aim to reduce transition costs, provide training, assist with credit and system design, and, finally, offer sampling coupons to reduce the cost of initial trials.

6.1. *Marketing tools*

From a consumer's perspective, we can divide the adoption procedure between being completely unaware of a product and eventually being a consumer of it into five stages: awareness, information search, evaluating alternatives, purchasing decision, and product feedback. In the awareness stage, consumers become aware of the product, which may prompt a further information search related to the product (i.e., the information search stage). During the stage of evaluating alternatives, consumers compare and evaluate the product against potential substitutes, and then enter the purchasing decision stage. Lastly, consumers might provide sellers some feedback regarding their experience with the product.

In each stage, some marketing tools can be used to facilitate the adoption of the product. Table 1 provides a list of marketing tools and identifies their use and their place in the adoption process. In what follows of this subsection, we will describe these marketing tools in detail.

Table 1. Some marketing tools under each adoption stage.

Adoption stages	Marketing tools
Awareness	Advertisements, demonstrations, salespeople, trade shows
Information search	Advertisement, demonstrations, salespeople, trade shows
Evaluating alternatives	Demonstrations, product training, salespeople, trade shows
Purchasing decision	Money-back guarantees, warranties, renting and leasing, providing credit, salespeople
feedback	Salespeople, trade shows

First, advertisements are the most widely used marketing tool, meant to increase awareness and trigger sales. There are different advertisement tools, and they evolve with technology. In the past, people advertised their products by singing or shouting at markets. They wrote and printed their advertisements on bulletin boards, store walls, and other surfaces. Advertisements became a major source of support to newspapers and then radio and TV. In the 21st century, pop-ups in search engines and the internet are major modes of advertisements. Advertisers may not know how effective their advertisements are, but they will pay more for well-targeted advertisements to direct their message to the appropriate demographic group.

One type of advertisement is announcements that market a new product or improvement. These are advertisements that announce a new product is born, or an existing product is now improved. These advertisements, on TV, in newspapers, or internet, are challenged to provide several details in limited space. They introduce to the world a new product or service with few details, hoping to raise consumers' curiosity so that they will dig further. Apple's introduction of the Mac was a fantastic commercial at the 1984 Super Bowl that raised buyers' curiosity about it. Introducing buyers to a new type of product or idea sometimes requires a long narrative or video trailer, which leads to the development of infomercials. As behavioral economics emphasizes, it is important to frame the presentation and give the consumer a reference point. Therefore, sometimes innovators who introduce a new product may compare it (favorably) to existing products. To add credibility, there may be a celebrity endorsement, often connected to the product, such as Michael Jordan with Nike.

Second, there are reminders. Kahneman (2011) distinguished between "slow" (deliberate) and "fast" (intuitive) thinking. Decision on day-to-day low-cost items is fast. When a consumer desires a soft drink, she will think "fast": If the first drink that comes to her mind is Coke, she will buy it rather than Pepsi. The role of advertisements, in this case, is to remind you about a product so you think about it rather than its competitors.

Third, there are timely advertisements. They provide critical, timely information that can lead to sales. A discount might spark interest among consumers who would otherwise find a product too expensive. Clearance sales are especially effective, as it puts a time limit on when the consumer can obtain the product.

Fourth, brands give a manufacturer identity and reduce uncertainty about quality and performance. A key element of the brand is familiarity as well as image and star appeal. Brands are important when it comes to reliability risk. When purchasing a product that is supposed to last for a long time, having a reliable brand is a major advantage. Brands are also very important when it comes to goods that are visible (e.g., clothes, cars). They indicate taste and ability to pay. Brands are assets for a company and their value can be estimated, in principle, by their contribution to increased demand and the market power they generate.

Fit uncertainty is a major barrier to adoption and demonstrations may address it. Demonstrations enable consumers to try the product before purchasing, and thus reduce fit uncertainty. All the shirts in a department store complete their primary purpose, but one should try one on before they walk out with a shirt that is too small or large (they also should make sure their significant other will like it). We can model fit risk quite simply: the outcome of consuming a product is a random variable. The benefit is B when the product fits with probability q. When the product does not fit, and cannot be used, the buyer has negative utility, L, representing the lost cost.

The maximum the individual will be willing to pay for the product with risky fit is $P_0 = Bq - L(1 - q)$. If the individual takes a demonstration, for example, a test drive, assumed to provide full information, they will now be willing to pay B, in case of fit, and 0 otherwise. So, the seller can charge more for the product with a demonstration. He may sell less, but the customers will be happy, enhancing long-run growth of the business; and if the demonstration is not expensive, it is worthwhile for the seller. If the lost cost is high, or the demonstration is time-consuming, it may be worthwhile for retailers to pay people to take a demonstration because otherwise, many people may not buy the product.

There are different types of demonstration — some include trying on clothes, driving a car, and others include watching how a machine works or trying a software program. Because of the complexity of supply chains, final buyers may not buy from producers but from retailers. Producers must market their products to wholesalers and retailers. One frequent tool is trade shows, which can provide opportunities for side-by-side demonstrations and comparisons. It also facilitates interaction between sellers and buyers, as well as between users and potential adopters.

Another tool to deal with fit risk is the money-back guarantee (MBG). Frequently, in the case of experience goods, where the assessment of value is difficult in advance, the buyer may be worried about lack of fit and losses associated with it. Money-back guarantees allow a buyer to return the product within a limited time frame (and sometimes with a penalty). The net benefit from purchasing a product priced at P under MBG is $B - P$ with probability q and $-RC$ with probability $1 - q$, where RC is the return cost including any possible penalty. Thus, the expected value of the purchase is $(B - P)\,q - RC\,(1 - q)$. The highest price one will be willing to pay to a product purchased with MBG is $P_{mbg} = [Bq - RC\,(1 - q)]/q$ which is greater than $Bq - L(1 - q)$, consumers' largest willingness to pay when there is no MBG.[6]

[6]Here we assume that the loss from owning an unfit product is larger than the return cost (i.e., $L > RC$).

The gain from money-back guarantees is greater when the fit risk (i.e., $1-q$) is smaller, the return cost is smaller, and the loss aversion is larger. One of the main advantages of a big retail store, like The Gap, is that the buyer can return their product at any location, which lowers the return cost. Once the product is returned, it might be readded to the rack or sold to "seconds" stores (e.g., outlet stores).

MBGs are not appropriate for every product. The offering of MBG may lead to a moral hazard, where people will buy a product they need for one event (e.g., a wedding gown), use it, and then return it. So MBG is appropriate with products that are used for a long time and require some experience for assessing their value and gaining from their use.

In addition to its role in reducing fit risk, MBG has been seen as a mechanism to signal quality. If the suppliers are confident that their products are good and that consumers will keep their products, they are more likely to offer the return option. This role is especially important in industries where most firms do not offer MBG, or when there are differences in the length of the return period. MBG has been used in agriculture for a long time. McCormick, who introduced the first reapers, used MBG to promote his product.

Demonstration and MBG serve a similar purpose. Demonstration provides presale tests and MBG allows reversing a decision. Sometimes they will be substitutes (if you have a good demonstration, you do not need an MBG), so a firm can decide which to use. In other cases, if the demonstration cannot remove all the fit risks, then they are complementary. The demonstration can screen and eliminate potential buyers that the product clearly does not fit and the MBG provides an option protecting buyers against misfits.

In cases of divisible products (e.g., seeds), providing free samples is a good way to reduce fit risk. When consumers are not familiar with a product or have a negative prejudice against it, a free sample may allow the testing that will lead to purchase. In some way sampling is a special case of a demonstration. Sampling, like a demonstration, may misfire and eliminate a potential buyer who had a bad sample and does not buy the product. However, overall, it is worthwhile to keep satisfied customers.

While MBG and demonstrations are mechanisms to address mostly fit risks, warranties are crucial in addressing performance risks. This is true especially for durable equipment (e.g., combines) which must be available during critical time periods. Warranty programs not only repair the products, but provide substitute products during the repair period. A warranty is a form of insurance and is also a signal of quality. The quality of the warranty and the MBG are important contributors to establishing brand quality.

There are other means to deal with fit risk. For instance, consumers may lease or rent a product before buying it. Moreover, secondhand markets reduce the need for MBGs. So, if someone finds that the product does not fit their needs then they may resell it, either in a market or online marketplace, like e-Bay, which reduces transaction costs even more. But prices in secondhand markets are significantly lower than the price of new products; because of asymmetric information, the buyer does not know the quality of the product. Thus, even in secondhand markets, demonstration and MBG could still be used to fetch a better price.

Rental and leasing have other purposes as well, especially their ability to address insufficient scale or credit. If the per period cost of owning the product, say, a combine, is denoted by I, and the gain per acre is π, then only farms of size $L \geq I/\pi$ should buy the product from a profitability perspective, while smaller firms can rent it, incurring a much lower per-period cost. In cases of durable goods, firms with insufficient credit may lease them. Leasing may enable a firm to overcome concerns about obsolescence, in that they avoid getting stuck with an older model when the new, improved one is available. However, buyers benefit from outright owning a product because they will be able to make the adjustments they see fit.

Marketing tools aim to reduce barriers to sales. Credit availability is one constraint and sellers frequently provide, or help attain, credit. Sellers of machinery and equipment provide credit to reduce transaction costs, and reduce the likelihood of buyer's remorse. One popular mechanism car dealers provide to reduce transaction costs is to purchase the older cars of potential new car buyers. People who do not want to take the time to sell their own car can take a loss and use the older car to finance the purchase of a new car. Furthermore, car dealers establish mechanic shops to provide customers with maintenance and repair.

Another important mechanism to reduce transaction costs is product training. Adopting new products requires changes in business practices as well as modification of existing arrangements along the supply chain. When a company purchases software, employees need to be trained on how to use, maintain, and repair it. Part of the warranty is addressing major repairs, but when it comes to daily operations, the sellers provide training. One of the key elements of franchising is that the franchisor trains the franchisee and their employees (e.g., McDonald's Hamburger University).

Salespeople are important for marketing in many circumstances. They are expensive but much more versatile. They are crucial to the wholesalers because they can approach potential retailers as well as build the relationships and the capabilities that will enable them to market the products to the public. Salespeople approach potential buyers, who are likely to be opinion makers, early in the diffusion process to introduce them to the product. They provide demonstration product support and assist with credit and early use.

When it comes to complex products, like irrigation systems and computers, companies may employ sales engineers who design the product to meet buyers' needs. These engineers serve as both salespeople and trainers. In some cases, potential buyers put a bid for a new product or service and the salespeople are the ones involved in preparing the bid and executing much of the contract. As the product gets cheaper and more widespread, the role of the salesperson declines. They were much more significant during the mainframe computer era than now during the personal computer era.

Price is perhaps the most important marketing tool. A firm can affect the speed of diffusion by modifying prices. Prices serve as signals of values and can be modified in response to existing and expected market conditions and consumer choices. Prices can be manipulated to allow for the learning of consumer preferences. For example, different price schemes may be used in different but similar markets to experiment with pricing schemes for products of different quality levels and different levels of service. Prices change over time and across locations. Early in the adoption process, a company may provide discounts to induce early adopters. In some cases, it may provide discounts to adopters who increase its value through their association with the product. For example, a car company may sell cars to Google or Apple at a discount because of the association (*Ford* car with a Google logo on it may be perceived as an implicit endorsement). Similarly, car companies may provide volume discounts to finalize a sale because large sales have lower transaction costs. Frequently, buyers may collaborate and form cooperatives to purchase in bulk. Companies may have fixed prices on relatively low-cost items sold on the floor, but when it comes to higher-priced items (cars or TVs), salespeople often offer a discount, increasing the value of the transaction from the buyer's perspective.

6.2. *Choice of marketing tools*

The choice of marketing tools is an economic choice like the choice of other inputs. The firm has an expected revenue function that is equal to sales times price. It also has costs, which include the cost of purchasing the products and of marketing. Revenues are a function of advertisements, demonstrations, and other marketing tools. For example, advertisements may increase the number of people attracted to a product and their willingness to pay for the product. If there is uncertainty regarding fit, demonstrations may reduce this uncertainty. It may reduce the number of potential buyers, but the willingness to pay among the buyers who remain is higher. MBG can reduce further the fit risk and thus increase willingness to pay for the product. Having a good brand and product support will increase the willingness to pay for the product. A firm needs to have an estimate of how each factor affects revenue.

With this information, the firm seeks to maximize expected revenue minus the cost of the marketing tool that it uses (e.g., demonstration, advertisement, money-back guarantee). The optimal level of advertisement is where the expected marginal revenue is equal to the marginal cost of advertisement. Similarly, the optimal level of demonstration is where the marginal revenue of providing demonstrations is equal to the marginal cost of demonstration.

To optimize the use of marketing tools, firms must be able to quantify the performance of the marketing tools they use. This is a major challenge. First, they need to track the impact of different marketing tools, which is difficult. For example, firms have little knowledge of the effectiveness of their advertisements. Subsequently, they may conduct surveys of consumers' awareness of their campaign, but still, these measurement tools are imperfect. Furthermore, they must respond to the competition and sometimes they must protect their product from "attacks" by competitors. They have to be aware of alternative products, and the strategies these companies employ. When Apple introduces a new product or service, Samsung, LG, and others need to respond. So, if a competitor offers a new warranty program, each competitor must decide how to respond. Managing marketing strategy is an ongoing process that relies on basic economic principles.

7. Conclusion

When conducting an economic analysis of a product, conventional microeconomics often focuses on the supply and demand for this single product and ignores the supply chain that makes the product available in the first place. This chapter has expanded this view by emphasizing on the entire supply chain of a product. Due to the special role of innovations in a supply chain, we stressed the intertwined relationship between innovations and supply chain. Two-, three-, and four-segment supply chains have been discussed in this chapter. Moreover, it discussed supply chain designs from both static and dynamic perspectives, employing the approach of optimization under constraints. Finally, the chapter carefully described several marketing tools that can facilitate consumers' adoption of a new product.

Supply chain designs have attracted increasing attention from agricultural economists since the outbreak of the COVID-19 pandemic which substantially disrupted the food supply chain around the world. Designing robust and resilient food supply chains has critical implications for farm income, food safety and security, as well as public health (Taylor *et al.*, 2020). Given the scant attention that conventional microeconomics has paid to supply chains as we noted above, economic analysis on supply chain designs and evaluation may prove to be a fertile area for future research, in both theoretical and empirical realms.

References

Becker, G.S. 1965. A Theory of the Allocation of Time. *The Economic Journal*, 493–517.

Belton, B., A. Hein, K. Htoo, L.S. Kham, U. Nischan, T. Reardon, and D. Boughton. 2015. *Aquaculture in Transition: Value Chain Transformation, Fish and Food Security in Myanmar* (No. 230981). Michigan State University, Department of Agricultural, Food, and Resource Economics.

Boas, M. and S. Chain. 1976. *Big Mac: The Unauthorized Story of McDonald's.* E.P. Dutton & Co., Boston.

Caswell, M.F. and D. Zilberman. 1986. The Effects of Well Depth and Land Quality on the Choice of Irrigation Technology. *American Journal of Agricultural Economics* 68(4): 798–811.

Chakravorty, U., E. Hochman, C. Umetsu, and D. Zilberman. (2009). Water Allocation under Distribution Losses: Comparing Alternative Institutions. *Journal of Economic Dynamics and Control* 33(2): 463–476.

Du, X., L. Lu, T. Reardon, and D. Zilberman. 2016. The Economics of Agricultural Supply Chain Design: A Portfolio Selection Approach. *American Journal of Agricultural Economics* 98(5): 1377–1388.

Kahneman, D. 2011. *Thinking, Fast and Slow.* Macmillan, London.

Khanna, M. and C.L. Crago. 2012. Measuring Indirect Land Use Change with Biofuels: Implications for Policy. *Annual Review of Resource Economics* 4(1): 161–184.

Khanna M. and D. Zilberman. 1997. Incentives, Precision Technology and Environmental Protection. *Ecological Economics* 23(1): 25–43.

Lancaster, K.J. 1966. A New Approach to Consumer Theory. *The Journal of Political Economy* 74(2): 132–157.

Levenstein, H.A. 2003. *Revolution at the Table: The Transformation of the American Diet* (Vol. 7). University of California Press.

Reardon, T., C.B. Barrett, J.A. Berdegué, and J.F.M. Swinnen. 2009. Agrifood Industry Transformation and Small Farmers in Developing Countries. *World Development* 37(11): 1717–1727.

Reardon, T. and C.P. Timmer. 2012. The Economics of the Food System Revolution. *Annual Review of Resource Economics* 4(1): 225–264.

Rosen, S. 1974. Hedonic Prices and Implicit Markets: Product Differentiation in Pure Competition. *Journal of Political Economy* 82(1): 34–55.

Schaefer, K.A. 2014. The Meat Racket: The Secret Takeover of America's Food Business. *American Journal of Agricultural Economics* 96(5): 1507–1508.

Schumpeter, J.A. 1934. *The Theory of Economic Development: An Inquiry into Profits, Capital, Credit, Interest, and the Business Cycle* (Vol. 55). Transaction Publishers, New Jersey.

Sunding, D. and D. Zilberman. 2001. The Agricultural Innovation Process: Research and Technology Adoption in a Changing Agricultural Sector. *Handbook of Agricultural Economics* 1: 207–261.

Swinnen, J.F. (Ed.). 2011. *The Economics of Beer.* OUP, Oxford.

Taylor, C.A., C. Boulos, and D. Almond. 2020. Livestock Plants and COVID-19 Transmission. *Proceedings of the National Academy of Sciences* 117(50): 31706–31715.

Taylor, R., D. Parker, and D. Zilberman. (2014). Contribution of University of California Cooperative Extension to drip irrigation. *ARE Update* 18(2): 5–8.

Zilberman, D., T. Reardon, J. Silver, and A. Heiman. 2022. From the Lab to the Consumer: Innovation, Supply Chain, and Adoption with Applications to Natural Resources. *Proceedings of National Academy of Sciences* 119(23): e2115880119.

Chapter 10

Health Risks, Food Security, and Food Safety

Food is a major contributor to health, and it is important to develop food and agricultural policies with an emphasis on health. Many food and agricultural policies aim to enhance consumers' nutritional status and address the challenges of food security, food safety, and environmental health. In this chapter, we will develop a framework to address human health risks associated with food. The framework could help us understand challenges such as hunger, safe food, and some of the environmental side effects of agriculture. Much of the chapter will review some of the literature on food security and food safety globally and in the United States, followed by a conclusion.

1. Analyzing Health Risks

While the economic literature on risk emphasizes income risks, a larger body of literature addresses health risks. A key element in this literature is the risk generation function (Lichtenberg and Zilberman, 1988; Zilberman and Jin, 2016), which determines the probability that a member of the population will die, get sick, or will be in undesirable health status (e.g., obesity) during a period. For example, a risk generation function may provide estimates of probabilities that members of a certain population will have an undesirable nutritional status (e.g., stunting) or are subject to the risk of morbidity or mortality due to the food situation. Regarding food safety, we can consider the probability of mortality due to poisoning or other food quality issues. Regarding environmental health, we can consider population decrease or even extinction probability to a species, be it a bird or other wildlife, caused by activities of food or agriculture.

The risk generation function reflects multidisciplinary models, and it is frequently used in epidemiological, toxicological, and engineering studies. Health risk is a product of multiple parameters that can be affected by individual and policy choices. Chances of death due to malnutrition, for example, are a function of several factors relating to an individual's access to food (Zilberman and Jin, 2016). Each of the factors that contribute to risk may be a random variable that represents variability: one aspect is heterogeneity, or how individuals vary in their capacity to withstand food shortages; another is randomness in weather; and a third concern is how a policymaker acts given the uncertainty in food supply.

Our model is inspired by the risk assessment framework of Wilson and Crouch (1987), and Robson *et al.* (2022). We assume a population with I groups, where $i = 1, \ldots, I$ is a group indicator. The size of the population of group i is denoted by N_i. Let $R_i = f_i(X, B_i)$ be the probability of a deleterious outcome (e.g., mortality or morbidity due to a pandemic, lack of food, or poisoning) to a member of group i during a specific period. It is affected by policy variable X and behavioral choices of the group denoted by B_i. The risk generation is an outcome of multiple processes, including the occurrence of a shock (i.e., emergence of an epidemic), exposure, and vulnerability. Policy responses may reduce the shock, for instance, by spraying or other treatments to slow the spread of the epidemic, by protective clothing and other mechanisms to reduce exposure, or by medical treatment, be it vaccine or pre-infection treatment to reduce vulnerability. Policymakers may need to determine the optimal level of intervention to minimize the expected cost. Here we use pandemic as an example, where the policymakers must make a choice between reducing mortality risk and reducing economic cost. Let us denote the value of statistical life (VSL) lost by V_i, which may vary by groups reflecting differences in age or other variables (Viscusi and Aldy, 2003). This concept applies to small risks and regional differences reflecting differences in endowment, but it does not encompass arbitrary judgments on different values of human life. There are several recent studies, Greenstone and Nigam (2020), for example, that use differences in health expenditures and labor market behavior to establish VSL as a function of age. Using our notations, the optimal policy choice problem is

$$\min_X \left\{ \left(\sum_{i=1}^{I} N_i \cdot f_i\left(X, B_i\right) \cdot V_i \right) + C(X) \right\}, \tag{1}$$

where C(X) is the cost of policy X, and the marginal costs are positive and increase with the magnitude of the policy intervention. X, in our example, is a scalar, but it can also be a vector. The optimal choice of X is reached when the expected value of marginal gain in lives saved is equal to the marginal cost of the policies,

$$-\sum_{i=1}^{I} N_i \cdot f_i^{'}(X, B_i) \cdot V_i = \mathrm{C}^{'}(\mathrm{X}), \tag{2}$$

where primes represent derivatives.

The COVID-19 pandemic led to many studies that evaluated policy intervention. For example, Kaplan *et al.* (2022) showed that an economic shutdown that reduced the U.S. GDP by about 25% was worthwhile given the number of lives that it was supposed to save. Goldstein and Lee (2020) presented a similar study about the economic cost of the pandemic under different assumptions. Since on average age of death for individuals who died from COVID-19 was about 11.7 years lower than the pre-pandemic life expectancy, an alternative approach to assess policies is to minimize the sum of the aggregate expected life years lost and the cost of policy intervention. Instead of using the VSL, one can use the value of quality-adjusted life year, which was $150,000 in the U.S. in 2015 (Young-Xu *et al.*, 2017).

Zilberman and Jin (2016) analyze policies to reduce the risk of death during a famine in a region. The risk generation function depends on the aggregate availability of food in the region, accessibility (dependent on distribution mechanisms), and vulnerability. The policy interventions considered were (1) increasing the amount of food shipped to the region, (2) distribution methods (by parachuting it from the air or providing meals through government or soup kitchens), and (3) medical intervention. In some situations where gangs may control parachuted food, it may be worthwhile to reduce the total supply of food and distribute it individually. There may be conditions that require both food supply as well as medical care. The World Food Programme developed an agile system that adjusted to different conditions in providing emergency food assistance (Cozzolino *et al.*, 2012). Wu *et al.* (2021) suggested that delaying the introduction of golden rice to the Philippines and Bangladesh resulted in a significant loss of life, particularly among children. Wesseler and Zilberman (2014) use the notion of VSL to assess the cost of delaying the introduction of golden rice to India. They show that, even with relatively low VSL, this delay may lead to the loss of tens of thousands of lives and cannot be easily justified. Wu and Khlangwiset (2010) estimate the health cost of aflatoxin in grains and food in Africa in terms of life years lost and identify the cost of reducing aflatoxin. They find that the health benefits of reducing aflatoxin far exceed the associated costs.

Thus far, we have established a conceptual framework to assess interventions that affect health risk. Below we discuss large bodies of literature documenting the extent of food security and food safety problems, and some policies that have been introduced to address these issues.

2. Food Security

According to United States Agency for International Development, food security means “having, at all times, both physical and economic access to sufficient food to meet dietary needs for a productive and healthy life".[1] Lack of food security results in malnourishment conditions that may include stunting[2], wasting (acute malnutrition during a short period of time that may lead to chronic stunting), and being underweight or overweight (United Nations Children's Fund (UNICEF) *et al.*, 2021). Close to 150 million children under the age of 5 suffered from stunting in 2020, mostly in developing countries (Nomura *et al.*, 2023). But these conditions are not limited to children. Body Mass Index (BMI), which is weight divided by height squared (km/m^2), is an indicator of health and nutritional situation. A person is obese if BMI is greater than 30, overweight if BMI is between 25 and 30, in the normal weight category if BMI is in the range of 18.5 and 25, and underweight if BMI is below 18.5, which is frequently associated with stunting. The classification is the same for men and women.

Bansal and Jin (2023) review the literature on the relationship between obesity and health at the global level. They find that average life expectancy increases with average BMI within a range and then declines, indicating that both undernutrition and obesity reduce average life expectancy. Since the 1960s, life expectancy has increased by about two months per year, and women on average live four years longer than men. Developed nations have higher obesity levels, which tends to reduce average life expectancy, but that is compensated by higher medical expenditure, indicating a substitution between medical costs and nutritional status (Bansal and Zilberman, 2020).

According to the Food and Agriculture Organization (FAO) of the United Nations, food insecurity refers to "lack[ing] regular access to enough safe and nutritious food for normal growth and development and an active and healthy life," and severe food

---

[1]Available at: https://www.usaid.gov/agriculture-and-food-security (accessed March 9, 2023).

[2]According to the World Health Organization (WHO), "stunting is the impaired growth and development experience from poor nutrition, repeated infection, and inadequate psychosocial stimulation. Children are defined as stunted if their height-for-age is more than two standard deviations below the WHO Child Growth Standards median." Available at https://www.who.int/news/item/19-11-2015-stunting-in-a-nutshell (accessed March 9, 2023).

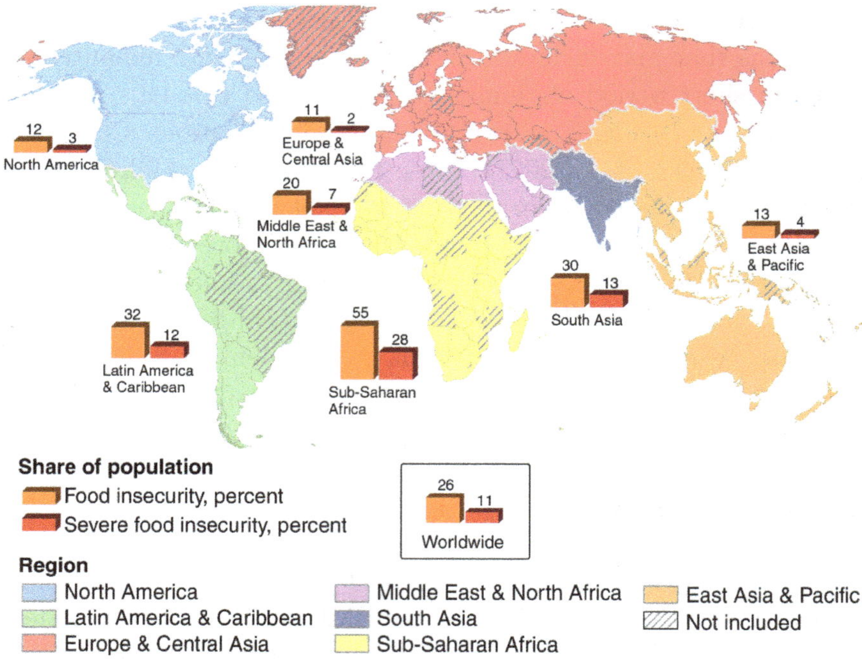

Figure 1. Food insecurity across the world.
Source: The graph is reproduced from Smith and Meade (2019), which is in the public domain.

insecurity refers to when one has "run out of food and gone a day or more without eating."[3] Globally, 26% of the population suffers from food insecurity, and 11% from severe food insecurity. Sub-Saharan Africa suffers from the worst rates of food insecurity, with 55% of its population food insecure. About 30% of the population of Latin America and South Asia suffer from food insecurity. We even observed more than 10% of food insecurity in Europe as well (see Figure 1).

Barrett's (2002) survey of the food security literature suggests that early lines of work emphasized the role of food availability in enhancing food security, the importance of increased

[3]Available at: https://www.fao.org/hunger/en/ (accessed January 27, 2024).

food productivity (especially in developing countries), as well as the important role of inventory, transportation, and supply chain (Barrett, 2002). Because of the randomness of food supply, the availability of reliable storage with low levels of food waste is essential. Lichtenberg and Zilberman (2002) presented a simple model of gains from storage to overcome seasonality and variability. Storage may require the use of pest control devices as well as temperature control. It increases social welfare and reduces environmental costs by reducing transportation costs. Inventory development requires public intervention because of the welfare gain to consumers that may not be fully captured by the industry. Williams and Wright (1991) analyze some of the complexity of inventory policy. Development of transportation systems enables countries to import food that they cannot produce from locations with comparative advantage, and it is crucial for intervention in cases of drought or crop failures (Bakker *et al.*, 2018).

With broader and more complex links between food origins and destinations, we are witnessing a transformation in global food supply chains. The food systems are affected by urbanization, changes in diets, intensification of production systems, expansion of intermediation, digitization, the transformation from commodities to differentiated products, and extensive regulation. The transformation may increase overall food availability but may lead to increased vulnerability to shocks, including climate change and pandemics. Thus, to assure supply availability, the resiliency of supply chain can be expanded by diversification of sources of input and production location, increased redundancy, and continuous innovation (Barrett *et al.*, 2022; Reardon and Timmer, 2014).

Another element that affects food security, according to Barrett (2002), is access to food. Access to food can be enhanced by physical means, investment in infrastructure, improved transportation, and storage. However, food accessibility is also affected by institutions and policies. Behrman (1997) emphasized the issue of intra-family allocation of resources based on the household production model, suggesting that different household members may have different preferences and different commands over resources within the family, with women and children tending to have inferior access to food. Heiman *et al.* (2001) introduced a framework for analyzing food consumption within the family. By using data from Israel, they showed that consumption differences are affected by cooking capacity, time availability, and income, among other factors. Their analysis suggests that food consumption outside the home is growing in importance with urbanization and food support programs, such as lunch at school. Heiman *et al.* (2019) emphasize the importance of cultural consideration, especially religion: using data from Israel, they found that the level of observance of religion's rules affects households' diet and food supply chains. Religion, thus, has an ambiguous effect, either leading to cooperation that increases food availability or constraints that reduce access to food.

A third element affecting food security is interaction with other factors, including health, employment, education, and housing. Sen (1982) emphasized the important impact of political economy factors on food security. Populations under colonialism are more vulnerable to severe famines because of a lack of political power. That was the case with the big famines of Bengal and Ireland. Similarly, famines are more likely under dictatorships, and thus introducing democracy, where the masses are given political power, would increase food security, as evidenced by India after liberalization. The pursuit of the Green Revolution and the increased food security after it was influenced by global awareness of food security risk may reflect the political powers of the masses in the post-World War II era. The literature reviewed by Barrett (2002) emphasizes the important link between food insecurity and poverty, which is linked to health. Food insecurity may harm health, and bad health reduces the capacity to produce income and leads to poverty and food insecurity, leading to a vicious cycle called the "poverty trap" (Barrett *et al.*, 2016).

Education is another important factor affecting food security. It affects individual income on the one hand, as well as their ability to make sound nutritional and health choices on the other hand. In the case of the COVID-19 pandemic, Alvi and Gupta (2020) found that lack of access to school as part of social distancing strategies affected access to school lunch programs and reduced food security.

Laborde *et al.* (2020) documented the negative impact of the pandemic on food security in developing countries, finding that loss of income because of unemployment, relocation, and lack of assets prevented the poor from buying food. While governments were able to develop various mechanisms to overcome or adapt to supply chain disruption during the pandemic, supply chains throughout the world were negatively affected by disruptions, especially in developing countries, where small enterprises lost access to customers and labor. On the other hand, supply chain modification through digitization and developing new channels (food delivery) allowed for overcoming some of the limitations of the pandemic. Schools' closures and other disruptions prevented access to food delivery mechanisms for the poor, and loss of employment reduced cash transfers that limited food consumption in developing countries.

Because food security is subject to random shocks, families and governments develop risk-coping mechanisms to address them. The World Food Programme and other aid organizations developed mechanisms to deliver food aid and health services during acute food crises. On a smaller level, networks through the community, religious organizations, and families can ease the burden on those dealing with food shortages. Food assistance programs, mostly by governments, are a major mechanism to address food security challenges. In this sense, it is useful to distinguish between domestic and international food assistance programs. Domestic food assistance programs include food aid programs such as food stamps in the United States, the Special Supplemental Nutrition Program for Women, Infants, and Children (WIC), food for work programs, food subsidies and price stabilization, micronutrient fortification programs (adding vitamins and other crucial micronutrients), and nutrition education programs. International food assistance programs include food aid, where a donor provides surplus food, usually for free, and food-related international finance that enables developing countries to purchase food. There is a large body of literature assessing these policies over multiple dimensions. Examining these policies and their design provides opportunities for future research. Food and nutrition policies should be evaluated on their efficiency (in terms of direct and indirect costs), incentive compatibility, equity, additionality (expanding food security), targeting (to whom the program is targeted and who benefits from it), as well as their flexibility and adaptability to changes over time (Barrett, 2002).

3. Food Insecurity in the United States

Despite its wealth, food insecurity is a major problem in the U.S. Food insecurity ranges from 5.4% in New Hampshire to 15.3% in Mississippi between 2019 and 2021. Figure 2 shows that food

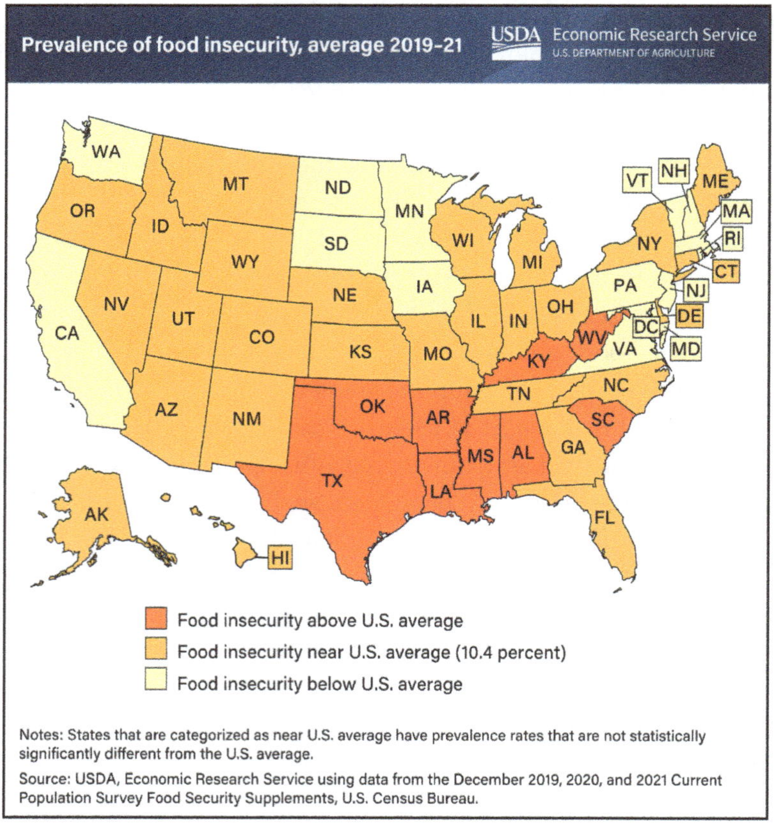

Figure 2. Food Insecurity in the U.S. over 2019–2021.
Source: Reproduced from Chart Gallery of ERS. Available at: https://www.ers.usda.gov/data-products/chart-gallery/gallery/chart-detail/?chartId=104693 (accessed March 9, 2023). Permission obtained.

insecurity is especially prevalent in the southern states, but even in the Corn Belt and California, food insecurity is substantial (U.S. Department of Agriculture (USDA), 2022). Figure 3 shows that obesity rates are especially high in states with food insecurity problems, and Figure 4 shows that again, lower life expectancy is connected to these regions. Bansal and Jin (2023) show evidence that high rates of obesity are associated with diseases such as diabetes, heart conditions, and other debilitating diseases, which end up requiring significantly increased health expenditures. Thus, addressing the issues of food and health has become a major policy concern in the U.S. and in the rest of the world.

Gundersen *et al.* (2011) survey the literature on the economics of food insecurity in the United States. Based on the results of the current population survey (CPS), they report that between 2001 and 2009, food insecurity among children in the U.S. increased between 18% and 24% and severe food insecurity between 9% and 12%. The literature has identified multiple factors that are associated with food insecurity; for example, African American or Hispanic households,

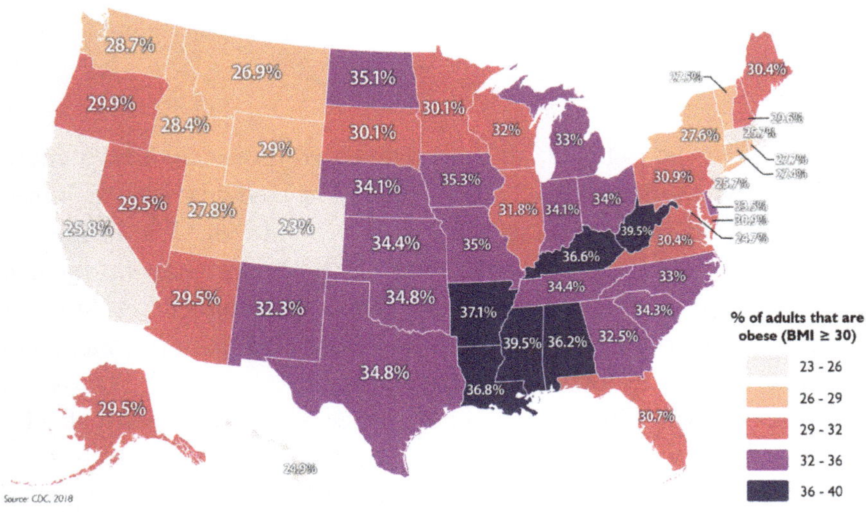

Figure 3. Obesity rate in the U.S.
Source: Map reproduced from Landgeist. Available at: https://landgeist.com/2021/05/07/prevalence-of-obesity-in-the-us/. Permission was obtained from Landgeist.

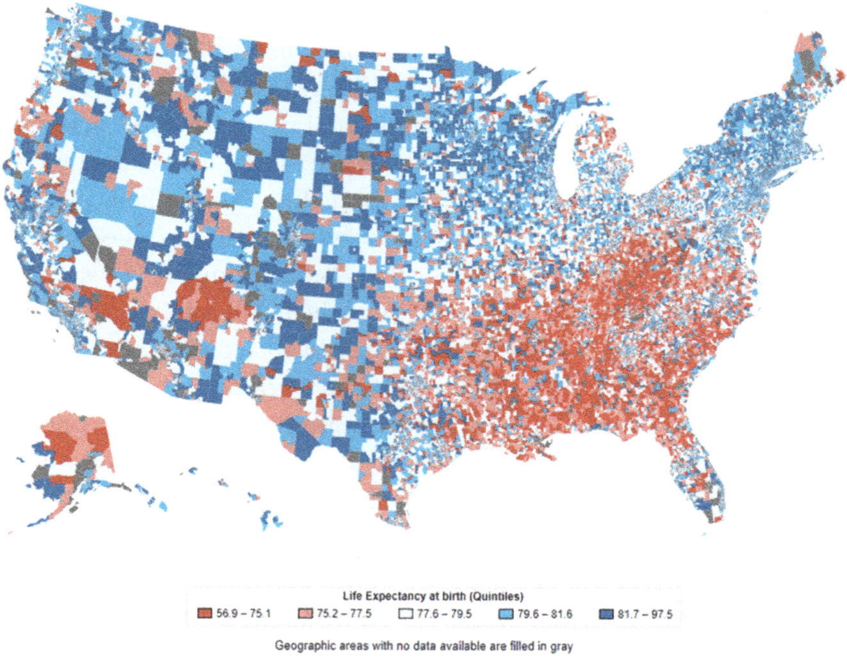

Figure 4. Life Expectancy at Birth for U.S. Census Tracts (2010–2015).
Source: National Center for Health Statistics, Centers for Disease Control and Prevention. Map was designed by Tejada-Vera *et al.* (2020) and is in the public domain.

single-parent households, and less-educated households are more likely to be food insecure. Furthermore, households with children are more food insecure than those without children. The likelihood of being food insecure is consistent with the permanent income hypothesis: average income is a better indicator than current income for food insecurity. Moreover, limited assets and unemployment are also major contributors to food insecurity.

The literature finds that food insecurity has severe health effects. Food insecurity during pregnancy is associated with birth defects, and food insecurity overall is associated with anemia, higher level of anxiety, asthma, behavioral problems, and chronic disease. However, there is a continued need to develop a more systematic understanding of the circular links between various health effects and food insecurity

(Gundersen *et al.*, 2011). Econometric tools could be useful, but the research may require multidisciplinary approaches and may develop predictive tools.

The U.S. has a wide array of food assistance programs. There has been a significant body of work on the historical food stamp program and now, the Supplemental Nutrition Assistance Program (SNAP). The food assistance programs in the United States were part of the Farm Bill and have reflected a political economic alliance between agricultural and urban regions (Pinstrup-Andersen, 1993). The design of a food assistance program is challenging, needing to set a limit on what goods can be purchased. There have been reports of the sale of food stamps for a discount, and thus the participants in the program may substitute food for income. Thus, some may argue that food support programs are inferior to income transfer programs. However, as Jensen and Wilde (2010) argue, there are restrictions as to what can be supported by the program (e.g., it cannot be used for cigarettes or lottery tickets). Furthermore, there is evidence that the programs improve nutritional choices and food security in the U.S. The SNAP program has been modified over the years to incorporate budgetary and political considerations, taking advantage of new electronic and data tools to make it more digital and effective. The entitlement requires income and asset tests, and the monthly benefits can reach $668 in 2010 dollars. Unfortunately, significant amounts of people who are entitled do not participate, maybe because of stigma, transaction costs, as well as low benefit-cost ratio for some families. Because of low participation in the program and data problems, it is not obvious to what extent SNAP programs contribute to addressing food insecurity in the U.S., and this is a subject for further research (Gundersen *et al.*, 2011).

The National School Lunch Program (NSLP) is another federal assistance program in the U.S. Half the participants receive subsidized lunches, and most pay nothing. In 2010, 31 million children participated in the program. The program aims to improve diets and health. School lunch programs are prevalent throughout the world, and some studies suggest that they provide significant benefits (Barrett, 2002). However, Gundersen *et al.* (2011) suggest that the methodological and data availability constraints make it difficult to quantify their impact.

Wide arrays of programs aim to improve nutritional intake, including economic incentives, subsidies, and income support, and educational efforts. For example, one mechanism to combat obesity is taxing sugary products and subsidizing healthy products, like vegetables (Cash *et al.*, 2005). There is significant literature on the impact of soda taxes, showing that they would change consumption patterns, especially when imposed in some locations and not others (Taylor *et al.*, 2019). There is momentum to expand the soda tax coverage globally, adjusting it to differences among countries (Roache and Gostin, 2017). Soda taxes may be much more beneficial in countries with high obesity rates, such as the U.S. and Mexico, but may even be harmful in countries with undernutrition. So, the design of food incentives should take into account heterogeneity and can improve with better data and monitoring tools. Furthermore, Just (2006) suggests that it is important to consider behavioral economic tools like nudging, as well as framing to modify food choice behavior.

4. Food Safety

Food safety concerns food that is toxic or otherwise endangers human health. It is an important component of food security. Every year, approximately 600 million people globally fall ill after consuming food contaminated by bacteria, viruses, parasites, or chemical substances, and among them, 420,000 die (Lee and Yoon, 2021). Belluz (2015) shows that food safety challenges are mostly attributed to vegetables and eggs, but also happen with meat and dairy.

The framework presented by Equations (1) and (2) has been applied to address issues of food safety, for example in the control of pesticides and water quality, as can be seen from the chapter on pesticides in this book, as well as from Lichtenberg (2002). The risk generation function is useful for modeling food safety problems. The risks can be viewed as the result of multiple processes, in particular, the emergence of a toxin, exposure, and vulnerability. Production processes control the emergence of toxicity, such as the use of pest control. Exposure can be reduced by preventive activities: boiling water, washing fruit, and other means of food-appropriate processing. Individuals who are allergic to various types of food can reduce their vulnerability simply by avoiding them; when an allergen attack occurs then medical treatment is needed.

Food safety is affected by multiple policies, including regulation of production processing, investment in health and safety education, and other procedures. Food safety may be either a complement or substitute for food security. Pest control activities to reduce spoilage increase the quantity of food supplied and its quality. Yet some food safety procedures (e.g., culling of animals suspected of carrying diseases like tuberculosis (Olmstead and Rhode, 2015)) may reduce food supply. Optimal food policy processes can be derived by minimizing the cost of health risk and of risk prevention activities.

Antle's (2001) survey of the economic literature on food safety emphasizes that food safety are outcome of all food systems, starting in production, going through processing, marketing, and returning. It is affected by pathogens in the soil, chemical residue in production, spoilage and treatment, and pathogens in processing. Reducing food safety hazards requires continuous monitoring throughout the food supply chain. There is a wide array of food safety regulations in the United States, starting with the Meat Inspection Act of 1906. Multiple agencies regulate food safety, including the Food and Drug Administration, U.S. Environmental Protection Agency, and the USDA, and there may be inefficiencies in regulation that need to be evaluated often. One aspect of food safety regulation, pesticide regulation, aims to minimize or eliminate harm. Since eliminating harm is not feasible, one big challenge is the "reasonable certainty of no harm." Lichtenberg and Zilberman (1988) suggested that, with a specific degree of statistical reliability in the risk assessment model, regulation can set a target level of risk, expanding the risk scope of the risk generation function. Another set of regulations stems from the Hazard Analysis Critical Control Points (HACCP) (Food and Safety Inspection Service, 1996), which involves monitoring and controlling food safety hazards throughout the food system. The strategies to monitor and reduce hazards need to be adapted over time based on new knowledge (including the occurrence of accidents) and new technologies. The regulatory efforts also include requirements to provide information and training to consumers, and labeling design can be modified as knowledge and technology improve (e.g., Wilson and Miao, in press). Since agricultural food products are traded globally, there is another set of food safety regulations affecting trade. On the one hand, for example, these policies must be strict to control invasive species, but on the other hand, these policies may be abused and serve as trade barriers. The International Agreement and the World Trade Organization are establishing some of these regulations, and economists need to reevaluate them over time.

The extent to which the government should regulate food safety is a subject of continuous research, especially given the uncertainty about food safety outcomes and their costs. Social cost-benefit analysis can contribute to effective food safety regulations, and to the sharing of responsibility between the public and private sectors in introducing and monitoring safety standards. Antle (2001) argues that companies may engage in food safety activities to protect their reputations and brands, and that consumers demand high safety standards. Products may be evaluated differently based on their perceived risk, which is a product characteristic. Food safety characteristics and information provision may affect market equilibrium, product quality, and market structure. Because of asymmetric information between producers and consumers, brands and pricing serve as signals that allow consumers to discriminate among products based on safety and other characteristics. There is large evidence of heterogeneity among consumers in terms of their demand for and understanding of food safety, which may lead to inefficiencies and a continuous need to redesign food safety features and regulations.

Henson and Caswell (1999) provide a detailed analysis of the categories of actions and division of responsibilities between the public and private sectors in food safety regulation. To develop sufficient regulation, it is important to have a sound framework for risk assessment that identifies hazards and the processes of generation and exposure. Risk assessment provides the grounds for risk management that evaluate hazards and treatment costs, and that develop monitoring strategies and interventions. Finally, there is an important role in risk communication since hazard control requires action from producers and consumers. The public sector affects food safety through direct regulation and product liability, and the private sector may affect food safety through self-regulation and certification. In most cases, public food safety regulations may be presented as standard, and once they are violated, the liability rules apply. Countries often have reasonable standards, but the implementation varies significantly. Consumers and the public, through non-profit organizations, frequently use the legal system to ensure that food safety standards are implemented.

Antle (2001) provides evidence that existing regulatory regimes may be suboptimal. There may be significant cases of excessive regulations that may raise the price of food and harm consumers. Studies by Just *et al.* (2006) also provide examples of inefficient regulations. For example, harmonizing pesticide regulation among countries and requiring that countries use more expensive and "safer" chemicals may be inefficient and costly for poorer countries. Finally, there is significant evidence that regulation of agricultural biotechnology has resulted in welfare loss and reduced the adoption of modern technologies, agricultural activity, and environmental quality.

5. Conclusion

Food security and safety are major global problems, and understanding them requires multidisciplinary approaches that combine the knowledge of the physical and economic processes that lead to food insecurity, as well as the medical challenges associated with treating it. Moreover, Clark *et al.* (2019) show how nutritional patterns and food availability affect both health and environmental outcomes and suggest the need for a holistic approach to address it.

Risk-generation function provides a mechanism to assess the processes behind food safety and security; in both cases, we can distinguish between the processes that generate risk, exposure, and vulnerability. These factors can be affected by regulations and innovation. Economists can play an important role in integrating different perspectives to assess the increasing availability of food and mechanisms linking the food supply chain to human and environmental health. But, economic analysis requires the integration of knowledge from other disciplines and combines both assessments of performance of past regulatory frameworks with the prediction of the performance of future regulatory frameworks.

The high rate of agricultural and medical innovation is challenged to increase food availability and improve human health efficiently and equitably. The economic research tools developed to address innovation, technology adoption, and impact assessment can apply to food availability and security issues. The same analytical approach that applies to understanding precision farming can be applied to precision medicine and to the notion of personal diet that is likely to develop first in the developed world, and then diffuses globally. The World Health Organization suggested the introduction of a "One Health" framework to integrate human and environmental health in an integrated way. Economic analysis can assist in framing and tools to provide solutions. The linkage between farming, food, and health has become a major issue of research.

References

Alvi, M. and M. Gupta. 2020. Learning in Times of Lockdown: How Covid-19 is Affecting Education and Food Security in India. *Food Security* 12(4): 793–796.

Antle, J.M. 2001. Economic Analysis of Food Safety. *Handbook of Agricultural Economics* 1: 1083–1136.

Bakker, C., B.F. Zaitchik, S. Siddiqui, B.F. Hobbs, E. Broaddus, R.A. Neff, J. Haskett, and C.L. Parker. 2018. Shocks, Seasonality, and Disaggregation: Modelling Food Security Through the Integration of Agricultural, Transportation, and Economic Systems. *Agricultural Systems* 164: 165–184.

Bansal S. and Y. Jin. 2023. Heterogenous Effects of Obesity on Life Expectancy: A Global Perspective. *Annual Review of Resource Economics* 15: 433–454.

Bansal, S. and D. Zilberman. 2020. Macrorelationship between Average Life Expectancy and Prevalence of Obesity: Theory and Evidence from Global Data. *Agricultural Economics* 51(3): 403–427.

Barrett, C.B. 2002. Food Security and Food Assistance Programs. *Handbook of Agricultural Economics* 2: 2103–2190.

Barrett, C.B., T. Garg, and L. McBride. 2016. Well-Being Dynamics and Poverty Traps. *Annual Review of Resource Economics* 8: 303–327.

Barrett, C.B., T. Reardon, J. Swinnen, and D. Zilberman. 2022. Agri-Food Value Chain Revolutions in Low- and Middle-Income Countries. *Journal of Economic Literature* 60(4): 1316–1377.

Behrman, J.R. 1997. Intrahousehold Distribution and the Family. *Handbook of Population and Family Economics* 1: 125–187.

Belluz, J. 2015. Fruits and vegetables poison more Americans than beef and chicken. News article published on Vox.com. Available at: https://www.vox.com/2015/3/6/8158289/food-poisoning (accessed March 9, 2023).

Cash, S.B., D.L. Sunding, and D. Zilberman. 2005. Fat Taxes and Thin Subsidies: Prices, Diet, and Health Outcomes. *Acta Agriculturae Scandinavica Section C* 2(3–4): 167–174.

Clark, M.A., M. Springmann, J. Hill, and D. Tilman. 2019. Multiple Health and Environmental Impacts of Foods. *Proceedings of the National Academy of Sciences* 116(46): 23357–23362.

Cozzolino, A., S. Rossi, and A. Conforti. 2012. Agile and Lean Principles In The Humanitarian Supply Chain: The case of the United Nations World Food Programme. *Journal of Humanitarian Logistics and Supply Chain Management* 2(1): 16–33.

Food Safety and Inspection Service. 1996. The final rule on pathogen reduction and HACCP. U.S. Department of Agriculture, Federal Register, 61, No. 144 (July 25) 38805–38855.

Goldstein, J.R. and R.D. Lee. 2020. Demographic Perspectives on the Mortality of COVID-19 and Other Epidemics. *The Proceedings of the National Academy of Sciences* 117(36): 22035–22041.

Greenstone, M. and V. Nigam. 2020. Does Social Distancing Matter? University of Chicago, Becker Friedman Institute for Economics Working Paper 2020–26.

Gundersen, C., B. Kreider, and J. Pepper. 2011. The Economics of Food Insecurity in the United States. *Applied Economic Perspectives and Policy* 33(3): 281–303.

Heiman, A., D.R. Just, B. McWilliams, and D. Zilberman. 2001. Incorporating Family Interactions and Socioeconomic Variables into Family Production Functions: The Case of Demand for Meats. *Agribusiness: An International Journal* 17(4): 455–468.

Heiman, A., B. Gordon, and D. Zilberman. 2019. Food Beliefs and Food Supply Chains: The Impact of Religion and Religiosity in Israel. *Food Policy* 83: 363–369.

Henson, S. and J. Caswell. 1999. Food Safety Regulation: An Overview of Contemporary Issues. *Food Policy* 24(6): 589–603.

Jensen, H.H. and P.E. Wilde. 2010. More Than Just Food: The Diverse Effects of Food Assistance Programs. *Choices* 25(3): 1–5.

Just, D. 2006. Behavioral Economics, Food Assistance, and Obesity. *Agricultural and Resource Economics Review* 35(2): 209–220.

Just, R.E., J.M. Alston, D. Zilberman. 2006. *Regulating Agricultural Biotechnology: Economics and Policy.* Springer Science & Business Media.

Kaplan, S., J. Lefler, and D. Zilberman. 2022. The Political Economy of COVID-19. *Applied Economic Perspectives and Policy* 44(1): 477–488.

Laborde, D., W. Martin, J. Swinnen, and R. Vos. 2020. COVID-19 Risks to Global Food Security. *Science* 369(6503): 500–502.

Lee, H. and Y. Yoon. 2021. Etiological Agents Implicated in Foodborne Illness World Wide. *Food Science of Animal Resources* 41(1): 1–7.

Lichtenberg, E. 2002. Agriculture and the Environment. *Handbook of Agricultural Economics* 2: 1249–1313.

Lichtenberg, E. and D. Zilberman. 1988. Efficient Regulation of Environmental Health Risks. *The Quarterly Journal of Economics* 103(1): 167–178.

Lichtenberg, E. and D. Zilberman. 2002. Storage Technology and the Environment. *Journal of Agricultural and Resource Economics* 27(1): 146–164.

Nomura, K., Bhandari, A.K.C., Matsumoto-Takahashi, E.L.A., and Takahashi, O. 2023. Risk Factors Associated with Stunting among Children Under Five in Timor-Leste. *Annals of Global Health* 89(1): 63.

Olmstead, A.L. and P.W. Rhode. 2015. *Arresting Contagion: Science, Policy, and Conflicts Over Animal Disease Control.* Harvard University Press.

Pinstrup-Andersen, P. 1993. *The Political Economy of Food and Nutrition Policies.* John Hopkins University Press.

Reardon, T. and C.P. Timmer. 2014. Five Inter-Linked Transformations in the Asian Agrifood Economy: Food Security Implications. *Global Food Security* 3(2): 108–117.

Roache, S.A. and L.O. Gostin. 2017. The Untapped Power of Soda Taxes: Incentivizing Consumers, Generating Revenue, and Altering Corporate Behavior. *International Journal of Health Policy and Management* 6(9): 489.

Robson, M.G., W.A. Toscano, Q. Meng, and D. A. Kaden (Eds.). 2022. *Risk Assessment for Environmental Health.* CRC Press.

Sen, A. 1982. *Poverty and Famines: An Essay on Entitlement and Deprivation.* Oxford University Press.

Smith, M.D. and B. Meade. 2019. Who Are the World's Food Insecure? Identifying the Risk Factors of Food Insecurity Around the World. Amber Waves, Economic Research Service, U.S. Department of Agriculture.

Taylor, R.L.C., S. Kaplan, S.B. Villas-Boas, and K. Jung. 2019. Soda Wars: The Effect of a Soda Tax Election on University Beverage Sales. *Economic Inquiry* 57(3): 1480–1496.

Tejada-Vera, B., B. Bastian, E. Arias, L.A. Escobedo, and B. Salant. 2020. Life Expectancy Estimates by U.S. Census Tract, 2010–2015. National Center for Health Statistics. Available at: https://www.cdc.gov/nchs/data-visualization/life-expectancy/ (accessed January 27, 2024).

United Nations Children's Fund (UNICEF), World Health Organization, The World Bank. 2021. *Levels and Trends in Child Malnutrition: Key Findings of the 2021 Edition of the Joint Child Malnutrition Estimates.* Geneva: World Health Organization.

U.S. Department of Agriculture. 2022. Food Insecurity Rates Differ across U.S. States. Available at: https://www.ers.usda.gov/data-products/chart-gallery/gallery/chart-detail/?chartId=104693 (accessed March 9, 2023).

Viscusi, W.K. and J.E. Aldy. 2003. The Value of a Statistical Life: A Critical Review of Market Estimates Throughout the World. *Journal of Risk and Uncertainty* 27: 5–76.

Wesseler, J. and D. Zilberman. 2014. The Economic Power of the Golden Rice Opposition. *Environment and Development Economics* 19(6): 724–742.

Williams, J.C. and B.D. Wright. 1991. *Storage and Commodity Markets.* Cambridge University Press.

Wilson, R. and E.A. Crouch. 1987. Risk Assessment and Comparisons: An Introduction. *Science* 236(4799): 267–270.

Wilson, N.L.W., and R. Miao. in press. Food Waste, Date Labels, and Risk Preferences: An Experimental Exploration. *Applied Economic Perspectives and Policy* 1–29. https://doi.org/10.1002/aepp.13507.

Wu, F., J. Wesseler, D. Zilberman, R.M. Russell, C. Chen, and A.C. Dubock. 2021. Allow Golden Rice to Save Lives. *Proceedings of the National Academy of Sciences* 118(51): e2120901118.

Wu, F. and P. Khlangwiset. 2010. Health Economic Impacts and Cost-Effectiveness of Aflatoxin-Reduction Strategies in Africa: Case Studies in Biocontrol and Post-Harvest Interventions. *Food Additives and Contaminants* 27(4): 496–509.

Young-Xu, Y., R. van Aalst, E. Russo, J.K.H. Lee, and A. Chit. 2017. The Annual Burden of Seasonal Influenza in the US Veterans Affairs Population. *PLoS One* 12(1): e0169344.

Zilberman, D. and Y. Jin. 2016. A Probabilistic Approach to Food Security. In *Food Security in a Food Abundant World.* Emerald Group Publishing Limited.

Chapter 11

Economics of Pesticides

Pesticides are chemicals used in controlling agricultural pests and include three major classes: *insecticides*, *fungicides*, and *herbicides*. The use of pesticides in agriculture presents some interesting aspects to be considered. First, they need to be chemically updated over time as pests build resistance. Second, they cause adverse human and animal health effects. The adverse human health effects of different types of pesticides depend on the similarity between human or animal biology and the biology of the target pest. Insecticides, for example, are generally worse for human health than fungicides.

From 1965 to 1980, growth in the relative price of labor increased the use of herbicide as a factor of production. This occurred because herbicide use was a substitute for labor. The 1970 creation of the Environmental Protection Agency (EPA) and an increase in energy prices led to a reduction in insecticide use through the 1970s. During the 1980s, lower agricultural commodity prices and reduced crop acreage led to a reduction in herbicide use. Overall, pesticide use in the past four decades in the United States has been quite stable. See Fernandez-Cornejo *et al.* (2014) for a comprehensive analysis of pesticide use in U.S. agriculture. In this chapter, we discuss how to incorporate pesticide use in production analysis and related policies.

1. Pesticides in a Damage Control Framework

Since pesticides are damage control agents, crop production can be modeled as

$$Y = g(Z)[1 - D(n)],$$

where Y is actual output, $g(Z)$ is potential output (i.e., the maximum output that can be produced in the absence of damage due to the presence of a pest), Z stands for all inputs not related to pest control, and $D(n) \in [0, 1]$ is the *damage function*, expressed as percent of output lost to pest damage and assumed to be function of the pest population, n.

The effect of pesticide use is that of controlling the pest population, according to

$$n = h(n_0, X, A),$$

where n_0 is the initial level of pest population before pesticide application, X is the level of applied pesticide, and A is some alternative pest control method, such as *Integrated Pest Management* (IPM). We assume that $h_X \equiv \partial h/\partial X < 0$ and $h_A \equiv \partial h/\partial A < 0$.

Obviously, there are costs associated with pesticide application. If the total damage from pests is less than the social cost associated with a single application of a pesticide to a field (including *marginal external cost*), then the welfare-maximizing level of pesticide use is zero. Note that this implies toleration of some pests in the field and the associated pest damage, such as less visibly appealing fruits and vegetables.

When the level of pest damage rises above the social cost of one pesticide application, then it is welfare-maximizing to apply the pesticide. Profit maximization in the private market will determine the **economic threshold**, $\bar{n}_0$, as the pest population level at which it becomes profit-maximizing to apply the pesticide. The economic threshold is determined by setting total pest damage equal to the total cost of a single pesticide application and solving for $\bar{n}_0$:

$$Pg(Z)D(\bar{n}_0) = w,$$

where P is output price and w is the total cost of a single pesticide application.

Given function forms for $g(\cdot)$ and $D(\cdot)$, one could solve the above equation for $\bar{n}_0$. In the models that follow, we assume that the pest population is above the economic threshold.

2. Model of Pesticide Use with Known Pest Population and Pest Control Alternatives

The optimal level of pesticide use is determined by solving

$$\max_{X,A} \{L = P \cdot g(Z)\,[1 - D(h(n_0, X, A))] - VA - wX\}, \tag{1}$$

where V is the unit cost of alternative control methods, and other symbols are as defined in the above section.

The first-order conditions are

$$\frac{dL}{dX} = -P \cdot g(Z) D_n h_X - w = 0, \tag{2}$$

$$\frac{dL}{dA} = -P \cdot g(Z) D_n h_A - V = 0. \tag{3}$$

Thus, one would maximize profits by applying pesticides until the value of marginal product (marginal benefit) of pesticide application equals the marginal cost of pesticide application. The model predicts that the use of pesticides will increase as a result of the following:

— an increase in initial pest population (n_0),
— an increase in the output price (P),
— an increase in potential output ($g(Z)$),
— an increase in the price of alternative controls (V), or
— a decrease in the price of pesticides (w).

Analogous results hold for the alternative pest control method.

2.1. *A model with a secondary pest*

Sometimes, a secondary pest may exist along with a primary pest, defined as those targeted by pesticide use due to their more severe effect on crops. Here we consider the presence of a secondary pest.

For simplicity, we do not consider any direct alternative controls besides the use of pesticides, but we assume a specific biological relationship between the two pest populations: both pests cause damage, both population levels are known, and pest 1 is a *predator* of pest 2.

The damage function, $D(\cdot)$, will be function of both pests' population levels: $D(n_1, n_2)$. Pest 1's population is directly affected by the pesticide so that $n_1 = h(n_0, X)$, while pest 2's population level is a decreasing function of pest 1's population level: $n_2 = \Psi(n_1)$, with $\Psi_{n_1} < 0$. In other words, using pesticide to control pest 1 may lead to an increase in the population of pest 2, since pest 1 is a predator of pest 2. Thus, the problem of determining the optimal level of pesticide to use becomes

$$\max_X \{P \cdot g(Z)\,[1 - D(h(n_0, X), \Psi(n_1))] - wX\} \tag{4}$$

with the first-order condition:

$$-P \cdot g(Z)[D_{n_1} h_X + D_{n_2} \Psi_{n_1} h_X] - w = 0.$$

Both the direct impact on n_1 and indirect impact on n_2 on crop damage have to be considered on determining the optimal level of X. Lack of recognition of the biological predator–prey relationships may lead to economically inefficient over-application of pesticides, since the beneficial effect of the predator pest on reducing pest 2 is ignored.

2.2. *Pesticide resistance*

Through the biological process of natural selection, pests exposed to pesticides gradually develop genetic resistance to pesticides. Higher levels of pesticide application may accelerate buildup of resistance due to genetic selection of resistant genes. Short run pesticide control problems in a given season will be inefficient if long term resistance effects are not considered. Therefore, the calculation of optimal dosage of pesticide should take into account (*i*) resistance buildup (pesticide effectiveness is an "exhaustible resource" and should be modeled as such) and (*ii*) use of alternative chemicals or alternative pest control methods (such as the use of alternative cropping methods, crop rotation, natural diseases, and predator–prey relationships) should be considered in order to reduce resistance buildup.

3. Unknown Pest Population and Pest Population Monitoring

When pest populations are unknown, as is usually the case, one can distinguish between *preventive* and *reactive* pesticide application. Contrary to what is considered common wisdom in human medicine, for agricultural pest control, preventing may be worse (less efficient) than reacting.

With **preventive application**, pesticides are applied without an attempt to determine potential pest populations. Instead, based on experience or historical data, the farmer makes educated guesses about the probabilities of various pest population levels occurring. The farmer then chooses a level of pesticide use to maximize expected profit. For example, suppose there are two possible initial pest population levels, low (n_1) with probability p and high (n_2) with probability $1-p$. Assuming preventive application, then the problem of deciding how much pesticide to apply is

$$\begin{aligned}\max_X E(\pi) &= p\{Pg(Z)[1 - D(h(n_1, X))] - wX\}\\ &\quad + (1-p)\{Pg(Z)[1 - D(h(n_2, X))] - wX\}.\end{aligned}$$

The first-order condition is

$$\begin{aligned}&p\{-Pg(Z)D_h h_X(n_1, X) - w\}\\ &\quad + (1-p)\{-Pg(Z)D_h h_X(n_2, X) - w\} = 0.\end{aligned}$$

Given specific g, D, and h functions, one could solve this first-order condition for X. Plugging the optimal value, X, back into the objective function would then give the level of expected profit associated with preventive pesticide application. Note that because the pest population is uncertain, X will be the same regardless of which pest population level, n_1 or n_2, actually occurs. This is inefficient because we would like to use less pesticide if n_1 occurs and more if n_2 occurs.

To decide between preventive and reactive application methods, we need to compare the level of expected profits under preventive pesticide application with the level of expected profits under the following model of reactive application.

With **reactive application**, a fixed monitoring cost, m, is paid to determine the pest population level, and then the optimal X is chosen for the specific pest level. This enables more precise pesticide use. The problem is then

$$\max_{X_1,X_2} E(\pi) = p\{Pg(Z)[1 - D(h(n_1, X_1))] - wX_1\} \\ + (1 - p)\{Pg(Z)[1 - D(h(n_2, X_2))] - wX_2\} - m.$$

The first-order conditions are

$$\frac{\partial E(\pi)}{\partial X_1} = p\{-Pg(Z)D_h h_{X_1}(n_1, X_1) - w\} = 0,$$
$$\frac{\partial E(\pi)}{\partial X_2} = (1 - p)\{-Pg(z)D_h h_{X_2}(n_2, X_2) - w\} = 0.$$

Given specific g, D and h functions, one could solve the first-order condition's for the optimal X_1 and X_2. Plugging X_1 and X_2 back into the objective function gives the level of expected profits under reactive pesticide application. Note that the resulting equation for expected profits will contain monitoring costs, m. With reactive application, there is a tradeoff between the monitoring costs and the savings in pesticide costs made possible by monitoring. Two points need to be underlined. First, if the difference between X_1 and X_2 is large, and m is relatively small, then reactive application will give a higher level of expected profits than would preventive application. Monitoring and reactive application are key components of modern IPM programs. Second, even if the difference between X_1 and X_2 is large, farmers may still prefer preventive application whenever the price of pesticides is very low or monitoring cost is very high to ensure higher expected profits. In order to combine the profit-maximizing decision with social-welfare maximization, an appropriate tax would be imposed on pesticides so that effective prices would reflect marginal external cost.

Pests do not recognize property rights. Pest control activities often lead to externality problems. For instance, a recent study published in *Science* shows that pest control approaches adopted by organic crop producers may increase overall pesticide uses on neighboring farms (Larsen *et al.*, 2024). Pest control districts are introduced to overcome these problems (e.g., mosquito control districts). The activities of such districts encompass joint effort in monitoring activities, coordinate crop management and rotation, and coordinate pesticide spraying.

4. Health-risk and Environmental Effects of Pesticide Use

Health risk is the probability that an individual selected randomly from a population contracts adverse health effects (mortality or morbidity) from a substance. The health risk-generating process contains three stages: *contamination*, *exposure*, and *dose–response.* **Contamination** is the presence of toxic pesticide or its derivatives on the agricultural product. It is direct result of pesticide application: the chemicals are spread through the air and water and become absorbed by the product. **Exposure** is the contact of toxic substances with human organisms, resulting from eating, breathing, or touching contaminated product by consumers or agricultural workers. **Response** translates exposure to probability of contracting certain diseases. We usually distinguish between acute and chronic risks. Acute risks are the immediate risks of poisoning. Chronic risks are risk that may depend on accumulated exposure and which may take time to manifest themselves (e.g., the higher incidence of certain type of cancer in populations that are exposed to a certain pesticide for a long time).

The processes that determine contamination, exposure, and the response relationship are often characterized by heterogeneity, uncertainty, and random phenomena (e.g., weather). Thus, contamination, exposure, and the response relationship need to be analyzed with models that accounts for the inherent uncertainty. *Risk assessment models* estimate health risks associated with pesticide application by making use of estimated probabilities.

Let r be the represent individual health risk. It can be expressed as

$$r = f_1(X, B_1)f_2(B_2)f_3(B_3),$$

where X is the level of pollution on site (i.e., the level of pesticide use), B_1 is the damage control activity at the site (e.g., protective clothing or re-entry rules), B_2 is the averting behavior by potentially exposed individuals (e.g., washing fruits and vegetables), and B_3 reflects the dosage of pollution (e.g., the type of pesticide residual consumed) or the level of medical treatment employed. The health risk of an average individual is modeled as the product of three functions. The first one is $f_1(X, B_1)$, the contamination function that relates contamination of an environmental medium to activities of an economic agent (i.e., relates pesticide residues on apples to pesticides applied by growers). The second is $f_2(B_2)$, the human exposure coefficient, which depends on an individual's actions to control exposure (e.g., relates ingested pesticide residues to the level of rinsing and degree of food processing an individual engages in). The last one is $f_3(B_3)$, the dose–response function which relates health risk to the level of exposure of a given substance (i.e., relates the proclivity of contracting cancer to the ingestion of particular levels of a certain pesticide), based on available medical treatment methods, B_3. Dose–response functions are usually estimated in epidemiological and toxicological studies of human biology.

The product $f_1(X, B_1)f_2(B_2)$ is the overall exposure level of an individual to a toxic material (e.g., the amount of pesticide present on an apple times the percentage *not* removed by rinsing the apple). The degree of overall exposure can be affected by improved technology and by a greater dissemination of information.

Estimating these functions involves much uncertainty. Scientific knowledge of dose–response relationships of pesticides is generally incomplete, especially for pesticides ingested in small doses over long periods of time. Contamination function depends partly on assimilation of pollution by natural systems, which can differ regionally (e.g., wind distributed residues). Exposure coefficient depends on education of population (e.g., consumers' awareness of pesticide residue averting techniques, such as washing).

Uncertainty could be included in the economic model by using a safety-rule approach. The policy goal of pesticide use regulation should be to maximize welfare subject to the constraint that the probability of health risk remains below a certain threshold level, R, and that the safety level, α, is above a certain threshold. Here α could be a measure of social risk aversion or the degree of confidence we have in our target risk. For any target level of risk and any degree of safety level, the model can be solved for the optimal levels of pesticide use, damage control activities, and averting behavior by consumers.

General implications of this way of approaching the modeling include the following. First, the optimal solution involves some combination of pollution control and exposure avoidance. Second, the cost of reaching the target risk level increases with the safety level α. And finally, the shadow price of meeting the risk target depends on the degree of significance (α) we have that the target is being met. The higher α, or the greater the uncertainty we have in our estimate of risk, the higher the shadow value of meeting the constraint.

Example 1 (a model without uncertainty):

Suppose there is no uncertainty regarding the health effects of pesticide use. That is, toxicologists know with certainty a point estimate of the dose–response function, $f_3(\cdot)$. Moreover, let

$Y = f(X, A)$ be the farm production function,
X = the level of pesticides used on a field,
A = the level of alternate pest control activities,
P = the value of farm output (e.g., the price of a basket of produce),
Y = the level of farm output,
W = the price of pesticide,
V = the price of alternative controls ($V > W$),
$R = f_1(X, B_1)f_2(B_2)f_3(B_3)$ be the level of health risk in society, where the notation is defined as before,

$C(R)$ = the cost to society of health risk R, and
$C(B_1, B_2, B_3)$ = the cost incurred by conducting B_1, B_2, and B_3. For simplicity, we assume away other production costs.

Then, the objective of the society is to

$$\max_{X,A,R,B_1,B_2,B_3} Pf(X, A) - C(R) - C(B_1, B_2, B_3) - WX - VA \quad (5)$$

subject to

$$R = f_1(X, B_1)f_2(B_2)f_3(B_3).$$

The optimization problem can be written in Lagrangian form as

$$\max_{X,A,R,B_1,B_2,B_3} L = Pf(X, A) - C(R) - C(B_1, B_2, B_3) - WX - VA$$
$$+ \lambda[R - f_3(B_3)f_2(B_2)f_1(B_1, X)].$$

The first-order conditions are

$$\frac{dL}{dA} = Pf_A - V = 0, \quad (6)$$

indicating that the marginal revenue product (MRP) of the alternative control equals the marginal cost of the alternative control, and

$$\frac{dL}{dR} = -C'(R) + \lambda = 0, \quad (7)$$

indicating that the marginal social cost of health risk equals the shadow value of risk (i.e., the marginal cost of risk in terms of social damages is equal to the shadow price of reducing societal risk).

Furthermore, we have

$$\frac{dL}{dX} = Pf_X - W - \lambda\left[f_3f_2\frac{df_1}{dX}\right] = 0, \quad (8)$$

$$\frac{dL}{dB_1} = -C_{B_1} - \lambda\left[f_3f_2\frac{df_1}{dB_1}\right] = 0, \quad (9)$$

$$\frac{dL}{dB_2} = -C_{B_2} - \lambda\left[f_3f_1\frac{df_2}{dB_2}\right] = 0, \quad (10)$$

$$\frac{dL}{dB_3} = -C_{B_3} - \lambda\left[f_2f_1\frac{df_3}{dB_3}\right] = 0. \quad (11)$$

We can rewrite Equations (8)–(11) using Equation (7) as

$$Pf_X = W + C'(R)\left[f_3 f_2 \frac{df_1}{dX}\right],$$

which implies that the marginal revenue product of pesticide use to the farm is equal to the marginal private cost of pesticides plus the product of marginal cost of risk and marginal contribution of pesticides to the risk;

$$C_{B_1} = -C'(R)\left[f_3 f_2 \frac{df_1}{dB_1}\right],$$

which implies that the marginal cost of damage control equals the product of avoided marginal cost of risk and marginal improvement in risk from engaging in damage control activities;

$$C_{B_2} = -C'(R)\left[f_3 f_1 \frac{df_2}{dB_2}\right],$$

which implies that the marginal cost of averting behavior equals the product of avoided marginal cost of risk and marginal improvement in risk from engaging in averting behavior; and

$$C_{B_3} = -C'(R)\left[f_2 f_1 \frac{df_3}{dB_3}\right],$$

which implies that the marginal cost of medical treatment equals the product of avoided marginal cost of risk and marginal reduction in risk from engaging in medical treatment.

The optimal solution involves equating all six first-order conditions. Equations (7)–(11) can be expressed as

$$\lambda = C'(R) = \frac{Pf_X - W}{\left(f_3 f_2 \frac{df_1}{dX}\right)} = \frac{-C_{B_1}}{\left(f_3 f_2 \frac{df_1}{dB_1}\right)} = \frac{-C_{B_2}}{\left(f_3 f_1 \frac{df_2}{dB_2}\right)} = \frac{-C_{B_3}}{\left(f_2 f_1 \frac{df_3}{dB_3}\right)},$$

which states that the optimal solution involves equating the shadow price of risk with a series of ratios. The denominator of each expression transforms marginal benefits or marginal costs of health-related activities into changes in health risk. When parameters are known, the model can be solved for the optimal levels. The model has some general implications. First, if there is no tax on pesticide use and no subsidy on farm-level damage control, then the farm will not recognize the effect of pesticide use on societal health, and will operate as if $\lambda = 0$. As a consequence, an inefficiently high level of pesticides will be used, and an inefficiently low level of damage control will be applied. Second, the optimal solution may involve a large level of pesticide use, little damage control, little medical treatment, and a high degree of averting behavior. Rinsing and washing produce might be the least expensive method of reducing health risk in society.

Example 2 (a model with uncertainty):

Let r be the probability of an individual contracting a disease and $r = c{\cdot}e{\cdot}d{\cdot}x$, where c stands for contamination probability, e exposure probability, d dose-response probability, and x amount of pesticide applied. Let

$$c = \begin{cases} 0.1 \text{ with probability } .5 \\ 0.2 \text{ with probability } .5, \end{cases}$$

$$e = \begin{cases} 0.1 \text{ with probability } .5 \\ 0.3 \text{ with probability } .5, \end{cases}$$

$$d = \begin{cases} 10^{-4} \text{ with probability } .5 \\ 10^{-5} \text{ with probability } .5. \end{cases}$$

Suppose $x = 1$, then we have

$$r = \begin{cases} 1 \times 10^{-6} \text{ with probability } 1/8 \\ 2 \times 10^{-6} \text{ with probability } 1/8 \\ 3 \times 10^{-6} \text{ with probability } 1/8 \\ 6 \times 10^{-6} \text{ with probability } 1/8 \\ 1 \times 10^{-7} \text{ with probability } 1/8 \\ 2 \times 10^{-7} \text{ with probability } 1/8 \\ 3 \times 10^{-7} \text{ with probability } 1/8 \\ 6 \times 10^{-7} \text{ with probability } 1/8. \end{cases}$$

Note that $r = 1 \times 10^{-6}$ means "one person per million people" contracts the disease. Here the expected risk is

$$\frac{13.2}{8} \times 10^{-6} = 1.65 \times 10^{-6},$$

or 1.65 people per one million people, on average, contract the disease.

Based on the distribution of r, the objective of the society is to maximize the expected net benefits from using pesticides. The objective function can be readily written by expanding optimization problem (5). In many cases, however, the highest value (worst case estimator) of each probability is used to solve optimization problem (5) when the risk generation processes are broken down to many sub-processes. This creates a "creeping safety" problem, in that the multiplication of many "worst case" estimates may lead to wildly unrealistic risk estimates. The variability and uncertainty associated with risk estimates can be reduced by expenditures on research and through information-sharing.

5. Pesticide Policy

Federal Insecticide, Fungicide and Rodenticide Act (FIFRA) was passed into law by Congress in 1972 and is enforced by the EPA, which has the power to prohibit the sale, distribution, or use of pesticides such as insecticides, fungicides, and rodenticides under the Act. If a threatened or endangered species could be adversely affected, the EPA can also issue an emergency suspension of certain pesticides. FIFRA requires that farmers, utility companies, and other users of pesticides register when they purchase pesticides, for which these individuals also have to pass a certification exam. FIFRA also contains provisions that require that all pesticides used in the United States be approved and licensed by the EPA. In 1972, the EPA banned the use of DDT (dichloro-diphenyl-trichloroethane), the pesticide featured in *Silent Spring* (Carson, 1962) and required extensive review of all pesticides. In 1996, the Food Quality Protection Act was passed to tighten standards for pesticides used to grow food, with special protections to ensure that foods are safe for children to eat. In 2015, EPA revised Agricultural Worker Protection Standards to increase protections from pesticide exposure for agricultural workers and their families in the US.

Modern pesticide policies tend to be triggered solely by health considerations: when a chemical is found to be carcinogenic or damaging to the environment, it is banned or "cancelled." The impacts of pesticide cancellation depend on the available alternatives. Cancellation often causes losses in crop yields due to higher pest damages and increases costs, since alternative methods of control, if there is any, are generally more expensive. To estimate overall short–term impacts, the impacts on yield per acre and cost per acre are evaluated using one of the following methods:

(1) *Delphi method*: The Delphi method was named after the famous "Oracle at Delphi" in ancient Greece. It uses "guesstimates by experts," which are often straightforward to obtain but are arbitrary and sometimes baseless.

(2) *Experimental studies*: These studies are based on data from agronomical experiments, but experimental plots often do not reflect real farming situations.

(3) *Econometric studies*: Statistical methods are based (ideally) on data gathered from real farming operations. However, these studies are often not feasible because of data limitations and the difficulty of isolating the specific effects of pesticides.

(4) *Cost budgeting method*: Let y_{ij} denote output per acre of crop i at region j with pesticide, P_{ij} price of crop i in region j, A_{ij} acreage of crop i in region j, Δy_{ij} yield reduction per acre because of cancellation, and Δc_{ij} cost increase per acre because of cancellation. Under a partial crop budget, impacts on farmers' surplus are estimated as

$$\sum_{i=1}^{I}\sum_{j=1}^{J}(P_{ij}\Delta y_{ij} + \Delta c_{ij})A_{ij}.$$

A pesticide cancellation causes losses in revenue from lowered yields and increased costs per acre, which is multiplied the total acreage in all regions and across all types of crop affected by the ban. This cost budgeting approach has at least two limitations. First, it ignores the effect of a change in output on output price. This tends to overestimate producer loss and underestimate consumer loss. Second, it ignores feedback effects from related markets. In general, this method does not consider the interaction of supply and demand,

and does not attempt to find the new market equilibrium after the application of a pesticide ban.

(5) *General equilibrium method*: This method is based on analyzing the impact of a pesticide ban on *equilibrium* prices and output, taking into account the interaction of supply and demand and any feedback effects from related markets. In addition, this method offers a better assessment of equity effects by computing welfare changes for various groups. As a result of a pesticide ban, marginal cost per acre increases, output declines, and output price increases. The magnitude of the change in output price depends on the elasticity of demand and any feedback effects from related markets, such as markets for substitute goods. General equilibrium analysis recognizes heterogeneity in welfare effects: the welfare of non-pesticide-using farmers increases due to the increase in output price, but the welfare of pesticide-using farmers decreases if demand is elastic (but may increase if demand is inelastic). Consumer welfare is harmed by price increases, but is enhanced by reducing health risk due to pesticide regulations. A recent study by Ye *et al.* (2021) provides an analysis on the impact of restricting glyphosate use on social welfare, considering the health, environmental, and economic impact of this herbicide. Chapter 5 in this book provides an analysis of the welfare impact of pesticide regulation accounting for the existence of other agricultural policies, such as price support policies.

Pesticide effects include several related issues such as food safety, worker safety, ground water contamination, and other environmental damage. Pesticide bans aim to address all these issues. However, a pesticide ban can be an inefficient policy because pesticide uses and impacts vary significantly across regions. Economic mechanisms (taxes and partial bans) that discriminate across different types of uses may eliminate most of the pesticide damage but retain most pesticide benefits. Although a pesticide ban may provide the incentive to develop new, less dangerous pest control methods, a pesticide tax may serve the same purpose and also allow a more gradual and efficient transition to the new technology. However, if a pesticide tax is used, policymakers should keep in mind that pesticide use patterns could shift significantly across geographic regions. Other policy tools can affect different stages of the risk generation process. For instance, regulations on pollution controls and protective clothing can affect contamination and exposure; regulations on residual tolerance standard can address food and water safety concerns; re-entry regulation can address worker and public safety concerns; and finally, water disposal regulation can reduce ground water contamination.

6. Conclusion

In this chapter, we have discussed the optimal pesticide use under various scenarios (e.g., known and unknown pest populations as well as the presence of a secondary pest). We have also discussed the health risk and environmental effects of pesticide use, followed by a brief discussion of pesticide policy in the United States. Pesticides are important inputs in agricultural production, and the tradeoff between their positive impact on production and negative impact on the environment will be a critical issue for societies in years to come. Tackling this issue has attracted much attention from researchers, policymakers, non-governmental organizations, and general public. Since pesticide use is closely related to agricultural production and is determined by farmers' choices, research in agricultural economics is well positioned to provide behavioral insights and policy recommendations. With the increased availability of data for pesticide use as well as for health and environmental measurement, a burgeoning field of study in economics has tried to quantify the adverse impact of pesticide uses on human health and the environment by using national or regional scale data (e.g., Li *et al.*, 2020; Dias *et al.*, 2023), complementing experimental or laboratory findings from natural sciences.

References

Carson, R. 1962. *Silent Spring.* Houghton Mifflin Harcourt.

Dias, M., R. Rocha, and R.R. Soares. 2023. Down the River: Glyphosate Use in Agriculture and Birth Outcomes of Surrounding Populations. *The Review of Economic Studies* 90(6): 2943–2981.

Fernandez-Cornejo, J., R. Nehring, C. Osteen, S. Wechsler, A. Martin, and A. Vialou, 2014. Pesticide Use in U.S. Agriculture: 21 Selected Crops, 1960–2008. U.S. Department of Agriculture, *Economic Research Service, Economic Information Bulletin* Number 124.

Larsen, A.E., F. Noack, and L.C. Powers, 2024. Spillover Effects of Organic Agriculture on Pesticide Use on Nearby Fields. *Science* 383(6689).

Li, Y., R. Miao, M. Khanna. 2020. Neonicotinoids and Decline in Bird Biodiversity in the United States. *Nature Sustainability* 3: 1027–1035.

Ye, Z., F. Wu, and D.A. Hennessy. 2021. Environmental and Economic Concerns Surrounding Restrictions on Glyphosate Use in Corn. *Proceedings of the National Academy of Sciences* 118(18): e2017470118.

Chapter 12

Economics of Space: Interaction of Urban and Rural Sectors

One of society's biggest challenges is allocating land between the urban sector, agriculture, forestry, and wilderness. Within agriculture, land allocation is also critical. Land management has been one of the main interests of economists for millennia, and we will cover some of the major findings in this section. We will start with one of the oldest economic models: the von Thünen land allocation model. Then, we will discuss market failures associated with land use, implications of land valuation, and targeting for environmental services. We will also discuss issues arising between energy prices, land, and housing, as well as the linkages between land use and climate change policies.

1. Models for Allocation of Land

The von Thünen model (Samuelson, 1983) represents a simple system for allocating resources over space, setting the central business district (CBD) of a region as an origin and reflecting everything else located in relation to it. This CBD can be considered a port, and all the producers are exporting their products to the port. A simple model allocates land over a line, where the zero point is a CBD. Let us assume that the distance of each particular point from the CBD is denoted by x and farmers can produce multiple activities. Let i

be an activity indicator, and i takes value from 1 to I. In our simple model, the net benefit per acre of production of activity i at location x is denoted by:

$$B_i(x, N) = b_i(x, N) - t_i \cdot x,$$

where the net benefit $B_i(x, N)$ is the difference between the gross benefit of production per acre, $b_i(x, N)$, and transportation costs per acre for activity i. For every activity, the gross benefits per acre are functions of location and population (N). We assume that the net benefit per acre of activities declines with location, while for the same location, the gross benefit per acre is lower for higher i (namely, $b_i(x, N) > b_{i+1}(x, N)$), and benefit per acre increases with the size of the population. We further assume that the transportation costs per acre tend to be lower for activities with higher i's ($t_i > t_{i+1}$).

Assuming that land is allocated under competition, under our assumption, the area under the CBD, from $x = 0$ *to* x_1^*, will be allocated to the highest value activity (activity 1). At the switching point, x_1^*, $b_1(x, N) - t_1 \cdot x = b_2(x, N) - t_2 \cdot x$. Similarly, the switching point, x_i^*, where $b_i(x, N) - t_i \cdot x = b_{i+1}(x, N) - t_{i+1} \cdot x$, separates the region where activity i is from the farther region where activity $i + 1$ is. The rent per acre for land at location x is equal to the net benefit per acre of the optimal activity for each location.

Figure 1 illustrates the outcome of the model: the envelope (the bold line) traces the rent as a function of location. The figure suggests five activities, and the wilderness area (the area between x_5^* and x_N^*), or the end of the region. The interpretation has varied: in much of the literature interpreting the von Thünen model, the area near the business circle is a commercial area, the next area is the residential area, and the agricultural area starts from high-value agricultural activities and moves to low-value agricultural activities. In some regions, livestock production is near the urban sector because of its relatively high transportation costs compared to field crops. In other regions, perishable high-value fruits and vegetables are closer to the city, followed by livestock, feedstock, and wildland. Clark (1973) also presents an exposition of the von Thünen model and demonstrates its applicability with historical data.

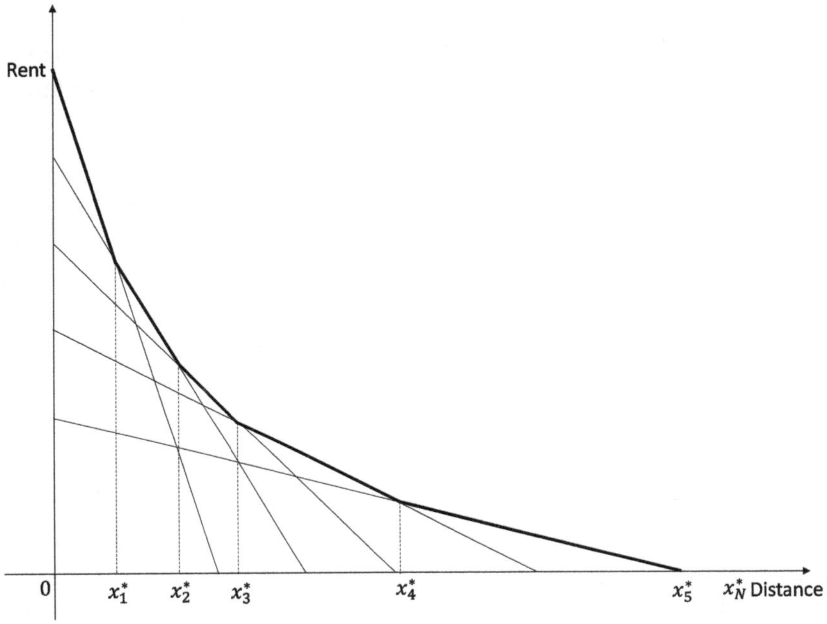

Figure 1. Net benefit and rent as a function of distance from CBD.

Because we assume that the benefit at each location is a function of the population, an increasing population tends to increase the benefit of all activities, and thus, is likely to increase the land rent and, furthermore, reduce the wildland area. Indeed, human settlement historically resulted in reductions in wildlands and biodiversity. While technological change has diminished the relevance of the von Thünen model since the 19th century, some of its features remain applicable. Over time, the model has been expanded and modified to address changing reality. Hochman *et al.* (1977) assume that some benefits from land use are associated with production and introduce production functions that rely on input (e.g., fertilizer) and pollution. Their model allows us to consider pollution from production activities as well as agricultural activities, and their analysis considers two types of externalities. First, pollution accumulates toward the urban center and causes damage there or on contiguous natural areas (normally bodies of water). In this case, social optimum requires introducing regulations, like taxes, that may reduce production intensity close to the urban area, and thus may change the rent structure, production intensity, or land use over space to reduce pollution generation. This approach, for example, is appropriate for designing policies that address the accumulation of pollution from farming activities along the Mississippi, or activities that result in a dead zone in the Gulf of Mexico (Rabotyagov *et al.*, 2014). The second type of externalities is those spread around the production area, such as odor or air pollution. These externalities can be controlled by penalties or zoning. For example, there was an attempt to reduce California's rice straw burning in order to reduce air pollution in Sacramento (Carey *et al.*, 2000).

Land use has major implications for greenhouse gas emissions. There is a large body of literature on the agricultural emissions that contribute to climate change and attempts to reduce emissions through land use changes, technological innovation, and better understanding of the interaction between the economy and ecological systems (Levin and Xepapadeas, 2021). Several outstanding studies by Karen Seto and collaborators established that increasing population and rising living standards are likely to contribute to greenhouse gas emissions and biodiversity loss (Seto *et al.*, 2011, 2012). They suggest that urbanization, especially in the developing world, is likely to double the urban landscape if there are no interventions. This will result in a significant loss of high-quality agricultural land that will further enhance deforestation and loss of biodiversity, contributing massively to climate change and mostly hurting the disadvantaged. Thus, policies increasing input-use efficiency on urban land, among other policies, could reduce the carbon footprint from the urban sector and offer benefits to agricultural production. Further understanding of the link between urban and agricultural development and policies to control the externalities of both are major research priorities and may require multidisciplinary collaboration.

Because climate change and other stock pollution problems (e.g. groundwater contamination) are dynamic phenomena, modeling them requires optimal control over space and time. Xabadia *et al.* (2008) develop a model where economic agents are heterogeneous and generating stock pollution over differing areas. The optimal intervention design is to maximize social welfare by maximizing the net present value of producer, consumer, environmental, and government surpluses. Through their approach, one can suggest a policy that sets the optimal pollution level to maximize social welfare. An optimal policy is spatially and temporally differentiated (varies by location over time). Real life has some limitations: lack of information and implementation capacity may lead to static and spatially uniform policy; or dynamic but spatially uniform policy; or static but spatially differentiated policy. Using a simulation based on data from California, they show that a simple, static, spatially uniform tax to control pollution results in about half of the gain of the optimal spatially and temporally differentiated policy, while policies that vary only by space or only by time may lose a quarter of the gain compared to the optimal policy. This analysis suggests a significant gain potential based on policies that can differentiate behavior over space and time. Certainly, designing such policies requires analytical tools to be developed.

The use of new remote sensing technologies and improved computational capacity led to the development of powerful tools that will eventually improve policies to incorporate variability over space and time. Spatial econometrics (Irwin and Geoghegan, 2001) modifies techniques of time series analysis to estimate technical and behavioral parameters over space and provides a foundation for quantitative policy making. Usually, there is a significant preference for open space and aesthetic values (Irwin and Bockstael, 2007), offering room for land use analysis to extend the von Thünen model to consider both distance from CBD and land value. One possible pattern of land use is consistent with maximizing utility from income and aesthetic value and assuming well-functioning land markets. For instance, the rich may live in areas with the best views next to the city and the poor may live near the city but in less appealing locations. Wu and Plantinga (2003) suggest that open space policies and aesthetic considerations are crucial for land use management and are likely to be an immigration magnet. Their analysis suggests that zoning can be a major mechanism affecting land use, taxation, and institutional arrangements (e.g., land distribution between municipalities).

According to Glaeser *et al.* (2005), housing shortages do not reflect physical restraints but are zoning-biased in favor of landlords and reduce housing supply. Glaeser and Khan (2004) argue that urban sprawl is mostly a result of technology (car-based living), and its main deficiencies relate to inequality in access and transportation use. Their analysis did not, however, consider the environmental externalities of sprawl (Seto *et al.*, 2011).

The analysis of land use in modern society, especially in the urban sector, has also discovered the importance of agglomeration economics, where productivity increases with density and the decline of the importance of transaction costs, leading to dense downtowns and urban sprawl (Glaeser and Gottlieb, 2009). Wu (2006) suggests that the geographic features of various locations, in addition to economic considerations, may explain changing density and non-contiguity along the urban–rural fringe and leapfrog development, segregation, and jurisdictional fragmentation. Newburn and Berck (2011) present evidence that exurban development, residential areas outside suburban areas, is comparatively more threatening to farmland and the natural environment than are the urban and suburban areas. They argue that while suburban development is constrained by water, especially sewer availability, the development of septic systems in the exurban areas is a major contributor to fragmentation and loss of intact agricultural and forested areas.

The literature on the evolution and economics of land use pattern development has benefited from improved empirical capabilities. New data sources allow using instrumental variables, matching techniques, differences-in-differences, regression discontinuity design, randomized controlled trials to understand individual land use choices in response to market conditions, policy incentives, and policy and market outcomes. Plantinga (2021) reviews recent progress in empirical studies of land use and suggests that new capabilities could provide new research opportunities, leading to improved understanding and, eventually, better policy choices.

Policy choices frequently reflect improved data, understanding of human behavior, and decision-making rules. The shift of agricultural policy to address environmental challenges led to the emergence of research on allocating resources to environmental amenities, which will be discussed in the following section.

2. The Economics of Payment for Ecosystem Services (PES)

For a long time, agricultural policies' main priorities were providing good and affordable food (consumer surplus), maintaining the well-being of farmers (producer surplus), and reducing government costs. This led to traditional agricultural policies that included land set-aside programs to control supply. Increased concern about environmental externalities and awareness of the importance of a sustainable environment for human well-being in the 1970s led to the introduction of programs with explicit environmental goals. Thus, the land set-aside program of the U.S. was converted in the 1980s to become a conservation reserve program, where landowners were paid to convert their land use from agricultural activities to less environmentally intensive activities that benefit the environment. This was a pioneering effort in establishing Payment for Ecosystem Services (PES). Over time, PES has become global tools for resource management in agriculture, forestry, and other resource forms (Bulte *et al.*, 2008; Engel *et al.*, 2008).

Currently, the United States has multiple agricultural PES.[1] A prominent example is the Conservation Reserve Program, a land set-aside program that provides environmental amenities like water protection, soil erosion reduction, wildlife habitat preservations, forest and wetland preservation, and enhanced resilience against natural disasters. Another example is the Environmental Quality Incentives Program (EQIP), a working land program that pays farmers to improve their production practices. PES programs may change over time to include support for activities that reduce greenhouse gas emissions and other objectives. The European Union's (EU)

---

[1]See Farm Service Agency's (FSA) conservation program webpage that is available at: https://www.fsa.usda.gov/programs-and-services/conservation-programs/index (accessed January 19, 2023).

Common Agricultural Policy (CAP) includes programs that aim to protect against environmental and biodiversity loss and contribute to climate change mitigation. These programs include payments for set-aside activities and working land programs. The requirements of the programs may also change over time to reflect changing food and agricultural contexts. For instance, the environmental payment and requirement may decline during tighter food supply situations.

There is growing economic literature on the economics of PES. One body of literature considers the issue of targeting budgets for environmental services payments. Babcock *et al.* (1997) developed a conceptual framework to associate allocating a budget to purchase agricultural land for environmental services. The model assumes that land within a region is heterogeneous (regarding productivity and environmental amenities). Each parcel of land has a fixed economic rent per acre (denoted by c, $0 \leq c \leq \underline{c}$). Assuming the environmental agency will pay the farmer the rent, then c reflects costs per acre for the environmental agency. Each piece of land also has a fixed environmental quality coefficient per acre (denoted by e, $0 \leq e \leq \underline{e}$). The density distribution of land is $f(c, e)$, and the total land (A) is $\int_{e=0}^{e=\underline{e}} \int_{c=0}^{c=\underline{c}} f(e, c)dcde = A$. In this case, land can be allocated by three criteria. First is cost targeting: when given a certain amount of budget B, the government buys all the land whose cost per acre is smaller than c^1 such that $\int_{e=0}^{e=\underline{e}} \int_{c=0}^{c=c^1} c \cdot f(e, c)dcde = B$ (the expenditure meets the available budget). The second criterion is environmental benefit maximization: the government buys all the land above a critical land quality e^2 so that $\int_{e=e^2}^{e=\underline{e}} \int_{c=0}^{c=\underline{c}} c \cdot f(e, c)dcde = B$. A third criterion is benefit-cost ratio maximization: the government buys all the land, where the benefit-cost ratio is greater than b_e, and this critical value is determined by solving $\int_{e=0}^{e=\underline{e}} \int_{c=0}^{c=e/b_e} c \cdot f(e, c)dcde = B$. In Figure 2, the areas that correspond to these three criteria are the area below the horizontal dashed line, the area to the right of the vertical dashed line, and the area below the sloping dashed line, respectively.

The cost targeting maximizes the acreage but is preferred by farmers because they are left with their best land. This cost targeting is also optimal from an environmental perspective if there is a

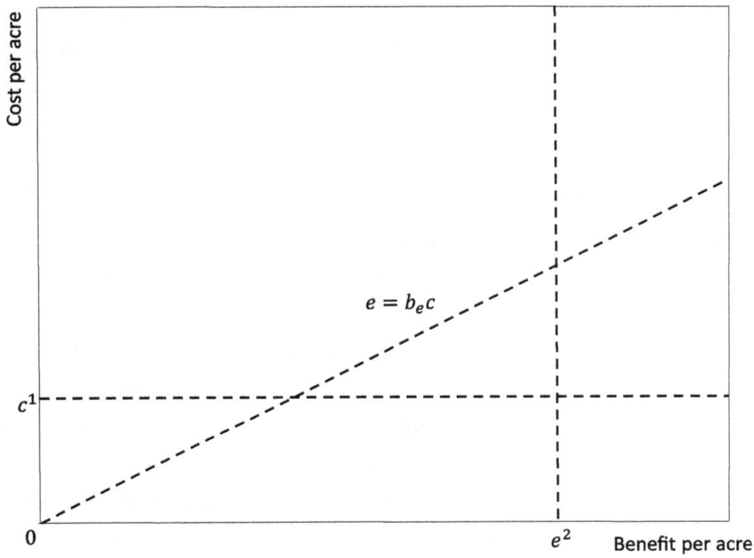

Figure 2. Targeting of environmental amenities.

full negative correlation between rent and environmental quality. In this case, buying the cheapest land will maximize environmental amenities. The environmental benefit maximization may result in the lowest purchase of land, but it would not maximize aggregate environmental benefit if some high-environmental-quality land has very high rent. Therefore, it may be worthwhile to buy cheaper lands, which together have higher aggregate environmental quality. The benefit-cost ratio targeting maximizes the environmental benefit for a given budget and should be considered by environmental agencies.

The analysis presented here is simple and can be expanded. Wu *et al.* (2001) consider the case where the industry faces negatively sloped demand, and differences in rent represent differences in land productivity. In this case, PES programs have expected negative consequences, such as slippage: if output demand is inelastic, the PES program increases agricultural prices leading to the farming of previously idle lands, potentially leading to a reduction of environmental benefits. Thus, PES may need to pay for keeping lands with high environmental services out of production. In this case, purchasing funds that are the sole buyer of environmental amenities may pay monopolistic pricing and short-change the landowners. PES programs also affect multiple agents in addition to government agencies and landowners. In particular, they affect consumers and farmworkers. Zilberman *et al.* (2008) develop a model that considers heterogeneity in both environmental and economic factors to assess the impact of PES programs. They argue that these programs tend to benefit landowners, but land diversion programs (from agricultural activities) may harm consumers by increasing prices and farmworkers by reducing employment opportunities. So, there may be a conflict between environmental protection and equity, especially in development. However, working land programs where farmers are paid for improved environmental amenities (more precise use of chemicals, water conservation, integrated pest management (IPA)) may benefit consumers by increasing supply and improving environmental quality. For workers, it may provide more employment opportunities and thus are desirable from an equity perspective. Quantifying the benefits and costs of PES programs is a significant and growing research topic.

The environmental benefit may have an agglomeration effect, namely that the benefit from an environmental amenity increases nonlinearly with the amount of land. For example, designing reserves for wildlife over space may require establishing corridors to allow wildlife movement. Furthermore, the same piece of land may provide multiple environmental amenities such as wetland protection, air quality protection, or wildlife shelter. Wu and Boggess (1999) developed an extended model to design PES that considers multiple attributes and agglomeration effects.

Over the years, land purchasing funds moved from targeting cheap land to using the benefit-cost criteria. The funds are used to achieve several objectives (e.g., soil erosion reduction, water quality protection, and wildlife habitat protection). The different features of parcels of land are quantified, and each feature is assigned a benefit weight. The benefit per acre is the sum of the benefits of the different features of the field. Each landowner should state a willingness to accept for providing environmental services. The environmental agencies select the plots with the highest environmental benefit per unit of land cost.

Political economy considerations of PES are important for designing PES programs. Different regions may benefit differently from emphasizing one program feature over another. For example, some regions may benefit from wetland protection, while others may benefit from improved air quality. So, weight and target of different features are subject to political negotiation. Furthermore, much of the environmental amenities are provided by non-governmental agents that benefit from government policies. For example, non-governmental organizations (NGOs) like the Nature Conservancy or World Wildlife Federation purchase environmental land or other resources with significant amenities, but their purchases may benefit from preferential tax treatment. Thus, understanding how tax policies affect land diversion to the agricultural sector is important for further research.

3. Land Pricing

The previous analysis suggests that land resources provide multiple benefits to agricultural, rural, urban, municipal, and environmental sectors. The von Thünen model and the analysis of PES suggest mechanisms for assessing land rents, namely, payments per unit of land per unit of time. However, the transition from land rent to land prices is quite tricky. According to Poterba *et al.* (1991), the return on housing investments is equal to a user cost, μ, which is

$$\mu = (1 - \theta)(t + r) + \delta + m + \alpha - g,$$

where θ is the marginal tax rate, r is the interest rate, t is the real estate tax rate, δ is depreciation, m is maintenance, α is the insurance risk premium, and g is expected capital gain. The ratio of net rent per acre to the price per acre is equal to the user cost. The net rent per acre in the von Thünen model is the periodical benefit per unit of land at a given location minus the user cost. For given agricultural activities and locations, the price of the land is equal to the net rent divided by the user cost, which suggests that land values increase when the interest rate, property tax, depreciation, maintenance costs, and insurable risk are declining, and when the expected capital gain is increasing. Just and Miranowski (1993) expanded the model to incorporate inflation and risk aversion, showing that expected capital gain, the opportunity cost of capital, and inflation (which tend to reduce prices) are important explanatory variables for price variability and profitability in the 1980s and 1990s, which suggests the importance of monetary policy and macro situations to the farm sector.

Agricultural land prices are affected directly by factors that affect agriculture. For example, increasing the price of food and introducing government programs that assure farm income, *ceteris paribus*, tend to increase the price of land. One reason farmers fight strongly for maintaining government support programs is that it benefits them directly in each period and enhances their wealth. The price-rent ratio formula above suggests that changes in taxes on land, macroeconomic policies that affect interest rates, and expectations for economic growth that affect land pricing affect the well-being of the farm sector. As such, farmers are keen on macro-policies. The link between macro policies and the agricultural sector is an area of importance (Rausser *et al.*, 1986) although not emphasized in this chapter.

The land market and the agricultural sector are closely linked to the energy sector. Wu *et al.* (2019) argued that over the 2007–2008 oil shock, the high-energy prices devastated the real estate market and triggered the financial crisis. The oil shock almost doubled the cost of transportation, thus reduced the willingness to pay for new houses farther away from cities. Land rent and house values declined faster with distance, and the expenditure of people who lived farther away from town increased. Thus, the net value of highly mortgaged individuals with houses farther from town became negative, and they declared bankruptcy and moved to towns to reduce their transportation costs. Many of the home bankruptcies during the financial crisis occurred in California. For example, home prices in commuting areas 40+ miles away from San Francisco, including Tracy, Stockton, and Antioch, declined more than 56 %. The increase in gas prices between 2005 and 2008 increased the transportation cost of individuals who paid $4,000 for commuting in 2005 to $7,600 in 2008 annually, and this difference may push people to insolvency and deter others from wanting to move to these locations. Similar losses occurred in southern California, resulting in more than $200 billion in bankruptcies.

As the von Thünen-type analysis suggests, the value of agricultural land is affected by the value of urban land, and shocks (e.g., financial crises) that reduce the value of residential land affect agricultural land as well, which suggests that the value of agricultural land is affected by energy prices through their impact on residential land. But energy prices also have a direct impact on agriculture. In some areas, an increase in energy price would also increase the price of transportation and fertilizers, thus reducing the price of agricultural land. In other areas — for example, the Midwest — higher energy prices incurred a search for substitutes (e.g., biofuels) that increased agricultural crop prices and land prices.

4. Conclusion

This chapter emphasized the importance of urban–rural relationships. The footprint of agriculture and its economy is affected by the economics and conditions of the adjacent urban center. Policies that affect the urban sector, in turn, impact rural regions and agriculture. We found that both urban and rural areas are affected by fuel and commodity prices as well as various government policies. In particular, taxation and interest rates, directly and indirectly, influence land rent and land prices. Zoning plays an important role in establishing agricultural regions and the borderline between urban and rural areas. Government policies in agriculture, specifically payment for ecosystem services, are affecting land use and income distribution and become an important part of agricultural policy packages. Analyses of the impact and design of these policies must recognize heterogeneity across locations and agents and use new analytical tools that take advantage of spatial information and advanced computational methods. One point that we must remember is that continued urban expansion, if not well-managed, will deprive us of much agricultural land and will worsen climate change. In conclusion, in order to obtain a full understanding of the agricultural sector and its environmental implications, one has to understand urbanization and urban–rural interactions, and there is much more to discover and research regarding the subject matter.

References

Babcock, B.A., P.G. Lakshminarayan, J. Wu, and D. Zilberman. 1997. Targeting Tools for the Purchase of Environmental Amenities. *Land Economics* 73(3): 325–339.

Bulte, E.H., L. Lipper, R. Stringer, and D. Zilberman. 2008. PES and Poverty Reduction: Concepts, Issues, and Empirical Perspectives. *Environment and Development Economics* 13(3): 245–254.

Carey, M., D.A. Sumner, and R.E. Howitt. 2000. The Value of Tradable Credits for Rice Straw Burning. *AIC Issues Brief* 12.

Clark, C. 1973. *The Value of Agricultural Land.* Elsevier.

Engel, S., S. Pagiola, and S. Wunder. 2008. Designing Payments for Environmental Services in Theory and Practice: An Overview of the Issues. *Ecological Economics* 65(4): 663–674.

Glaeser, E.L. and M.E. Kahn. 2004. Sprawl and Urban Growth. In *Handbook of Regional and Urban Economics*, Vol. 4, pp. 2481–2527. Elsevier, Amsterdam.

Glaeser, E.L., J. Gyourko, and R.E. Saks. 2005. Why Have Housing Prices Gone Up? *American Economic Review* 95(2): 329–333.

Glaeser, E.L. and J.D. Gottlieb. 2009. The Wealth of Cities: Agglomeration Economies and Spatial Equilibrium in the United States. *Journal of Economic Literature* 47(4): 983–1028.

Hochman, E., D. Pines, and D. Zilberman. 1977. The Effects of Pollution Taxation on the Pattern of Resource Allocation: The Downstream Diffusion Case. *The Quarterly Journal of Economics* 91(4): 625–638.

Irwin, E.G. and J. Geoghegan. 2001. Theory, Data, Methods: Developing Spatially Explicit Economic Models of Land Use Change. *Agriculture, Ecosystems & Environment* 85(1–3): 7–24.

Irwin, E.G. and N.E. Bockstael. 2007. The Evolution of Urban Sprawl: Evidence of Spatial Heterogeneity and Increasing Land Fragmentation. *Proceedings of the National Academy of Sciences* 104(52): 20672–20677.

Just, R.E. and J.A. Miranowski. 1993. Understanding Farmland Price Changes. *American Journal of Agricultural Economics* 75(1): 156–168.

Levin, S. and A. Xepapadeas. 2021. On the Coevolution of Economic and Ecological Systems. *Annual Review of Resource Economics* 13(1): 355–377.

Newburn, D. and P. Berck. 2011. Exurban Development. *Journal of Environmental Economics and Management* 62(3): 323–336.

Plantinga, A.J. 2021. Recent Advances in Empirical Land-Use Modeling. *Annual Review of Resource Economics* 13: 1–15.

Poterba, J.M., D.N. Weil, and R. Shiller. 1991. House Price Dynamics: The Role of Tax Policy and Demography. *Brookings Papers on Economic Activity* 2: 143–203.

Rabotyagov, S.S., C.L. Kling, P.W. Gassman, N.N. Rabalais, and R.E. Turner. 2014. The Economics of Dead Zones: Causes, Impacts, Policy Challenges, and a Model of the Gulf of Mexico Hypoxic Zone. *Review of Environmental Economics and Policy* 8(1): 58–79.

Rausser, G.C., J.A. Chalfant, H.A. Love, and K.G. Stamoulis. 1986. Macroeconomic Linkages, Taxes, and Subsidies in the US Agricultural Sector. *American Journal of Agricultural Economics* 68(2): 399–412.

Samuelson, P.A. 1983. Thünen at Two Hundred. *Journal of Economic Literature* 21(4): 1468–1488.

Seto, K.C., M. Fragkias, B. Güneralp, and M.K. Reilly. 2011. A Meta-Analysis of Global Urban Land Expansion. *PloS One* 6(8): e23777.

Seto, K.C., B. Güneralp, and L.R. Hutyra. 2012. Global Forecasts of Urban Expansion to 2030 and Direct Impacts on Biodiversity and Carbon Pools. *Proceedings of the National Academy of Sciences* 109(40): 16083–16088.

Xabadia, A., R.U. Goetz, and D. Zilberman. 2008. The Gains from Differentiated Policies to Control Stock Pollution When Producers are Heterogeneous. *American Journal of Agricultural Economics* 90(4): 1059–1073.

Wu, J.J. 2006. Environmental Amenities, Urban Sprawl, and Community Characteristics. *Journal of Environmental Economics and Management* 52(2): 527–547.

Wu, J.J. and W.G. Boggess. 1999. The Optimal Allocation of Conservation Funds. *Journal of Environmental Economics and Management* 38(3): 302–321.

Wu, J.J. and A.J. Plantinga. 2003. The Influence of Public Open Space on Urban Spatial Structure. *Journal of Environmental Economics and Management* 46(2): 288–309.

Wu, J.J., S. Sexton, and D. Zilberman. 2019. Energy Price Shocks, Household Location Patterns and Housing Crises: Theory and Implications. *Energy Economics* 80: 691–706.

Wu, J.J., D. Zilberman, and B.A. Babcock. 2001. Environmental and Distributional Impacts of Conservation Targeting Strategies. *Journal of Environmental Economics and Management* 41(3): 333–350.

Zilberman, D., L. Lipper, and N. McCarthy. 2008. When Could Payments for Environmental Services Benefit the Poor? *Environment and Development Economics* 13(3): 255–278.

Chapter 13

Climate Change and Agriculture

Climate change is humanity's most challenging issue, and it is changing agriculture and agricultural policy worldwide. There is a large body of research addressing climate change, and every few years, a report is published by the Intergovernmental Panel on Climate Change (IPCC) to assess scientific findings related to climate change.[1] In this chapter, we present some of the modeling and policy issues, emphasizing the impact of climate change on agriculture and the possible role of agriculture in adaptation and mitigation. Adaptations are changes in behavior that will allow us to withstand the impact of climate change, and even prosper. Effective adaptation builds resilience. Mitigation involves activities that will allow to slow or even reverse the buildup of greenhouse gases (GHGs). Agriculture and food systems must adapt to climate change, and this can be a major contribution to its mitigation. Adaptation and mitigation are substitute activities. Mitigation may slow the pace of climate change and reduce the high cost of adaptation. It will be useful for policymakers to be able to quantify the cost-optimal mitigation strategies given the level of mitigation and optimize adaptation and mitigation strategies.

[1]For instance, the most recent report, the Sixth Assessment Report, can be found at: https://www.ipcc.ch/assessment-report/ar6/ (accessed October 21, 2023).

After a brief review of the impact of climate change on agriculture, this chapter will address how policies, both direct and indirect, can affect how agriculture will adapt and how agriculture can contribute to mitigating climate change. The first section of the chapter will assess the impact of climate change on agriculture, and then we will present several perspectives on how agriculture will adapt to climate change. We will consider impacts and adaptation in the context of individual markets, as well as supply chains for mitigation. The final section will discuss changes in policy and perception that are important to address climate change.

1. Impact of Climate Change on Agriculture

The IPCC reports list the effects of climate change, including shift of climate from the tropics to the poles, rising sea levels, greater likelihood of extreme weather events, melting snowpack, and more (Rosenzweig and Tubiello, 2007). These impacts will damage ecosystems, increase human vulnerability, and increase political instability.

Most models predict that warmer climates will shift from the tropics to the poles, and temperatures will rise. More concretely, we could see the environmental conditions in Mexico appear in California, while that in California could shift to Oregon. Most of Texas and Oklahoma are set to become deserts, but parts of Canada could become agriculturally viable. Similarly, there could be areas in Russia and northern Europe that are also viable for agriculture, but more southern areas will become uninhabitable. Expansion of the Sahel could expand political instability in the region.

Historically, those working in agriculture have been able to adapt to certain conditions. Farmers will change the input and switch crops. Water systems will be redesigned and reconstructed. Areas close to the equator will be deserted, and some near the poles will be farmed. Therefore, it is important to distinguish between the aggregate and regional effects. Lu, Buchsbaum, and Zilberman (2021) develop a conceptual model to assess the impact of climate change on agriculture. The model assumes heterogeneity across locations, where l is the locational variable, varying from 0 (e.g., equator) to $\underline{L}$ (e.g., the North Pole). They assume that only two crops are available, and i is the crop indicator, which is assuming the value 1 for a warmer-temperature crop (e.g., corn) and 2 for a lower-temperature crop (e.g., wheat). The production function per unit of land at time t for crop i at location l is $y_{it}(l) = f(h(s_t, l), t)$, where y_{it} is output, $h(s_t, l)$ is the temperature, which depends on the time t carbon stock s_t and location l. It is assumed that output increases with technological change, which, itself, increases over time. Output first increases and then decreases in temperature (thinking of extreme heat that causes crop damages). Temperature increases with the stock of carbon s_t and declines (for a given s_t) as l increases (i.e., locations get closer to the poles). At each location, a producer must allocate land between the two crops. Let δ_{it} denote the land share of crop i such that $\delta_{1t}(l) + \delta_{2t}(l) \leq 1$.

We assume that producers aim to maximize profits; profits per unit of land at location l are given by:

$$\begin{aligned}\pi_t(l) = \delta_{1t}(t)[&p_{1t}y_{1t}(l) - c_1(y_{1t}(l)) - T_1(t)]\\ &+ \delta_{2t}(t)[p_{2t}y_{1t}(l) - c_2(y_{2t}(l)) - T_2(t)],\end{aligned}$$

where p_{1t} and p_{2t} are prices of goods 1 and 2 at period t, c_1 and c_2 are the cost of production per acre as functions of output. We assume that marginal cost is positive and increasing in output and that there are transition costs from increasing the share of crop i, at period t. We denote this transition cost per unit of land as $T_i(t)$. So, land allocation at period t and location l is determined by choosing the land share of the technologies and their output per acre to maximize profits per acre, $\pi_t(l)$. This is a micro-land allocation problem. By aggregating over all land to obtain supply to each of the crops, as equated with demand, one can solve a macro-problem that determines prices and aggregate quantity of the two crops.

The solution to the micro and macro problems is discussed by Lu *et al.* (2021). Their analysis suggests that climate change will invoke a transition away from the equator and toward the poles. Some lands near the equator will be deserted, and some lands near the poles will be reclaimed. Because of the transition costs, there may be a delay in the transition to a new land that may affect supply. However, their analysis suggests that the total agricultural productivity on a global level may not necessarily decrease with climate change after some adjustments, as production in the areas in Canada and Russia may replace lost productivity in Oklahoma and China. Furthermore, if technology continues to increase resiliency, there might not be a loss in production. The conceptual model thus suggests that total food production may not decrease under a changing climate. However, it may have very severe negative distributional effects; there may be new opportunities in Canada and Russia, but domestic markets in Mexico and several African countries will be damaged. So, the challenge of climate change is how to deal with these severe spatially heterogeneous effects.

There are several significant bodies of literature on the impact of climate change on agriculture. The Ricardian approach, pioneered by Mendelsohn *et al.* (1994) assesses the impact of climate change on yield and cost over space (translated as land rent per unit of land), suggesting the aggregated effect is not as big as the distributional effect. However, the approach was criticized for ignoring irrigation and other effects and a new econometric literature emerged, estimating the impact of climate change on crop yields (Schlenker *et al.*, 2005; Schlenker and Roberts, 2009; Deschênes and Greenstone, 2007; Fisher *et al.*, 2012; Burke and Emerick, 2016; Miao *et al.*, 2016; Malikov *et al.*, 2020).

Carter *et al.* (2018) connect the past performance of crop breeding with restricted capacity to indicate that technological innovation may overcome much of the yield losses caused by rising temperatures. Ortiz-Borbea *et al.* (2021) find that climate change might have reduced agricultural productivity gains in agriculture by 21%, but the losses are more substantial in developing countries. Since the utilization of agricultural biotechnology and other advanced technology in the developing world has been limited, there seems to be a significant possibility of maintaining and improving yield despite the effects of climate change in many regions, and this, combined with new farming opportunities in cold areas, suggest that aggregate food supply is much less of a problem associated with climate change than the significant losses in different locations.

While the effects of changing environmental conditions directly on agriculture are spatially determinant, the expansion of areas habitable for pests paints a darker picture. Skendžić *et al.* (2021) suggest that climate change would increase the range of multiple insects, the transmission of plant diseases, and the risk of overwintering the survival of insects and their invasiveness. Adaptation will require fast development and modification of pest control strategies.

Assessment of the impact of climate change on agriculture is a multistage process. One approach is to assess impacts on yield distributions at various locations, which depends on climatic scenarios, technology improvement, and policies. Yield changes will affect the profitability of different crops, potentially resulting in changes in land use, supplies of crops, and input demands. These changes, in turn, will affect prices and welfare distribution among groups. Several alternative modeling strategies to assess these impacts are reviewed by McCarl and Hertel (2018).

Yield effects were estimated econometrically and through simulations. Blanc and Schlenker (2017) review econometric studies using large panel data. These studies have identified nonlinear response functions that may indicate significant yield loss as temperatures increases. Lobell *et al.* (2011) suggest that global maize and wheat yields may decline significantly with climate change, eliminating the gains from technological improvement. However, the role of temperature in relation to soil humidity on yield is subject to ongoing research: a recent study by Lobell *et al.* (2020) documents that U.S. corn yield has become increasingly sensitive to drought, citing the increased plant density as one of many possible reasons.

Several papers present more ways agricultural economics can function with other fields of science to study the impact of climate change on agriculture. For instance, agricultural economists can work with scientists and obtain their assessment of yields, technologies, and pest dynamics, incorporate these impacts on supply to generate supply functions, and then intersect it with demand relationships to assess the overall effect. Adams *et al.* (1990) presented an early model integrating relationships from atmospheric science, plant science, and agricultural economics, along with the impact of climate change on temperature and carbon, suggesting that land-use patterns in the United States will shift with a growing reliance on irrigation, and the overall effects depend on the specification of the model. Fei *et al.* (2017) develop a simulation relying on multiple models of the impact of climate change on yields under different conditions, as well as a model of the grain market, indicating the relocation of wheat production could increase the relative share of soybean compared to corn, and reduce the acreage of cotton. Beach *et al.* (2015) combine economics, agronomy, and forestry simulations to assess the impact of climate change in the U.S., comparing scenarios where climate change is mitigated to those where it is unabated. The results suggested that there could be gains from enacting mitigation policies (e.g., carbon sequestration), particularly for agriculture, forestry, and ranchlands.

There is also plenty of literature concerning sea-level rise, an important consideration with vulnerabilities to coastal agriculture. For example, much of the population in Bangladesh and Pakistan is vulnerable to floods, and this vulnerability will drastically increase from climate change. Sea water intrusion will affect the land supply and groundwater supply. Global rice production could decline by 3%, increasing prices substantially (Chen *et al.*, 2012). Melting snow pacts mean that water storage is even more crucial: irrigation water supply stands to decrease by 40% in areas such as Central Asia, the Western U.S., and the Andes (Qin *et al.*, 2020). Mitigation to confront these effects includes building dams to contain and store runoff water.

2. Adaptation to Climate Change

Climate change will increase the likelihood of extreme events, including floods, storms, and typhoons. Thus, climate change adaptation will have to consider not only responses to average scenarios but also how to improve resiliency to extreme events. Mechanisms to protect against these events are crucial, such as dikes, grain silos, and even emergency response plans. The development of these mechanisms and capacities is a multidisciplinary effort where economists can gain input from other disciplines, and it is one of the challenges of future research.

Predictive capacity for weather and climate is another step to resiliency in the face of climate change, as one of the main challenges of engaging in both adaptation and mitigation strategies is uncertainty regarding the impacts of climate change at the macro and micro levels. Lemoine and Rudik (2017) develop a recursive integrated assessment model to develop decision trees and make decisions that involve major uncertainties at the macro level. At the micro level, being able to assess when and where snowmelt will occur is important to discover alternative water supplies. In this sense, increased resilience is a result of policy geared toward protecting and evacuating victims when the situation arises.

Fankhauser (2017) reviews some of the economic modeling approaches that are taken to assess adaptation strategies. An integrated assessment model that represents both the economic and biophysical conditions associated with a changing climate can be a starting point for assessing adaptation strategies, and they can provide a background on the conditions that require adaptation, as well as an assessment of changes in economic and climatic conditions over time (Kling *et al.*, 2017).

Econometric analysis is important to assess individual behavioral responses to different types of shocks and opportunities. For example, one could figure out how likely certain people are to adopt some technology within different locations, as well as the factors that shift the capacity to adopt. Burke and Emerick (2016) employ a long-differences approach to study the adaptation within U.S. agriculture; using corn as an example, they found that the long-run responsiveness of corn yield to overheating temperature changes is not statistically different from the short-run responsiveness. They, therefore, conclude that there is no clear adaptation in the corn yield to climate change. Yu *et al.* (2021) expand the long differences approach by allowing the responsiveness to differ over two periods far apart (e.g., 50 years) and find that there is a significant adaptation of U.S. corn and soybean yields to overheat temperature over the past six decades. Zhang *et al.* (2023) further expand the long differences approach by allowing the responsiveness of crop yield to climate to vary across both time and space. They find that for corn, about half of the studied counties experience adaptation while the other half experience no adaptation or even maladaptation to climate change.

On a more aggregated level, it is important to be able to use an economy-wide simulation model that may include general equilibrium models and programming models. Khanna and Zilberman (2012) demonstrate how different models that may address different degrees of detail can be used together to assess the impact of policies; in their case, land use changes that are associated with policies that aim to reduce greenhouse gas emissions. When it comes to specific situations, various decision-making tools have been proposed to address choices in specific situations, considering both economic and technological uncertainties. There are several microeconomic tools to assess individual choices, including cost-benefit analysis, cost-effectiveness analysis, as well as others to assess different dimensions of the impact of adaptation policies (Fankhauser, 2017). These calculations also distinguish between choices in the private and public sectors that point toward future collaboration, and the constraints on lower-income individuals with limited resources and those who are either climate deniers or have negative attitudes toward adaptation (Fankhauser, 2017).

There are further considerations that have to be taken into account for large-scale individual behavior: large-scale geoengineering that modify the vulnerability of continents requires international agreements and thus may result in conflict (Schneider, 1996). In this sense, geoengineering should be an extreme measure, a last resort that may be utilized only when mitigation has not been effective (Brown, 2010).

Zilberman *et al.* (2012) identify several strategies for adaptation to climate change in agriculture. First is investment and support for research and development that result in technological and institutional innovations. Second, once appropriate solutions for technologies are identified, mechanisms to enhance the adoption of new technologies and crops should be introduced. Frequently, adaptation to climate change may require shifting of crops across regions, as well as the development of new crop varieties that can overcome some of the challenges of climate change (e.g., drought-tolerant varieties). A third strategy that may occur when economic variability is limited is migration, a drastic strategy. The development of an international environment that will enable migration is a major challenge and the global community needs to develop mechanisms to enable migration and relocation of climate refugees. On this line, institutions have to focus on the changes stemming from shifting economic and trade activities, which would allow capitalizing on new conditions in response to climate change (Dellink *et al.*, 2017).

Regarding the first strategy mentioned above (i.e., innovations), a recent study by Moscona and Sastry (2023a) shows that agricultural innovation reduces the negative impact of climate change on U.S. agriculture by only 20%, indicating that innovation should not be relied upon as a sole approach of adaptation. Moreover, technological innovations mainly occur in developed countries, and those adaptations may not transfer well to developing countries. In another paper, Moscona and Sastry (2023b) show that this technology mismatch reduces global agricultural productivity by 58% while increasing inequality of productivity by 15%. It is crucial, therefore, to focus on R&D in developing countries to avoid such disparities.

The build-up of large inventories of commodities and the capacity to utilize them is another useful mechanism to stabilize uncertain supply situations, especially in agriculture (Wright, 2012). Insurance mechanisms for farmers and intermediaries can allow investment, stabilize income, and prevent some of the instability associated with climate change, but the design of a solid insurance program is a major challenge, and insurance may even hinder innovation (Surminski *et al.*, 2016; Miao, 2020). Additionally, consumers and producers who rely on supply chains will be even more vulnerable when adaptation is stunted (Reardon and Zilberman, 2018). For example, frequent droughts or floods may harm affected regions, as well as regions that export products to producers in the affected regions. Therefore, suppliers may develop diversified sourcing and enhanced inventory. However, the capacity to adapt will vary among different economic agents, and some groups may become more vulnerable to shocks. In these cases, transportation and infrastructure will have to change to include safeguards in the event of a shock. Finally, adaptation strategies should recognize the likelihood that major disaster events may occur, and the development of emergency aid is an important strategy for climate change adaptation.

3. Mitigation

Agriculture is a major contributor to climate change, especially through emissions of carbon and non-carbon dioxide GHGs, such as methane and nitrous oxide. Agriculture can contribute to mitigation by reducing the emission of these GHGs, providing cleaner alternatives to fossil fuels, and by sequestering carbon through various agricultural and biological practices.

Paustian *et al.* (2001) suggest three avenues for agricultural mitigation of GHGs. First, sequestering carbon by moving to low and non-tillage practices as well as growing more environmentally friendly cover crops. They furthermore suggest that grazing practices can be enhanced by using improved species, sowing legumes, fertilizing, and irrigating. Other activities for carbon sequestration are restoring degraded soils and ecosystems, reforesting and afforesting, retiring marginal land through programs such as the conservation reserve program, and controlling desertification. Second, farmers could reduce nitrous oxide emissions through more precise nitrogen application, planting genetically improved varieties, and the use of cover crops, and better management of animal and food waste to reduce leakages, involving the storage of wastes anaerobically. Third, methane emission could be reduced through fermentation from livestock manure, reduction of waste of livestock, and residue burning. This may require technology like introducing new varieties, changing feeding ratios, changing waste management, and improving storage practices. Production of biofuels is another important avenue for reducing GHG emissions as they replace more carbon-intensive fossil fuels.

Rosenzweig and Tubiello (2007) suggest that carbon sequestration can be an effective mitigation strategy that prevents carbon emissions from agriculture and restores soil carbon that was emitted in the past. Regarding sequestration, the strategy addresses the one-third of carbon dioxide emissions in the atmosphere that come from land use (Lal, 2004), but it may only capture up to half of this total. Therefore, mitigation has to be considered in relation to adaptation (Rozenweig and Tubiello, 2007). However, farmers themselves may stand to gain through mitigation strategies, as they often involve more efficient yields.

Introducing all these new technological changes requires significant policy changes and incentives to modify behavior, such as changes in land use practices, adoption of new technologies, and improved management of waste products from animal and agricultural production. Policies must be incorporated at multiple levels—the national and international levels—since GHGs are global externalities that will not be managed correctly unless some mutual agreement, monitoring, and accounting exist. One key element to successful policy is full GHG accounting from all agricultural activities, both in terms of land use, crop production, and animal waste. This calls for the use of the tools of life cycle analysis that can and should be adjusted to incorporate economic principles (Rajagopal *et al.*, 2017). Effective emission accounting needs to be able to assign responsibility for emissions to the source: there has to be a way to track carbon fees and subsidies and evaluate compliance with regulation. Because many agricultural emissions are non-point sources, mechanisms have to point to observable behavior. For example, one may estimate greenhouse gas emissions based on known acreage, crop production, and technologies employed on-farm.

One of the main challenges of policies to reduce greenhouse gas emissions is dealing with additivity issues, especially permanence. A farmer may move to non-tillage, and their land may sequester carbon for multiple years, but changes in prices or other conditions may lead a farmer to de-plow the field and emit much of the sequestrated carbon. Incentives can be important to reducing the risk of deplowing and retaining the appeal of sequestration activities for landowners (Thamo and Pannell, 2016). Feng *et al.* (2002) develop a dynamic model to investigate the optimal path of emission sequestration and carbon stocks. They suggest efficient carbon sequestration with three mechanisms: a pay-as-you-go system, contracting, and carbon annuities. Van't Veld and Plantinga (2005) suggest that the timing of sequestration may be affected by the price of carbon, and when one expects carbon price to decrease over time, conservation will be delayed. Another challenge is to make sure individuals get paid for GHG mitigation activities that would not have been done rather than activities that would have been performed anyway (Konidari and Mavrakis, 2007).

McCarl and Schneider (2001) develop a mathematical programming model that relies on multidisciplinary data to assess the costs and impacts of greenhouse gas mitigation in agriculture and forestry in the U.S. They show that optimal policies depend on the price of carbon. Their analysis incorporates the agricultural crop, livestock, and forestry sectors. They find that local strategies to reduce carbon mitigation include carbon sequestration, afforestation, and livestock-related non-carbon emissions. High-price carbon mitigation may lead to changes in forestry practices and biofuels. Van Meijl *et al.* (2018) project that, by assessing integration, partial equilibrium, biophysical crop models, and computer-generated equilibrium models, there would be a negative but small impact on agriculture by 2050. However, mitigation strategies that aim to contain temperature increases by 2°C have a significant impact on global agricultural production. Their results vary based on modeling, basic economic assumptions, and policy.

Climate change mitigation may play a major role in agriculture in the future, depending on policies. Different mitigation strategies may be introduced at different locations, and mitigation strategies will change land use patterns as well as patterns of trade. Developing the capacity to assess the impact of mitigation is a major challenge to economists and will require further development of predictive multidisciplinary models.

4. Climate Smart Agriculture

The current centuries have witnessed both the unraveling of the Kyoto Protocol and the limitations of the Paris Climate Accords. There has been a realization, then, that environmental adaptation does not take precedence over all societal factors. Climate-smart agriculture (CSA), which harmonizes the development of food systems, especially in developing countries (Lipper *et al.*, 2014), with other objectives by having incentive-compatible mechanisms (Groves and Ledyard, 1987), will really be smart in achieving its objectives.

The notion of CSA led to a research agenda that aimed to develop technological solutions and policy tools that result in changes in agricultural systems that will both enhance productivity and well-being, as well as address climate change. The notion of climate-smart agriculture and its associated policies have evolved with climate change policies. As far back as the Kyoto Protocol, CSA was offering a framework for projects in developing countries that could earn the support of the people and governments there. Over time, climate-smart agriculture activities emphasize both adaptation and mitigation activities that provide new income opportunities and growth. It entails researching, utilizing, and adopting new technologies that provide new opportunities to address climate change and contribute to sustainable growth. Thus, CSA is consistent with the utilization of modern biotechnologies and other advanced technologies in developing countries around the world (Lipper *et al.*, 2017).

A key element of CSA is the development of innovation and associated supply. However, there exist several obstacles to implementation, and policies have evolved to overcome these constraints. A lack of technical knowledge on the impact of climate change and the properties of different solutions requires investment in R&D and mechanisms for technology transfer across locations. Access to technologies may be hampered by intellectual property, and thus it is useful to develop mechanisms that would allow special access to technologies, especially those that serve developing countries

(Graff and Zilberman, 2001). Another constraint is regulation: precaution is often warranted, but regulation has to balance benefits with the risks in order to avoid missing the adoption of beneficial technologies. Adoption of some of the new climate-smart solutions needs to enhance community participation, and therefore to develop technologies that fit the needs of the community. Solutions require finance, and because of the positive externalities associated with CSA, it is important to have targeted farms, and the global-social benefit will be considered so that the cost of finance will be reduced. As noted previously in the chapter, effective solutions need to account for barriers to adoption, so it is useful to integrate incentives such as including extension activities, demonstrations, and discounted pricing that will accelerate adoption and lead to learning by doing and learning by using (Lipper *et al.*, 2017).

Adaptation to climate change requires a new environmental thinking and framework. The traditional thinking of environmental groups is to preserve, protect, and conserve. However, in a changing world, one must transition to methods of controlling climate change and sustaining the improvements to human wellbeing (Gates, 2022). Preservation is challenging in an evolving world, and we need to find a new balance of change with environmental protection. One must recognize that different priorities in the developing world result in diverging policies. While the developing world is interested in food security and increasing well-being, the developed world places more emphasis on preservation. CSA represents a strategy that enforces mitigation while maintaining preservation ideals, and it embraces new technologies that may enable sustainable development (Belton *et al.*, 2020).

5. Conclusion

Climate change will dramatically affect agricultural systems, so developing policies and technologies to address climate change should be a major emphasis of environmental policy research. This research should assess the impacts of climate change on agriculture, identify alternative mechanisms for adaptation and mitigation, and recognize that the solutions to climate change need to be achieved using climate-smart policies that address other societal issues.

Climate change consideration emphasizes the development and adoption of innovations that allow adaptation and mitigation. They include drought and heat tolerance, pest control strategies, technologies that enhance input-use efficiency of water and other inputs, mechanisms to quickly identify and respond to changes in weather, mechanisms that lengthen shelf life, and resilience of livestock to respond to weather conditions. In addition to technological innovation, there is a need to develop institutions to facilitate peaceful migration and relocation in response to climate change, mechanisms to relocate rights to natural resources that will become productive as the weather is changing, institutions that will allow low-cost flood protection and storage facilities (Lipper *et al.*, 2017). Many of these new technologies require the use of modern biotechnologies and innovations. In some cases, these technologies will lead to drastic changes in land use and may affect ecosystems, sometimes negatively, at least in the short run.

Several promising technological directions have been identified to address climate change, including carbon capture and sequestration, battery storage systems, improved air conditioning, solar microgrids, nuclear energy, and new porous materials. These technologies have mostly relied on breakthroughs in physics, but the 21st century is likely to enjoy new capabilities developed by the life sciences and biology. These solutions include modern biotechnologies, like GMOs and CRISPR, that develop new traits to accelerate photosynthesis, fix nitrogen, and produce alternative meats. Algae can play a major role in sequestering carbon, insects can provide new sources of protein and minimize waste and thus reduce emissions, soil and plants can sequester carbon, compost can serve as a carbon sink, biofuels can provide fuel for airlines, trucks, and boats, especially for the reduction of emissions associated with the production of nitrogen, and lumber can be used for housing. Finally, wind and solar energy represent further solutions, but they are likely to compete with agriculture for land. Pascaris (2021) suggests that introducing solar energy in rural locations encounters objection because of its impact on land use, but developing technology and policies that enhance cooperation between energy and agriculture may increase income and are part of smart government policies (Miao and Khanna, 2020).

Developing new technological solutions requires significant institutional and policy change, challenging agricultural and environmental policy research. This research should have multiple priorities. First, assess the benefit of new technologies combining economic and scientific knowledge. Second, design solutions that allow efficient resource allocation, inducing economic agents to pay the price of carbon emissions. Third, understand public acceptance of new technologies and develop new policies that enhance the adoption of socially desirable technologies. Fourth, understand the political economy of climate change and assist in developing international and domestic mechanisms to address the issues of climate change in general and especially in climate change and natural resources. Fifth, better understand the operation of the supply chain in natural resources and develop mechanisms that lead to a more efficient market and supply chain (Rausser and Zilberman, 2022).

References

Adams, R.M., C. Rosenzweig, R.M. Peart, J.T. Ritchie, B.A. McCarl, J.D. Glyer, R.B. Curry, J.W. Jones, K.J. Boote, and L.H. Allen. 1990. Global Climate Change and US Agriculture. *Nature* 345: 219–224.

Beach, R.H., Y. Cai, A. Thomson, X. Zhang, R. Jones, B.A. McCarl, A. Crimmins *et al.* 2015. Climate Change Impacts on US Agriculture and Forestry: Benefits of Global Climate Stabilization. *Environmental Research Letters* 10(9): 095004.

Belton, B., T. Reardon, and D. Zilberman. 2020. Sustainable Commoditization of Seafood. *Nature Sustainability* 3(9): 677–684.

Blanc, E. and W. Schlenker. 2017. The Use of Panel Models in Assessments of Climate Impacts on Agriculture. *Review of Environmental Economics and Policy* 11(2): 258–279.

Brown, M.A. 2010. Policy Update: The Multiple Policy Dimensions of Carbon Management: Mitigation, Adaptation and Geoengineering. *Carbon Management* 1(1): 27–33.

Burke, M. and K. Emerick. 2016. Adaptation to Climate Change: Evidence from US Agriculture. *American Economic Journal: Economic Policy* 8(3): 106–140.

Carter, C., X. Cui, D. Ghanem, and P. Mérel. 2018. Identifying the Economic Impacts of Climate Change on Agriculture. *Annual Review of Resource Economics* 10: 361–380.

Chen, C.C., B.A. McCarl, and C.C. Chang. 2012. Climate Change, Sea Level Rise and Rice: Global Market Implications. *Climatic Change* 110(3–4): 543–560.

Dellink, R., H. Hwang, E. Lanzi, and J. Chateau. 2017. *International Trade Consequences of Climate Change.* OECD Trade and Environment Working Papers, OECD Publishing.

Deschênes, O. and M. Greenstone. 2007. The Economic Impacts of Climate Change: Evidence from Agricultural Output and Random Fluctuations in Weather. *The American Economic Review* 97(1): 354–385.

Fankhauser, S. 2017. Adaptation to Climate Change. *Annual Review of Resource Economics* 9: 209–230.

Fei, C.J., B.A. McCarl, and A.W. Thayer. 2017. Estimating the Impacts of Climate Change and Potential Adaptation Strategies on Cereal Grains in the United States. *Frontiers in Ecology and Evolution* 5: 62.

Feng, H., J. Zhao, and C.L. Kling. 2002. The Time Path and Implementation of Carbon Sequestration. *American Journal of Agricultural Economics* 84(1): 134–149.

Fisher, A.C., W.M. Hanemann, M.J. Roberts, and W. Schlenker. 2012. The Economic Impacts of Climate Change: Evidence from Agricultural Output and Random Fluctuations in Weather: Comment. *American Economic Review* 102(7): 3749–3760.

Gates, B. 2022. *How to Avoid a Climate Disaster: The Solutions We Have and the Breakthroughs We Need.* Penguin Random House LLC, New York.

Graff, G., and D. Zilberman. 2001. Towards an Intellectual Property Clearinghouse for Agricultural Biotechnology. *IP Strategy Today* 3: 1–13.

Groves, T. and J. Ledyard. 1987. Incentive Compatibility since 1972. *Information, Incentives, and Economic Mechanisms: Essays in Honor of Leonid Hurwicz* 84(2): 48–111.

Khanna, M. and D. Zilberman. 2012. Modeling the Land-Use and Greenhouse-Gas Implications of Biofuels. *Climate Change Economics* 3(3): 1250016.

Kling, C.L., R.W. Arritt, G. Calhoun, and D.A. Keiser. 2017. Integrated Assessment Models of the Food, Energy, and Water Nexus: A Review and an Outline of Research Needs. *Annual Review of Resource Economics* 9: 143–163.

Konidari, P. and D. Mavrakis. 2007. A Multi-Criteria Evaluation Method for Climate Change Mitigation Policy Instruments. *Energy Policy* 35(12): 6235–6257.

Lal, R. 2004. Soil Carbon Sequestration Impacts on Global Climate Change and Food Security. *Science* 304(5677): 1623–1627.

Lemoine, D. and I. Rudik. 2017. Steering the Climate System: Using Inertia to Lower the Cost of Policy. *American Economic Review* 107(10): 2947–2957.

Lipper, L., P. Thornton, B.M. Campbell, T. Baedeker, A. Braimoh, M. Bwalya, P. Caron *et al.* 2014. Climate-Smart Agriculture for Food Security. *Nature Climate Change* 4(12): 1068–1072.

Lipper, L., N. McCarthy, D. Zilberman, S. Asfaw, and G. Branca. 2017. *Climate Smart Agriculture: Building Resilience to Climate Change*. Springer Nature.

Lobell, D.B., J.M. Deines, and S.D. Tommaso. 2020. Changes in the Drought Sensitivity of US Maize Yields. *Nature Food* 1, 729–735.

Lobell, D.B., W. Schlenker, and J. Costa-Roberts. 2011. Climate Trends and Global Crop Production since 1980. *Science* 333(6042): 616–620.

Lu, X., J. Buchsbaum, and D. Zilberman. 2021. Economics of the Impact of Climate Change on Agriculture, F. Castillo, M. Wehner and D.A. Stone (Eds.), *Extreme Events and Climate Change: A Multidisciplinary Approach*. Elsevier, Amsterdam.

Malikov, Emir, R. Miao, and J. Zhang. 2020. Distributional and Temporal Heterogeneity in the Climate Change Effects on U.S. Agriculture. *Journal of Environmental Economics and Management* 104: 1–10.

McCarl, B.A. and T.W. Hertel. 2018. Climate Change as an Agricultural Economics Research Topic. *Applied Economic Perspectives and Policy* 40(1): 60–78.

McCarl, B.A. and U.A. Schneider. 2001. Greenhouse Gas Mitigation in US Agriculture and Forestry. *Science* 294(5551): 2481–2482.

Mendelsohn, R., W.D. Nordhaus, and D. Shaw. 1994. The Impact of Global Warming on Agriculture: A Ricardian Analysis. *The American Economic Review* 89: 753–771.

Miao, R. 2020. Climate, Insurance, and Innovation: The Case of Drought and Innovations in Drought-Tolerant Traits in U.S. Agriculture. *European Review of Agricultural Economics* 47(5): 1826–1860.

Miao, R. and M. Khanna. 2020. Harnessing Advances in Agricultural Technologies to Optimize Resource Utilization in the Food-Energy-Water Nexus. *Annual Review of Resource Economics* 12: 65–85.

Miao, R., M. Khanna, and H. Huang. 2016. Responsiveness of Crop Yield and Acreage to Price and Climate. *American Journal of Agricultural Economics* 98(1): 191–211.

Moscona, J. and Sastry, K. 2023a. Does Directed Innovation Mitigate Climate Damage? Evidence from US Agriculture. *Quarterly Journal of Economics* 138(2): 637–701.

Moscona, J. and Sastry, K. 2023b. Inappropriate Technology: Evidence from Global Agriculture. Working Paper. Harvard University.

Ortiz-Bobea, A., T.R. Ault, C.M. Carrillo, R.G. Chambers, and D.B. Lobell. 2021. Anthropogenic Climate Change Has Slowed Global Agricultural Productivity Growth. *Nature Climate Change* 11(4): 306–312.

Pascaris, A.S., C. Schelly, L. Burnham, and J.M. Pearce. 2021. Integrating Solar Energy with Agriculture: Industry Perspectives on the Market, Community, and Socio-Political Dimensions of Agrivoltaics. *Energy Research & Social Science* 75: 102023.

Paustian, K., B. Babcock, J.L. Hatfield, R. Lal, B.A. McCarl, S. McLaughlin, C. Rice *et al.* 2001. Agricultural Mitigation of Greenhouse Gases: Science and Policy Options. In *2001 Conference Proceedings, First National Conference on Carbon Sequestration*. Washington, DC: Conference on Carbon Sequestration, 2001.

Qin, Y., J.T. Abatzoglou, S. Siebert, L.S. Huning, A. AghaKouchak, J.S. Mankin, C. Hong, D. Tong, S.J. Davis, and N.D. Mueller. 2020. Agricultural Risks from Changing Snowmelt. *Nature Climate Change* 10(5): 459–465.

Rajagopal, D., C. Vanderghem, and H.L. MacLean. 2017. Life Cycle Assessment for Economists. *Annual Review of Resource Economics* 9: 361–381.

Rausser, G. and D. Zilberman. 2022. Resource Economics and Modern Science to the Rescue. *Annual Review of Resource Economics* 14: v–xvi.

Reardon, T. and D. Zilberman. 2018. Climate Smart Food Supply Chains In Developing Countries in an Era of Rapid Dual Change in Agrifood Systems and the Climate, L. Lipper, N. McCarthy, D. Zilberman, S. Asfaw, G. Branca (Eds.), *Climate Smart Agriculture: Building Resilience to Climate Change*, pp. 335–351. Springer Nature.

Rosenzweig, C. and F.N. Tubiello. 2007. Adaptation and Mitigation Strategies in Agriculture: An Analysis of Potential Synergies. *Mitigation and Adaptation Strategies for Global Change* 12: 855–873.

Schlenker, W., W.M. Hanemann, and A.C. Fisher. 2005. Will U.S. Agriculture Really Benefit from Global Warming? Accounting for Irrigation in the Hedonic Approach. *The American Economic Review* 95(1): 395–406.

Schlenker, W., and M.J. Roberts. 2009. Nonlinear Temperature Effects Indicate Severe Damages to U.S. Crop Yields Under Climate Change. *Proceedings of the National Academy of Sciences* 106(37): 15594–98.

Schneider, S.H. 1996. Geoengineering: Could — Or Should — We Do It? *Climatic Change* 33(3): 291–302.

Skendžić, S., M. Zovko, I.P. Živković, V. Lešić, and D. Lemić. 2021. The Impact of Climate Change on Agricultural Insect Pests. *Insects* 12(5): 440.

Surminski, S., L.M. Bouwer, and J. Linnerooth-Bayer. 2016. How Insurance Can Support Climate Resilience. *Nature Climate Change* 6(4): 333–334.

Thamo, T. and D.J. Pannell. 2016. Challenges in Developing Effective Policy for Soil Carbon Sequestration: Perspectives on Additionality, Leakage, and Permanence. *Climate Policy* 16(8): 973–992.

van Meijl, H., P. Havlik, H. Lotze-Campen, E. Stehfest, P. Witzke, I.P. Domínguez, B.L. Bodirsky *et al.* 2018. Comparing Impacts of Climate Change and Mitigation on Global Agriculture by 2050. *Environmental Research Letters* 13(6): 064021.

Van't Veld, K. and A. Plantinga. 2005. Carbon Sequestration or Abatement? The Effect of Rising Carbon Prices on the Optimal Portfolio of Greenhouse-Gas Mitigation Strategies. *Journal of Environmental Economics and Management* 50(1): 59–81.

Wright, B.D. 2012. International Grain Reserves and Other Instruments to Address Volatility in Grain Markets. *The World Bank Research Observer* 27(2): 222–260.

Yu, C., Miao, R. and Khanna, M. 2021. Maladaptation of U.S. Corn and Soybeans to a Changing Climate. *Scientific Reports* 11: 12351.

Zhang, J., E. Malikov, R. Miao, and P. Ghosh. Geography of Climate Change Adaptation in U.S. Agriculture. Working paper (2023), the Department of Agricultural Economics and Rural Sociology, Auburn University.

Zilberman, D., J. Zhao, and A. Heiman. 2012. Adoption Versus Adaptation, with Emphasis on Climate Change. *Annual Review of Resource Economics* 4: 27–53.

Epilogue: Sustainable Development

Sustainable development has become a major guiding principle for policymaking around the world. The notion of sustainable development, in a way, is an oxymoron given that "sustainable" implies preserving and staying in place, and "development" means moving forward. In practice, sustainable development is a compromise between the desire of the developed world to preserve and protect the environment and the developing world's wishes for progress. The Brundtland Commission defines sustainable development as "*development that meets the needs of the present without compromising the ability of future generations to meet their own needs*" (Brundtland, 1987). This definition of sustainable development is amenable to economic interpretation as optimization, subject to constraint. This definition comes from an anthropocentric perspective, as the benefits are viewed from human perspectives and may not be acceptable to some environmentalists.

There is a growing economic perspective on sustainable development. First, we will review some macro-economic approaches to sustainable development and then the micro approaches. In both cases, we will emphasize the implications of the notion to policymaking.

1. The Macro-Economic Approach to Sustainable Development

The surveys by Pearce *et al.* (1994) and Zilberman (2014) provide an overview of the growing macroeconomics of sustainable development, where the analysis of sustainable development is built on economic growth theory (Jones, 2016). One approach to sustainable development is to maximize the net present value of average utility under the constraint that average utility doesn't decline over time. A question is: What is the source of average utility? Is it solely consumption, or does it come in a multi-dimensional form? Many policymakers view sustainable development as a three-legged stool that includes economic, social, and environmental sustainability (Sachs, 2015), which may imply that utility comes from consumption, environmental amenities, and social well-being. Therefore, environmental policy has a role in public policy, given that environmental amenities provide utility. Furthermore, given heterogeneity among people and the concern about social sustainability, the pursuit of sustainable development may aim to protect the utility of the poor (say, the bottom 10%) over time and ensure that it does not decline. To do so, policymakers can either employ the max-min approach to maximize the utility of the lowest-well-being group over time or reduce the variability of the income of the poor.

Economic research on sustainable development also recognizes that the environment and society are subject to random shocks, such as natural disasters, pandemics, financial crises, political dramas, and wars. Therefore, resilience is a growing emphasis as a key element of sustainable development (Perrings, 2006). Namely, sustainable development policies must be developed to allow economic systems to withstand and recover from shocks, which implies that analysis of sustainable development must incorporate randomness and uncertainty, and solutions may need to be multiple-dimensional. Sustainable development policies may also require diversification of economic activities and increased capacity to move resources in response to shocks.

Consumption and environmental amenities are outcomes of production activities, and economic growth models have a specification of production systems. Some theoretical growth models, originating from Solow's pioneering work, present output as the outcome of variable inputs, especially labor and physical capital (Solow, 1994). However, as we model sustainable development, we have to recognize that there are even more variants of capital, including human, natural, and social. The stock of each type of capital changes over time. Physical capital could increase with investment and decline with depreciation. Human capital, which is the knowledge and skills of humans, could increase with education and investment in research and development but decline due to aging and depreciation. Natural capital, a combination of the regulatory forces of nature that provide environmental services (Bulte *et al.*, 2008), could decrease through mining and exploitation but, in turn, increase through restoration and care. Finally, social capital represents a difficult concept to define and measure, although it is generally viewed as a stock of social cohesion which includes trust, collective action, and reduced transaction costs. Several lines of research emphasize the importance of social arrangement and organization for economic growth, underlying the major contributions of social capital. Nobel Laureate Elinor Ostrom (2009) emphasizes the role of social arrangement in sustaining effective water systems in developing countries. Acemoglu *et al.* (2005) stress the crucial role of institutions in economic growth. Development of indicators of institutions and arrangements and other factors that contribute to social capital, and the factors that affect economics, is a major challenge.

Much economic analysis considers population growth is given. But, as Becker *et al.* (1999) argued, population choices are economic activities. Furthermore, countries like China and India have implemented policies that aim to affect population growth. Population change has also been crucial to understanding the environmental side of sustainable development.

The research on the economics of sustainable development distinguishes between the notion of weak sustainability and strong sustainability. The notion of weak sustainability recognizes significant substitution between different types of capital goods and the capacity of economic activities to restore and improve environmental conditions. The notion of strong sustainability limits the substitution between different types of capital and other inputs and emphasizes concern about irreversible outcomes. The assumptions of weak sustainability lead to increased investments in research and development and taking environmental risks; for example, increased mining of resources with the belief that alternatives will be available over time. Strong sustainability assumes that thresholds of environmental protections are very costly to exceed and, thereby, suggests more constraints in action. Leading economists developed a foundation for macroeconomics based on the two ideas, which we will demonstrate later in this epilogue. Most of this analysis assumes weak sustainability. One paramount scientific challenge is identifying humanity's constraints and where and when the weak or strong sustainability assumptions hold.

2. Quantitative Foundation for Measuring Sustainable Development

There is significant quantitative modeling of the macroeconomics of sustainable development based on the economic growth literature, which is a large and sophisticated literature. In this section, we provide an overview and some references that can lead the readers to study the topic in depth.

2.1. *Technological change as a function of economic activity*

Macro-analysis of sustainable development is constructed significantly upon the works of Robert Solow. Solow (1957) and other scholars of economic growth stated as a limitation of their models that changes in input like capital and labor could not explain all the changes in output. Solow's (1957) econometric analysis utilized time series of national data on the output and input of various nations to demonstrate that economic growth, measured by output, is caused by traditionally measured inputs plus a "residual." This residual, called *Total Factor Productivity* (TFP), measures the economy's long-term technological change.

The unexplained residual has been attributed to major factors associated with technological change, such as innovation, learning, and technological improvement. Early studies considered this technological change to be determined by forces outside the economic system, but new endogenous growth theories argue that technological change is an outcome of economic activities and is determined within the economic system (Romer, 1994). Technological change is frequently originated in research activities that result in knowledge, which has properties of a public good in that a large population can utilize it simultaneously. This property of research may lead to increasing economics of scale to production when inputs for innovation and knowledge are considered (Jones, 2022).

The challenge of sustainable development is substituting non-renewable resources and natural capital with human, physical, and social capital. Solow espouses the economic perspective toward sustainability by saying that almost all the natural environment and resources are substitutable (except for, perhaps, rare minerals and unique locations like Yosemite and the Grand Canyon). This perspective is consistent with "*Weak Sustainability*" to be distinguished from "*Strong Sustainability*", which limits the substitution of one form of capital or resource with another (Daly, 1990).[1,2]

2.2. *Alternative approaches to model weak sustainability*

There are two different approaches to modeling weak sustainability, which assumes that resources are interchangeable. One approach, which we will refer to as the Solow–Rawls (SR) approach, is more normative in that it aims to find a unique resource allocation over

---

[1]These two concepts of sustainability were first presented by Professor Daly at the Conference on Human Demography and Natural Resources, Stanford University, Hoover Institution and Morrison Institute, February 1–3, 1989, p. 15. See: www.popline.org/node/360084#sthash.gwfL2zbx.dpuf.

[2]Under Strong Sustainability, economic growth should be optimized subject to specific constraints setting a threshold that limits the extraction or depletion of specific resources. These concepts are explored in the following subsection.

time that will maximize the net expected discounted utility of consumption per capita, subject to three constraints: technological capacity, limits to various capital, and non-decreasing consumption. This approach calculates for each period the amount of capital and physical labor utilized, the output produced, resources extracted, and pollution generated, subject to the equation of motions of various types of capital and a constraint that the utility of consumption per capita does not decline over time. An illustration of this approach considers the case in which individuals gain utility from consumption and environmental quality, insofar as the aggregate utility does not decline over time.

A variation of this approach, referred to herein as the Arrow–Dasgupta (AD) approach, assumes greater flexibility of the utility function such that utility does not decline below some threshold over time (Arrow *et al.*, 2004). The AD approach has a strong element of accounting and measurement of actual national and global performance. It aims to measure whether actual aggregate resource allocation is consistent with the definition of sustainability by the Brundtland Commission. This approach developed several criteria before one can assess whether the evolution of the economies of nations follows a path leading to sustainable development. A major advantage of this approach is that under certain assumptions,[3] resource allocation can be achieved by a competitive economy with price incentives (taxes and subsidies) for non-market goods or externalities (Arrow *et al.*, 2004).

The AD approach starts from the assumption that sustainable development occurs when *intertemporal social welfare* is not declining over time, where intertemporal social welfare is defined as the sum of the net present values of the aggregate utility of consumption at a given moment in time, given the equations of motion of the various types of capital.[4] Arrow *et al.* (2004) suggest that this

[3]The aggregate production function demonstrates diminishing returns of scale and non-decreasing marginal costs.

[4]This sustainability criterion holds true if the sum of the net discounted present values of the utility of consumption from now to infinity is smaller or equal to the sum of the infinite discounted present values of utility of consumption from next year to infinity.

sustainability criterion holds if the economy's *productive base*, the sum of all the capital stocks used for the production and provision of services, does not decline over time. Thus, this sustainability criterion—of non-declining intertemporal social welfare—is akin to the non-declining productive base.

Further, this criterion implies that the value of the sum of all types of capital will not decline over time. This interpretation assumes that one can monetize the value of all types of capital and sum them. In a well-functioning economy, the value of each type of capital at each moment represents the sum of the discounted value of future benefits that this capital good will provide. The value of the sum of all types of capital can also be referred to as *genuine wealth*, and the change in the value of genuine wealth can be referred to as a *genuine investment*. This first sustainability criterion, which we denote AD1.1, states that the *rate of change of genuine investment is not declining over time.*

However, Arrow *et al.* (2004) realized that this sustainability criterion must be adjusted for population growth and technological change. Therefore, they suggested a modified criterion for sustainable development that compares the rate of change of genuine capital and population growth. This sustainability criterion, denoted as AD2.1, states that the *genuine investment per capita will not decline over time.* However, this criterion does not consider technological change (i.e., the Solow residue). Thus, the third criterion for sustainable development, which we denote as AD3, is that the *genuine investment per capita adjusted for technological change will not decline over time.* In particular,

$$\frac{genuine\ Investment}{genuine\ capital} - \frac{population\ growth}{Population\ size} - \frac{Total\ Factor\ Productivity}{output\ elasticity\ of\ genuine\ capital} \geq 0,$$

where the *output elasticity of genuine capital* (EGP) measures the contribution of genuine capital to growth. This technological change contributes to societal welfare at a growth rate equivalent to TFP/EGP in genuine capital. The inclusion of this fraction generates a measure of the overall change in productive capacity per capita, including the contribution of technology.

The AD sustainability indicators are a practical tool applied by Arrow *et al.* (2004) to various countries and regions. In general, the AD approach is especially valuable for assessing the state of resource allocation at present (based on AD3), but the present condition does not imply that it will hold in the future. The AD measures of sustainability provide an overall assessment of excess consumption (of our overall capital), interpreted as a suboptimal genuine investment. Arrow *et al.* (2004) highlighted several important findings:

(1) During the last three decades of the 20th century, genuine investment (AD1.1) was positive in most regions but negative in sub-Saharan Africa and the Middle East (where resource extraction was most concentrated).
(2) On the other hand, the growth rate of genuine capital per capita (AD2.1) was negative for most of the developing world (except China) due to the high rate of population growth in exceeding the rate of growth of genuine capital.
(3) The AD3 criterion may result in different outcomes predicted by the constrained expected net present value maximization, which accounts for environmental amenities and resource dynamics. Yet policies that aim to reduce pollution or set the optimal price for renewable or non-renewable resources, based on constrained net present value optimization, are likely to enhance sustainability measured by AD3.
(4) AD3 measurements show that sustainability declined in Sub-Saharan Africa and the Middle East, but did not change much in developing countries like Bangladesh, India, and Pakistan, and grew substantially in China (due to high investment rates in manufacturing and human capital). These findings indicate that AD3 tends to be lower than the growth rate of the Gross National Product (GNP). Some countries with a significant growth rate of GNP have a low negative measure of sustainability, like AD3.

The AD measures of sustainability are a work in progress. For instance, the monetizing of forest depletion and greenhouse gas

(GHG) emissions, as well as other elements contained in AD3, are lively debated and subject to much uncertainty. Therefore, presenting a confidence interval where the sustainability estimates may lie in with a high degree of statistical significance may be valuable. Furthermore, as we learn more about the costs of climate change and the value of biodiversity, the measure of sustainability may change. Finally, technology is evolving quickly and will remain a key source of uncertainty, captured by the Solow residue.

The AD and SR measures of sustainable development are complementary. The AD approach uses *ex-post* measurements reflecting choices made in the past and indicates the urgency of intervention in the future. The SR measures are *ex-ante* and suggest the best plan for future performance. However, these measures address issues of inter-temporal equity by providing conceptual frameworks and asking: do humans consume too much (globally and regionally)? Is the overall environmental situation improving — and which regions need to improve most? Answering these big questions is important, and thinking, in general, is crucial to developing an effective set of strategies to address environmental challenges. But policy implementation depends on the specifics. For example, the importance of focusing on a single species in developing environmental policies points to the emphasis on strong sustainability.

The macro perspective on sustainable development suggests the importance of enhancing the stock of different types of capital over time through physical investment, education, environmental protection, restoration, and action to improve trust and social cohesion. This range of activities, combined with efficient use of resources to increase net social benefit, is a policy foundation to pursue sustainable development. Developing rigorous theoretical and empirical economic research on sustainable development is a major challenge for the future. The studies mentioned above are the beginning of quantifying sustainable development, especially assuming weak sustainability. It is challenging to expand the theoretical foundation to analyze cases of strong sustainability and determine when each set of assumptions is appropriate. These lines of research are likely to change national accounting to incorporate environmental and social considerations.

3. Micro-Level Analysis of Sustainable Development

To develop management practices and policies based on sustainable development in agriculture, it is important to assess the impact of this concept at the micro-level (Zilberman, 2014). Sustainable development has implications both for analytical approaches and policy strategies. The implications of sustainable development in relation to research methodologies include:

(1) **Emphasis on multidisciplinary work:** As with environmental and resource economics, a basic understanding of biophysical relationships is crucial for economic modeling. To manage water well, one must understand the basic principles of hydrology and soil-water relationships. Pest control analysis requires an understanding of entomology and toxicology. This does not imply that the technologists need to be specialists in the field. Still, they need to understand key relationships and collaborators who can provide specific details. As Khanna (2022) suggested, applied economists not only need to have depth in economics but also some breadths in other fields to combine multidisciplinary work.

(2) **Production, pollution, and risk function:** Economics emphasizes the role of the production function that relates outputs to inputs. But economic activities have side effects that are important to consider in developing sustainable solutions. Therefore, pollution functions that relate different types of pollution to economic input and output levels are essential for the complete analysis of systems that consider externalities. Similarly, many economic activities, such as the use of pesticides, may result in risk. So, risk-generating functions that relate mortality probabilities to economic activities and recognize the procedures of contamination, exposure, and dose-response are essential to complete the analysis of economic activities.

(3) **Heterogeneity and randomness:** The simple economic analysis assumes certainty and identical firms. In reality, agents are different, and production activities are subject to random shocks. Therefore, it is important to explicitly recognize these conditions and develop policies that allow adaptations to different conditions and shocks. The notion of precision is increasing the productivity of inputs while reducing pollution; and resilience to shocks is crucial to develop sustainable solutions. Our analysis of the risk of adoption emphasizes the response to randomness and heterogeneity. The development of improved monitoring solutions (e.g., remote sensing and global positioning system), communication tools (e.g., the internet), better analytic tools (e.g., artificial intelligence), and better mobility tools (e.g., drones) allow the development of increased precision and fast adaptation to shocks.

(4) **Input-use efficiency:** The distinction between applied and effective inputs as well as the externalities caused by input residues are key features of agricultural systems. The development of methods that increase input-use efficiency, and thus conserve resources and reduce waste is necessary. But, having more precise technologies does not mean that they will be adopted, so policy intervention and supply chain design should be considered.

(5) **Supply chain and life cycle analysis:** Agriculture is part of the supply chain of food, fuels, and other products. Therefore, complete analysis in search of sustainable development requires analysis of the complete supply chain. Furthermore, innovation and product supply chains are associated with economic activities (Zilberman *et al.*, 2022). Because of the multiple links between economic activities and markets throughout the value chain, assessing the environmental impact of policies may require life cycle analysis from birth to death. Life cycle analysis methods have been developed by engineers and may need adjustment to be used in economic analysis. But this adjustment is essential and has some foundations to guide it (Rajagopal, 2017).

4. Conclusion: Avenues for Achieving Sustainable Development Solutions

We conclude by discussing several avenues for achieving sustainable development solutions. First, the transition from non-renewable resources to renewable resources. In principle, non-renewable resources are depletable, so their use is not sustainable. But even when they are abundant, their use may cause negative externalities, as with fossil fuels. Thus, transitioning to a renewable economy is one of the guiding principles of sustainable development. We can distinguish between two types of renewable resources. The first is physical renewables, such as energy from the sun, wind, and water. The second is living organisms, such as plants, animals, and others. Early in human history, humans mostly harvested living organisms. But, with the emergence of agriculture, they moved to animal husbandry systems. Humans invested in breeding and raising living organisms because they acquired higher yields and more controllable and cheaper harvesting. We transitioned from hunter-gatherer to agriculture; we now have a transition toward aquaculture, and with research, we may breed other species.

Second, adoption of conservation strategies to improve input-use efficiency and reduce residue. Such strategies are essential for adapting and mitigating climate change (Zilberman *et al.*, 2012). Policy design and implementation are necessary to create conservation technologies, adapt them for different applications (crops and environment), and enhance adaptations.

Third, recycling. Reusing materials reduces the financial and environmental toll of production. Additionally, recycling plays a valuable role in the global economy, as second-hand markets for products, like clothes and cars, provide an efficient means for goods to make their way to developing countries. Recycling is especially critical when it comes to non-renewable resources like metals. One of the most notable causes of crime worldwide is reusing equipment (car parts) and precious materials. So, there is an important role in analyzing the economics of recycling, its implications, and the role of policies to improve it.

Embedded within the idea of recycling is the circular economy. Every good and product goes through processes of life and death, and its residues are recycled. Production systems have been, historically, linear, considering the inputs and outputs that are needed and useful while ignoring the residues. In contrast, a circular economy recognizes these residues and treats them. Policies to control environmental side effects may transform the linear economy into a circular economy and lead to increased resource conservation and reuse.

Lastly, the bioeconomy. The bioeconomy is an economic sector that utilizes natural resources and takes advantage of new biological capabilities. It has a traditional component, which involves agriculture, fishery, forestry, agrotourism, bioenergy, and green chemistry, and was essential for the development of human civilization to build the capacity to preserve food and enhance health. The modern component of the bioeconomy involves science-based discoveries among medical treatment, sequestration of carbon, and the development of new modes of production of chemicals and energy. These, according to Zilberman *et al.* (2013), have important implications for continued advancements in longevity for humanity and the environment.

However, there are a few major challenges for the development of bioeconomy. First of all, regulations have to improve procedural safety. Currently, regulations are inconsistent globally and do not provide incentives to integrate biotechnology solutions across nations. Regulatory inconsistency and uncertainty are the major barriers to the expansion of the bioeconomy and deter investments and product development. Some countries are even considering banning modern biotechnology. Moreover, there must be investment in research for biotechnological innovations. The scientific knowledge base for the bioeconomy is in its infancy, and further expansion of research and education in the life sciences, microbial and cell biology, and related organismal technology will identify new mechanisms and technological opportunities. However, technology development is likely to encounter many barriers, especially when it comes to technologies that can address environmental challenges and provide solutions to problems that afflict the poor and developing nations. Therefore, introducing policies that will further support the commercialization of biotechnologies that can address the challenges of climate change and food security may require government support. Policies that will provide incentives to address climate change, e.g., support for carbon sequestration or reduction of greenhouse gas emissions, may benefit the bioeconomy. Finally, the bioeconomy may provide capabilities that may endanger humanity, e.g., biological weapons. International institutions must develop mechanisms to avoid such development and use while allowing biotechnological research to advance.

References

Acemoglu, D., S. Johnson, and J.A. Robinson. 2005. Institutions as a Fundamental Cause of Long-Run Growth. *Handbook of Economic Growth* 1: 385–472.

Arrow, K., P. Dasgupta, L. Goulder, G. Daily, P. Ehrlich, G. Heal, S. Levin *et al.* 2004. Are We Consuming Too Much? *Journal of Economic Perspectives* 18(3): 147–172.

Becker, G., E.L. Glaeser, and K.M. Murphy. 1999. Population and Economic Growth. *American Economic Review* 89(2): 145–149.

Brundtland, G.H. 1987. *World Commission on Environment and Development. Our Common Future.* Oxford University Press, Oxford.

Bulte, E.H., L. Lipper, R. Stringer, and D. Zilberman. 2008. Payments for Ecosystem Services and Poverty Reduction: Concepts, Issues, and Empirical Perspectives. *Environment and Development Economics* 13(3): 245–254.

Daly, H.E. 1990. Sustainable Development: From Concept and Theory to Operational Principles. *Population and Development Review* 16: 25–43.

Jones, C.I. 2016. The Facts of Economic Growth. *Handbook of Macroeconomics* 2: 3–69.

Jones, C.I. 2022. The Past and Future of Economic Growth: A Semi-Endogenous Perspective. *Annual Review of Economics* 14: 125–152.

Khanna, M. 2022. Breakthroughs at the Disciplinary Nexus: Rewards and Challenges for Applied Economists. *American Journal of Agricultural Economics* 104(2): 475–492.

Ostrom, E. 2009. A General Framework for Analyzing Sustainability of Social-Ecological Systems. *Science* 325(5939): 419–422.

Pearce, D.W., G.D. Atkinson, and W.R. Dubourg. 1994. The Economics of Sustainable Development. *Annual Review of Energy and the Environment* 19(1): 457–474.

Perrings, C. (2006). Resilience and Sustainable Development. *Environment and Development Economics* 11(4): 417–427.

Rajagopal, D., C. Vanderghem, and H.L. MacLean. 2017. Life Cycle Assessment for Economists. *Annual Review of Resource Economics* 9(1): 1–21.

Romer, P.M. 1994. The Origins of Endogenous Growth. *The Journal of Economic Perspectives* 8(1): 3–22.

Sachs, J.D. 2015. *The Age of Sustainable Development.* Columbia University Press.

Solow, R.M. 1957. Technical Change and the Aggregate Production Function. *The Review of Economics and Statistics* (1957): 312–320.

Solow, R.M. 1994. Perspectives on Growth Theory. *Journal of Economic Perspectives* 8(1): 45–54.

Zilberman, D. 2014. Fellows Address: The Economics of Sustainable Development. *American Journal of Agricultural Economics* 96(2): 385–396.

Zilberman, D., J. Zhao, and A. Heiman. 2012. Adoption versus Adaptation, with Emphasis on Climate Change. *Annual Review of Resource Economics* 4(1): 27–53.

Zilberman, D., E. Kim, S. Kirschner, S. Kaplan, and J. Reeves. 2013. Technology and the Future Bioeconomy. *Agricultural Economics* 44(s1): 95–102.

Zilberman, D., T. Reardon, J. Silver, L. Lu, and A. Heiman. 2022. From the Laboratory to the Consumer: Innovation, Supply Chain, and Adoption with Applications to Natural Resources. *Proceedings of the National Academy of Sciences* 119(23): e2115880119.

Appendix A

Elements of Optimization Theory

In this appendix we briefly introduce some basic techniques for static and dynamic optimization that are often used in agricultural economics. These techniques include Kuhn–Tucker conditions for constrained optimization, linear programming with constraints, the bordered Hessian and its applications in comparative statics, decision-making over time, and finally, optimal control. For complete treatment of these topics, we refer readers to Chiang (1992), Dixit and Pindyck (1994), as well as Simon and Blume (1994).

1. Kuhn–Tucker Conditions

With reference to Figure 1, consider the problem

$$\max_{x} f(x)$$

$$\text{s.t.} \quad x \geq 0,$$

where $f(\cdot)$ is a concave function.

If function $f(x)$ is f^A as depicted in Figure 1, the optimum occurs at x_1, where $(df^A/dx)|_{x^*=x_1} = 0$. In the case of f^B in Figure 1, the global maximum is not achievable so that the constrained optimum

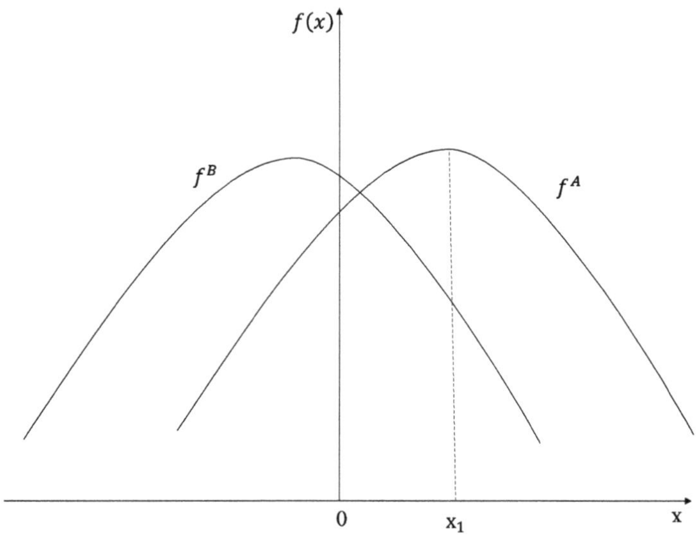

Figure 1. A constrained maximization problem.

occurs at $x = 0$, where $(df^B/dx)|_{x^*=0} < 0$. Therefore, in a general case, the first-order conditions can be characterized by

$$f_x(x^*) \leq 0, \qquad x^* f_x(x^*) = 0,$$

where $f_x(x)$ is defined as $df(x)/dx$.

Consider now

$$\max_{\mathbf{x}} f(\mathbf{x})$$

$$\text{s.t.} \quad g(\mathbf{x}) \leq \mathbf{b}, \quad \text{and} \quad \mathbf{x} \geq 0,$$

where $\mathbf{x} = (x_1, \ldots, x_n)'$, $g(\mathbf{x}) = (g^1(\mathbf{x}), \ldots, g^m(\mathbf{x}))'$, and $\mathbf{b} = (b_1, \ldots, b_m)'$.

Form the Lagrangian

$$L = f(\mathbf{x}) + \boldsymbol{\lambda}'[\mathbf{b} - g(\mathbf{x})],$$

where $\boldsymbol{\lambda} = (\lambda_1, \ldots, \lambda_m)$.

Then the Kuhn–Tucker conditions can be written as

$$L_{x_i} = f_{x_i}(\mathbf{x}^*) - (\boldsymbol{\lambda}^*)' g_{x_i}(\mathbf{x}^*) \le 0, \quad \forall i = 1, \ldots, n, \tag{1}$$

$$x_i^* \cdot L_{x_i} = x_i^*[f_{x_i}(\mathbf{x}^*) - (\boldsymbol{\lambda}^*)' g_{x_i}(\mathbf{x}^*)] = 0, \quad \forall i = 1, \ldots, n, \tag{2}$$

$$L_{\lambda_j} = b_j - g^j(\mathbf{x}^*) \ge 0, \quad \forall j = 1, \ldots, m, \tag{3}$$

$$\lambda_j^* L_{\lambda_j} = \lambda_j^*[b_j - g^j(\mathbf{x}^*)] = 0, \quad \forall j = 1, \ldots, m, \tag{4}$$

$$\mathbf{x}^* \ge 0, \tag{5}$$

$$\boldsymbol{\lambda}^* \ge 0. \tag{6}$$

These conditions are sufficient if $f(\cdot)$ is quasiconcave and $g(\cdot)$ is quasiconvex.

2. Linear Programming and Constrained Optimization

2.1. *Primal vs. Dual*

Consider the following optimization problem:

$$\max_{\mathbf{x}} \mathbf{c}'\mathbf{x}$$

$$\text{s.t.} \quad A\mathbf{x} \le \mathbf{b}, \text{ and } x \ge 0,$$

where $\mathbf{x}$ is an $n \times 1$ vector of choice variables (e.g., production levels); $\mathbf{c}$ is an $n \times 1$ vector of net returns of the choice $\mathbf{x}$; A is the $m \times n$ matrix of technical coefficients, where the element $\{a_{ij}\}$ indicates the requirement of resource i needed to support one unit of choice j; and $\mathbf{b}$ is the $m \times 1$ vector of resource availability. In this problem, we have n variables and m constraints, with $n > m$.

It is an optimization problem subject to inequality constraints. An optimal solution can be characterized by the necessary Kuhn–Tucker conditions. We first write the Lagrangian as

$$L = \mathbf{c}'\mathbf{x} + \boldsymbol{\lambda}'[\mathbf{b} - A\mathbf{x}],$$

where $\boldsymbol{\lambda}$ is an $m \times 1$ vector of *shadow prices*.

The optimality conditions are given by

$$L_{\mathbf{x}} = \mathbf{c} - A'\boldsymbol{\lambda} \leq 0,$$
$$L_{\boldsymbol{\lambda}} = \mathbf{b} - A\mathbf{x} \leq 0,$$

and the following *complementary slackness conditions*:

$$x_i L_{x_i} = x_i[c_i - \sum_{j=1}^{m}(\lambda_j a_{ji})] = 0, \quad \forall i = 1, \ldots, n,$$

$$\lambda_j L_{\lambda_j} = \lambda_j[b_j - \sum_{i=1}^{n}(a_{ji}x_i)] = 0, \quad \forall j = 1, \ldots, m.$$

This problem is called the *primal.*

Now consider the following:

$$\min_{\boldsymbol{\lambda}} \boldsymbol{\lambda}'\mathbf{b}$$
$$\text{s.t.} \quad A'\boldsymbol{\lambda} \geq \mathbf{c}, \text{ and } \boldsymbol{\lambda} \geq 0,$$

where the parameters are defined as above. This optimization problem is called the dual.

The fundamental result in linear programming is that the primal and the dual have the same first-order necessary conditions. Readers can easily prove this conclusion by using Kuhn–Tucker conditions (hint: for the Lagrangian of the dual problem, set the Lagrangian multipliers as $\mathbf{x}$). These lead to some of the following results:

1. At the optimal solution, $\mathbf{c}'\mathbf{x}^* = \boldsymbol{\lambda}^{*\prime}\mathbf{b}$ or, in a scalar notation,
$$\sum_{i=1}^{n} c_i x_i^* = \sum_{j=1}^{m} \lambda_j^* b_j;$$
2. if $\sum_{i=1}^{n} a_{ji}x_i^* < b_j$ then $\lambda_j^* = 0$;
3. if $\sum_{j=1}^{m} a_{ji}\lambda_j^* > c_i$, then $x_i^* = 0$.

2.2. *The bordered Hessian and its applications*

Consider the following optimization problems:

$$\begin{array}{c|c} \max_{\mathbf{x}} f(\mathbf{x}) & \min_{\mathbf{x}} f(\mathbf{x}) \\ \text{s.t. } \mathrm{g}(\mathbf{x}) = \mathbf{b} & \text{s.t. } \mathrm{g}(\mathbf{x}) = \mathbf{b} \end{array}$$

where $\mathbf{x}$ is an $n \times 1$ vector of decision variables, $\mathbf{b}$ is an $m \times 1$ vector of resource availability, $f : \mathbb{R}^n \to \mathbb{R}$, and $g : \mathbb{R}^n \to \mathbb{R}^m$.

Using Lagrange multiplier techniques, these problems become

$$\max_{\mathbf{x}} f(\mathbf{x}) + \boldsymbol{\lambda}'[\mathbf{b} - g(\mathbf{x})] \quad \Big| \quad \min_{\mathbf{x}} f(\mathbf{x}) + \boldsymbol{\lambda}'[\mathbf{b} - g(\mathbf{x})],$$

where $\boldsymbol{\lambda}$ is a $m \times 1$ vector of Lagrange multipliers. The first-order conditions for both problems are

$$\underbrace{\nabla_x f(\mathbf{x})}_{n\times 1} - \underbrace{\nabla_x g(\mathbf{x})}_{n\times m} \underbrace{\boldsymbol{\lambda}}_{m\times 1} = \underbrace{\mathbf{0}}_{n\times 1}$$

$$\underbrace{\mathbf{b} - g(\mathbf{x})}_{m\times 1} = \underbrace{\mathbf{0}}_{m\times 1}.$$

The bordered Hessian of these problems is

$$H = \left[\begin{array}{c|c} \overbrace{\mathbf{0}}^{m\times m} & \overbrace{-(\nabla_{\mathbf{x}} g(\mathbf{x}))}^{m\times n} \\ \hline \underbrace{-(\nabla_{\mathbf{x}} g(\mathbf{x}))'}_{n\times m} & \underbrace{\nabla^2_{\mathbf{xx}} f(\mathbf{x})_{n\times 1} - \nabla_{\mathbf{x}}[\nabla_{\mathbf{x}} g(\mathbf{x})\boldsymbol{\lambda}]}_{n\times n} \end{array}\right].$$

The second-order conditions of the maximization and minimization problems are

$$\begin{array}{c|c} \underline{\text{maximum}} & \underline{\text{minimum}} \\ (-1)^r H_r > 0 \quad \forall r = m+1, \ldots, n, & (-1)^m H_r > 0 \quad \forall r = m+1, \ldots, n, \end{array}$$

where H_r is the $(m + r)^{\text{th}}$ leading principal minor of the bordered Hessian, H. Note that H_r consists of the first $m+r$ rows and columns of $|H|$, and $H_n = |H|$.

2.3. *Example of application*

Consider the problem

$$\max_{\mathbf{x}} f(\mathbf{x})$$
$$\text{s.t.} \quad g(\mathbf{x}) = \mathbf{b},$$

with $\mathbf{x} \in \mathbb{R}^3$, $\mathbf{b} \in \mathbb{R}^2$, $f : \mathbb{R}^3 \to \mathbb{R}$, and $g : \mathbb{R}^3 \to \mathbb{R}^2$. That is, it is a problem with three variables and two constraints. The Lagrangian for this problem can be formed as

$$L = f(\mathbf{x}) + \lambda_1[b_1 - g^1(\mathbf{x})] + \lambda_2[b_2 - g^2(\mathbf{x})],$$

with the first-order conditions:

$$\begin{aligned} \nabla_x f(\mathbf{x}) - \nabla_x g(\mathbf{x})\boldsymbol{\lambda} &= 0, \\ \mathbf{b} - g(\mathbf{x}) &= 0, \end{aligned}$$

or, in scalar notation,

$$\begin{aligned} f_{x_1} - g^1_{x_1}\lambda_1 - g^2_{x_1}\lambda_2 &= 0, \\ f_{x_2} - g^1_{x_2}\lambda_1 - g^2_{x_2}\lambda_2 &= 0, \\ f_{x_3} - g^1_{x_3}\lambda_1 - g^2_{x_3}\lambda_2 &= 0, \\ b_1 - g^1(\mathbf{x}) &= 0, \\ b_2 - g^2(\mathbf{x}) &= 0. \end{aligned}$$

To simplify notation, we let g^1_1 denote $g^1_{x_1}$, f_{12} denote $f_{x_1x_2}$, and so on. The bordered Hessian is

$$H = \begin{bmatrix} 0 & 0 & (-g^1_1) & (-g^1_2) & (-g^1_3) \\ 0 & 0 & (-g^2_1) & (-g^2_2) & (-g^2_3) \\ (-g^1_1) & (-g^2_1) & \begin{matrix}(f_{11} - g^1_{11}\lambda_1 \\ -g^2_{11}\lambda_2)\end{matrix} & \begin{matrix}(f_{12} - g^1_{12}\lambda_1 \\ -g^2_{12}\lambda_2)\end{matrix} & \begin{matrix}(f_{13} - g^1_{13}\lambda_1 \\ -g^2_{13}\lambda_2)\end{matrix} \\ (-g^1_2) & (-g^2_2) & \begin{matrix}(f_{21} - g^1_{21}\lambda_1 \\ -g^2_{21}\lambda_2)\end{matrix} & \begin{matrix}(f_{22} - g^1_{22}\lambda_1 \\ -g^2_{22}\lambda_2)\end{matrix} & \begin{matrix}(f_{23} - g^1_{23}\lambda_1 \\ -g^2_{23}\lambda_2)\end{matrix} \\ (-g^1_3) & (-g^2_3) & \begin{matrix}(f_{31} - g^1_{31}\lambda_1 \\ -g^2_{31}\lambda_2)\end{matrix} & \begin{matrix}(f_{32} - g^1_{32}\lambda_1 \\ -g^2_{32}\lambda_2)\end{matrix} & \begin{matrix}(f_{33} - g^1_{33}\lambda_1 \\ -g^2_{33}\lambda_2)\end{matrix} \end{bmatrix}.$$

2.4. *Comparative statics*

By totally differentiating the first-order conditions, the following comparative statics results can be derived:

$$H\begin{bmatrix} d\lambda_1 \\ d\lambda_2 \\ dx_1 \\ dx_2 \\ dx_3 \end{bmatrix} = \begin{bmatrix} -1 & 0 \\ 0 & -1 \\ 0 & 0 \\ 0 & 0 \\ 0 & 0 \end{bmatrix} \begin{bmatrix} db_1 \\ db_2 \end{bmatrix}.$$

We have

$$\begin{bmatrix} d\lambda_1 \\ d\lambda_2 \\ dx_1 \\ dx_2 \\ dx_3 \end{bmatrix} = H^{-1} \begin{bmatrix} -db_1 \\ -db_2 \\ 0 \\ 0 \\ 0 \end{bmatrix}.$$

Note that

$$H^{-1} = \frac{1}{|H|}\begin{bmatrix} C_{11} & C_{21} & C_{31} & C_{41} & C_{51} \\ C_{12} & C_{22} & C_{32} & C_{42} & C_{52} \\ C_{13} & C_{23} & C_{33} & C_{43} & C_{53} \\ C_{14} & C_{24} & C_{34} & C_{44} & C_{54} \\ C_{15} & C_{25} & C_{35} & C_{45} & C_{55} \end{bmatrix},$$

where C_{ij} is the (i, j)th cofactor of matrix H. Specifically, $C_{ij} = (-1)^{i+j}|H_{-i,-j}|$, where $H_{-i,-j}$ is a submatrix of H obtained by deleting the ith row and jth column of matrix H. Therefore, we further have

$$\begin{bmatrix} d\lambda_1 \\ d\lambda_2 \\ dx_1 \\ dx_2 \\ dx_3 \end{bmatrix} = \frac{1}{|H|}\begin{bmatrix} -C_{11}db_1 - C_{21}db_2 \\ -C_{12}db_1 - C_{22}db_2 \\ -C_{13}db_1 - C_{23}db_2 \\ -C_{14}db_1 - C_{24}db_2 \\ -C_{15}db_1 - C_{25}db_2 \end{bmatrix}.$$

Solving, for example, for dx_3/db_1, one obtains

$$\frac{dx_3}{db_1} = -\frac{C_{15}}{|H|} = -(-1)^{1+5}|H_{-1,-5}|/|H|.$$

From the second-order conditions we know that the determinant of H is negative. Therefore, the sign of dx_3/db_1 is the same as that of $|H_{-1,-5}|$.

3. Decision-Making Over Time

A meaningful analysis of the agricultural and resource system cannot be done without understanding their evolution over time. Some of the most important decisions that economists are asked to evaluate are investment decisions, which entail assessments of dynamic flows of incomes and expenditures. In this section, we discuss two concepts that are critical to such assessments: discounting and interest rate.

There is a basic theoretical explanation for determination of the interest rate (sometimes we use the term discount rate). It is an equilibrium price for a one-period delay in use of one unit of value (e.g., a dollar). Figure 2 illustrates the determination of the discount rate.

The curve AB is a production possibility frontier, and it denotes all the possible tradeoffs between consumption in period t and period $t+1$. Point B corresponds to a situation with maximum consumption in period t and no consumption in period $t+1$. At A, all the consumption is delayed to period $t+1$, and the points connecting A to B correspond to positive consumption in both periods. The figure is drawn under the assumption that delay in consumption will lead to expanded resource availability. At point D, BE units of resource are not consumed in period t and lead to the availability of OG units of resources in period $t+1$. The assumed concavity of the tradeoff curve is the reason for this outcome. Each of the curves I_0, I_1, and I_2 is a locus of consumption patterns that result in the same level of utility; therefore, consumers are indifferent to movements between points on the same curve. Higher indifference curves correspond to higher utility levels. The optimal resource allocation is at D where

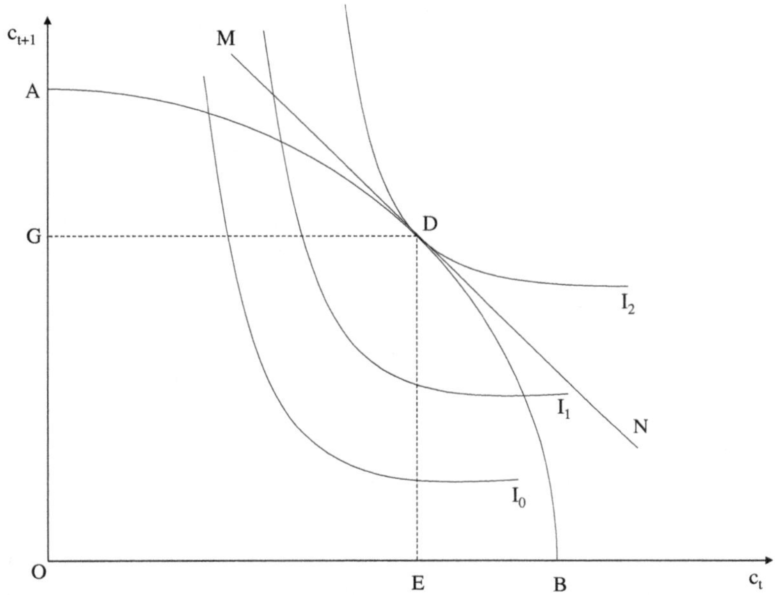

Figure 2. Consumption decision over time.

the highest feasible indifference curve is tangent to the production possibility frontier. The absolute value of the slope of the tangency line MN is $1 + r$, where r is defined as the discount rate.

Under certain assumptions (competition, full information, and no externalities), the market gives rise to the socially optimal discount rate. These conditions are not likely to hold in many cases, and market discount rates are likely to be different and, in most cases, higher than the social interest rate. The importance of monetary policy considerations in the determination of interest rates is one reason for the difference between market rates and socially optimal rates. Market rates may be higher for the following reasons:

(a) Risk considerations: Society has a much better capacity than any individual to carry risks, especially ones that are not correlated. Since society has many members that carry and share uncorrelated risks, the risk cost to the society approaches zero, and societal choices should be conducted using an interest rate reflecting risk neutrality.

Many market rates reflect risk aversion. This argument was first introduced by Arrow and Lind (1970).

(b) Externality considerations: When individuals decide about future investments, they consider only the benefits to themselves and their direct families in the future. However, their sons or daughters may get married, and other unrelated people may benefit from the activities generated by this investment. However, these benefits are not taken into account by the private parties. Therefore, they tend to underinvest from a social perspective and that can be interpreted as having a private interest rate that is higher than the social one (note that higher interest rates mean that benefits in the present are weighted more heavily relative to benefits in the future). This argument was advanced by Marglin (1963). Moreover, the interest rates paid by producers and consumers are adjusted to incorporate a lot of other elements besides society's equilibrium value of time preference, such as inflation and transaction costs associated with facilitation of loans.

3.1. *The decomposition of interest rates*

Let I denote interest rates paid by individuals to organizations, which can be decomposed into several elements: real market discount rate (R), rate of inflation (RI), transaction cost (TC), and risk factor (RF). That is, $I = R + RI + TC + RF$.

Examples:

- Banks pay to Federal Reserve: $R + RI$.
- Low-risk customers of banks pay prime interest rate: $I = R + RI + TC_m + RF_m$, where TC_m and RF_m are factors that reflect minimum traction and risk cost levels.
- Loans backed by assets generally pay lower interest rates than loans that are not backed by assets, reflecting risk factor.
- Credit ranking and other devices are used by lenders to assess riskiness of loan and to determine the risk factor.
- Lenders assess riskiness of investment and new projects before financing them.

- If the real interest rate is 3%, the inflation rate is 4%, and the risk and transaction cost of banks is 1%, then it could be that
  - Federal Reserve loan to banks at 7%,
  - the consumer-paid interest rate is 8%.
- If home mortgage loans are 9%, then it could be that
  - lender receives 7%,
  - risk-transaction cost is 2%.
- If the nominal interest rate is 12%, then it could be that
  - inflation rate is 14%,
  - real interest rate is –2%.

When interest rates are higher, individuals are less likely to invest money in projects and instead will deposit their money in banks and buy government bonds.

3.2. *Methodology to assess investments*

Here we only consider deterministic scenarios and refer readers to Dixit and Pindyck (1994) for a comprehensive treatment of investments under stochastic scenarios. Two steps are involved to assess investments in risk-free scenarios: (1) Assess economic cost and benefit over time and (2) use discount rate to compute net present value or compute internal rates of return.

For a potential investment project, let B_t be benefits and C_t be costs in period t. The net present value (NPV) of this project is $\sum_{t=0}^{N}(1/(1+r))^t(B_t - C_t)$ in a discrete time framework and is $\int_0^T e^{-rt}(B_t - C_t)dt$ in a continuous time framework. Investment on a project will make sense if its NPV is positive.

An alternative way to determine whether to invest is to calculate the internal rate of return (IRR) by using equation $\sum_{t=0}^{N}(1/(1+IRR))^t(B_t - C_t) = 0$. If IRR is greater (respectively, less) than the market interest rate, then the investment should (respectively, should not) be made.

Example. Suppose a project will need \$100 million to be established. Once established, it will last for two years, generating benefits at \$66 million in year one and \$60.5 million in year two.

Assuming that the interest rate is 10%, then the NPV of this project is $-100+66/(1+0.1)^1+60.5/(1+0.1)^2 = 10$. The IRR of this project is solved from equation $-100+66/(1+IRR)^1+60.5/(1+IRR)^2 = 0$: $IRR \approx 17.5\%$. If the benefits in each year were to be $70 million, then the NPV of this project would be $-100+70/(1+0.1)^1+70/(1+0.1)^2 \approx 21.5$, and the IRR would be about 25%.

Paradox of Internal Rate of Return. Consider a flow of net benefits $-a, b, -c$ across three periods. The IRR solves

$$-a + \frac{b}{1+IRR} - \frac{c}{(1+IRR)^2} = 0.$$

The quadratic equation may have two positive solutions. To see this, suppose $a = 10$, $b = 30$, and $c = 20$. In this case,

$$\begin{aligned} -10(1+IRR)^2 + 30(1+IRR) - 20 = 0 \\ \Rightarrow 1+IRR = \frac{30 \pm \sqrt{100}}{20} = \frac{30 \pm 10}{20} \\ \Rightarrow (1+IRR) = \begin{cases} 1 \\ 2. \end{cases} \end{aligned}$$

What is the true IRR? How to analyze investments? To avoid such a paradox, one could use IRR only in cases when there is one switch of the signs of net benefits across periods (e.g., investment occurs first and returns later). Or, one could just use the NPV approach in most cases.

4. Dynamic Systems

Dynamic systems are widely applied in agricultural economics such as water management models and soil carbon sequestration models. Optimal control is often used to derive optimal policies for a dynamic system. The analytic methodology for deriving the optimal solution to deterministic dynamic problems was developed by Pontryagin *et al.* (1962) and has been applied to a wide range of economic problems. In this section, we first obtain optimality conditions for discrete optimal control problems and then analyze the necessary optimality conditions of a continuous control problem.

4.1. *Discrete time optimal control*

A dynamic system typically has a policy variable (labeled x_t) and a stock variable (labeled s_t), where the policy variable is chosen in each period by the decision maker and the stock variable is influenced by the choice. The relationship between s_t and x_t is reflected by an equation of motion, $g_t(s_t, x_t, \boldsymbol{\theta}_t)$, where $\boldsymbol{\theta}_t$ stands for a set of exogenous model parameters. The goal of the decision maker is to optimize his or her objective function value, $f_t(x_t, s_t, \boldsymbol{\theta}_t)$, under initial conditions and any given constraints. A discrete time deterministic control model can be written as

$$\max_{x_t} \sum_{t=0}^{T} \beta^t f(x_t, s_t, \boldsymbol{\theta}_t) + \beta^{T+1} V(s_{T+1})$$

$$\text{s.t.} \quad s_{t+1} - s_t = g(s_t, x_t, \boldsymbol{\theta}_t), \quad \forall t = 0, \ldots, T, \text{ and}$$

$$s_0 = \bar{s_0},$$

where $\beta = 1/(1+r)$ is a discounting coefficient and r is interest rate.

For example, $f(x_t, s_t, \boldsymbol{\theta}_t)$ can be the profits from a fishing operation, s_t may be the stock of fish, x_t may be the fishing effort, and $\boldsymbol{\theta}_t$ may be a vector of prices. The equation of motion may denote the change in the fishing population and may combine the effect of fishing (reduces stock) and growth. The function, $V(s_{T+1})$, is the terminal value of the stock of fish at the end of the planning horizon.

The Lagrangian approach may be useful for solving this problem (we omit $\boldsymbol{\theta}_t$ for convenience):

$$L = \sum_{t=0}^{T} \left(\beta^t \underbrace{f(x_t, s_t)}_{\substack{\text{period } t \\ \text{net benefit}}} - \lambda_t [s_{t+1} - s_t - g(s_t, x_t)] \right) + \beta^{T+1} \underbrace{V(s_{T+1})}_{\text{scrap value}},$$

subject to the initial condition $s_0 = \bar{s_0}$.

The first-order conditions are

$$L_{x_t} = \beta^t f_{x_t} + \lambda_t g_{x_t} = 0, \quad t = 0, \ldots, T, \tag{7}$$

$$L_{s_t} = \beta^t f_{s_t} + \lambda_t(1 + g_{s_t}) - \lambda_{t-1} = 0, \quad t = 1, \ldots, T, \tag{8}$$

$$L_{\lambda_t} = s_{t+1} - s_t - g(s_t, x_t) = 0, \quad t = 0, \ldots, T, \tag{9}$$

$$L_{s_{T+1}} = \beta^{T+1} V_{s_{T+1}} - \lambda_T = 0, \tag{10}$$

given s_0.

The Lagrange coefficient, λ_t, denotes the marginal value (i.e., shadow price) of extra units of stock at the end of period t discounted to period 0.

Condition (7) suggests that the decision variable, x_t, is set so that its discounted marginal net benefit at period t is equal to its marginal costs in terms of stock growth. We expect $g_{x_t} < 0$.

Conditions (8) and (10) can be rewritten as

$$-(\lambda_t - \lambda_{t-1}) = \beta^t f_{s_t} + \lambda_t g_{s_t}, \quad t = 1, \ldots, T, \tag{11}$$

$$\lambda_T = \beta^{T+1} V_{s_{T+1}}. \tag{12}$$

Equations (11) and (12) provide a set of difference equations establishing the dynamics of the shadow price of the stock. The shadow price of time T is equal to the discounted marginal contribution of the residual stock at time $T + 1$. All shadow prices are discounted to time 0, so we do not have a time difference problem.

The net shadow price of stock increases as time approaches period zero because the right-hand side of Equation (11) is positive. The increase $(\lambda_{t-1} - \lambda_t)$ reflects the marginal contribution to production (f_{s_t}) and growth (g_{s_t}) of the stock at this extra period. Note the earlier the stock is introduced, the more it can contribute because it lasts longer.

The difference equations (11) and (12) reflect the dynamics of the dual variables (shadow price of stock variables), while the difference equation (9) with the initial s_0 sets the dynamics of the real stock variables. Therefore, we have to solve for both the dynamics of (shadow) price and quantities in solving optimal control problems.

To better understand the problem, $f(s_t, x_t)$ may be viewed as profits from fishing, i.e., $f(s_t, x_t) = p_t k(s_t, x_t) - w_t x_t$, where p_t is the fish price, $k(s_t, x_t)$ is the quantity of catch, s_t is the fish stock, x_t is the effort, and w_t is the cost per unit of effort. The stock equation may be $s_{t+1} - s_t = h(s_t) - k(s_t, x_t)$, where $h(s_t)$ denotes the stock growth. The shadow price, λ_t, is the discounted value of fish *in the water.*

4.2. *Continuous time optimal control*

It is much more convenient and elegant to use a continuous optimal control model for analytic purposes. We derive the optimality conditions rather heuristically using the approach of Intriligtor (1971). The continuous version of the model presented earlier is

$$\max_{x_t} \int_0^T e^{-rt} f(x_t, s_t)\, dt + e^{-rT} V(s_T)$$

$$\text{s.t.} \qquad \dot{s}_t = g(s_t, x_t).$$

One can write the Lagrangian function

$$L = \int_0^T \{e^{-rt} f(x_t, s_t) - \lambda_t [\dot{s}_t - g(s_t, x_t)]\} dt + e^{-rT} V(s_T), \tag{13}$$

where λ_t is the dynamic shadow price of the equation of motion. It reflects the discounted marginal value of stock added at time t. This Lagrangian function can be rewritten in an alternative way. To see it, note

$$L = \int_0^T e^{-rt} f(x_t, s_t) dt - \int_0^T \lambda_t \dot{s}_t\, dt + \int_0^T \lambda_t g(s_t, x_t)\, dt + e^{-rT} V(s_T).$$

Since

$$\int_0^T \lambda_t \dot{s}_t\, dt = (\lambda_t s_t)\Big|_0^T - \int_0^T \dot{\lambda}_t s_t dt$$

by using integration by parts, the alternative formulation of the Lagrangian is

$$L = \int_0^T [e^{-rt} f(x_t, s_t) + \dot{\lambda}_t s_t + \lambda_t g(s_t, x_t)]dt + V(s_T)e^{-rT} - \lambda_T s_T + \lambda_0 s_0, \tag{14}$$

where $s_0 = \bar{s_0}$.

The optimality conditions are obtained by differentiating L, using Equation (13) or (14) as appropriate:

$$\frac{\partial L}{\partial x_t} = e^{-rt} f_{x_t} + \lambda_t g_{x_t} = 0, \quad \text{(using equation (13))},$$

$$\frac{\partial L}{\partial s_t} = e^{-rt} f_{s_t} + \dot{\lambda}_t + \lambda_t g_{s_t} = 0, \quad \text{(using equation (14))},$$

$$\frac{\partial L}{\partial \lambda_t} = \dot{s}_t - g(s_t, x_t) = 0, \quad \text{(using equation (13))},$$

$$\frac{\partial L}{\partial s_T} = \lambda_T - e^{-rT} V'(s_T) = 0, \quad \text{(using equation (14))},$$

$$\frac{\partial L}{\partial \lambda_0} = s_0, \quad \text{(using equation (14))}.$$

Pontryagin *et al.* (1962) have derived a simple approach to obtain this optimality condition. They define the Hamiltonian function where

$$H(x_t, s_t, \lambda_t) = e^{-rt} f(x_t, s_t) + \lambda_t g(s_t, x_t)$$

and proved that at each t the optimality conditions are

$$\frac{\partial H}{\partial x_t} = e^{-rt} f_{x_t} + \lambda_t g_{x_t} = 0, \tag{15}$$

$$\dot{s}_t = \frac{\partial H}{\partial \lambda_t} = g(s_t, \lambda_t), \tag{16}$$

$$-\dot{\lambda}_t = \frac{\partial H}{\partial s_t} = e^{-rt} f_{s_t} + \lambda_t g_{s_t}, \tag{17}$$

given s_0 and $\lambda_T = e^{-rt} V'(s_T)$.

These sets of conditions allow one to solve a dynamic optimal control problem as a succession of static choice problems corrected by the dynamics of stock variables and their shadow prices. The dynamic of stock is given by Equation (16) and $s_0 = \bar{s_0}$, and the dynamic of shadow prices is presented by Equation (17) and $\lambda_T = e^{-rt}V'(s_T)$.

4.3. *Optimal control techniques and applications*

In the previous section, we presented the optimality conditions using shadow prices discounted to period 0. Many times we are interested in temporary prices and values, rather than discounted ones. To obtain such prices, we derive first temporary optimality conditions. Consider the problem discusses earlier:

$$\max_{x_t} \int_0^T e^{-rt} f(x_t, s_t)\, dt + e^{-rT} V(s_T)$$

$$\text{s.t.} \qquad \dot{s}_t = g(s_t, x_t).$$

The (*discounted*) Hamiltonian of this problem is

$$H_D = e^{-rt} f(x_t, s_t) + \lambda_t^D g(s_t, x_t),$$

where λ_t^D is the shadow price of the equation of motion (or the shadow price of stock in time t) in values *discounted* to time 0. The optimality conditions are

$$\frac{\partial H^D}{\partial x_t} = e^{-rt} f_{x_t} + \lambda_t^D g_{x_t} = 0, \tag{18}$$

$$\dot{s}_t = \frac{\partial H^D}{\partial \lambda_t^D} = g(s_t, x_t), \tag{19}$$

$$-\dot{\lambda}_t^D = \frac{\partial H^D}{\partial s_t} = e^{-rt} f_{s_t} + \lambda_t^D g_{s_t}, \tag{20}$$

$$\lambda_T^D = e^{-rT} V'(s_T), \tag{21}$$

given s_0.

Let $H = e^{rt} H^D$ denote the temporal (or current value) Hamiltonian and $\lambda_t = e^{rt} \lambda_t^D$ denote the temporal shadow price of the stock.

The alternative presentation of the optimality condition is

$$\frac{\partial H}{\partial x_t} = f_{x_t} + \lambda_t g_{x_t} = 0, \tag{22}$$

$$\dot{s}_t = \frac{\partial H}{\partial \lambda_t} = g(s_t, x_t), \tag{23}$$

$$-\dot{\lambda}_t + r\lambda_t = \frac{\partial H}{\partial s_t} = f_{s_t} + \lambda_t g_{s_t}, \tag{24}$$

$$\lambda_T = V'(s_T), \tag{25}$$

given s_0.

To see that conditions (18)–(21) and (22)–(25) are consistent, note that

$$-\dot{\lambda}_t = -r\lambda_t - e^{rt}\dot{\lambda}_t^D = -r\lambda_t + e^{rt}\frac{\partial H^D}{\partial s_t} = -r\lambda_t + \frac{\partial H}{\partial s_t}.$$

4.3.1. *The simple model of economic growth*

The first and perhaps the most important early applications of optimal control in economics pertain to the study of economics growth. These are macro models, but the analysis can apply to micro problems. The economic growth model presented here considers the case when one good is both consumed and invested. Suppose the production function is

$$y_t = f(k_t),$$

where y_t is the output and k_t is the capital stock. Let c_t be consumption in time t and investment is $y_t - c_t = f(k_t) - c_t$.

Utility derived from consumption is measured by $u(c_t)$, where $u(\cdot)$ is a utility function with $u' > 0 > u''$. Thus, the objective is

$$\max_{c_t} \int_0^{\infty} e^{-rt} u(c_t) dt,$$

and the equation of motion is

$$\dot{k}_t = f(k_t) - c_t - \gamma k_t.$$

Capital increases at the investment rate but may decline because of depreciation where γ is the depreciation coefficient. The initial capital stock is k_0. The temporary Hamiltonian is

$$H = u(c_t) + \lambda_t[f(k_t) - c_t - \gamma k_t],$$

and the optimality conditions are given by

$$\frac{\partial H}{\partial c_t} = u_c - \lambda_t = 0, \tag{26}$$

$$-\dot{\lambda}_t + r\lambda_t = \frac{\partial H}{\partial k_t} = \lambda_t f_k - \lambda_t \gamma, \tag{27}$$

$$\dot{k}_t = \frac{\partial H}{\partial \lambda_t} = f(k_t) - c_t - \gamma k_t. \tag{28}$$

First, optimality condition (26) equates the shadow price of the stock to marginal utility of consumption; this is reasonable since a unit of the good is either traded or invested and marginal benefit from both activities has to be equal at the optimal solution. The rate of change in the nominal shadow price is affected by three elements (from Equation (27), we can obtain $\dot{\lambda}_t/\lambda_t = r - f_k + \gamma$). They are as follows: (1) discounting, which has the effect of increasing nominal prices over time, (2) depreciation, which has a similar effect as that of discounting, and (3) marginal productivity of capital (i.e., f_k), which operated by reducing nominal prices over time. The higher f_k is, the more capital will be available in the future and the less valuable it is.

4.3.2. *The dynamics of consumption*

Total differentiation of Equation (26) yields $u_{cc}\dot{c}_t - \dot{\lambda}_t = 0$. From (27), we obtain $\dot{\lambda}_t = \lambda_t(r - f_k + \gamma)$. Thus, $u_{cc}\dot{c}_t - \dot{\lambda}_t = 0$ becomes

$$u_{cc}\dot{c}_t + \lambda_t[f_k - r - \gamma] = 0.$$

Since $u_c = \lambda_t$, the expression leads to a condition defining the rate of changes in consumption over time:

$$\frac{\dot{c}_t}{c_t} = -\frac{u_c}{u_{cc}c_t}[f_k - r - \gamma].$$

Let us define $\eta(c_t) = \frac{u_c}{u_{cc}c_t}$. It can be interpreted as the elasticity of demand for the good. To see this point, suppose we have a utility-maximizing consumer who derives additive utility from c and expenditure. The optimal consumption choice of this individual is

$$\max_c\{u(c) + I - pc\},$$

where I is the income and p is the commodity price. Optimality condition is $u_c - p = 0$. Total differentiation of this condition yields

$$u_{cc}dc - dp = 0 \Rightarrow \frac{dc}{dp} = \frac{1}{u_{cc}} < 0.$$

Therefore,

$$\frac{dc}{dp}\frac{p}{c_t} = \frac{u_c}{u_{cc}c_t} = \eta(c_t) < 0.$$

Using this definition, note that

$$\frac{\dot{c}_t}{c_t} = -\eta(c_t)[f_k - r - \gamma]. \tag{29}$$

If $f_k - r - \gamma > 0$, then the productivity of capital is substantial and the shadow prices decline over time. In this case, Equation (29) suggests that consumption increases and the increase in consumption is inversely related to the demand elasticity. The intuition is as follows. The price of today's consumption is today's investment. If the demand elasticity is smaller (i.e., more negative), then the decision maker will reduce today's consumption and increase investment, which results in larger increase in tomorrow's consumption.

4.3.3. *Steady state*

At steady state, both state and co-state (shadow price of stocks) variables do not change over time. Economists are interested in knowing if steady-state situations exist, what will be the dynamic path which leads to them, and whether they are stable. They are stable when the system returns to steady state in spite of some random shocks that move it away. Economists are enamored with

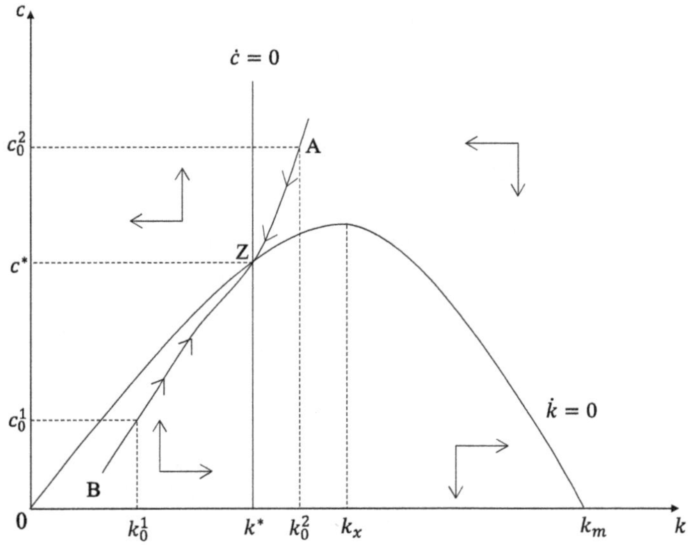

Figure 3. A phase diagram.

steady states because they are the dynamic equivalent of long-run equilibria, which represent the outcome for which the system converges.

In the growth theory model, steady state occurs when

$$\dot{k} = f(k) - c - \gamma k = 0, \tag{30}$$

$$\dot{c} = \dot{\lambda} = f_k(k) - r - \gamma = 0. \tag{31}$$

Figure 3 presents a phase diagram. The loci of all the k and c combinations that lead to $\dot{k} = 0$ and $\dot{c} = 0$ are depicted as well as their intersection(s) which are the steady states of the system.

The locus of all the points with $\dot{c} = 0$ is at $k = k^*$. The curve $c = f(k) - \gamma k$ is the locus of all the points with $\dot{k} = 0$. It intersects $c = 0$ at $k = 0$ and $k = k_m$. The steady state of the system occurs in our case at Z with $k = k^*$ and $c = c^*$.

To study the dynamic properties of the system, note that the diagram indicates that consumption deceases when $k > k^*$ and consumption increases when $k < k^*$. Similarly, k declines above the curve with $\dot{k} = 0$ (when $f(k) - \gamma k - c < 0$) and increases below it.

The curve AZB denotes optimal consumption-capital path. If initial capital is k_0^1, initial consumption should be c_0^1 and movement along BZ will lead to equilibrium. If initial capital is k_0^2, initial consumption should be c_0^2 and, for a period before steady state, consumption will be greater than production.

The analysis here denotes the importance of time preference. If $r = 0$, optimal solution will be at $k_x > k^*$. But with $r > 0$, even if initial stock is k_x, there will be periods of excess consumption along the line AZ until the steady-state capital at $k = k^*$ is attained.

References

Arrow, K.J. and R.C. Lind. 1970. Uncertainty and the Evaluation of Public Investment Decisions. *The American Economic Review* 60(3): 364–378.

Chiang, A.C. 1992. *Elements of Dynamic Optimization.* Waveland Press, Inc. Long Grove, Illinois.

Dixit, A.K. and R.S. Pindyck. 1994. *Investment under Uncertainty.* Princeton University Press. Princeton, NJ.

Intriligator, M.D. 1971. *Mathematical Optimization and Economic Theory.* Prentice-Hall, Inc., Englewood Cliffs, NJ.

Marglin, S.A. 1963. The Social Rate of Discount and The Optimal Rate of Investment. *The Quarterly Journal of Economics* 77(1): 95–111.

Pontryagin, L.S., V.G. Boltyanskii, R.V. Gamkrelidze, E.F. Mischenko. 1962. *The Mathematical Theory of Optimal Processes* (trans: Tririgoff KN; Neustadt LW (ed)). Wiley, New York, NY.

Simon, C.P. and Lawrence Blume. 1994. *Mathematics for Economists.* W. W. Norton & Company, Inc. New York, NY.

Appendix B

Problem Sets

In this appendix, we present six problem sets that can be used during teaching agricultural economics and policy. The first two problem sets focus on production and the third on risk analysis. The last three problem sets are comprehensive and can be used as exercises or exams. The solutions to the first three problem sets are provided in Appendix C.

Problem Set 1

(1) Assume that a product is used initially without any regulation. The price, which is equal to the marginal cost of producing the product, is equal to 2 and the quantity is equal to 8. We know that the demand is linear and, at the initial outcome, the price elasticity is

$$\eta_D = -\frac{\partial Q}{\partial P}\frac{P}{Q} = \frac{1}{4},$$

where Q is output and P is price. Suppose that the marginal social cost of externality is $MSC = Q$.

A. What is the social optimum and the resulting price and quantity of the output?

B. What is the consumer surplus, producer surplus, government revenue, and environmental cost before the regulation and (1) under pollution tax, (2) under pollution reduction subsidy, and (3) under tradable permits?
C. Suppose that the product is sold by a monopoly. What is the optimal pollution policy in this case?

(2) The micro-level production function is Von-Liebig

$$y = ax \text{ for } x \leq \bar{x},$$

where y is output per acre, x is water, and a is the land fertility parameter. The land density function as a function of fertility is

$$g(a) = M - na, \;\; g(a) \geq 0.$$

A. Given output price, P, and water price, W, what is aggregate supply? What is aggregate water demand?
B. Attempt to derive an aggregate production function and interpret its coefficient.

(3) Let the *ex-ante* production function be

$$Y = AK^{\alpha} L^{1-\alpha},$$

where Y is output, K is capital, and L is labor. Let P denote output price and W denote wage rate. Suppose output price is increasing at rate γ, wage rate at rate δ, and $r>\delta>\gamma$ where r is the discount rate. In a putty-clay framework, write a model to answer the following:

A. What is the optimal capital/output and labor/output ratio of a new plant?
B. What is the planned economic life of this plant?
C. How will the optimal life of capital change as γ and δ increase?

Problem Set 2

(1) A crop is produced with a constant return-to-scale technology using land and effective water (water attaining the plants).

The production function is

$$q = f(e),$$

where q is output per acre and e is effective water per acre. Effective water is a production of applied water per acre, a, and land quality (α) $0 \leq \alpha \leq 1$, i.e.,

$$e = a\alpha.$$

Let P denote the output price and w water price.

A. How will per-acre output supply and actual and effective water demands be affected by changes in P, w, and α?
B. Assume a competitive land market. How will the rental rate behave as a function of P, w, and α?
C. Assume the production function is a C.E.S. Derive (1) per-acre output supply and water demands and (2) the rental-rate function.

(2) Suppose a household is managed like a business. It controls $\bar{N}$ hours of labor. It runs a small enterprise that produces output Y with N_h hours of labor, with a Just–Pope production function $Y = f(N_h) + \alpha N_h \varepsilon$. The production function f is concave and $\alpha > 0$. The price of output is p and ε is a random variable with mean 0. Family members can also work outside the firm and earn w dollars per hour.

A. Establish the appropriate assumptions and find the optimal decision rules for time allocation under risk neutrality. What is the likelihood of an internal solution (when family members diversify their time between work in the family business and the labor market) for a risk-neutral individual? How will a change in the price of the variable input or the output affect the time allocation and the input use?
B. Suppose that the family is risk averse and utility is a function of wealth with initial wealth denoted by W_0 What are the optimal allocation rules for a risk-averse household? Derive the first-order conditions and interpret them. How will changes in the price of output and the wage rate affect time allocation and expected output?

C. Compare analytically the output of a risk-averse family with a risk-neutral one. If the family has an initial wealth of W_0, how a change in wealth affects its labor allocation and expected output?

D. Solve the problem for the case where the household has a negative exponential utility function and the random variable is distributed normally (specify the assumptions). How will an increase in the variance of the random variable affect the time allocation?

E. Thus far the household was modeled as a firm. Explain how your modeling will change if we consider a household that gains utility from both income and leisure and total labor is not given but is a decision variable.

Problem Set 3

(1) A risk-averse individual evaluates the following five portfolios:

I		**II**		**III**		**IV**		**V**	
X	$P(X)$	X	$P(X)$	X	$P(X)$	X	$P(X)$	X	$P(X)$
3	1/6	5	1/3	2	1/4	3	1/3	2	1/6
7	1/6	7	1/6	6	1/12	7	1/6	8	1/6
10	1/3	12	1/12	10	1/3	12	1/12	9	1/3
13	1/6	14	1/12	14	1/12	14	1/12	11	1/6
17	1/6	15	1/3	16	1/4	17	1/3	17	1/6

A. Order the distributions (whenever possible) according to their riskiness using the mean-preserving spread concept.

B. Using the second-order stochastic dominance concept, order these distributions. What are the implications of the ordering?

C. Order the distribution using a mean-variance criterion.

D. Using Roy's minimum probability rule — min $[P(X \leq 6)]$ — to order these distributions.

E. Using Kataoka's safety-fixed rule — Max d, s.t., $P(X \leq d) \leq 1/6$ — order these distributions.

F. Using $U(X) = ln\ (X + 1)$ to order these distributions.

G. Compare and evaluate the different orderings.

(2) A farmer operates L acres of land using the production function defined on a per-acre basis:

$$q = f(l, m) + g(l, m)\varepsilon,$$

where ε is a random variable, $f_l > 0$, $f_m > 0$, $g_l > 0$, and $g_m < 0$ — f and g are concave in m and l.

Let the total profit be

$$\Pi = L \cdot (pq - wl - rm) - F,$$

where p is output price, r and w are input prices, and F is fixed cost.

A. Assume the farmer maximizes the expected utility of income with $u' > 0$, $u'' < 0$, and $E(\varepsilon) = 0$.

   i. How has behavior under uncertainty differed from behavior under certainty when $\varepsilon \equiv 0$?
   ii. Assuming decreasing absolute risk aversion, how does reduction in fixed costs affect input use?
   iii. Assuming constant relative risk aversion, how will increase in farm size affect input use?

   Prove all your results mathematically.

B. Assume $\varepsilon \sim N(0, \sigma^2)$, and $U(\Pi) = 1 - e^{-\delta\Pi}$.
   What are the optimal decision rules of the farmers? How are they affected by farm size and the fixed cost level?
C. Assume that ε is gamma distributed — $E(\varepsilon) = 1$. What are the optimal decision rules?
D. Assume that $\varepsilon \sim N(0, \sigma^2)$ and the farmer pursues Kataoka's safety-fixed rule. What are his optimal decision rules?
E. Compare the behavior under the alternative models.

Problem Set 4

(1) Consider L units of land and many farms. There is heterogeneity because different locations are exposed differently to pest damage, but otherwise land productivity is the same. The industry is producing an output with a constant return to scale

technology and the production function per acre is a damage control function $y = f(z)\,[1 - d(N, j)]$, where y is output per acre, $f(z)$ is potential output per acre, z is fertilizer use per acre, and $d(N, j)$ is pest damage that assumes value from 0 to 1. The pest damage function increases with the pest population per acre N, which assumes values from 0 to $\bar{N}$ and is affected by pest control treatment j. It can assume three values, $j = 0$ when there is no treatment, $j = 1$ when there is a chemical treatment, and $j = 2$ when GMO is introduced. The damage function $d(N, j) = h(N)g(j)$ can be decomposed to $h(N)$, damage without interference, and $g(j)$, fraction of damage after treatment j. We assume that $g(0) = 1$ (when $j = 0$ there is no damage reduction). We also assume that $1 \geq g(1) \geq g(2) \geq 0$, namely there is more damage after treatment with chemical pesticides than GMO (this is hypothetical). For example, when $g(1) = 0.5$ and $g(2) = 0$, the chemical treatment eliminates half the damage and GMO all of it. Let output price be denoted by P, fertilizer price by V, and the prices of the pest control treatment j, $w(j)$ where $w(0) = 0$, $0 < w(1) \leq w(2)$. The pest exposure per acre is a random variable with a density function $\psi(N)$ where $\int_0^{\bar{N}} \psi(N)dN = 1$. So, if the marginal land operating has a pest population $0 \leq N_a \leq \bar{N}$, the total land in production is $L \int_0^{N_a} \psi(N)dN$.

A. First consider the case where the two pest control treatments are not available, so $j = 0$. Write the optimization problem of a farm with initial pest level N. If farms maximize profits, what will be the aggregate output of the industry (hint, first define a critical level of N above which production is not profitable and then aggregate). Show how output will change in response to changes in P and V.
B. Suppose the chemical pesticide is becoming available, so either $j = 0$ or $j = 1$. Analyze the adoption of the pesticide. What subgroup of farms will adopt it? What will be the impacts on land use and output? How will changes in output price or pesticide price affect adoption?

C. Suppose the GMO is available. So j may assume three values (0, 1, or 2). Write the farmer optimization problem. Identify conditions under which the GMO will be adopted, and in particular when it will be adopted by all farmers or only by subgroups of farmers (with or without adoption of chemical pesticides). How will the introduction of the GMO affect supply and pesticide use? Derive supply for various conditions. How will the adoption of pesticides affect fertilizer use?
D. Consider the case where the agriculture industry is facing inelastic demand. Discuss graphically how the introduction of GMO will affect prices and quantity of output.

(2) An entrepreneur is considering producing a new biofuel. He considers a processing plant to refine the biofuel from a feedstock crop. He can either grow the feedstock or buy if from farmers. The entrepreneur has limited initial credit that he has to allocate among the refinery and feedstock production faculties that he may invest in.

A. Develop a model to present the entrepreneur's decision problem.
    i. Find the optimal decision rules: How much biofuel to produce? How much feedstock to produce in-house and how much to buy from others? Interpret the optimality conditions.
    ii. How will the credit constraint affect the outcome?
B. Suppose the refinery receives the subsidy for greenhouse gases that the biofuel saves relative to gasoline. Expand the model to include the subsidy and analyze its implications.
C. Suppose the entrepreneur is risk averse and has an exponential utility function. Assumes that the cost of processing of one unit of feedstock has a random component with a Normal distribution.
    i. What will be the optimal allocation rule? How will the risk aversion affect the overall production and feedstock production choices?

ii. Now suppose also that the cost of feedstock is a linear combination of a deterministic and random component with a Normal distribution. Derive the supply chain design problem and characterize the solution.

(3) Buyers want to buy a product that provides the benefit of b if it fits and 0 otherwise.

The probability of fit is q. The buyer has three options — (1) to buy it with a money-back guarantee (MBG) at a price P_G that allows return and refund if the product does not fit, but with a return fee of R dollars, or (2) to buy it without guarantee at price P_N, or (3) not to buy.

A. Under what condition will a buyer utilize the MBG option? What is the value of the option as a function of the key parameters?
B. There are M buyers and the probability of fit is distributed uniformly from q_L to 1. How many people will buy the product with the MBG? How many people will buy the product without the MBG?
C. Suppose the buyer has a disappointment cost of S if the product does not fit. How will it affect the answers to B?
D. Suppose that a buyer can pay a fee of D dollars and take a demonstration that with probability γ will tell whether the product fits or not — while keeping the buyer uncertain with probability $1-\gamma$. Under what conditions will the buyer prefer the demonstration to the MBG?

(4) A small project.
Write a brief (2 pages) on an agriculture or agribusiness region, organization, or a company (e.g., California, Monsanto, John Deere, Iowa, UC cooperative extension) providing

A. Basic facts — what is unique about the region or company?
B. What are the main challenges and opportunities?
C. What policies (actions) will you recommend?

Problem Set 5

(1) A farmer is growing wheat with a Just–Pope production function, where the output and input are denoted by y and x, respectively. The prices of the output and the input are p and w, respectively.

A. Establish the appropriate assumptions and find the optimal decision rules for input choice under risk aversion and risk neutrality.

B. Compare input use and expected output under both risk neutrality and risk aversion, under various assumptions about the technology (e.g., risk-increasing or risk-decreasing technologies).

C. How will an increase in the initial wealth of the farmer affect input use?

D. Solve the problem for the case where the farmer has a negative exponential utility function and the random variable is distributed normally (specify the assumptions).

E. For the case of normal distribution of the random element of the yield function, what will be the decision rule if the firm wants to maximize the level of profits that will be exceeded 95% of the time (the 5% of the profits distribution)?

(2) A. Compare the optimal stock of groundwater in a steady state to the one arising from a decentralized, private property solution.

B. Give some intuition for why they differ as they do.

C. Discuss the role of natural recharge.

D. Discuss how an increase in water use efficiency would change the steady-state level of pumping or the groundwater stock.

(3) A. What is the difference between diffusion and adoption? What are the measurements of these concepts?

B. What are the main theories explaining observed diffusion patterns? What are the main assumptions and implications? What are their strengths and weaknesses?

C. Derive a threshold model for the adoption of an irrigation technology where output per acre y depends on effective input αx where α is a land quality index assuming value from 0 to 1. Modern technology costs I dollars per acre but doubles input use efficiently. Fixed cost per acre regardless of water cost is F. Output price is p and water price is w. Prices of inputs vary over time. There is a distribution of land quality with density function $g(\alpha)$ where $\int_0^1 g(\alpha)d\alpha = L$ and L is total land.

i. Establish basic assumptions. Derive the microlevel optimization rule for each period.
ii. Divide lands into three groups: adopters, non-adopters, and idle. What will determine to which category each land quality belongs? Derive aggregate supply.
iii. If the fixed cost of the technology will decline over time, how will it affect diffusion? How will an increase in output price affect diffusion?
iv. How does risk consideration affect the outcomes?

(4) A. What are the main stages in the evolution of U.S. agriculture, and correspondingly in the evolution of U.S. agricultural policy?
B. To what extent did agricultural policy serve to enhance efficiency versus other social objectives?
C. How does agricultural policy affect the environment?
D. What institutions, policies, and arrangements have emerged to address various types of risks in different contexts?
E. What are likely to be the economic impacts of these institutions and policies (e.g., how are they likely to affect prices, quantities, welfare of various agents, etc.)?
F. What are the likely drawbacks of some of these arrangements?
Use basic models to illustrate some of your answers.

Problem Set 6

(1) A firm is producing a product using energy with a production function $y = f(x)$, where the output and input are denoted

by y and x, respectively. The production function has normal properties. The prices of the output and the input are p and w, respectively. The price of energy w is a random variable $w = \bar{w}\varepsilon$, where ε has a zero mean.

A. Establish the appropriate assumptions and find the optimal decision rules for input choice under risk aversion and risk neutrality.
B. Compare input use and expected output under both risk neutrality and risk aversion.
C. Suppose there is an energy tax of t dollars per unit. Show how will it affect the optimal energy use.

(2) On pesticide use.

A. Explain the damage control function approach to analyze pesticide use. Use this specification to develop a model where output depends on fertilizer use and pest population. The pest population is affected by initial pest population and pesticide treatment. Specify your assumptions.
B. Show how changes in the initial pest population and changes in the prices of output, pesticides, and fertilizers will affect pesticide and fertilizer uses, pest damage, and output in the case of a profit-maximizing firm.
C. Suppose there is an upper bound limiting pesticide use. Show how it will affect fertilizer use and output.
D. Suppose there is a pesticide tax. How will it affect optimal choices?
E. What will the regulated farm prefer: A pesticide tax or an upper bound of pesticide use? Explain.
F. Suppose a new genetically modified variety is available. It reduces pest damage but requires extra cost. Expand the model and identify the conditions under which it will be adopted. How will it affect output, pesticide use, and fertilizer use?

(3) Consumers derive utility from health and fun. They consume three goods. Each good has fixed coefficients of fun and health per unit consumed. Good A has the highest fun-to-health ratio,

good C has the lowest fun-to-health ratio, and the fun-to-health ratio of good B is in between.

A. Develop a model to analyze the choices of a consumer with a given income. Specify your assumptions.
B. How will a change in the price of Good A affect its consumption? Explain. How will it affect the consumption of fun and health?
C. An investor is considering introducing a new product that will dominate all existing products. What are the requirements it must meet?

(4) On U.S. agricultural policies.

A. How have the agricultural policies of the U.S. changed over time? Please explain these changes.
B. Discuss how the energy situation and climate change affect agriculture.
C. Discuss how the energy situation and climate change are likely affecting agricultural and related policies.

Appendix C

Solutions to Selected Problem Sets

Solutions to Problem Set 1

(1) Solution

A. What is the social optimum and the resulting price and quantity of the output?

Since demand is linear, $P = 2$ and $D = 8$, based on

$$\eta_D = -\frac{\partial Q}{\partial P}\frac{P}{Q} = \frac{1}{4},$$

we have

$$\frac{\partial Q}{\partial P} = -\frac{1}{4} \times \frac{Q}{P} = -\frac{1}{4} \times \frac{8}{2} = -1.$$

Thus, we know that the linear demand curve has a slope of -1. Given the slope and a point on the demand curve (i.e., $P = 2$ and $D = 8$), we can readily check that the demand is $Q = 10 - P$ and the *inverse demand is* $P = 10 - Q$.

Since the marginal cost of producing the product is 2 and the marginal social cost of externality is Q, the total social marginal cost of producing the product is $2+Q$. So, at the social optimum, we have $10 - Q = 2 + Q$ so $Q^* = 4$ and $P^* = 6$.

B. Before Regulation:

CS^0 (*consumer surplus*) $= (10 - 2) \times 8/2 = 32$
PS^0 (*producer surplus*) $= 0$
EC^0 (*externality cost*) $= 8 \times 8/2 = 32$
SS^0 (*social surplus*) $= 0$

Under a pollution tax:

Because the marginal cost of the product is 2 and because the socially optimal price and quantity are 6 and 4, respectively, the socially optimal tax is 4. Under this tax, the equilibrium quantity demanded is 4. Therefore,

$CS^T = (10 - 6) \times 4/2 = 8$
$PS^T = 0$
EC^T (*externality cost*) $= 4 \times 4/2 = 8$
GR^T (*Government revenue*) $= 4 \times 4 = 16$
$SS^T = CS^T + PS^T - EC^T + GR^T = 16$

Under a pollution reduction subsidy:

Under such a subsidy, the producer takes actions to mitigate the externality. Assuming the cost of the actions is equal to the marginal externality cost. Then the optimal subsidy rate is 4. In this case, the producer will only invest in pollution reduction technology for the first 4 units of product because investing in the pollution reduction technology for the 5th unit will reduce the profit. Readers can readily check this.

$CS^S = (10 - 6) \times 4/2 = 8$
$PS^S = 4 \times 4/2 + 4 \times 4 = 24$
EC^S (*externality cost*) $= 0$
$GR^S = -16$
$SS^S = 16$

Under a tradable permit:

$Subsidy = Tax = 0$
$CS^R = (10 - 6) \times 4/2 = 8$
$PS^R = 4 \times 4 = 16$

$EC^R = 4 \times 4/2 = 8$
$GR^R = 0$
$SS^R = 16$

C. Outcome under a Monopoly:

$MR = 10 - 2Q$

At Monopoly optimum $MR = MC \rightarrow 10 - 2Q = 2$. So, $Q^M = 4$, $P^M = 6$

$CS^M = (10 - 6) \times 4/2 = 8$
$PS^M = 4 \times 4 = 16$
$EC^M = 4 \times 4/2 = 8$
$SS^M = 16$

Monopoly results in social optimum in this case.

(2) Solution

A. Farmers will produce only if profits are positive, i.e., if

$$\pi = pax - wx \geq 0,$$

or

$$a \geq \frac{w}{p}.$$

If profits are strictly positive, they will produce the maximum amount possible per acre, i.e., $y = a\bar{x}$. Aggregate supply is therefore given by the aggregated maximum output of each fertility grade of land that can be farmed profitably, or

$$Y(P, W) = \int_{\frac{W}{P}}^{\frac{M}{n}} a\bar{x}(M - na)da = \bar{x}\left[\frac{M^3}{6n^2} - \frac{M}{2}\left(\frac{W}{P}\right)^2 + \frac{n}{3}\left(\frac{W}{P}\right)^3\right]$$

and aggregate demand for water by

$$X(P, W) = \int_{\frac{W}{P}}^{\frac{M}{n}} \bar{x}(M - na)da = \bar{x}\left[\frac{M^2}{2n} - M\left(\frac{W}{P}\right) + \frac{n}{2}\left(\frac{W}{P}\right)^2\right].$$

B. Solving the water demand equation for W/P yields

$$\frac{W}{P} = \frac{M}{n} - \sqrt{\frac{2X}{n\bar{x}}}$$

and substituting this into the supply equation gives the aggregate production function

$$\begin{aligned} Y(X) &= \bar{x}\left[\frac{M^3}{6n^2} - \frac{M}{2}\left(\frac{M}{n} - \sqrt{\frac{2X}{n\bar{x}}}\right)^2 + \frac{n}{3}\left(\frac{M}{n} - \sqrt{\frac{2X}{n\bar{x}}}\right)^3\right] \\ &= \left[\frac{M}{n} - \frac{2}{3}\sqrt{\frac{2X}{n\bar{x}}}\right] X. \end{aligned}$$

(3) Solution

A. A producer building a new plant chooses capital, labor, and the planned economic life of the plant (denoted T) so as to maximize the discounted sum of expected gross profits less the cost of capital. The optimization problem is, therefore,

$$\max_{K,L,T} \int_{t=0}^{T} e^{-rt}[P_t A K^\alpha L^{1-\alpha} - w_t L]dt - K$$

subject to the no-shutdown condition

$$P_t A K^\alpha L^{1-\alpha} - w_t L \geq 0.$$

Using that

$$\begin{aligned} P_t &= P_0 e^{\gamma t} \\ w_t &= w_0 e^{\delta t}, \end{aligned}$$

where P_0 and w_0 are initial price and wage rate. We can rewrite the objective function as

$$\max_{K,L,T} P_0 A K^\alpha L^{1-\alpha} \frac{(1 - e^{(\gamma - r)T})}{r - \gamma} - w_0 L \frac{(1 - e^{(\delta - r)T})}{r - \delta} - K.$$

The first-order conditions are (assuming an interior solution)

$$K: \quad \alpha P_0 AK^{\alpha-1}L^{1-\alpha}\frac{(1-e^{(\gamma-r)T})}{r-\gamma}-1=0$$

$$L: \quad (1-\alpha)P_0 AK^{\alpha}L^{-\alpha}\frac{(1-e^{(\gamma-r)T})}{r-\gamma}-w_0\frac{(1-e^{(\delta-r)T})}{r-\delta}=0$$

$$T: \quad P_0 AK^{\alpha}L^{1-\alpha}e^{(\gamma-r)T}-w_0 Le^{(\delta-r)T}=0,$$

whence

$$k=\frac{K}{AK^{\alpha}L^{1-\alpha}}=\alpha P_0\frac{(1-e^{(\gamma-r)T})}{r-\gamma}$$

$$l=\frac{L}{AK^{\alpha}L^{1-\alpha}}=(1-\alpha)\frac{P_0}{w_0}\frac{(1-e^{(\gamma-r)t})}{(1-e^{(\delta-r)t})}\frac{(r-\delta)}{(r-\gamma)}$$

and

B. $$T=\frac{\ln\left[\frac{p_0}{w_0}A\left(\frac{K}{L}\right)^{\alpha}\right]}{\delta-\gamma}=\frac{\ln\left[\frac{p_0}{w_0}A\left(\frac{k}{l}\right)^{\alpha}\right]}{\delta-\gamma}.$$

C. Plugging k and l into the above equation and using the implicit function theorem, readers can obtain comparative statics of $\mathrm{dT}/\mathrm{d}\delta$ and $\mathrm{dT}/\mathrm{d}\gamma$.

Solutions to Problem Set 2

(1) Solution

A. The producer's optimization problem is

$$\max_a [Pf(a\alpha)-wa]$$
$$\text{subject to } Pf(a\alpha)-wa\geq 0$$

with first-order condition (assuming an interior solution)

$$Pf_e\alpha-w=0.$$

Applying the implicit function theorem to this condition, we find

$$\frac{da}{dP} = -\frac{f_e\alpha}{Pf_{ee}\alpha^2} = -\frac{f_e}{Pf_{ee}\alpha}$$

$$\frac{da}{dw} = \frac{1}{Pf_{ee}\alpha^2}$$

$$\frac{da}{d\alpha} = -\frac{Pf_e + Pf_{ee}a\alpha}{Pf_{ee}\alpha^2} = -\frac{f_e}{f_{ee}\alpha^2} - \frac{a}{\alpha}$$

Thus,

$$\frac{de}{dP} = \alpha\frac{da}{dP} = -\frac{f_e}{Pf_{ee}}$$

$$\frac{de}{dw} = \alpha\frac{da}{dw} = \frac{1}{Pf_{ee}\alpha}$$

$$\frac{de}{d\alpha} = \alpha\frac{da}{d\alpha} = -\frac{f_e}{f_{ee}\alpha} - a$$

and

$$\frac{dq}{dP} = f_e\frac{de}{dP} = -\frac{f_e^2}{Pf_{ee}}$$

$$\frac{dq}{dw} = f_e\frac{de}{dw} = \frac{f_e}{Pf_{ee}\alpha}$$

$$\frac{dq}{d\alpha} = f_e\frac{de}{d\alpha} = -\frac{f_e^2}{f_{ee}\alpha} - af_e.$$

B. The rental rate will equal profits as a function of land quality:

$$r(\alpha) = \pi(\alpha) = Pf(a\alpha) - wa.$$

By the envelope theorem, we need only consider the direct effects of changes in P, w, and α on this rate, so that

$$\frac{dr}{dP} = \frac{d\pi}{dP} = f(a\alpha)$$

$$\frac{dr}{dw} = \frac{d\pi}{dw} = -a$$

$$\frac{dr}{d\alpha} = \frac{d\pi}{d\alpha} = pf_e a,$$

all evaluated at the optimal solution.

C. If the production function is CES, we have

$$Q = (c_1 E^\rho + c_2 L^\rho)^{1/\rho},$$

where E denotes total effective water demand and L denotes land.

Written in intensive form (i.e., in per-acre basis), this becomes

$$q = (c_1 e^\rho + c_2)^{1/\rho}.$$

The producer's optimization problem is therefore

$$\max_a [P \cdot (c_1 \alpha^\rho a^\rho + c_2)^{1/\rho} - wa].$$

The first-order condition

$$P \cdot (c_1 \alpha^\rho a^\rho + c_2)^{(1/\rho)-1} c_1 \alpha^\rho a^{\rho-1} - w = 0,$$

implicitly defines the optimal actual water demand

$$a^* = a^*(c_1, c_2, P, w, \alpha, \rho).$$

The effective demand, output supply, and rental rate are therefore given by

$$\begin{aligned} e^* &= \alpha a^* \\ q^* &= (c_1 \alpha^\rho (a^*)^\rho + c_2)^{1/\rho} \\ r^* &= P \cdot (c_1 \alpha^\rho (a^*)^\rho + c_2)^{1/\rho} - wa. \end{aligned}$$

(2) Solution

A. If there is an internal solution, the profit-maximization problem under risk neutrality becomes very simple:

$$\max\nolimits_{N_h} \pi = p\,(f\,(N_h)) - wN_h.$$

The first-order condition is:

$$\frac{d\pi}{dN_h} = p(f'(N_h)) - w = 0$$
$$N_0 = \bar{N} - N_h.$$

If $p(f'(0)) < w$, $N_h = 0$. If $p(f'(\bar{N})) > w$, $\bar{N} = N_h$. One can readily check that an increase in output price will increase the optimal time allocated to the small enterprise, whereas if the opportunity cost of the labor (w) increases then the optimal time allocated to the enterprise will decrease.

B. Assume an internal solution. Here, we need to consider the entire income of the household.

$$max_{N_h}\, EU(W_0 + p\,(f\,(N_h) + \alpha N_h \varepsilon) + \left(\bar{N} - N_h\right) w).$$

The first-order condition is:

$$EU'\,(\cdot)\,(p(f'\,(N_h) + \alpha\epsilon) - w) = 0$$

$$pf'\,(N_h) = w + \frac{-E[U'\,(\cdot)\,p\alpha\epsilon]}{EU'\,(\cdot)}.$$

The value of the marginal product of labor is equal to the wage plus a risk element that reflects the negative correlation between marginal utility and ϵ. Based on the discussion in the chapter about risk and uncertainty, one can show that $E[U'\,(\cdot)\,p\alpha\epsilon] < 0$. By comparing the first-order condition here with that under risk neutrality, one can see that the optimal input under risk aversion will be smaller than that under risk neutrality.

C. A risk-averse family will produce less than a risk neutral one based on our interpretation of the first-order conditions. The impact of a change in initial wealth depend on the decision maker's risk preference. Under decreasing (respectively, constant or increasing) absolute risk aversion in wealth, an increase in the initial wealth will increase (respectively, have no impact or decrease) expected output and increase labor use inside the household (relative to outside the household).

D. Based on Chapter 4, if we have negative exponential utility and a normal distribution, the objective function of the firm is to maximize mean profit minus measure of absolute risk aversion times variance divided by 2 (i.e., a mean-variance utility function). Note that $E\left(1 - e^{-r\pi}\right) = 1 - E\left(e^{-r\pi}\right)$ and that $E\left(e^{-r\pi}\right)$ is a moment-generating function of random variable π at r. The moment-generating function of a random variable x is e^{tx}. If x is normally distributed with mean μ and variance σ^2, then the moment-generating function is $e^{t\mu + \frac{1}{2}\sigma^2 t^2}$. If we replace t with $-r$, maximizing exponential utility is equivalent to maximizing $\mu - \sigma^2 r/2$.

We denote the measure of absolute risk aversion as r. Thus the objective function (in case of internal solution) is

$$max_{N_h}\, pf\left(N_h\right) - N_h w - \frac{1}{2} r\alpha^2 N_h^2 \sigma^2 p^2.$$

The first-order condition is:

$$pf'\left(N_h\right) - w = r\alpha^2 N_h \sigma^2 p^2.$$

Obviously, risk reduces labor inside the household, and higher variance does the same.

E. In this case, we have a household production function, but now the household gains utility from leisure. In this case, we add another variable, N_l, and the time allocation constraint is $\bar{N} = N_h + N_l + N_o$. In this case, one can have several formulations. If we have expected utility, we get utility from income and leisure, and the optimization problem becomes:

$$\max_{N_h, N_l} EU(W_0 + p(f\left(N_h\right) + \alpha N_h \varepsilon) + \left(\bar{N} - N_h - N_l\right) w,\, N_l).$$

In this case, you have utility from wealth, which is initial wealth plus income, and leisure.

Solutions to Problem Set 3

(1) Solution

A. According to the mean-preserving spread criterion, portfolios with the same mean may be compared. In this case, I, II, and IV have $E(X) = 10$. The means of III and V are 9.5 and 28/3, respectively. The variances of portfolios I to V are 19.3, 19.8, 27.4, 35.8, and 19.6, respectively. Riskier portfolios have "more weight in the tail." The following figure shows the probability density for portfolios I, II, and IV.

By observing the figure, we can draw the following conclusions: II dominates IV (i.e., IV is a mean-preserving spread of II); I dominates IV; and I and II cannot be compared because, for

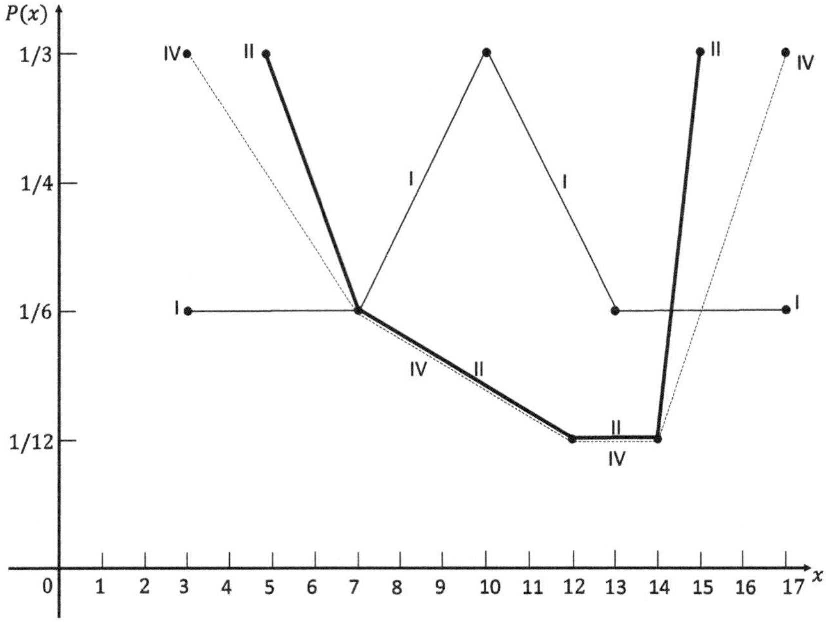

a small tail, I is riskier; but for a large tail, II is riskier. To better see that I and II cannot be compared, note that conditional on I and II having equal means, I is a mean-preserving spread of II if and only if for any x, the area to the left of x under the cumulative distribution function (CDF) curve of portfolio I should be larger than or equal to that under CDF curve of portfolio II. Mathematically, the condition can be expressed as,

$$S^I(x) \equiv \int_{-\infty}^{x} F^I(t)dt \geq S^{II}(x) \equiv \int_{-\infty}^{x} F^{II}(t)dt, \quad \forall x,$$

where $F^I(\cdot)$ and $F^{II}(\cdot)$ are the CDFs of portfolios I and II, respectively. One can easily check that $S^I(3) = S^{II}(3) = 0, S^I(5) = 1/3 > S^{II}(5) = 0, \quad S^I(7) = S^{II}(7) = 2/3$, and $S^I(10) = 10/6 < S^{II}(10) = 13/6$, showing that the condition does not hold (see the following figure).

B. Second-order stochastic dominance: It is necessary to calculate and plot $S^I(x)$ to $S^V(x)$ as a function of x described above. Any

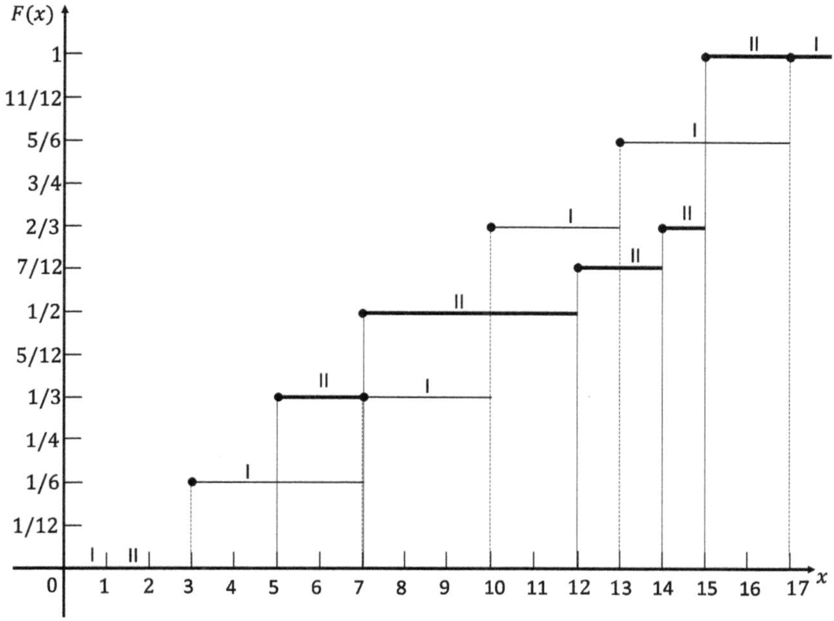

portfolio for which the plot lies wholly to the right of another dominates the other.

Conclusions: I dominates III, IV, and V; II dominates III and IV but not V. I and II are not comparable in the sense of second-order stochastic dominance.

C. Order the distributions using the mean-variance criterion.

I >II because it has the same mean and lower variance.

I >III because it has a higher mean and a lower variance.

I >IV because it has the same mean and lower variance.

I >V because it has a higher mean and a lower variance.

II >III because it has a higher mean and a lower variance.

II >IV because it has the same mean and lower variance.

Therefore, the ordering is I >II >III and IV and I >V. III and IV, III and V, as well as IV and V are not comparable without knowing further information about the penalty that the mean-variance criterion puts on variance.

D. Order the distributions using Roy's minimum probability rule: min $[P(X \leq 6)]$.

Portfolio	I	II	III	IV	V
$P(X \leq 6)$	1/6	1/3	1/3	1/3	1/6

So, I and V are preferred to II, III, and IV.

E. Order the distributions using Kataoka's safety-fixed rule: Maximize d subject to $P(X \leq d) \leq 1/6$.

	I	II	III	IV	V
max d	7 - ε	5 - ε	2 - ε	3 - ε	8 - ε.

where ε is a positive infinitesimal number. Thus, V >I >II >IV >III.

F. Order the distributions using $U(X) = \ln(X + 1)$.

$$E(U) = \Sigma P(X)\ ln\ (x + 1)$$

	I	II	III	IV	V
$E(U)$	2.2984	2.3075	2.1702	2.2115	2.2127

Thus, II >I >V >IV >III.

G. The mean-preserving spread, second-order stochastic dominance, mean-variance criterion, and Roy's minimum probability rule (min $[P(X \leq 1/6)]$) give partial orderings only. Kataoka's safety-fixed rule and the utility function give complete orderings.

The mean-preserving spread and second-order stochastic dominance give rankings (albeit partial) and the basis of any risk-averse utility function. That is, the orderings implied by these two methods will be true for any risk-averse individual. Note that the partial orderings implied by these two methods are consistent with the orderings implied by the utility function.

The orderings implied by the mean-variance criterion are consistent with expected utility maximization if the utility function is defined over only the mean and variance (or if the utility function is exponential and the distributions are all normally distributed). Note that the orderings implied by $M - V$ are not consistent with those implied by the log utility function.

The orderings implied by the safety rules are not consistent with any sort of utility or expected utility maximization.

(2) Solution

A. The farmer maximizes his expected utility of income:

$$\max_{\ell,m} EU\left[L[pf(\ell,m)+pg(\ell,m)\cdot\varepsilon - w\ell - rm] - F\right].$$

The first-order condition with respect to ℓ is:

$$\frac{\partial EU}{\partial \ell} = E\left(U'\cdot[L(pf_\ell + pg_\ell\cdot\varepsilon - w)]\right) = 0,$$

where U' is shorthand for $U'(L[pf(\ell,m)+pg(\ell,m)\cdot\varepsilon-w\ell-rm]-F)$ (the same for the below-mentioned U''). Based on this first-order condition and on a property of the expected value of the product of two random variables (i.e., $E(X\cdot Y) = E(X)\cdot E(Y) + cov(X,Y)$), we have

$$E(U')\ (Lpf_\ell - Lw) + Lpg_\ell \operatorname{cov}(U',\varepsilon) = 0.$$

Since $E(\varepsilon) = 0$,

$$pf_\ell - w = \frac{-pg_\ell \operatorname{cov}(U',e)}{E(U')}.$$

With $g_\ell > 0$ and $\operatorname{cov}(U',\varepsilon) < 0$, this indicates that $pf_\ell - w > 0$.

Under certainty, $\varepsilon = 0$, which implies that cov $(U', \varepsilon) = 0$. Therefore, with complete certainty, $pf_\ell - w = 0$. With diminishing returns to the factor 1 (i.e., $f_{\ell\ell} < 0$), this implies that, with uncertainty, less of the input will be used. The result is, of course, that, with everything else the same, the output will be less. This seems intuitive for increased use of the input l increases not only the expected yield but also the variation in yield. A risk-averse farmer would, therefore, limit the use of the input because, by so doing, he reduces the risk.

Analogously, we can study the optimal condition for input m:

$$\frac{\partial EU}{\partial m} = E\left(U'[L(pf_m + pg_m\cdot\varepsilon - r)]\right) = 0,$$

$$L\cdot E(U')\ (pf_m - r) + L\ pg_m \operatorname{cov}(U',\varepsilon) = 0$$

$$pf_m - r = \frac{-pg_m \operatorname{cov}(U',\varepsilon)}{E(U')}$$

because $g_m < 0$, we can conclude that $pf_m - r < 0$.

As above, certainty (or risk neutrality) implies that $\mathrm{cov}(U', \varepsilon) = 0$ and, hence, $pf_m - r = 0$. Comparing the case of certainty with that of uncertainty, it is clear that more of the input m is used when uncertainty is introduced, because increasing m reduces the variance in yield.

Comparative statics

To examine the effect of a change in fixed costs and a change in farm size on input use, we differentiate totally the two first-order conditions with respect to ℓ, m, f, and L.

The total derivative of first-order condition $E[U'\,\Pi_\ell] = 0$ can be written as,

$$\underbrace{E\left[U'\Pi'_{\ell\ell} + U''\Pi_\ell\Pi_\ell\right]}_{h_{11}} d\ell + \underbrace{E\left[U'\Pi_{\ell m} + U''\Pi_\ell\Pi_m\right]}_{h_{12}} dm$$
$$+ \underbrace{E\left[U'\Pi_{\ell F} + U''\Pi_\ell\Pi_F\right]}_{a_{11}} dF + \underbrace{E\left[U'\Pi_{\ell L} + U''\Pi_\ell\Pi_L\right]}_{a_{12}} dL = 0.$$

For first-order condition $E\left[U'\Pi_m\right] = 0$, the result of total differentiation is

$$\underbrace{E\left[U'\Pi_{m\ell} + U''\Pi_m\Pi_\ell\right]}_{h_{21}} d\ell + \underbrace{E\left[U'\Pi_{mm} + U''\Pi_m\Pi_m\right]}_{h_{22}} dm$$
$$+ \underbrace{E\left[U'\Pi_{mF} + U''\Pi_m\Pi_F\right]}_{a_{21}} dF + \underbrace{E\left[U'\Pi_{mL} + U''\Pi_m\Pi_L\right]}_{a_{22}} dL = 0.$$

In sum, we have

$$\begin{bmatrix} h_{11} \; h_{12} \\ h_{21} \; h_{22} \end{bmatrix} \begin{bmatrix} d\ell \\ dm \end{bmatrix} + \begin{bmatrix} a_{11} \; a_{12} \\ a_{21} \; a_{22} \end{bmatrix} \begin{bmatrix} dF \\ dL \end{bmatrix} = 0,$$

where

$$\begin{aligned}
\Pi_\ell &= L(pf_\ell + pg_\ell \cdot \varepsilon - w)\\
\Pi_m &= L(pf_m + pg_m\varepsilon - r)\\
\Pi_{\ell\ell} &= L(pf_{\ell\ell} + pg_{\ell\ell} \cdot \varepsilon)\\
\Pi_{\ell m} &= L(pf_\ell m + pg_{\ell m} \cdot \varepsilon)\\
\Pi_{m\ell} &= L(pf_{m\ell} + pg_{m\ell} \cdot \varepsilon)\\
\Pi_{mm} &= L(pf_{mm} + pg_{mm} \cdot \varepsilon)\\
\Pi_{\ell F} &= 0\\
\Pi_{mF} &= 0\\
\Pi_{\ell L} &= (pf_\ell + pg_\ell \cdot \varepsilon - w)\\
\Pi_{mL} &= (pf_m + pg_m \cdot \varepsilon - r)\\
\Pi_F &= -1\\
\Pi_L &= (pf + pg\varepsilon - w\ell - rm).
\end{aligned}$$

Solving for d_ℓ and d_m, we obtain:

$$\begin{bmatrix} d\ell \\ dm \end{bmatrix} = \frac{1}{|H|}\begin{bmatrix} h_{22} & -h_{12} \\ -h_{21} & h_{11} \end{bmatrix}\begin{bmatrix} -a_{11} & -a_{12} \\ -a_{21} & -a_{22} \end{bmatrix}\begin{bmatrix} dF \\ dL \end{bmatrix},$$

where $H \equiv \begin{bmatrix} h_{11} & h_{12} \\ h_{21} & h_{22} \end{bmatrix}$.

From this, we can see that:

$$\begin{aligned}
\frac{d\ell}{dF} &= \frac{1}{|H|}\left[-a_{11}h_{22} + h_{12}a_{21}\right]\\
\frac{dm}{dF} &= \frac{1}{|H|}\left[a_{11}h_{21} - a_{21}h_{11}\right].
\end{aligned}$$

If we substitute for a_{11} and a_{21}, we obtain:

$$\frac{d\ell}{dF} = \frac{1}{|H|}\left[(E[U''\Pi_\ell])h_{22} - E\left[U''\Pi_m]\right)\right] \cdot h_{12}\right].$$

To sign this expression, we assume that the second-order condition for the maximization problem hold, i.e., H is a negative definite matrix. This implies that h_{11} and h_{22} are negative and that, with an even number of decision variables (namely, ℓ and m), $|H|$ is positive. To sign the term $E\left[U''\Pi_\ell\right]$, we can proceed as what we have discussed in the production chapter:

$$E\left[U'' \cdot L(pf_\ell + pg_\ell \cdot \varepsilon - w)\right] \gtreqless 0.$$

Define $\tilde{\Pi}$ as a point where $L(pf_\ell + pg_\ell\varepsilon - w) = 0$. If $pf_\ell + pg_\ell\varepsilon > w$, then $\Pi > \tilde{\Pi}$ and, with decreasing absolute risk aversion, $R_a\,(\Pi) < R_a(\tilde{\Pi})$. If $pf_\ell + pg_{\ell\varepsilon} < w$, then $\Pi < \tilde{\Pi}$ and $R_a(\Pi) > \mathrm{R}_a(\tilde{\Pi})$. Then, for all values of $pf_\ell \cdot pg_{\ell\varepsilon} - w$,

$$\begin{aligned}
&R_a(\Pi)\ (pf_\ell + pg_\ell\varepsilon - w) < R_a(\tilde{\Pi})\ (pf_\ell + pg_\ell\varepsilon - w) \\
&\Rightarrow -\frac{U''(\Pi)}{U'(\Pi)}(pf_\ell + pg_\ell\varepsilon - w) < R_a(\tilde{\Pi})\ (pf_\ell + pg_\ell\varepsilon - w) \\
&\Rightarrow -U''(\Pi)(pf_\ell + pg_\ell\varepsilon - w) < R_a(\tilde{\Pi})\ U'(\Pi)\ (pf_\ell + pg_\ell\varepsilon - w) \\
&\Rightarrow -E\Big[U''(\Pi)(pf_\ell + pg_\ell\varepsilon - w)\Big] < R_a(\tilde{\Pi})\ E\Big[U'(\Pi)\,(pf_\ell + pg_\ell\varepsilon - w)\Big].
\end{aligned}$$

Hence, $E\left[U''\Pi_\ell\right] > 0$ because $E\left[U'\Pi_\ell\right] = 0$ from the first-order condition. By an analogous argument, we should be able (in principle) to show that $E\left[U''\Pi_m\right] < 0$. If this is the case and if we can assume that $h_{12} < 0$, then $(d\ell/dF) < 0$ and $(dm/dF) > 0$. These results indicate that under decreasing absolute risk aversion, reduction in fixed costs will increase the use of "risk-increasing" input ℓ and decrease the use of "risk-decreasing" input m. This is intuitive because when fixed costs F decreases, the decision maker has more wealth and thus becomes less sensitive to risk. Therefore, she is more willing to use risk-increasing input and less willing to use risk-decreasing input.

To examine the effect of farm size on input use, we look at the expressions

$$\begin{aligned}
\frac{d\ell}{dL} &= \frac{1}{|H|}(-a_{12}\,h_{22} + a_{22}\,h_{12}) \\
\frac{dm}{dL} &= \frac{1}{|H|}(a_{12}\,h_{21} - a_{22}\,h_{11}).
\end{aligned}$$

Although it has not been shown mathematically, the intuitive answer to this is that, with constant relative risk aversion, $(d\ell/dL) = (dm/dL) = 0$. That is, when the farm is large, the farmer is just as unwilling to risk, say, 5% of his farm as he is when it is small. As a result, the level of input usage per acre should remain exactly the same as it was when the farm was small. Intuitively, because the decision maker is constant-relative-risk averse, a proportional change in her wealth does not affect her decisions.

B. The farmer's maximum expected utility is:

$$\begin{aligned} E(U) &= 1 - E\left[e^{-\delta\Pi}\right] \\ &= 1 - E\left[e^{-\delta[L(pf+pg\varepsilon-w\ell-rm-F)]}\right] \\ &= 1 - e^{-\delta[L(pf-w\ell-rm-F)]}\ E\left[e^{-\delta Lpg\varepsilon}\right]. \end{aligned}$$

Because $\varepsilon \sim N(0, \sigma)$, for any number t, we have $E\left(e^{t\varepsilon}\right) = e^{t^2\sigma^2/2}$. If we define $t = -\delta Lpg$, then $E\left[e^{-\delta Lpg\varepsilon}\right] = e^{\delta^2 L^2 p^2 g^2 \sigma^2/2}$. Therefore, to maximize $E(U)$, we maximize

$$\begin{aligned} E(U) &= 1 - e^{-\delta[L(pf-w\ell-rm-F)]}\ e^{\delta^2 L^2 p^2 g^2 \sigma^2/2} \\ &= 1 - e^{-\delta[L(pf-w\ell-rm-F)] + \delta^2 L^2 p^2 g^2 \sigma^2/2}. \end{aligned}$$

The first-order condition is:

$$\begin{aligned} &\frac{\partial E(U)}{\partial \ell} = e^{-\delta[\cdot]}\left[-\delta L(pf_\ell - w) + \frac{1}{2}\delta^2 L^2 p^2 2gg_\ell\sigma^2\right] = 0 \\ &\Rightarrow pf_\ell - w = \delta L p^2 g g_\ell \sigma^2. \end{aligned}$$

With g and $g_\ell > 0$, this implies that $pf_\ell - w > 0$. This means that less of input ℓ is used as compared with the case of complete certainty ($\sigma^2 = 0$) or the case of risk neutrality ($\delta = 0$), both of which imply that $pf_\ell - w = 0$.

$$\frac{\partial E(U)}{\partial m} = 0 \Rightarrow pf_m - r = \delta L p^2 g g_m \sigma^2.$$

Because $g_m < 0$, this implies that $pf_m - r < 0$. In this case, more of input m is used as compared to the case of complete certainty or risk neutrality.

Comparative statics

Because fixed costs do not appear in the first-order conditions, a change in fixed costs will not affect the level of input use (unless the increase in fixed costs is so great that it becomes unprofitable for the firm to produce and it is shut down).

To determine the effect of a change in farm size, we differentiate totally the two first-order conditions and obtain:

$$\underbrace{\left[pf_{\ell\ell} - \delta L p^2 \sigma^2 \left(g g_{\ell\ell} + g_\ell^2\right)\right]}_{h_{11}} d\ell + \underbrace{\left[pf_{\ell m} - \delta L p^2 \sigma^2 (g g_{\ell m} + g_\ell g_m)\right]}_{h_{12}} dm$$

$$\underbrace{-\delta p^2 g g_\ell \sigma^2}_{a_1} dL = 0.$$

$$\underbrace{\left[pf_{\ell m} - \delta L p^2 \sigma^2 \left(g g_{m\ell} + g_m g_\ell\right)\right]}_{h_{21}} d\ell + \underbrace{\left[pf_{mm} - \delta L p^2 \sigma^2 (g g_{mm} + g_m^2)\right]}_{h_{22}} dm$$

$$\underbrace{-\delta p^2 g g_m \sigma^2}_{a_2} dL = 0.$$

Therefore, we have,

$$\begin{bmatrix} h_{11} \; h_{12} \\ h_{21} \; h_{22} \end{bmatrix} \begin{bmatrix} d\ell \\ dm \end{bmatrix} + \begin{bmatrix} a_1 \\ a_2 \end{bmatrix} dL = \begin{bmatrix} 0 \\ 0 \end{bmatrix}$$

$$\Rightarrow \begin{bmatrix} \frac{d\ell}{dm} \end{bmatrix} = \frac{1}{|H|} \begin{bmatrix} h_{22} & -h_{12} \\ -h_{21} & h_{11} \end{bmatrix} \begin{bmatrix} -a_1 \\ -a_2 \end{bmatrix} dL$$

$$\Rightarrow \begin{cases} \dfrac{d\ell}{dL} = \frac{1}{|H|} \left(-h_{22} a_1 + h_{12} a_2\right) \\ \dfrac{dm}{dL} = \frac{1}{|H|} \left(h_{21} a_1 - h_{11} a_2\right). \end{cases}$$

To sign these two expressions, we assume that the second-order condition for the maximization problem holds, i.e., H is a negative definite matrix. This implies that h_{11} and h_{22} are negative and that, with an even number of decision variables (namely, ℓ and m), $|H|$ is positive. By inspection, it is clear that a_1 <0 and a_2 >0. If $h_{12} = h_{21} < 0$, then $d\ell/dL < 0$ and $dm/dL > 0$. Intuitively, these results are reasonable. The exponential utility function implies increasing relative risk aversion ($R_r = \delta \cdot \Pi$). Thus, as farm size increases, it seems likely that the farmer will use less of the risk-increasing input, ℓ, and more of the risk-decreasing input, m. However, as may be seen from an examination of the expression h_{12}, the sign of this term will depend on how f_ℓ and g_ℓ change with m (and how f_m and g_m change with ℓ). Note, however, that $h_{12} < 0$ is a sufficient condition; if its sign should change, this sign on $d\ell/dL$ and dm/dL could remain as above.

C. Assume now that $\varepsilon \sim$ gamma with $E(\varepsilon) = 1$. We saw that

$$E(U) = 1 - e^{-\delta[L(pf - w\ell - rm - F)]}\, E\left[e^{-\delta Lpg\varepsilon}\right].$$

For the gamma distribution, $E(e^{t\varepsilon}) = (1 - \beta t)^{-\alpha}$, where α, β are parameters of the distribution, and $E(\varepsilon) = \alpha\beta = 1$; $V(\varepsilon) = \alpha\beta^2$; $\alpha, \beta > 0$; and ε >0. If we define $t = -\delta\ Lpg$, we have

$$E(U) = 1 - e^{-\delta[\cdot]}\,(1 + \beta\delta Lpg)^{-\alpha}.$$

The problem for the farmer is to maximize

$$\begin{aligned} E(U) &= 1 - e^{-\delta[\cdot]}(1 + \beta\delta Lpg)^{-\alpha} \\ \Rightarrow \frac{\partial E(U)}{\partial \ell} &= -e^{-\delta[\cdot]}(1 + \beta\delta Lpg)^{-\alpha}\,(-\delta\,[L(pf_\ell - w)]) \\ &\quad - e^{-\delta[\cdot]}\,(-\alpha)\ (1 + \beta\delta Lpg)^{-\alpha-1}\beta\delta Lpg_\ell = 0 \\ &\Rightarrow pf_\ell - w = \frac{-\beta pg_\ell\alpha}{1 + \beta\delta Lpg}. \end{aligned}$$

Now let us assume that there is no risk. Replacing ε with 1 in the production function, profit maximization yield first-order condition $pf_\ell - w = -pg_\ell < \frac{-\beta pg_\ell\alpha}{1+\beta\delta Lpg} = \frac{-pg_\ell}{1+\beta\delta Lpg}$. Note that the last equality holds because $E(\varepsilon) = \alpha\beta = 1$. Therefore, we can see that with risk, less ℓ will be used than under the case of certainty. Similarly, we have

$$\frac{\partial E(U)}{\partial m} = 0 \Rightarrow pf_m - r = -\frac{\beta pg_m \alpha}{1+\beta\delta Lpg} = -\frac{pg_m}{1+\beta\delta Lpg} < -pg_m.$$

The last inequality holds because $g_m < 0$. This implies that more of input m will be used than under complete certainty.

D. Assume that $\varepsilon \sim N(0,\sigma^2)$. The farmer acts under Kataoka's safety-fixed rule:

$$\text{Maximize } d \text{ s.t. } p(\Pi \leq d) \leq \alpha.$$

If $\varepsilon \sim N(0,\sigma_\varepsilon^2)$, then $\Pi \sim N([L\cdot(pf - w\ell - rm - F)], (Lpg\sigma)^2)$, or $\Pi \sim N(u_\pi, \sigma_\pi^2)$. Thus,

$$p\left(\frac{\Pi - u_\pi}{\sigma_\pi} \leq \frac{d-u_\pi}{\sigma_\pi}\right) = \alpha$$

or

$$\frac{d-u_\pi}{\sigma_\pi} = \Phi^{-1}(\alpha),$$

where $\Phi(\cdot)$ is the cumulative distribution function of standard normal distribution. Suppose $\alpha = 0.05$, then $\Phi^{-1}(\alpha) = -1.64$.

$$\begin{aligned}
d &= u_\pi + \Phi^{-1}(\alpha)\sigma_\pi \\
d &= L(pf - w\ell - rm - F) - 1.64\ Lpg\sigma \\
\frac{\partial d}{\partial \ell} &= L(pf_\ell - w) - 1.64\ Lpg_\ell\sigma = 0 \\
pf_\ell - w &= 1.64\ pg_\ell\ \sigma > 0.
\end{aligned}$$

Again, note that, since $pf_\ell - w > 0$, less of input ℓ will be used than certainty ($\sigma = 0$). Similarly,

$$\frac{\partial d}{\partial m} = 0 \Rightarrow pf_m - r = 1.64\ pg_m\sigma < 0.$$

Because $pf_m - r < 0$, more of input m will be used than under uncertainty.

E. The behavior implied by all of the models was very similar. As compared with the certainty case, less of input λ was used and more of input m was used. The precise levels of usage of these inputs differed from model to model. In general, however, the level of input use depended on the risk-averseness of the farmer (e.g., δ and α) and the degree of riskiness of production (e.g., σ and ϕ).

Index

U

V

W

Z

www.ingramcontent.com/pod-product-compliance
Lightning Source LLC
Chambersburg PA
CBHW071215060126
37764CB00004B/178
9789811299162